PERUVIAN PREHISTORY

PERUVIAN

PREHISTORY

An overview of pre-Inca and Inca society

Edited by
RICHARD W. KEATINGE

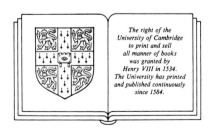

The right of the
University of Cambridge
to print and sell
all manner of books
was granted by
Henry VIII in 1534.
The University has printed
and published continuously
since 1584.

CAMBRIDGE UNIVERSITY PRESS

Cambridge   New York   New Rochelle   Melbourne   Sydney

Published by the Press Syndicate of the University of Cambridge
The Pitt Building, Trumpington Street, Cambridge CB2 1RP
32 East 57th Street, New York, NY 10022, USA
10 Stamford Road, Oakleigh, Melbourne 3166, Australia

First published 1988

Printed in Great Britain at the University Press, Cambridge

British Library cataloguing in publication data
Peruvian prehistory:
an overview of pre-Inca and Inca society.
1. Indians of South America – Peru – Antiquities
2. Peru – Antiquities
I. Keatinge, Richard W.
985'.01   F3429

Library of Congress cataloguing in publication data
Main entry under title:
Peruvian prehistory.
Bibliography.
Includes index.
1. Indians of South America – Peru – Addresses, essays, lectures.
2. Incas – Addresses, essays, lectures.
I. Keatinge, Richard W.
F3429.P453 1988   985'.01   85–29059

ISBN 0 521 25560 0 hard covers
ISBN 0 521 27555 5 paperback

In memory of
JUNIUS B. BIRD
Colleague, friend,
and pioneer in
Peruvian prehistory

CONTENTS

ILLUSTRATIONS

CONTRIBUTORS

RICHARD L. BURGER, Department of Anthropology, Yale University

CLAUDE CHAUCHAT, Institut de Quaternaire, Centre National de la Recherche Scientifique, Université de Bordeaux I

WILLIAM J. CONKLIN, The Textile Museum, Washington DC

ROSE FUNG PINEDA, Programa Académico de Arqueologia, Universidad Nacional Mayor de San Marcos, Lima

CHARLES M. HASTINGS, Museum of Anthropology, University of Michigan, Ann Arbor

WILLIAM H. ISBELL, Department of Anthropology, State University of New York, Binghamton

RICHARD W. KEATINGE, Leucadia, California

CRAIG MORRIS, Department of Anthropology, American Museum of Natural History, New York

MICHAEL E. MOSELEY, Department of Anthropology, University of Florida

PATRICIA J. NETHERLY, Department of Anthropology, University of Massachusetts, Amherst

JEFFREY R. PARSONS, University of Michigan, Ann Arbor

J. SCOTT RAYMOND, Department of Archaeology, University of Calgary

JOHN W. RICK, Department of Anthropology, Stanford University

PREFACE

Some forty years ago, in July of 1947, a conference on Peruvian archaeology sponsored by the Viking Fund and the Institute of Andean Research was convened in New York City. The purpose of the conference was to evaluate the progress of research in Peruvian prehistory, focusing on various questions of chronology, stylistic relationships, and culture history. The conference volume, *A Reappraisal of Peruvian Archaeology*, assembled by Wendell Bennett and published by the Society for American Archaeology in 1948, stands as a landmark in the assessment of Peruvian archaeology. However, in the years since its publication there has been no comparable comprehensive evaluation and review of Peruvian archaeology by a group of active scholars such as was represented in the 1947 conference volume. While a number of important syntheses of Peruvian culture history have been published since that time (Bennett and Bird 1949, Bushnell 1956, Mason 1957, Lanning 1967, Lumbreras 1969, 1974, Kauffman Doig 1970, Willey 1971, Ravines, 1982), virtually all represent interpretations of single individuals rather than the collective analyses of a group of specialists.

The purpose of this volume is to provide an overview of the status of Peruvian archaeology today. Since the 1947 conference and particularly in the last fifteen years, a wealth of new material has been recovered by archaeologists working in Peru, much of it still unpublished. It seems, then, an appropriate moment for stocktaking – a time for an examination of recent research results and their ramifications for more traditional interpretations and approaches. In attempting to fulfill this goal, each participant in the present volume has been asked to review a specific period of Peruvian prehistory in which he or she has a particular interest and expertise. While such a scheme inevitably results in some overlap, it also assures complete coverage of the spectrum of cultural evolution in Peru.

The framework for the volume is provided by the chronological scheme suggested by Max Uhle and magnified by John Rowe (1960). Though increasingly challenged, this scheme is still the one most generally accepted amongst scholars working in Peru. This framework is based on the subdivision of pre-ceramic and ceramic stages into a number of different periods. The ceramic

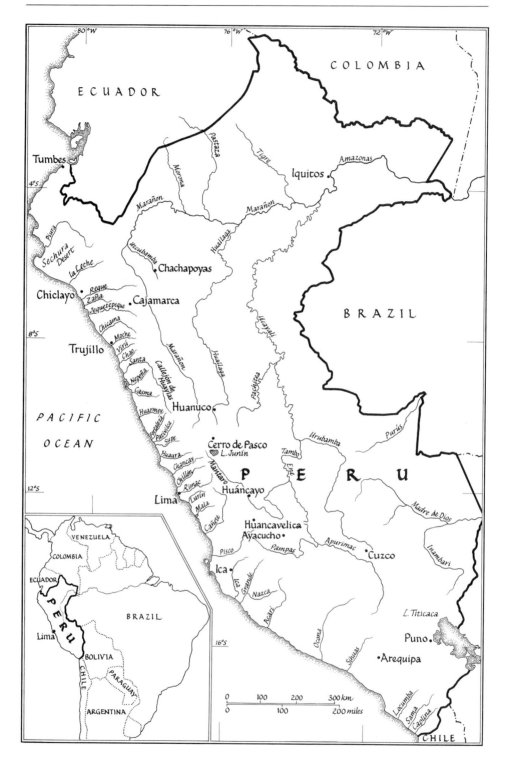

stage, in particular, is divided by alternating Horizons and Periods, a distinction based on the contrast of time periods characterized by a wave of stylistic influence sweeping beyond parochial regional boundaries (Horizons) and time periods characterized by regional styles with much less pan-Andean impact (Periods). Combined with the preceramic subdivisions suggested by Lanning and Patterson (Lanning 1967: 25), subdivisions which are severely criticized in this volume by John Rick and Claude Chauchat (chs. 1 and 2), the standard chronological framework for Peruvian prehistory can be presented as follows:

Late Horizon	AD 1476–1534
Late Intermediate Period	AD 1000–1476
Middle Horizon	AD 600–1000
Early Intermediate Period	200 BC–AD 600
Early Horizon	900–200 BC
Initial Period	1800–900 BC
Preceramic Period VI	2500–1800 BC
Preceramic Period V	4200–2500 BC
Preceramic Period IV	6000–4200 BC
Preceramic Period III	8000–6000 BC
Preceramic Period II	9500–8000 BC
Preceramic Period I	?–9500 BC

Part I, covering the preceramic periods, begins with the appearance of the first inhabitants and focuses on the evolution of subsistence economies together with the trend towards sedentary village life in different regions of Peru. For the highlands, John Rick examines the earliest evidence for human occupation of the sierra region, emphasizing the effects of climate and ecological zonation on the behavior of hunter-gatherer society in the movement towards settled village life based on domesticated plants and animals. For the coastal region, Claude Chauchat reviews the evidence of early human occupation and discusses the ecological determinants which played a role in the adaptive behavior of these early inhabitants. Chauchat critically analyzes the empirical data on which traditional preceramic coastal chronology is based and argues that this periodization cannot be supported on the basis of the evidence.

Following the contrastive discussions of the highland and coastal zones during the preceramic stage, Rosa Fung's analysis focuses on developments which began at the end of the Preceramic and continued into the Initial Period. Her contribution thus provides a transitional chapter dealing with the complexity of cultural development characterizing this period. In addition to the introduction of ceramics and other important items in the cultural inventory, the Initial Period provides the first evidence for what later blossomed into the "Chavín phenomena" of the Early Horizon. Fung reviews the developments on the coast and in the highlands relevant to the beginning of the politico-religious organization of Chavín, thus setting the stage for a consideration of the florescence of complex society in Part II.

Part II begins with Richard Burger's discussion of the religious manifestation referred to as the "Chavín cult" during the Early Horizon. In an exceptional discussion which draws upon his own excavations at several important sites, including the highland site of Chavín de Huántar, Burger presents an evaluation of the development and inter-regional connections of Chavín. Following Burger's chapter, William Conklin and Michael Moseley discuss the Early Intermediate Period. Utilizing pattern analysis, they contrast cultural development in different regions in terms of settlement distribution, road patterning, and irrigation networks as well as a variety of other cultural remains during a period of dynamic regional development.

There follows an essay by William Isbell in which the critical developments of the Middle Horizon are discussed. This period is characterized, though not necessarily dominated, by the two great centers of Huari (in the highlands near the modern town of Ayacucho) and Tiwanaku (on the southern shore of Lake Titicaca in what is now Bolivia). Isbell examines the stylistic evidence for a relationship between these two sites as well as their impact on cultural development in other regions, emphasizing a number of major problems in our current understanding of this critical period in Andean prehistory. Finally, to close Part II, Jeffrey Parsons and Charles Hastings review the status of research on the Late Intermediate Period, seen as a transitional period between the collapse of Huari and Tiwanaku and the formation of the Inca Empire. In discussing the Late Intermediate Period, the authors focus on four principal regions of the coast and highlands, reviewing the archaeological record and suggesting a number of guidelines for future investigation.

Part III deals with two closely related topics: the pan-Andean empire of the Incas and the importance of ethnohistoric research. Craig Morris's contribution is devoted to a review of research on the Inca Empire, including discussions of chronology, variation in artifacts, functional studies, and structural approaches to ideology and principles of organization. Following Morris's chapter, and his call for a methodology combining the efforts of specialists in anthropology and history, Patricia Netherly provides a demonstration of the potential of such an approach. In her chapter, Netherly clearly outlines the merits of research which combines the use of ethnohistoric sources with data obtained from the archaeological record.

In Part IV, Scott Raymond deals with the often-neglected tropical forest region and the impact of this important area on the evolution of Andean civilization. He discusses the archaeological evidence for exchange between the Peruvian highlands-coast and the tropical forest, and presents a number of interaction models, one involving highland settlement of the montaña during the Early Intermediate Period and the other the exploitation of the tropical forest as a resource base during the Middle Horizon.

The final section of the volume, Part V, offers a synthesis of the major ideas presented by the book as a whole, examines current trends in the study of Peruvian prehistory, and suggests possible research directions for the future.

This is the first collective assessment of Peruvian archaeology for a generation. We hope it will attract those with no specialist interest in Peru as much as existing students, and will play at least a small part in making the extraordinary richness of Andean culture more widely known and appreciated in the English-speaking world. If so, we will have been amply rewarded.

RICHARD W. KEATINGE

I
EARLY INHABITANTS
AND SETTLEMENT

The character and context of highland preceramic society

———— *J O H N   W.   R I C K* ————

Any discussion of preceramic Andean cultures must define its limits. A strict consideration of totally non-food-producing societies would leave aside the great majority of preceramic remains from the Peruvian highlands. While the earliest human arrivals in this area may not have brought important domesticated plants and animals, domesticates do show up shortly after their arrival. In a more realistic vein, this chapter considers societies organized around relatively small residential groups, perhaps in the 20–50 person range, that subsisted mainly on wild foods, and probably had relatively egalitarian relations.

This isolates a Non-Complex Preceramic, which excludes large sites such as Kotosh (Izumi and Terada 1972) and complex preceramic evidence in or near the Callejón de Huaylas (Burger and Burger 1980, Bueno Mendoza and Grieder 1979). These sites show evidence of elaborate ceremonialism, probably involving a specialized and status-differentiated society. While these developments are underway by at least 2500 BC, a more traditional, small-group and egalitarian existence continued in other Andean areas.

The environment, character, and adaptation of these societies in the Peruvian highlands will be the focus of this chapter. In keeping with current trends in the study of prehistoric hunter-gatherers, I will avoid extensive comparisons of chronologies, stone tools and other artifacts, and instead examine socio-cultural adaptations to the specific environmental conditions of the highland Central Andes.

Since different adaptations were evolving at varying speeds in contrasting highland ecological situations, wide-ranging chronologies such as those of Lanning (1967a) and MacNeish, Patterson, and Browman (1975) are of limited use here. Rather than describe preceramic archaeological remains from all known phases in all known areas, I will make general observations about two broad periods: an early glacial period, prior to 9000 BC, and a post-glacial preceramic of 9000 to 1800 BC.

HIGHLAND ENVIRONMENTS AND PALEOENVIRONMENTS

Natural resource characteristics, such as seasonality, behavior and distribution, greatly influence hunter-gatherer adaptation. This is in contrast to

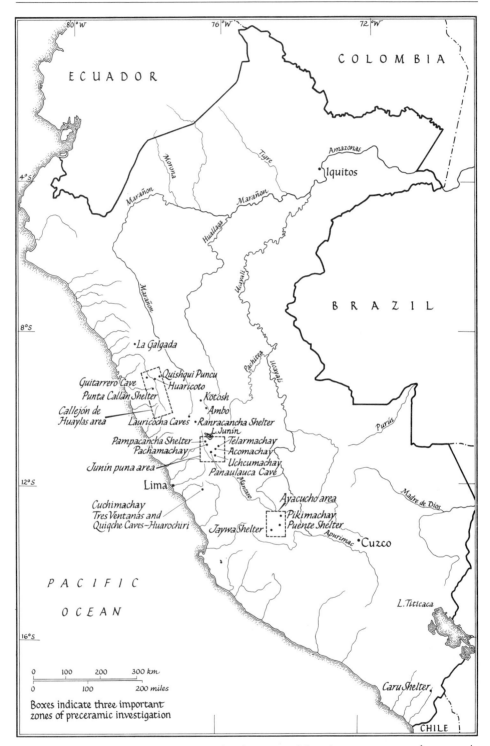

Fig. 1.1 Major preceramic sites mentioned in the text, and three important zones of preceramic investigation.

advanced food-producing societies with storage facilities, which are capable of altering ecosystems to their advantage and storing foods across seasonal gaps in availability. Since highland preceramic cultures depended mostly on wild foods, the Andean ecosystem provides an important foundation for our consideration of these early peoples.

Evidence of human occupation in Peru may be 20,000 years old, so the significant climatic changes at the end of the Pleistocene are of concern. In the highly altitude-stratified Andean environment, any change in temperature or rainfall would have shifted present zones upwards or downwards. Such changes in resource distribution have serious implications for hunter-gatherer occupation. Pleistocene ice cover over large areas of the Andes, potentially limiting or eliminating highland occupation, represents an even greater impact (Lynch 1980: 311, Hester 1973). To cover these possibilities I will briefly describe the modern highland environment, and then review evidence for climate change.

Modern environment

Crossing the Andes chain from east to west anywhere in Peru, zones are highly stratified in synchrony with the steep altitude gradients. Starting at the top of the Andes and moving down, we can recognize the snow and periglacial zone, the puna zone, and below this the highland valley macrozone, an internally complex biotic area. Still lower is the lush tropical vegetation to the east of the Andes, and a contrasting riparian-xerophytic-littoral-fog-meadow complex along the western coastline – but these areas are beyond the geographic range of this discussion.

Snow and periglacial zone. As the name implies, this very high altitude wasteland above 5,000 m is either covered by permanent ice and snow, or seasonally frozen or snow-covered. The very limited range of resources, low biomass, and rugged topography make this zone of dubious value for human subsistence.

Puna zone. This is the highest area fit for human occupation, consisting of rolling grasslands spotted with flat lakeshore plains and crossed by a network of perennial streams (Fig. 1.2). The altitude range of the puna, from about 3,900 to 5,000 m, has rather little effect on puna ecology, especially in central Peru. More significant are moisture-retention and heat-protection differences due to a variety of topographical, ground-water, and bedrock-exposure conditions. In general, the puna is best considered a fine-grained mosaic environment, which contains scattered plant resources such as berries, tubers, and seeds, but with ideal grassland areas for grazing of abundant wild camelids (Fig. 1.3) and deer. Lakeshore areas may have been productive for waterfowl, aquatic plants, and amphibians.

The puna, like all highland environments, varies considerably between northern and southern Peru. In the north the puna is largely lacking, due to heavy erosional dissection of the Andes (Fig. 1.4). Central Peru has a large puna girdle at about 11° S latitude. This expanse is surprisingly non-seasonal, varying more in precipitation than temperature between the wet (November–April) and dry (May–October) seasons. Modern puna herders maintain their grazing animals the year round on the same pastures, since the grasses are productive across the seasons. In far southern Peru the snowline is higher, and there is a greater contrast between wet and dry seasons. Nevertheless, the vicuña, a camelid which needs year-round productive territories, are as at home as they are in the central puna.

The puna of southern Peru has been described as an unpredictable environment with reference to modern herder-agriculturalists (Winterhalder and Thomas 1978). Given their reliance on domestic plants and animals not totally adapted to the zone, this is a reasonable view. But for much of the central puna's natural food sources, predictability may have been rather high with a

Fig. 1.2 Typical puna landscape. This is the central Peruvian puna (4,200 m) in the dry season, looking towards the Western Cordillera of the Andes, which is about 60 km away.

medium overall resource density, without strong spatial or seasonal aggregation. The puna's fine-grain mosaic resource distribution and lack of pronounced seasons give relatively even resource availability across space and time. The frigid climate of this altitude limits the growth of leafy and herbaceous plants, permitting grasses and grazing animals to take a front seat in the human resource arena (see Cardich 1976). A possible exception to this dispersion are the lakeshores, where ameliorated temperature regimes allow concentration of waterplants and waterfowl.

Highland valley macrozone. The highland valley's highly stratified ecology is strongly influenced by altitude, and even more by rainfall (Fig. 1.5). A pan-Andean view of the highland valleys must consider more than altitude, since rainshadow areas are highly distinct from more moist environments of the same altitude. In such a water-limited situation, major watercourses are of great importance. The relatively drier condition of the highland valleys accentuates the contrasts between wet and dry seasons, highly affecting productivity across the yearly cycle. Lack of perennial grazing or browsing resources would have led to a much lower density of large game than the puna offered. Because of their own storage needs, and because of the freedom from heavy frosts, valley plants would have been more productive, but seasonal, resources for hunter-gatherers.

Fig. 1.3 Band of vicuña in the punas of Junín, 4,200 m altitude. These deer-sized wild camelids were an important, non-seasonal resource to early hunters of the high grasslands.

A reconstruction of the biotic resources characterizing the modern highland valleys is hampered by the great environmental modification of two or three millenia of intensive agriculture. Many forests, in particular, were removed long ago by field clearing and firewood collection.

Microzones present in most highland valleys would be 1) narrow riparian corridors following major streams, with low trees, shrub vegetation, and some herbaceous growth; 2) barren xerophytic areas away from streams at lower altitudes and in rainshadows; and 3) increasingly more abundant shrubby and

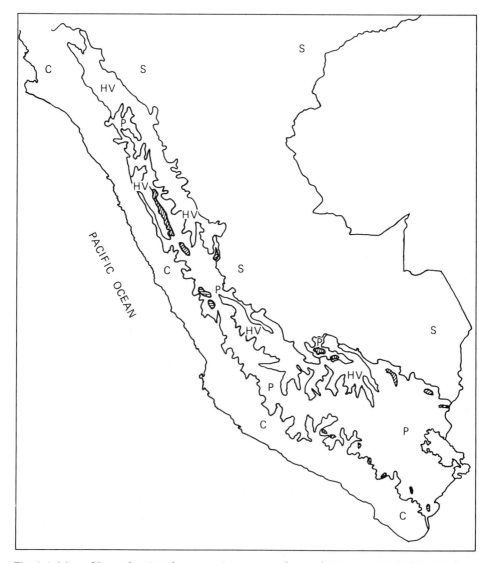

Fig. 1.4 Map of Peru, showing the approximate area of coastal (C), puna (P), highland valleys (HV), and the selva or jungle area (S). Hatched zones are the major snow and periglacial areas. Compiled from pp. 143, 175 of Instituto Nacional de Planificacion (1969).

thorn-forest vegetation as a level of 3,600 m is reached, above which the trees and shrubs thin to puna grassland. For technical reasons, terms such as "humid" and "forest" have appeared in environmental classifications of Peru (see Tosi 1960). These are not, however, the moisture levels or tree growth the average person might envision. Even "humid" areas have less than 500 mm of highly seasonal rainfall. "Forests" were mostly of low-standing, spiny trees (see esp. Smith 1980b).

In sum, highland valley areas show significant seasonality, with seasonal desiccation of lower zones and, to a lesser degree, of the higher valley areas. During dry seasons, resources would have concentrated around water sources, much as in the Kalahari desert, as animals sought out remaining green vegetation. Wet-season conditions would encourage the dispersal of food resources, with lower areas becoming relatively more productive. Resources therefore probably ranged from somewhat aggregated to quite dispersed, and density probably was low in terms of overall biomass compared to the puna. Predictability was rather low; any rainfall variation would have a striking

Fig. 1.5 Highland valley scene. This view looks eastward from the mouth of Pikimachay Cave (Ayacucho), towards higher, more vegetated zones.

effect on vegetation and game movements, since the environment is water-limited to begin with.

It is worth while to evaluate the relative surface area included in these zones. Most investigators have viewed the puna as a fringe which rings the allegedly more important highland valleys. This may in part reflect the prevalence of modern population centers in highland valleys rather than in the puna. However, using Tosi's (1960) ecological zonation for Peru, which includes the huge expanses of low eastern tropical vegetation (58% of Peru), zones assignable to the puna total 14.1% of Peru, while a liberal estimate of highland valleys is 11.4%. This large proportion of puna is further compounded, since the northern third of Peru has no puna at all – making the lower two-thirds of the country very puna-rich indeed (Fig. 1.4). This suggests a zone that is more than just an upper valley edge, but rather one of greater area, of large, unbroken extensions, and of greater natural resource productivity than highland valleys.

Environmental change

There is little reliable information from highland Peru concerning climates of the recent past. Most studies have relied upon the more solid records from outside Peru, including Van Der Hammen's Quaternary Project in Colombia (1973), Heusser's Chilean pollen record (1966), or Mercer's Patagonian glacial evidence (1972). Changes in such distant locations cannot be assumed to have occurred in Peru, especially if they represent minor trends. Peru itself has a few studies of glacial stages and snowline depression, one non-archaeological pollen study just completed, and a smattering of archaeological pollen, plant, and animal remains studied in on-site contexts.

The best-documented evidence is of snowline depression and major climate change during the last stadial of the Pleistocene. Human occupation in the sierra might have been restricted by ice cover at this time, according to Hester (1973) and Lynch (1980). A number of studies examine snowline depression for the Pleistocene (Clapperton 1972, Hastenrath 1967, Nogami 1976), but there is little assurance that these studies document the latest, as opposed to earlier Pleistocene, advances. Wright (1980) suggested, on the basis of field studies coupled with carbon dates, that the last major ice advance in central Peru occurred around 12,000 BP, and involved a 300–500 m lowering of snowline. A more recent series of dates from the same area now suggest termination of glacial conditions by at least 13,000 BP (Wright, personal communication). During this last major glacial advance, ice may have descended to 4,600–4,500 m altitude, according to Wright (1980). Hastenrath (1967) documents a Pleistocene glaciation as low as 3,700 m in northern Peru, and 4,300 in the central area. But, as mentioned above, the lowest glaciations may have preceded human occupation.

The more conservative estimates suggest that most of the Peruvian sierra was not recently under ice. Even parts of the puna of central Peru were ice-free in the last advance. While it was more frigid and less productive than at present, it still may have been inhabitable. Highland valleys would have been quite productive, perhaps reflecting somewhat higher life zones than they do today. A depression of ecological zones seems probable, given the 2° C temperature drop and greater precipitation that Wright (1980) uses to explain snowline depression. Cardich (1964) presents a moraine sequence from the Lauricocha puna, which he correlates with known Pleistocene sequences elsewhere. However, independent dating is lacking to support these correlations.

Records from outside Peru have varying dates for the end of Pleistocene glaciation, but all agree that most areas were ice free by 12,000–10,000 BP. No glaciers or climate changes of Pleistocene magnitude are found after this date. A few small, undated advances are known from Junín, indicating short periods of colder/wetter climate (Wright 1980, 1984). Times of greater warmth than the present day have been mentioned for areas outside Peru by Gonzalez, Van Der Hammen, and Flint (1965) and others. But from within Peru itself, the most convincing evidence to date for postglacial climate comes from a deep, carbon-dated pollen core retrieved by H. E. Wright, Jr, and his colleagues from Lake Junín (Hansen, Wright, and Bradbury 1984). The pollen stratigraphy implies that east Andean forests were lowered in elevation or reduced in density during the last glacial maximum. The Holocene record shows uniform climate and vegetational conditions, broken some time after 3,000 years ago by an advance of local glaciers. This post-preceramic ice began a final retreat before 1,100 years ago. Therefore, after the retreat of Pleistocene glaciation, there is little evidence for changing highland climate during the preceramic period.

Other evidence for postglacial climate is based mostly on archaeological assemblages. Implicit in archaeological data is the human role in the accumulation of pollen, and plant and animal remains. Kautz (1980) clearly shows that much of the pollen record for Guitarrero Cave in the Callejón de Huaylas is a result of human contributions. MacNeish *et al.* (1980) reconstruct environments on the basis of animal remains from archaeological levels, although admitting that the various climatological data from this project are not in agreement. For Smith (1980a) the abundant plant remains from Guitarrero Cave speak for a rather constant plant environment after about 8000 BP, and Pearsall's (1980) extensive carbonized plant identifications from Pachamachay Cave in the Junín puna show no significant quantities of non-puna species since 12,000 BP, and no trends suggestive of climate change.

None of these records argues for a totally constant climate, but, in conjunction with pollen evidence, it seems safe to suggest that no radical changes capable of substantially altering subsistence patterns occurred in postglacial preceramic times. Glacial periods would have seen zone depression, but no total elimination of major zones for human habitation.

HIGHLAND PRECERAMIC: THE EARLIEST SITES

Rather than reconstruct late glacial environments, it is better to see if the archaeological evidence from this period is sufficient to test environmentally derived models of human occupation. Radiocarbon dates for human presence prior to 11,000 BP or 9000 BC come from three well-described sites: Pikimachay in Ayacucho, Pachamachay in Junín, and Guitarrero Cave in the Callejón de Huaylas. Undated remains from Uchcumachay Cave in Junín are felt to belong to this period (Pires-Ferreira, Pires-Ferreira, and Kaulicke 1976).

Evidence for occupation in these sites in the glacial period is not very strong. Pachamachay Cave has a date of 11,800 ± 930 BP for the second lowest of 33 undisturbed strata (Rick 1980). The layer associated with this date produced 42 chert tools, 162 carbonized seeds, 13 animal bones, and 580 g of stone-tool waste. The stone tools consist of 14 retouched or utilized flakes, 6 finished bifacial projectile pounts, 5 larger, unfinished or fragmentary bifaces, and 17 unifacially retouched tools. With minimal stylistic differences, all these tools fit perfectly within the tool traditions that continue at this site for at least another 8,000 years. The remains are relatively scanty compared with later layers, and do not represent a major cultural phenomenon. The standard deviation on the single date is so large that this stratum could be as early as 11,600 BC, or as late as 8000 BC. Given the similarity of tool industry and function, the human adaptation represented probably is like that of later strata.

The earliest Guitarrero Cave date of 12,560 ± 360 BP now has the companionship of four other dates ranging from 9140 ± 90 to 9790 ± 240 BP, coming from the same stratigraphic unit (Lynch 1980: 32). It seems probable that this material is mostly, if not all, from postglacial times, and is best seen as part of the later preceramic assemblage.

The undated Uchcumachay site (Fig. 1.6) bases its antiquity on a lowest layer containing extinct Pleistocene fauna, along with one well-defined tool and seven retouch flakes (Pires-Ferreira, Pires-Ferreira, and Kaulicke 1976). The fauna are the basis for dating this culturally silent layer to 7000–10,000 BC. Significantly, this stratum is overlain immediately by a clearly cultural deposit containing 78 stone artifacts, and about 550 retouch flakes cross-dated to 7000–5500 BC. The chances of one artifact's having been transferred to a lower level, along with a few retouch flakes, seems rather high. If the association is good, there is still little evidence upon which to deal with adaptation, even including the eight animal bones present.

Finally, at the risk of joining a wearying battle, the now-famous Pikimachay materials from Ayacucho must be considered (MacNeish 1979, Lynch 1974). MacNeish has argued at length for the antiquity of his Pacaicasa and Ayacucho-phase strata from Pikimachay Cave (Fig. 1.7), which he dates to between 20,000 and 11,000 BC. The dates for the phases are derived entirely from animal bone, and have been questioned previously by Lynch (1974). Although the dates are widely known, confusion remains since one date is alternatively reported as 18,250 BC ± 1050 and 18,250 BC ± 105, and another is either 17,650 BC ± 1200 or 17,650 BC ± 3000 (MacNeish 1979: 18, 25). An undated occupation is cited as 20,500 BC ± 2500 as if carbon dated, which it is not (*Ibid*. p. 19).

I will avoid topics covered in previous discussions, and make a few new observations on these two early phases. I am one of the few archaeologists other than Ayacucho Project personnel to have examined in detail the entire collection of Pacaicasa and Ayacucho-phase tools in the Museum of the University of San Marcos. I am indebted to MacNeish himself for allowing this examination. In my opinion, the Pacaicasa materials are so eroded that it is effectively impossible to determine their tool status, especially since they are almost all rocks from the tuff bedrock of the cave itself. Two very crude tools of non-cave rock are also present. MacNeish's photographs are excellent testimony to the condition of the tuff fragments (Fig. 1.8). As an archaeologist with experience in lithic analysis and replication, I am not convinced that these either are, or are not, tools. Any conclusive evidence for manufacture or use was long ago eroded from their surfaces. They certainly are not extensively

Fig. 1.6 Uchcumachay shelter, located at 4,050 m in the southern puna of Junín. An excavation conducted by P. Kaulicke in the foreground produced bones of Pleistocene mammals, in possible association with stone-tool materials.

worked items, nor is there consistent shape, or even selective use of particular rock-fragment forms. Nor is the soft tuff very appropriate for tool use, especially when more appropriate materials are near by. One of the two non-tuff tools is described as a burin, found near a "cut sloth rib, a scratched and polished sloth rib, and two different fragments of polished and scratched long bones of large mammals" (MacNeish 1979: 27). While this certainly suggests human activity, the associated bone tools are not illustrated in the final report of the project, restricting outside evaluation (MacNeish *et al.* 1980).

Evidence for human presence in Pacaicasa layers includes horizontal bone and rock distributions characterized as "non-random" (MacNeish 1979: 41). Any demonstration of non-randomness remains to be seen, for rather random distributions, and rather arbitrary activity areas, are seen in floor plots (*Ibid.* pp. 11–14).

A few other problems are also present. There is no evidence of fire, which could be due to very short visits, but, with a minimum of four occupations, it is rather surprising. Also, the faunal assemblage suggests successful hunting of big – and in the case of puma, ferocious – game, yet no tools such as projectile

Fig. 1.7 Pikimachay Cave (Ayacucho). The dark spot in the center of the photo is the mouth of the cave, located at 2,850 m.

Fig. 1.8 Possible stone tools from Pacaicasa-phase levels in the Pikimachay site, Ayacucho. MacNeish describes these as hammer core choppers (1, 2); worked flake (3); plane scraper (4); burin (5); spokeshaves (6–8); and denticulate (9). From Humphrey, R. L., and D. Stanford, eds., *Pre-Llano Cultures of the Americas: Paradoxes and Possibilities.* Copyright 1979 by the Anthropological Society of Washington.

points or sharp knives useful to such an adaptation are present. While this can be fitted to a pre-projectile point stage, evidence of an appropriate technology would be reassuring.

In sum, there is little solid, unquestionable evidence of humans in the Pacaicasa phase, but neither is there conclusive evidence that the materials are non-cultural. Many key questions remain to be answered, perhaps through analysis of floor distributions, taphonomic techniques to assure that representation of game body parts is not due to non-human carnivores, and microscopic analysis of bone scratches.

The subsequent Ayacucho-phase materials are in a different category, because there are significant numbers of non-tuff, human-made tools from this phase. I noted when examining the collection that these definite tools are accompanied by tuff pieces as well. The tools most frequently illustrated are the non-tuff ones (MacNeish 1979: 44, 45). Unfortunately, the final report on these materials is organized in such a way that which materials were used in each phase cannot be determined (MacNeish *et al.* 1980). Some tools could have slipped downwards from later layers through the porous rockfall which directly overlies the Ayacucho strata, but it is possible they are *in situ*. Spatial organization of these strata seems more complex than in the preceding phase, although there is still no solid evidence for use of fire.

MacNeish's (1979) interpretations of various activity areas as seasonal microband occupations find little supporting evidence. It does seem likely that these would be *short-term* occupations, but "seasonal" implies consistent presence in a specific season, which is not evident in the published data. Just what a microband is has not been made clear. If it is an analogy to historic hunter-gatherers, no evidence is presented to show why these early hunters of such different prey, and with such different technology, should have a similar organization.

Out of the total 206 tools listed for the Ayacucho phase, an unknown number are unmistakably tools. Therefore, it seems possible that around 12,000 BC there was human activity at Pikimachay at least partially involved with exploiting Pleistocene game. The presence of puma and other large cat remains in most of these layers suggests that not all of these animals were killed by humans, however. As MacNeish himself states, "any attempt to relate these three ill-defined complexes to other equally poorly defined assemblages in the New World is at best, speculation" (1979: 46). Attempting to explain these scanty materials as adaptations to paleoenvironmental conditions would be premature at this point.

Therefore, the evidence for Pleistocene occupation in highland Peru is at best nebulous, and even the strongest case does not contribute much information on past culture. In fact, it is significant that immediately after this period there is an explosion of undoubted human cultural remains in the Andes. This suggests that either Pleistocene hunters did not exist, or they were so different in habits, so small in numbers or unsuccessful in adaptation as to leave them nearly archaeologically invisible.

POSTGLACIAL PRECERAMIC CULTURES

Starting around 9000 BC, and blossoming by 8000 BC, there is major human occupation throughout the sierra of Peru. Various sites are known in the Callejón de Huaylas (Lynch 1971, 1980), from the Huanuco puna at Lauricocha (Cardich 1958, 1964), from the Junín puna (Lavallée and Julien 1975, Matos Mendieta 1975, Pires-Ferreira, Pires-Ferreira, and Kaulicke 1976, Rick 1980), from Huarochiri (Engel 1970c), from Ayacucho (MacNeish *et al.* 1980, MacNeish *et al.* 1981), and from the far southern highlands (Ravines 1967, 1972), to mention the more well-known areas (see Fig. 1.1). Not only do these manifestations occur suddenly, but the chipped stone-tool industries are relatively uniform. Stone tools from sierra sites generally are quite numerous, in contrast to the coast (compare Lanning 1963a with Lynch 1980, MacNeish *et al.* 1980, Rick 1980). As a result, sierra tools have been used extensively as chronological indicators in highland, coastal, and Peru-wide sequences. For instance, the pan-Andean projectile-point sequence of Lanning and Hammel (1961) was based largely on tools from the Lauricocha puna.

Early chronologies were based on as little as one radiocarbon date and partial stratigraphic superposition. Changes in stone tools form the basis for archaeological periods, which are used as if having ultimate validity or value. More useful temporal divisions are based on significant changes in prehistoric adaptation, which may not be observed adequately in stone-tool – especially projectile-point – form. Changes in tool form in any area are thought to be in synchrony with form changes throughout Peru. In the rugged and geographically variable Andes, such uniform changes would require sweeping economic transformations, rapid transfer of style between innovator and acceptor, or fast expansion of a style-bearing population. None of these processes has been demonstrated adequately for the Andean area.

Therefore, wide-ranging, fine-scale correlations based on stone tools are rather uncertain, and it is difficult to explain why they would exist. Given the few independently dated sites, I will emphasize adaptation and leave details of material culture and chronology to others. Lynch (1980: 317) conveniently has provided the term "Central Andean Preceramic Tradition," applicable to the Non-Complex Preceramic of 9000–1800 BC. Lynch includes only the Central and North-Central Sierra within this tradition. It is difficult to exclude the Ayacucho area, however, so I use the term for the entire central Andean area of Peru. The outside observer should have some idea of the remains, sites, and site distributions of this tradition. After building this material foundation

I will examine the subsistence organization and interaction proposed for the Central Andean Preceramic.

Material remains

Chipped stone tools are the only widely distributed, uniformly preserved artifacts of the Andean preceramic. As mentioned, assemblages throughout this period are similar, but only at the general level. That is, the same tool technology and functions are seen at most sites: small projectile points of various forms, a flake uniface complex of "scrapers" or "knives," and an admixture of larger core tools with probable chopper function (Figs. 1.9, 1.10). A few other tool types include notched, denticulate, or pointed forms, mostly made on flakes. Whether blades or microblades are an important, intentional aspect of this industry is not well resolved (Lynch 1980, Rick 1980, Stothert 1980), but utilized flakes and other casual non-retouched tools are an important, often-ignored component.

On a more specific level, the proportions of different functional types of tool vary notably across both space and time. Chauchat (1972), Pires-Ferreira, Pires-Ferreira, and Kaulicke (1976), and Rick (1980) all show that there is a

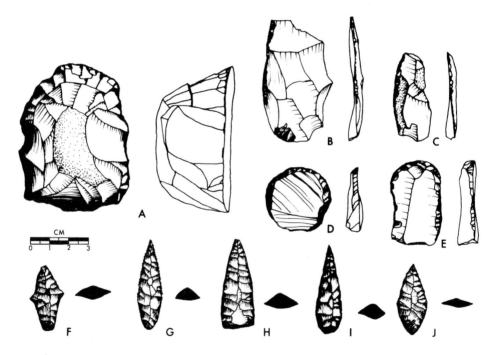

Fig. 1.9 Stone tools from Pachamachay (Junín): core chopper (A), straight-edged unifaces (B, C), curved-edge unifaces (D, E), and projectile points from various periods (F–J). While these are exclusively from one puna site, they are typical tools of the Central Andean Preceramic Tradition.

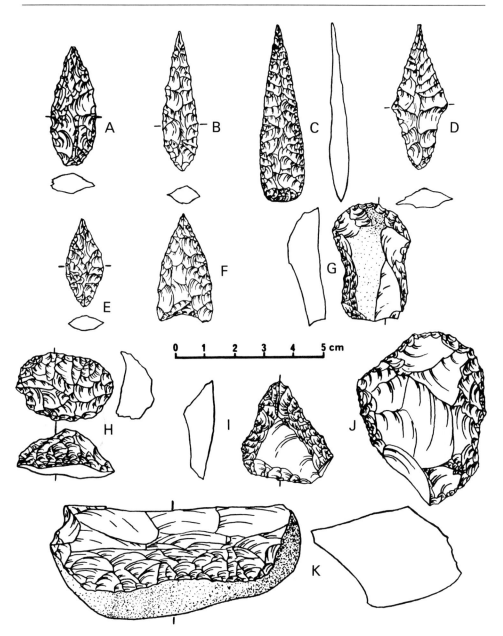

Fig. 1.10 Chipped stone tools from Guitarrero Cave, Callejón de Huaylas. Note the generally similar form, technology, and size with Pachamachay tools (fig. 1.9). Lynch describes these tools as projectile points (A–F); flake endscraper (G); steep-scraper (H); graver-scraper (I); scraper (J); steep-scraper (K). From Thomas F. Lynch, *Guitarrero Cave: Early Man in the Andes.* Copyright 1980 by Academic Press. Reprinted by permission.

general increase in projectile-point proportion in puna assemblages across time. Data from highland valley contexts generally do not confirm this trend (Lynch 1980, MacNeish *et al*. 1980). Lynch (1971) has shown that neighbouring puna sites generally have higher proportions of projectile points than do lower sites in the valley area of the Callejón de Huaylas.

On a more local level, proportions of unifaces and chopping tools differ between hunting and base camps in the puna (Rick 1980). Variation in general functional tool-class proportions likely reflects different economic processes in different ecological zones, and perhaps across time. Vierra (1975) suggests that temporal variation in stone-tool proportions at the Puente site in Ayacucho is not economically significant because faunal remains vary indifferently to tools. It is equally likely that faunal remains are very heavily affected by varying site-formation processes, and may not be the yardstick against which to measure the meaning of stone tools.

Certain functional classes, such as projectile points, have been amenable to further classification into stylistic types. Temporal change in these types has fueled the cultural chronologies of the preceramic. The existence and validity of these sequences varies widely from area to area, but a general trend is for shouldered points to occur early, followed by leaf-shaped points, and smaller or less elongate points are found last. This trend has been supported by Lynch (1967), MacNeish, Nelken-Terner and Garcia Cook (1970), and Rick (1980), but it probably is so coarse and variable that it will not serve for fine cross-dating.

Some believe that similar projectile points from all parts of the Andes must be exactly coeval (MacNeish 1980), but there is evidence to the contrary. Shouldered forms may occur earlier in the north and later in the south (Rick 1980: 319). Concave-base, triangular forms are the earliest-known points from the central puna, and are terminal preceramic artifacts in the south. Projectile points from the 30-km distant puna base-camp sites of Pachamachay and Panaulauca in Junín show notably different forms in contemporary levels. Given the limited range of forms in the small and thick Andean projectile points, less-than-identical points widely separated in space may not indicate contemporaneity.

Ground or pecked stone tools are rare compared to chipped stone tools, although hammerstones are reasonably frequent. Milling-stone fragments are notably scarce, and are little modified by use or manufacture. They are a little more common in highland valley than in puna sites, suggesting a greater use of plant resources at lower altitudes (compare Nelken-Terner [1980] with Rick [1980]). Ornamental, non-utilitarian items include quartz crystals, a variety of beads, and paint-grinding tools – all in relative rarity.

Bone tools such as awls, needles, flakers, or fleshers are characteristic of this period (Fig. 1.11), but, like ground stone, are relatively scarce and not elaborate. There may be many casually used and rarely recognized bone tools, especially in game-rich and wood-poor puna areas. Perishable artifacts are well reported only at Guitarrero Cave (Lynch 1980). Although looter-mixed strata are a great problem at this site, the range of wood and fiber artifacts illustrates what must be missing under less dry conditions, including fire drills, cordage, basketry, and textiles (Fig. 1.12).

Subsistence remains vary considerably from zone to zone. Wing (1977) has found that a diversity of game is represented in highland valley sites, while the puna bag is composed primarily of camelids and deer. Unfortunately, it has not yet proved possible definitely to separate the four camelids – the domesticated llama and alpaca and the wild vicuña and guanaco – on the basis of their remains. Plant resources are less well documented, given preservation problems, and the reticence of Andean archaeologists to accept flotation techniques. With rare exceptions, plant recovery has been oriented towards early domesticated species, so our knowledge of wild plant utilization is quite poor (see, however, Pearsall 1978). Pearsall (1980) has identified a surpris-

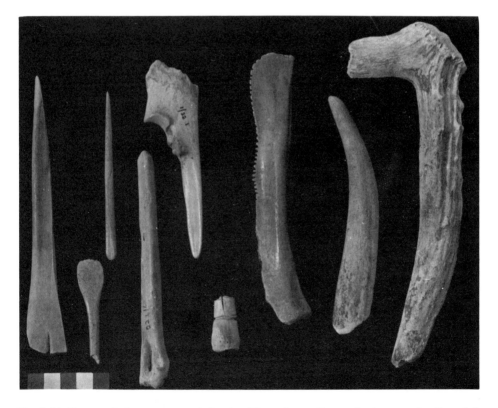

Fig. 1.11 Bone tools from preceramic levels of Panaulauca Cave, a Junín puna site. From left to right are simple awl, spatulate tool, fine awl or needle, pressure flaker, ulna awl, bone grooved for cutting beads, scapula flesher or comb, taruca deer antler pressure flaker, and taruca deer cylindrical antler hammer. Scale at bottom measures 5 cm in length.

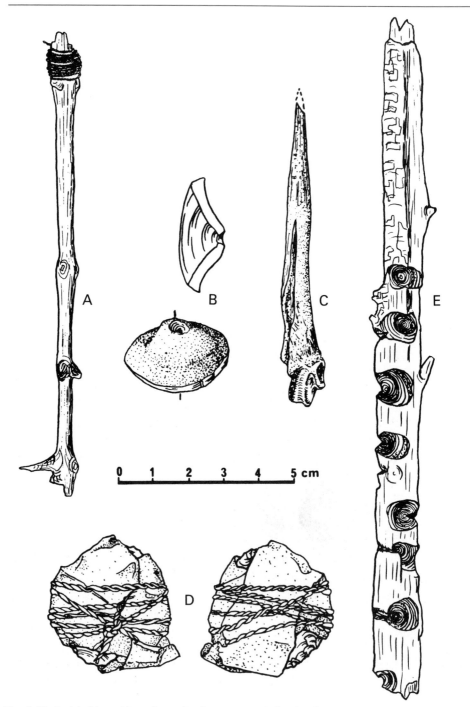

Fig. 1.12 Perishable artifacts from the dry preceramic levels of Guitarrero Cave, Callejón de Huaylas. Stick with cemented and bound end (A); top to gourd container (B); bone awl (C); hide-wrapped scraper (D); fire-drill hearth (E). From Thomas F. Lynch, *Guitarrero Cave: Early Man in the Andes*. Copyright 1980 by Academic Press. Reprinted by permission.

ingly wide range of plant resources in Junín puna sites. Included are grains and cactus fruit, as well as a series of probable medicinal herbs and food plants.

Domesticated plants show up rather early in the highland valley preceramic, with well-documented beans and peppers present at about 8500 BC (Smith 1980a, Kaplan 1980). A wider variety of domesticates including maize and other grains, gourds, squash, tubers, grains, and fruits are known by 3000 BC (Pearsall 1978). Particularly striking is the absence of almost all domestic plants in the puna preceramic.

Domestication of the llama and guinea pig has yet to be clearly identified, in spite of a number of important studies (Pollard and Drew 1975, Pires-Ferreira 1975, Wheeler, Cardoza, and Pozzi-Escot 1977, Wing 1977). From all evidence, it seems probable that the llama was domesticated sometime during the preceramic, but the exact location, species, and period involved are currently unknown. Domesticated alpacas, however, may have been present in some parts of the Junín puna around 4,000 BC (Wheeler 1984).

Architecture from the Non-Complex Preceramic is rare, and is found primarily in cave sites. Known structures are small, stone or post-walled structures, which appear to be dwellings (Fig. 1.13). Constructions are present in puna base-camps as far back as 10,000 BC (Rick 1980), and are apparent in the Huarochiri site of Tres Ventanas (Engel 1970c).

Burials and associated offerings are known mostly from Lauricocha Cave L-2 (Cardich 1964), Junín sites (Julien, Lavallée, and Dietz 1981), and Tres Ventanas and Quiche caves of Huarochiri (Beynon and Siegel 1981). Most burials are flexed, and many are lying on their sides (Fig. 1.14). In Lauricocha, the three children among the eleven burials received more material offerings – food, stone tools, beads, colorants – than the adults. The lack of preceramic burials in other sites suggests systematic disposal in a place or manner that avoids archaeologists' attentions.

Rock art, mostly in the form of red-colored pictographs, is found throughout Peru. There appears to be a clustering of art in the puna between Lauricocha and Huarochiri in the Central Sierra. There is some evidence that art in this area dates specifically to the preceramic (Rick 1980: 241). Usual subjects are animals, interpreted as camelids, occasionally pursued by hunters or accompanied by geometric designs (Fig. 1.15; see also Cardich 1964).

Preceramic site distribution

The known location of preceramic sites is a mixture of sampling bias and true distribution, and care is required to distinguish between the two. Significantly, there are no Non-Complex Preceramic sierra sites below 2,500 m that have attracted archaeological attention, and only three lie below 3,000 m (see Table 1, p. 36). MacNeish, for instance, may have located such sites in the lower reaches of the Ayacucho Valley, but they evidently did not merit excavation.

Were notable sites present in lower areas, in all likelihood at least one would have been investigated. Since the lower valley areas lead to the Amazonian lowlands, this may be a significant absence. Alternatively, it could be an artifact of a lack of good facilities and agreeable conditions for archaeological field work in lower areas.

A less secure observation is the tendency for sites to be in caves. Two major open-air sites that have been described, Quishqui Puncu (3,040 m) in the Callejón de Huaylas (Fig. 1.16; Lynch 1970), and Ambo (2,065 m) near Huánuco (Ravines 1965), are among the lower known preceramic sites. Puna cold would make cave shelter very desirable, and the heat of the valleys might make cool caves attractive. Either more open sites are present and awaiting excavation, or else this is a true cave-dwelling culture.

The abundance of preceramic sites in different ecological zones cannot be easily compared, since no large-scale intensive preceramic surveys have yet been reported. Two small surveys in the Junín puna yielded site density between about .13 and .07 sites per km^2 (Rick 1980, Lavallée and Julien 1975). Survey in the Ayacucho area seems to have yielded about .03–.08 sites per km^2 (MacNeish *et al.* 1980) – perhaps not a significant difference, given variation in survey and recording techniques.

Fig. 1.13 Late preceramic structure (1800 BC) at Pachamachay Cave, puna of Junín. Rocks are the foundation of a 3 m-diameter structure, whose entrance is indicated by the trowel. A hearth is present in the lower center of structure, at which point the floor is interrupted by an earlier excavation.

Fig. 1.14 Preceramic burial of adult male from 3000 BC layers of Panaulauca Cave, puna of Junín. Note the individual's tightly flexed position, resting on left side, with head oriented north. No clear offerings were present, and this burial was covered with sizeable rocks.

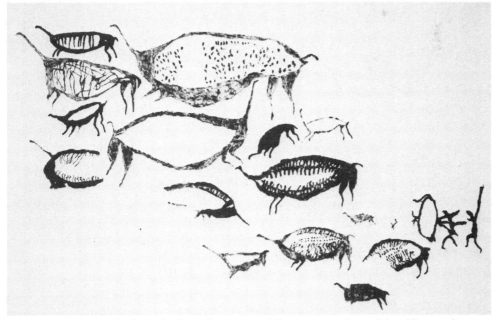

Fig. 1.15 Pictographs from Cuchimachay (Lima). These groups of camelid and human figures adorn the walls of a large cave at 4,200 m in the sierra of Lima. They are executed in red, with the largest figure about 3.5 m across. Drawing by Grace M. Oseki.

Fig. 1.16 Excavations at the open preceramic site of Quishqui Puncu at an altitude of 3,040 m in the Callejón de Huaylas. Photograph courtesy of Thomas Lynch.

INTERPRETING THE CENTRAL ANDEAN PRECERAMIC

There have been few attempts to characterize the adaptations of highland pre-ceramic peoples beyond their material culture and diet. Those who have dared to infer social or subsistence organization and seasonal habits are in surprisingly little agreement about basic patterns. The most synthetic of these studies are worth considering at length.

Mobility, seasonality, and sedentism

A major problem of the preceramic is human utilization of the major Andean ecological zones and their differing resources. Apparent resource complementarity of different life zones suggests to some that transhumance, or systematic zone visitation during productive seasons by mobile peoples, was an optimal adaptation. In the earlier of his formulations, Lynch (1967, 1971) proposed a seasonal round spanning sierra and coastal areas, based on the complementary seasonality of highland valleys (dry between May and October) and the coastal *lomas* fog meadows (dry between December and July). The green season in *coastal valleys*, however, is not due to local rainfall, but to runoff descending from the *highlands*. This takes place during the December-to-March period, producing a coastal bloom complementary to that of the *lomas*. Patterson (1971c) suggested a more probable seasonal round contained within the coastal areas, and Lynch (1980) more recently has agreed that coast–highland transhumance is not a widespread preceramic pattern.

Transhumance has been proposed also for groups inhabiting puna caves quite near the coast in central Peru (Engel 1970c). In this very low rainfall puna, a movement between the coast and westernmost sierra might be necessary. The same situation may apply to the far south of Peru, where the puna is seasonally arid. Here Ravines (1972) has documented a number of sites believed to belong in a transhumance system.

Lynch's (1980) more recent views suggest that transhumance within the highland valleys, reaching into the puna zone, would have been more probable than coastward transhumance. The proposed movement would be motivated by water-dependent green seasons and their accompanying game distributions. In essence, the first zones to dry out are the lowest. Hence the occupation of lower areas would be during times of maximum rainfall (December–March), with groups thereafter departing for the higher areas, reaching the puna during the most arid season (June–September). Whether game migrated across these zones in this way is not known, but lower-area aridity would be a stimulus. The puna of central Peru, however, provides good pasture during the dry season, often remaining verdant the year round.

This seasonal round is specifically suggested for the Callejón de Huaylas, the only major sierra valley that drains westward instead of east to the

Amazon (Fig. 1.1). The Callejón can be envisioned as a long, straight valley which gradually ascends southward until it reaches puna altitude. Lynch designed his reconstruction around a series of known sites, ranging from 2,580 to 4,130 m altitude. The lower sites, such as Guitarrero Cave (Lynch 1980) and Quishqui Puncu (Lynch 1970), are near the valley bottom around 2,500–3,000 m, and presumably served as wet-season camps within the round. A number of higher sites are known, both in the mountains west of the valley and in the puna area to the south. Groups from the valley sites could move either west or south to obtain dry-season resources. The difference is considerable – going west to the puna from Guitarrero Cave would be a 10–30 km trek, while the southern puna would require about 100 km of travel. But if Guitarrero people travelled to the south puna, were they the only existent group, or did they pass through adjacent upriver territories on their way to the puna? More than one preceramic group likely inhabited the Callejón, since the area exceeds 5000 km². Valley groups probably would have used nearby puna resources in short seasonal movements, permitting a series of groups to exploit resources found on east–west transects of the valley.

MacNeish, Patterson, and Browman (1975) have suggested a series of mobility and seasonality patterns for the preceramic of Ayacucho. They propose a very similar seasonal movement from low-altitude (2,800 m) valley camps to high-valley or puna camps (3,300–4,000 m) for the period of 10,000–2500 BC. In their last preceramic phase of 2500–1750 BC, less mobile and larger groups specialized in low- or high-altitude areas, maintaining themselves through considerable exchange of resources.

A very different pattern is favored by investigators working on puna sites not directly adjacent to lower valleys. Puna dwellers who had large expanses of puna resources would likely have remained there year-round, according to Cardich (1964, 1976) and Rick (1980). Low-puna and high-puna areas supposedly were used during wet and dry seasons respectively (MacNeish, Patterson, and Browman 1975), but the central puna expanse is a tableland with little major relief, and no such zones ever have been defined conclusively. The area is quite inhabitable all year, since major game resources never leave. Plant resources are a little more seasonal, with tubers and seeds more available in the dry season, and herbaceous, leafy growth more common in the wet season. As suggested above, resources are of medium density, but rather high predictability. These characteristics, in combination with the slight seasonality, would allow for not only year-round occupation, but probably relatively sedentary groups as well (Rick 1980).

How can these different hypothesized settlement systems be reconciled, and what evidence is there for each of them? The first problem is simple: in an area as varied as the Andes, with not only differing zones, but variable zone proximity and breadth, would not a single pattern of settlement be unlikely? With the resource distributions outlined earlier in this chapter, there should be considerable variation in seasonal movement *and* general levels of mobility, depending upon resource characteristics. Given the sparser, more seasonal, and less predictable resources of the highland valleys, a pattern of seasonal movement is probable. The more secure, productive, and non-seasonal puna resources would likely have led to little mobility, seasonal or otherwise.

The puna is most commonly seen as a zone where both humans and grazing animals would go in the highland valley dry season. This ignores the likelihood of year-round human and animal occupants of the puna, who might have been reticent to share puna resources with seasonal visitors. Puna edges bordering the highland valleys, perhaps unpopulated because of their lower productivity, might have been utilized by valley populations. The Telarmachay site, on the edge of the Junín puna, seems to show predominantly wet-season occupation (Lavallée, Julien and Wheeler 1982). While this confirms seasonal occupation, it is surprising to see wet-season, as opposed to the predicted dry-season, use. However, the puna often covers large expanses, and is greater in area than the highland valleys (Fig. 1.4). Even if all highland valley populations seasonally had swept to the puna, they probably would have utilized only a small fraction of the resources available. Permanent puna residence by at least part of the population would be a much more efficient utilization of resources. The level of sedentism likely to occur in the puna will be highest in the larger, continuous puna areas of central Peru, and will decrease in the southern seasonal puna, and where the puna is in small, isolated segments.

What then, is the evidence for any of these seasonal patterns? In Lynch's case there is a series of excavated shelters and open sites at different altitudes, but they have not yielded remains of known seasonality. He suggests (Lynch 1971, 1980) that Guitarrero Cave (Fig. 1.17) is a wet-season base camp, but the rugged terrain and relatively slight amount of cultural material in this shelter, as well as the emphasis on fiber materials, seems to indicate a special-function camp. The nearby open site of Quishqui Puncu is in a much more inviting setting. Although poor in preservation and heavily mixed by tilling, it contains many more lithic artifacts. Higher-altitude sites generally have small floor areas, leading Lynch to believe that these are short-term hunting sites for small groups of hunters.

Because of artifact similarities, Lynch suggests a strong cultural linkage among all these scattered sites. While a degree of contemporaneity and interaction existed between the makers of these tools, were they the same people, shifting from high to low altitudes and back? Stone-tool raw material studies might determine the total range of the group occupying a site, since curated tools should reflect lithic resources available at sites visited throughout the year. Identification of seasonal occupations, and intensive survey of territory-sized areas, must be undertaken before transhumance can be confirmed. Still, some level of mobility within the highland valleys remains a strong probability.

Fig. 1.17 Guitarrero Cave (Callejón de Huaylas). The site is located in the rock outcrop near the center of the photograph, at 2,580 m. The Santa River intervenes between the photographer and the slope in which the cave is located.

Ayacucho settlement diagrams (Fig. 1.18) offer a picture of a very concrete series of seasonal movements between different zones. There is very little data to confirm the seasonal character of these sites, and some site seasonality was assigned before major analysis had been performed on ecofacts (see MacNeish *et al.* 1981). Also, the majority of sites in the diagrams are known only from

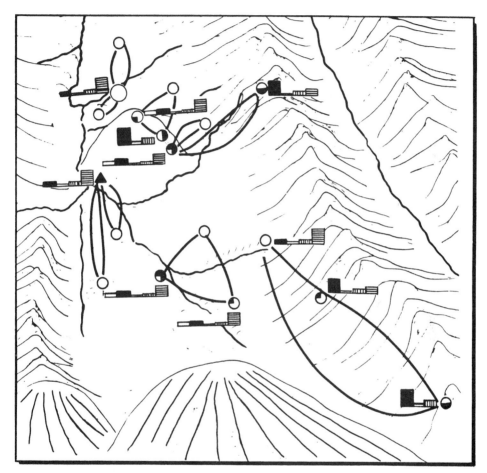

Settlement Pattern

◑ Summer (January–March) Microband Camp   ◯ Macroband Camp

◐ Fall (April–June) Microband Camp   ▲ Hamlet

◓ Winter (July–September) Microband Camp

◑ Spring (October–December) Microband Camp

Subsistence Activities

▥ Hunting   ▥ Plant Collecting

▢ Trapping   ▤ Seasonal Agriculture

Fig. 1.18 Reconstructed settlement and subsistence pattern of the Ayacucho Basin for the period of 4200 to 2500 BC. From Richard S. MacNeish, *The Science of Archaeology?* Copyright 1978 by Wadsworth Publishing Company, Inc. Reprinted by permission.

surface materials, which limits confidence in assigned season of occupation, or group size (microband, macroband). Part of the Ayacucho research design was to sample sites in a variety of highland-valley and, to a lesser degree, puna areas. Excavated sites were therefore far flung, so it is unclear that they are sites of specific groups moving in the manner portrayed. As before, it is probable that linkages of this type existed, but these are not confirmed by published data.

Stone-tool similarities between Ayacucho sites cannot be verified, in spite of a voluminous final report on the lithic materials (MacNeish *et al.* 1980). Tools from different sites were grouped by type and described *en masse*, so it is not possible to tell if significant morphological or raw-material differences exist between sites. Again, correspondences between tools from high- and low-altitude sites are likely, but the degree of linkage they imply is far from clear.

Somewhat more can be said for the puna. Seasonality of preceramic sites is not totally clear, but the Pachamachay site (Fig. 1.19) produced both wet-season camelid remains and dry-season plant remains (Wing, personal communication, MacNeish 1980, Rick 1980). While only hinting at all-year occupation, this is the most convincing evidence to date. A small, intensive puna survey revealed a developed settlement pattern in a small (200 km^2) area, included entirely within the puna zone (Fig. 1.20). The pattern of base camp surrounded by temporary camps is not a likely result of temporary or short seasonal occupation. The degree of linkage between these sites is somewhat clearer than in the highland valley situation, due to identical raw materials and exact duplication of finely defined projectile-point types. Additionally, the very small distances between sites, with no intervening sites or unsurveyed areas, help confirm occupation and use by the same groups. Significant differences between base- and temporary-camp functional tool assemblages have been documented. Rock art is common in temporary hunting camps, but is absent in base camps of the area.

Additional evidence for year-round puna occupation is the total lack of non-puna materials in the numerous remains from the puna base camp of Pachamachay (Rick 1980). Stone-tool materials there are only puna cherts, and there is no evidence of non-puna plants or animal foods, and relatively slight evidence for non-puna firewood.

The sedentism proposed for the puna includes the use of a base camp over long periods, with occasional short-term use of hunting camps located at relatively short distances from the base camp. This pattern is difficult to support archaeologically, but some evidence is present (Rick 1980). The Pachamachay base camp yielded a huge quantity of cultural material in a very small sample of the site (Table 1). The great amount of material in this site cannot be due to short occupation by large groups, given the very limited usable floor surface, and so must represent extended occupation by small groups. Evidence of permanence is in the form of living structures in the cave mouth area, and in extensive cleaning or displacement of trash away from the major occupation surface, which is atypical of short-term camps (see, e.g., Yellen 1977). Of the total archaeological material estimated for the territory-sized area, better than 85% is in the base camp, with only 15% estimated for all the outlying sites. This concentration of remains is likely a result of preferential and long-term use of a single base camp, with relatively infrequent trips out to other sites. Such a concentration does not appear at highland valley sites, where remains are more evenly scattered.

It is instructive to compare the tool densities, total tools, and altitudes of well-published excavated sites of the highland preceramic (Table 1). In many cases these are extremely crude estimates, since information on excavated area or volume of excavated deposits is sketchy at best. However, even with a large error factor, some clear trends are apparent. First, both total stone tools and stone-tool density are positively correlated with altitude (see Figs. 1.21a, 1.21b). Secondly, there are relatively few excavated sites between 3,300 and

Fig. 1.19 Pachamachay (Junín). The cave is the dark spot in the rock outcrop, and site midden continues down to the corrals in the foreground. The site is at 4,300 m.

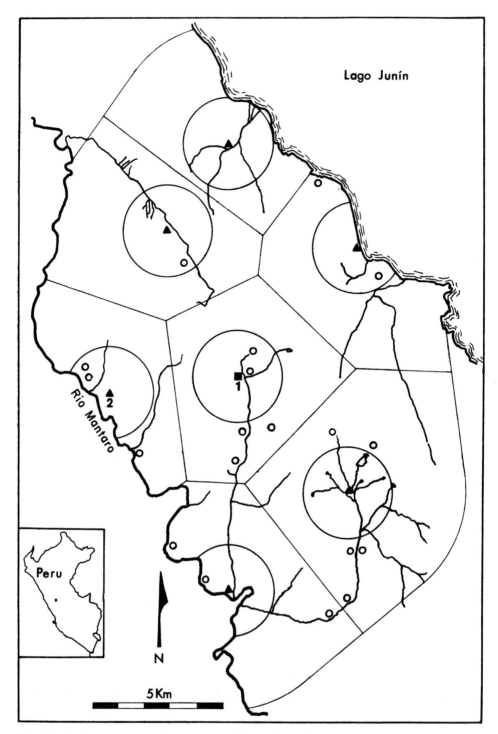

Fig. 1.20 Settlement pattern of sites surrounding Pachamachay Cave, puna of Junín. Base camp of Pachamachay is square site 1, excavated secondary site of Pampacancha is triangle 2. Other triangles represent principal secondary sites, small circles are very light-density preceramic occupations. Large circles represent zones of high vicuña density as determined by available stream-based vicuña territories. Polygons are equidistantly spaced between major camps, representing areas likely exploited from these loci.

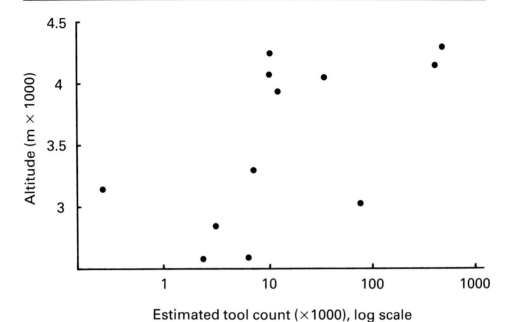

Fig. 1.21a Scatter diagram of stone-tool counts (log scale), estimated for published preceramic sites, against altitude of sites. Correlation coefficient $(r) = .58$, significant at the .05 level.

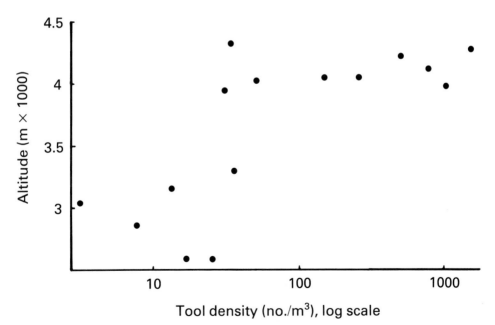

Fig. 1.21b Scatter diagram of stone-tool density (log scale) per site, against altitude of sites. Correlation coefficient $(r) = .73$, significant at the .01 level.

Table 1 *Basic data from excavated highland preceramic sites*

Site	Altitude (m)	Estimated per cent of site excavated	Number of tools recovered	Estimated total no. of tools in site	Approximate tool density in excavation (tools per m³)	Reference
Guitarrero Cave	2,580	25	580	2,300	25	Lynch 1980
Quishqui Puncu	3,040	1.5	1,129	75,000	3	Lynch 1970
Punta Callan Shelter	4,000	U[a]	U	U	1,000	Lynch 1971
Lauricocha Cave U1	4,020	U	582[b]	U	50	Cardich 1958
Lauricocha Cave L2	3,950	1.5[c]	177[b]	11,800	30	Cardich 1964
Ranracancha Shelter	4,340	U	60	U	33	Cardich 1959
Pampacancha Shelter	4,074	3	297[b]	10,000	250	Rick 1980
Pachamachay	4,300	3[c]	15,159	460,000	1,500	Rick 1980
Acomachay A	4,250	1?	108	10,000+	490	Lavallée and Julien 1975
Panaulauca Cave	4,150	0.3	1,129	380,000	750	Rick (field notes)
Uchcumachay	4,050	3	1,012	33,000	145	Pires-Ferreira, Pires-Ferreira and Kaulicke 1976
Pikimachay	2,850	33	985	3,000	7.5	MacNeish (various)
Puente Shelter	2,582	66	3,443	5,200	17	MacNeish (various)
Jaywa Shelter	3,300	30	2,105	7,000	35	MacNeish (various)
Caru Shelter	3,150	5?	13	260	13	Ravines 1967

[a] U = Unknown
[b] Many casual tools present in addition to this sum, but not fully reported
[c] Preceramic levels only

3,900 m of altitude. Lynch (1971, 1980) and MacNeish (1969) apparently did not excavate sites found in this altitude range, suggesting either difficult field conditions or, more probably, a relative lack of remains.

How can puna sites containing 100 times as much material as valley sites be explained? Two important factors must be kept in mind: 1) that many chipped stone tools may be hunting tools, likely to be more common in the game-rich puna; and 2) that the cold climate of the puna might have restricted occupation to caves more than was so in highland valleys, generating a more tool-dense record. But even so, the limited excavations and relatively lower degree of archaeological effort in the puna have produced a much richer archaeological record. If, in fact, plant foods were so important in valley areas, there are few appropriate processing tools to confirm it.

Two models can account for the data. The first, which is rather improbable, is that numerous, near-permanent puna occupants occasionally visited the highland valleys on a very temporary and perhaps seasonal basis, leaving a sparse record. The second puts two major populations in the highlands: a relatively sparse one in the highland valleys, who perhaps used nearby puna-edge resources on occasion, but contributed little to the total puna record; and a relatively larger puna population, who did not commonly venture outside of the zone. Any attempt to make the puna part of a highland valley seasonal round must account for the large quantity of puna remains, found mostly in sites within the large puna expanses not adjacent to highland valleys.

On the basis of this information, I would venture a further guess about subsistence behavior in the highland valleys. As environments in which water availability exerted strong influence over resource density and distribution, the wet season would allow maximum resource dispersal during the lowest area's most productive time. Dry seasons would cause a maximum concentration of green plants and animals around running watercourses, which mostly would be restricted to the higher reaches of the highland valleys. Major rivers flowing all year at lower altitudes might be an exception, but the dry-season productivity would still be quite low and spatially restricted. Ideally, preceramic peoples would be maximally dispersed and rather mobile in wet seasons, since resources would also be widely scattered. In dry seasons, aggregation would be necessary near the water with its plant and game concentrations. Further movements to puna areas would relieve some dry-season pressures, but demand greater mobility, and could engender conflict with puna natives.

This corresponds well to the observed data, for even *within* highland valleys there is an increasing density of stone tools in higher sites. Total tools has a lower, but still significant, correlation with altitude within highland valleys (Fig. 1.21a). The lack of important known sites in the 3,300–3,900 m range could indicate isolation of highland-valley groups from the puna, or simply that the pull of puna resources was strong enough to make a sizable, direct jump to the puna worth while.

For both mobility and seasonality, it is very important to avoid imposing models transplanted from different ecologies. Most of Peru, lying near the Equator, is not subject to the climatic imperatives of the fiercely hot summers and icy winters in which transhumant cultures are found (Flannery 1965, Davis 1963). Complementary productivity of resource zones may not be sufficient reason for transhumance if the gain is slight, or if one of the zones lacks a season of resource depression (Rick 1983). Our models increasingly should reflect realistic reconstruction of Andean ecology.

Interaction

Major interaction between distant highland valley, puna, and coastal groups has been suggested for the preceramic by MacNeish, Patterson, and Browman (1975). Given the general similarity of Central Andean Preceramic tools, some level of interaction must have existed. "Splitters" and "lumpers" who regard tools as either very different or very similar have differing opinions about the level of such interactions. Given our inability to translate tool similarity into any specific human interaction phenomenon, tools may be poor evidence for long-distance interaction.

Raw materials that are far enough from their origins can imply one type of interaction – trade. One distinctive Andean stone-tool raw material that can be traced to its source is obsidian (Burger and Asaro 1978). Contrary to assertions about the widespread occurrence of obsidian tools in preceramic times (MacNeish, Patterson, and Browman 1975), obsidian occurs mostly in areas near its sources (Burger 1980). Junín sites, Laurichocha, the Callejón de Huaylas sites, and other north-central Non-Complex Preceramic sites almost entirely lack obsidian tools, while Ayacucho sites – near the sources – have many obsidian tools. In fact, the short distance obsidian travelled is quite striking, compared to other areas of the world with cultures of similar level.

Lack of obsidian movement suggests relatively little interaction along the highland axis, but what of coast–highland interaction? Shell is a durable item that is extensively traded in other parts of the world. Although used on the coast, shell is notably absent in almost all highland preceramic components. Junín, Ayacucho, and the Callejón de Huaylas generally lack preceramic shell artifacts (Lynch 1980, MacNeish *et al.* 1980, Rick 1980). Notable exceptions are the Huarochiri sites reported by Engel (1970c), and shell burial offerings in Junín (Julien, Lavallée, and Dietz 1981). The rarity of shell in the highland Andes preceramic is striking when compared with western North America, where significant amounts of shell travelled hundreds and even thousands of kilometers during the hunter-gatherer periods. Interaction must have been slight between coast and sierra, minimizing shell movement.

Other remains worthy of consideration are plants or animals transported from their zones of origin. To MacNeish, Patterson, and Browman (1975), the widespread distribution of domestic plants indicates interaction between zones, but moving a domestic plant requires only one instance of contact, if the plant can be grown in the new environment. The presence of plants or animals outside of zones that possibly could have nurtured them is a much better piece of evidence. Such conditions can be difficult to document, but the Junín puna situation is persuasive. The only possible domesticate present at Pachamachay is *quinoa*, which is indigenous to the zone. At times when corn, beans, squash, and a wide variety of plants are being grown in the highland valleys, the puna is bereft of the slightest import of these plants. The botanical samples from Pachamachay are of significant size, and well identified – it seems unlikely that domesticates were present here and remain undetected (Pearsall 1980). Off-hand, fruits, vegetables, and grains that cannot be grown in the puna would seem ideal foci for trade or interaction, but puna peoples do not appear to have received them from their highland-valley neighbors.

What then, of interaction? Certainly some form of contact probably did exist, and intensity of interaction probably varied according to perceived and real needs of the populace. In all likelihood, such needs were not uniformly distributed in highland environments. The meaning of different types of displaced materials must be clarified before the nature of interaction is clear. Does interaction mean trade, mate exchange, warfare, or population displacement? Current evidence points to a comparatively low level of interaction, whatever its nature.

Domestication and the origins of complexity

Probably the most pressing problem in the preceramic period is the degree to which subsistence was based on domesticated plants or animals during this 8,000-year timespan. The highland valleys are clearly a zone of domestication or early use of domesticated plants, while evidence thus far allows the puna little role in this area (Matos Mendieta 1980, Pearsall 1978). The puna has been suggested as the likely zone of camelid domestication (MacNeish, Patterson, and Browman 1975, Pires-Ferreira, Pires-Ferreira, and Kaulicke 1976). Studies at puna-edge Telarmachay suggest the presence of domesticated alpaca by 3500 BC (Wheeler 1984). Time will tell whether the late preceramic puna was dominated everywhere by herding subsistence, but central puna occupation characteristics such as settlement pattern and degree of social complexity seem remarkably unaltered at least until the ceramic horizon (Rick 1980). Even more important than the presence of domesticates is the impact of domestication on lifeways. Early puna groups seem to retain their simple organizations relatively longer than groups in any other inhabited zone. The relatively predictable puna resource base probably did not reward innovations leading to domestication, and so natural – or slightly modified – resources were used for a longer period.

In highland valleys the less predictable and secure resource base may have imposed a low threshold upon which the benefits of domestication were more clearly felt. It will be very important to investigate how much the early domesticates demanded of their human recipients. How was mobility, group size, or interaction modified by the necessities of the domesticates? A more unexplored area of study hardly exists.

The transition out of the Non-Complex Preceramic, however, is a telling phenomenon. The clearly complex late preceramic cultures of the coast are thus far matched only in two highland areas. Both are in highland valleys, and at quite low altitudes. Kotosh (1,900 m), in a major valley leading to the eastern selva (Izumi and Terada 1972), and La Galgada (1,500 m) and Huaricoto (2,700 m), in the westward-draining Callejón de Huaylas, show signs of notable complexity in preceramic times. This low-altitude position in valleys that span considerable ecological diversity is clearly important. Security of natural resources may have been low, and successful use of domesticates may have required extensive organization, and perhaps even irrigation. Many of the requisite conditions for extensive use of domesticates are present here, correlated with early trends to societal complexity.

CONCLUSION

In this short space, I probably have complicated the problem of Pleistocene human presence in Peru. This is fitting, since the situation is far from clear cut.

There is some evidence for human presence, but it is not totally convincing, and it is far from illuminating about how these early arrivals might have adapted to their environments. The climates and landscapes of this time are not well known, either, although current knowledge points to an environment fit for human habitation throughout at least the later Pleistocene, and perhaps not so very foreign to the present-day situation. Post-Pleistocene climate does not appear to have varied sufficiently to have been in itself a major impetus for cultural change.

I have chosen to treat the postglacial Central Andean Preceramic synchronically, as if there were no evolution of adaptations across the 7,500 years of time. This stems not from a belief that there was no progressive change but rather from the fact that such changes have not yet been well documented. Rick (1980) suggested some trends towards increasing sedentism and perhaps conservatism in puna groups, Pires-Ferreira, Pires-Ferreira, and Kaulicke (1976) developed an outline of animal domestication, and MacNeish, Patterson, and Browman (1975) attempted to show the development of agriculture and other phenomena within a Peru-wide framework. It is tempting to describe the highland preceramic as if it were a uniformly evolving adaptation in all areas. But it clearly did not progress at similar speeds and with identical characteristics in the different zones. The fragmentary record is not yet sufficient to write a definitive history of these different cultural vectors, much less fully to explain them.

The adaptation of non-complex Andean peoples who depended largely on natural foods was based on the structure of resources within highland ecology. I hope to have shown that a likely response to diversity was not one all-encompassing strategy that included all resources, but rather a partial specialization. There can be little doubt that cultural systems that can span and control all Andean zones are at great advantage over those entirely restricted to any particular zone. But the benefits are very different for small-group egalitarian societies, where the primary access to resources is by travelling to them, as compared with state-level societies that have major resource redistribution. Although I have suggested that two basic adaptations existed for puna and highland-valley areas respectively, at times these probably intergraded, and there may be variants different from any combination of the two. Perhaps one of the most important lessons of the Andes is that of human response to diversity. This diversity is not only the tight packing of ecological zones, but also differing widths, proximities, and characteristics within and between these zones. This variability must have had impact on early humans. If we make predictions based on this ecology, and then let archaeological data determine the validity of those predictions, giant steps will be taken towards understanding preceramic societies.

Early hunter-gatherers on the Peruvian coast

CLAUDE CHAUCHAT

The early occupation of the Peruvian coast by hunter-gatherers has been much underestimated by archaeologists, for several reasons. The complex and brilliant agricultural societies of later periods have prompted more and more scholarly interest over the years, first because of the wealth of sites and materials, and secondly because of the outstanding potential of these societies for unravelling ecological and socio-cultural mechanisms with more general application. Attention has been focused on highly visible architectural remains, middens, cemeteries, etc., thus neglecting the more unobtrusive lithic scatters. Moreover, due to the present clear-cut partition between barren desert and fertile valleys – a direct by-product of this agricultural history – many archaeologists have behaved as if there was nothing to find beyond the valley margins. Within the valleys themselves, intensive and deep plowing as well as probable recent alluvial deposition long ago destroyed any evidence of hunter-gatherers. It is no wonder, then, that the first discoveries of the remains of hunter-gatherers resulted from accidents or isolated endeavors rather than systematic regional surveys. Very little more than the modern irrigated valleys have been explored and sites less visible than the ever-present *huacas* were often overlooked. More recently, though, the example of the Chan Chan–Moche Valley Project has shown that attitudes are changing and that more complete and careful surveys will be successful.

ECOLOGICAL DETERMINANTS

The ultimate factors affecting the climate on the Peruvian coast result from the rotation of the planet. The Coriolis force tends to deviate any moving fluid at a right angle from its original direction. This and other factors create a pattern of air and water circulation which determines the existence of permanent, stationary high-pressure zones near the center of the oceans in both hemispheres. In this case, the South Pacific high is situated near Easter Island. Centrifugal winds radiate from this zone, pushing surface water along. This surface water is in turn forced to the west and, near the Peruvian coast, tends to move away from the shore, where it is replaced by a deep, cold-water

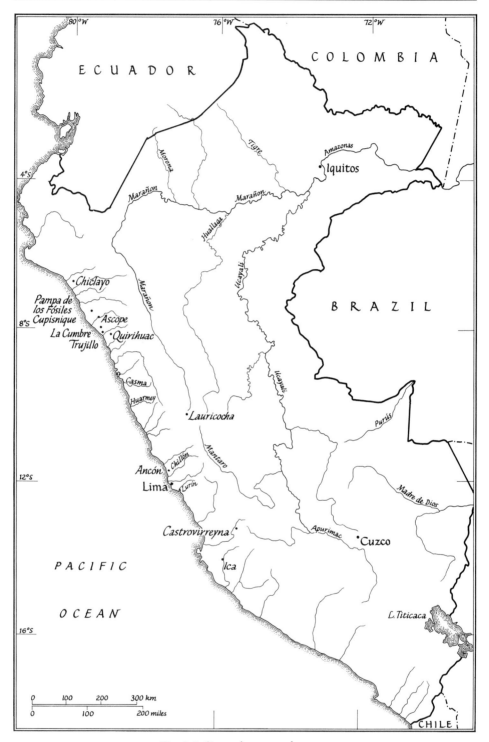

Fig. 2.1 Sites relevant to the text.

current. The permanence of superficial cold water along the coast of Peru as well as the coast of northern Chile is of utmost importance for the ecology and even human economy of the region. As a direct consequence, the evaporated water is prevented from condensing as rain over the coastal plain by the existence of a stable temperature inversion layer located between 300 and 500 m above sea level. However, fog is allowed to form, especially during the winter, and is blocked below this inversion layer. When hills intervene at the same height, fog-dependent oases composed of plant species thriving on the condensed air moisture are formed. The lush patches of this fog-dependent greenery in an otherwise barren desert are locally referred to as *lomas*. It is clear from this description that the extent of the *lomas* vegetation is dependent on world-wide climatic factors. This peculiar foggy desert of the coastal plain cannot exist very far from the ocean shore. Since light reflected from the bare ground is considerably stronger than that from the ocean, the intense radiation tends to dissipate these fogs at a distance from the shore, depending on the strength of the various intervening factors. On the central Peruvian coast the coastal plain is generally so narrow that this phenomenon cannot occur. Rather, the extension of the fog is blocked by the steep Andean slope. This climatic pattern results in an ecological zonation which parallels the coast and follows altitudinal zones. As one moves north, however, a gradual lowering of this ecological zonation can be observed. This is due to the weakening of marine influence and the progressive strengthening of proper latitudinal factors as well as influence from the Cordillera. As a result, vegetation appears on the plain at about 8° latitude and the desert is generally sunny with occasional summer rains.

Another consequence of the upwelling of the cold coastal current must not be forgotten. Nutrients are prevented from falling slowly to the ocean floor and are forced to remain in the immediately subsurface waters where photosynthesis is at its maximum. From phytoplankton to birds and sea mammals, the whole marine ecosystem is thus multiplied and the Peruvian ocean swarms with life. It is natural, then, that almost from the beginning marine resources have been important to the inhabitants of the Peruvian coast.

THE FIRST DISCOVERIES

Evidence of the remains of hunter-gatherers on the coast was first published independently by Junius Bird and Rafael Larco Hoyle in 1948. Heinrich Ubbelohde-Doering claimed to have found "artifacts of palaeolithic character" as early as 1933 but did not disclose his discovery until 1959, after Augusto Cardich's first publication of the Lauricocha caves sequence (Cardich 1958) had given the antiquity of man in Peru wide acceptance. A little before, Frédéric Engel had reported the results of his own visit to the same sites (Engel 1957a). All these very brief notes refer to the Cupisnique desert between the

Chicama and Jequetepeque valleys, some 100 km north of the modern city of Trujillo. None of them provides any description of the artifacts involved except in very general terms. Larco Hoyle (1948), Ubbelohde-Doering (1967), and Engel (1957a) published photographs of some of the collected artifacts, consisting mainly of massive bifacial fragments and a distinctive elongated projectile point with a long narrow stem. The exact numbers and locations of the sites are unclear. The apparent association on the same surface with extinct fauna and ceramics is mentioned by all these authors. Bird is of the opinion that the lithic artifacts may be contemporaneous with the faunal remains. His argument that these artifact types are completely unreported in the well-known later cultures of the North Coast is well taken. The combination of projectile points of unusual size and occasional apparent association with Pleistocene animals led to the hypothesis that these points were morphologically adapted to big-game hunting (see, e.g., Lanning 1967a: 54).

Subsequently, this poorly described assemblage became known in the literature as the Paiján–Pampa de los Fósiles complex, as the result of the imposition by Larco Hoyle of inadequate place names for some of the sites. Later, these scarce data were included by Lanning and Hammel (1961) in a somewhat premature attempt at synthesis involving lithic artifacts from half the continent. Though researchers were convinced that there was indeed some interesting material on the North Coast, there were nevertheless no grounds on which to assign any chronological or cultural status to these finds. This situation was to last until the beginning of the 1970s.

THE CENTRAL COAST SEQUENCE

In the mean time, the main bulk of data was produced by coordinated research around the bay of Ancón and in the lower Chillón Valley just north of Lima. Edward P. Lanning (1963a) must be credited with describing pre-agricultural settlements in the Ancón area while Thomas C. Patterson (1966) published the first descriptive account of the Cerro Chivateros and Cerro Oquendo sites on the lower Chillón. At the same time, some attempts were made to organize these two independent sets of data into a regional sequence and to describe associated subsistence and settlement patterns (Lanning 1965, 1967a, Patterson and Lanning 1964, Lanning and Patterson, 1967).

It cannot be denied that the results obtained in this area were and still are important for the understanding of early Peruvian prehistory. It is unfortunate, however, that the two preliminary reports were not followed by comprehensive descriptions of the evidence.

Chivateros and Oquendo

Patterson's (1966) report deals with the description of lithic assemblages found in two quarry sites on the right bank of the Chillón river, less than 2 km from the present seashore. Excavation at Cerro Chivateros is said to have exposed several soil zones that are deemed equivalent to depositional layers. The lowest soil zone (the "Red Zone") and its assemblage is seriated first, before the assemblage found isolated at Cerro Oquendo. The Chivateros 1 and 2 assemblages are seriated next. The two earliest assemblages are described as including tools made of retouched flakes or tabular pieces of rock, such as notches, denticulates, and burins. Elongated thick bifaces as well as "spear-points" appear in the later assemblages. An uncharred piece of wood found associated with the Chivateros 1 assemblage gave a radiocarbon date accepted by the author as proof of great antiquity (Patterson 1966: 150). This result (UCLA 683) is listed in Table 1 (p. 47).

Several problems are raised by the Oquendo–Chivateros sequence. First, the existence of a complex stratigraphy in the Chivateros quarry site has been questioned almost from the beginning. Fung, Cenzano, and Zavaleta (1972) describe the existence of stratigraphy but do not assign any of the layers to depositional phases. As Lynch (1974: 362) has already noted, these layers are really soil zones in a pedological sense, i.e., were developed after the deposition.

Other problems arise from the lithic artifacts themselves. Judging from the illustrations in Patterson (1966: pl. XX), Lanning (1967a: 42, 1970: fig. 21), and Willey (1971: 35), most of the pieces in the Red Zone and Oquendo assemblages are unconvincing as artifacts. It is suggested here that a combination of naturally fractured pieces of rock and occasional flakes resulting from human activity, but subjected to repeated crushing during the quarrying operations, form the majority of these controversial assemblages.

By contrast, the Chivateros complex seems quite straightforward. Massive bifaces knapped by hammerstone percussion are clearly shown in all the publications. A smaller number of "thrusting spearpoints" are also illustrated (Lanning 1967a: 43, c, Lanning and Patterson 1967: 48, i and l). These finer, slender pieces appear to have been chipped by soft-hammer percussion, a technique not recognized by any of the authors. Other technological misinterpretations are "pseudo-Levallois cores" and "denticulates" (Lanning 1970: 99, e, f), which are only bifaces. The massive Chivateros bifaces sometimes have been called preforms (e.g., in Fung, Cenzano, and Zavaleta 1972: 64), but without explaining for which tools they are preforms.

The radiocarbon date obtained from the uncharred piece of wood found associated with Chivateros does not seem to have been challenged seriously, though doubts have been expressed by Lynch (1974: 362). Contamination by earlier charcoal or organic matter is much harder to come by in natural circumstances and must be massive to have some effect, while contamination by younger material is much more common. This early date has been put into proper perspective by recent research, as is shown below.

What, then, can we reasonably infer from these publications? There is no doubt that remains of an early human occupation are found at Cerro

Chivateros. There are strong doubts, however, about intentional human activity as the cause for the Oquendo material. All the available evidence points to quarries and workshops for the manufacture of massive bifaces and more slender foliate pieces. No campsite is associated with these quarries. Our knowledge of Chivateros stoneworkers' material equipment is limited to these bifacial pieces. No inference regarding the subsistence economy of these stoneworkers can be made.

The Ancón sequence

Lanning's (1963a) paper describes several surface sites around the bay of Ancón, located about 20 km north of the mouth of the Chillón river. The sites actually form two separate clusters, one at the foot of the northern hills, the other further inland on a group of low hills dividing the Ancón depression from the Chillón Valley. The sites can therefore be labelled the northern and eastern group, respectively. These sites generally consist of lithic scatters and very thin refuse, with some of them described as being quite large. The sites are interpreted as campsites by Lanning and, since they occur in areas of extinct *lomas*, they are supposed to testify to a subsistence economy oriented toward the exploitation of this *lomas* zone. The view that Ancón campsites are located on extinct *lomas* stands is supported only by the presence of dead landsnail colonies on the same surface. The cause for the disappearance of the *lomas* is another matter. The post-Conquest introduction of European cattle may have been a later factor with the same result (Lynch 1964: 362).

It is noteworthy that these two clusters of sites contain different lithic assemblages. This two-fold partitioning of sites and assemblages probably forms the basis of Lanning's seriation. Six lithic complexes are recognized in the 1963 report and seriated in the following chronological order: Piedras Gordas, Luz, Arenal, Canario, Corbina, Encanto. The first three complexes are located in the eastern group, the others in the northern group. Again, the seriation is based on stylistic changes observed on the lithic artifacts. However, the number and chronological placement of these complexes has changed in later papers: Piedras Gordas has been lumped with Luz because it was thought to consist of "nothing more than exceptionally poor Luz sites" (Patterson and Lanning 1964: 120 n. 5), and Arenal was seriated first because four radiocarbon dates applying to the Luz–Piedras Gordas sites were younger than had been thought previously (Table 1).

As with Chivateros and Oquendo, several difficulties arise from a careful examination of the literature. Again, we are faced with preliminary reports and synthetic articles without any attempt at exhaustive description. Moreover, several misconceptions are patent. Seriation based on morphological changes of two or three artifact types, without consideration of either the context or the composition of the total assemblage, ought not to be con-

Table 1 *Central Coast early radiocarbon dates*

Site name or cultural affiliation	Nature of sample	Sample number	Age determination (BP)
Cerro Chivateros	Uncharred wood	UCLA 683	10,430 ± 160
Ancón: Luz complex	(not specified)	UCLA 201	7,300 ± 100
Ancón: Luz complex	(not specified)	UCLA 202	7,140 ± 100
Ancón: Luz complex	(not specified)	Y 1303	7,300 ± 120
Ancón: Luz complex	(not specified)	Y 1304	6,600 ± 120
Ancón: Canario complex	(not specified)	UCLA 203	6,700 ± 100

sidered a scientific procedure. There is nothing in the artifact itself that allows its placement at one point of a sequence rather than another. Seriation criteria are never stated explicitly in Lanning's papers, nor are we told if the advocated types are built on a handful of specimens or a more substantial sample.

A serious lack of knowledge in lithic technology and typology is also obvious from several details in the description and interpretation of lithic artifacts. The "awls" illustrated in Lanning (1963a: 364, h, i) are simply Luz point tips. There is more variation within the Canario complex than between Arenal, Canario, Corbina, and Encanto. The Corbina complex seems to be separated from the others solely on the basis of different raw material. The identification of so-called pointed tools (beaks and borers) as pressure flakers is somewhat hasty. There is no known experiment to support this hypothesis.

Again we must ask: what is left when all the misinterpretations are eliminated and the lack of descriptive data accounted for? A close examination of the material shows that two assemblages stand clearly against each other. The first is the Luz complex, whose projectile-point shape is unquestionably outside the range of variation of the others. We will accept provisionally the combination of the Piedras Gordas complex with the Luz complex although the reasons for this are not clearly explained. Undoubtedly, the Luz complex is related to the North Coast Paiján complex, but its placement within the Ancón sequence cannot be decided on local evidence alone. Neither can the cited radiocarbon dates applying to this complex (Table 1) be dismissed, though it must be remembered that they come from superficial sites with no indication of the circumstances of sampling.

The four other complexes are related to one another and to the highland lithic industries. However, this does not permit their placement at any point in the chronology, since in the High Andes all implement types can be followed from the origins to the Conquest and vary only in their relative amounts (Chauchat 1972). There is nothing in Lanning's reports that would allow for this distinction of four complexes, at least on the basis of lithic artifacts. This does not mean, however, that examination of organic remains, for instance, would not support such a seriation.

One of the by-products of Lanning and Patterson's research on the Central Coast was the elaboration of a periodic sequence involving the whole pre-ceramic stage (Lanning 1967a: 25). If the Chivateros–Oquendo sequence is non-existent and the Ancón sequence drastically reduced (and, moreover, not well supported by empirical data), then this periodization is not sufficiently supported by the evidence and must be abandoned. This is the reason that pre-ceramic periods I to IV are not mentioned here.

NEW INVESTIGATIONS ON THE NORTH COAST: THE MOCHE VALLEY DATA

Paul P. Ossa's research on the Moche Valley "lithic stage" was conducted within the Chan Chan–Moche Valley Project in 1969–70 and summarized in several papers (Ossa 1978, Ossa and Moseley 1972) as well as an unpublished dissertation (Ossa 1973). Unsuspected and important sites were discovered on both sides of the valley as the result of careful survey going well beyond the valley margin zone and into the desert. The most important cluster of sites was found north of the valley and comprises the large open-air site of La Cumbre. In addition, on the southern margin of the valley, at Quirihuac, the first inhabited shelter on the Peruvian coast was discovered and excavated.

La Cumbre

The La Cumbre lithic assemblage is clearly identical to the Paiján material as it was published earlier and already exhibited in several Peruvian museums. However, more systematic collection procedures and sophisticated descriptive methods have provided considerably more information about the artifacts and the site. Recognized artifacts have been organized into a type-list of 12 main categories, thus allowing some idea of their quantitative relationships to be formed. Artifact categories are: projectile points, scrapers, "slugs," notches, beaks, denticulates, pebble-scrapers, pebble-tools, bifacials, retouched pieces, diverse pieces, and cores. Over 4,500 artifacts were collected (Ossa and Moseley 1972: 2).

Most of the projectile points are virtually identical to the already known specimens from Paiján. The most distinctive features are their dimensions – about 10 cm in length, a narrow stem, and an exceedingly long, thin tip. Within a general stemmed class there is a good deal of variation affecting the dimensions of the body and the shape and dimension of the stem. Scrapers are all sidescrapers, judging from the texts. Pebble-scrapers are a pebble-tool variety, the cutting edge being distinctly long, convex, and carefully retouched. "Slugs," a translation of the French *limace*, are strongly reminiscent of this type, defined on the European Mousterian (see, e.g., Bordes 1961). This well-defined type is scarce in La Cumbre and may be a kind of multi-purpose scraper or knife. Bifacials are the most numerous class in all the Moche Valley sites and are long, foliate, bifacially chipped pieces.

Two supposedly intrusive artifacts have been found. The first is a triangular, convex-sided obsidian projectile point or knife (Ossa 1973: fig. 93, no. 3). This shape is very similar to the obsidian points or knives of the Paracás and Ica region that are associated with ceramic-stage sites. An analysis of the La Cumbre obsidian point by Burger and Asaro (1979: 303) has shown the material to be identical to the obsidian of the Quispisisa quarry near Castrovirreyna (Department of Huancavelica), a fact which betrays a later intrusion in La Cumbre rather than early trade. A small Early Intermediate Period settlement exists, furthermore, several hundred meters from the lithic site.

The second controversial find is a fragment of a fluted fishtail point made of green stone, called "chert" by Ossa (1976) but which is actually a variety of dacite. Although the Ei Inga–Fell's cave complex to which this point is supposed to belong is not well dated, this complex is thought to be early and even antecedent to the Paiján complex. This projectile point could be a piece collected by one of the Paiján people. This kind of dacite is not found near La Cumbre but exists more to the north in the Cupisnique area and, at any rate, probably can be found at many places (like all cinerites or lavas), given the volcanic geology of the Peruvian coast.

Test excavations have been prompted by the presence of bone splinters on the surface. These test pits have disclosed bone concentrations attributed at least to a mastodon and a horse in a fine-grained compact sediment beneath the superficial sand. Although Ossa and Moseley (1972) discuss at length the possibility of association between those extinct animals and the lithic implements on the surface, there is little doubt that they come from two different geological contexts. However, the radiocarbon analyses performed on the apatite fraction of the mastodon bone gave surprisingly late dates (Ossa and Moseley 1972). The first sample (GX 2019) was taken from a small gully out of which were eroding several pieces of bone; the second was taken *in situ* (see Table 2).

Quirihuac

Quirihuac Shelter is a huge granite boulder fallen from a nearby rocky hill in a small dry valley, some 2 km from the cultivated fields and 25 km from the present-day seashore (Fig. 2.2). At the base of this boulder is a low overhang, which provided sheltered space from the sun or occasional rains. At the time of excavation the surface under this overhang was covered by a 20 cm-thick layer of natural flakes from superficial exfoliation of the granite boulder – a common phenomenon in arid lands. Under this layer is a loose, fine-grained sediment without any granite flakes but containing a human occupation layer with a small lithic assemblage very similar to the La Cumbre artifacts: stemmed projectile-point fragments, bifacial fragments, biface chipping flakes, etc. Along with these lithic debris were numerous landsnail shells, charcoal flecks, and two human skeletons (a child and an adult).

From this almost ideally preserved context, several radiocarbon determinations have been made (Ossa 1973, 1978) on charcoal samples from single square meters each and on bone samples from each skeleton. The apatite fraction was used on both bone samples (Table 2). If the dates refer to a single occupation it is rather difficult to choose which one is closest to the real date. It can be summarized that the completely treated samples have given results between 10,000 and 13,000 BP and that the bone samples are reasonably close to this period, though younger. This interval should then represent a good estimate of the age of the Quirihuac occupation and consequently an estimate of the age of the Paiján complex.

These results are considerably older than those given by Patterson and Lanning (1964), listed in Table 1. Even assuming a slow rate of expansion along the coast, the difference should be expressed in centuries rather than in millenia. A second consequence of these results is that contemporaneity can still be maintained with the faunal remains from La Cumbre.

Fig. 2.2 Quirihuac Shelter, a huge granite boulder fallen from a mountain on Moche Valley's southern margin, yielded to Paul P. Ossa the first sealed Paijanense occupation layer ever found on the Peruvian coast. Photo courtesy of Paul Ossa, La Trobe University, Bundoora, Australia.

Table 2 *Moche Valley early radiocarbon dates*

Site name	Nature of sample	Chemical retreatment	Sample number	Age determination (BP)
La Cumbre	Mastodon bone apatite	Complete	GX 2019	10,535 ± 280
La Cumbre	Mastodon bone apatite	Complete	GX 2492	12,360 ± 700
Quirihuac	Charcoal	Complete	GX 2021	12,795 ± 350
Quirihuac	Charcoal	Complete	GX 2024	10,005 ± 320
Quirihuac	Charcoal	(incomplete)	GX 2020	12,400 ± 750
Quirihuac	Charcoal	(incomplete)	GX 2022	8,645 ± 370
Quirihuac	Charcoal	(incomplete)	GX 2023	4,740 ± 210
Quirihuac	Child burial bone apatite	Complete	GX 2493	9,930 ± 820
Quirihuac	Adult burial bone apatite	Complete	GX 2491	9,020 ± 650

Source: Ossa 1973

Discussion

There are several drawbacks to the field methods employed at La Cumbre, probably due to the short duration of the field work. Though it cannot be denied that quantitative results are a great improvement in our knowledge of the Paiján complex, these results must not be taken at face value. Because of the enormous amount of chipped material present on the surface, collecting procedures were not exhaustive but affected only those artifacts specifically recognized as tools in the field; all other artifacts were left on the site. The extent of the collection depends then on the archaeologist's ability to recognize rapidly lithic tools on the ground and also on what she or he generally considers to be tools. Given these conditions of field work it is impossible for all the materials to be evaluated and collected accurately. Moreover, this procedure depends on previous knowledge of the industry and in this case this knowledge was very nearly non-existent. As a consequence, only clearly retouched tools were collected. For instance, what Bordes (1970) calls *a posteriori* tools, which are flakes or blocks modified by use alone, without intentional retouch, went completely unnoticed. Ossa was not aware, either, that artifacts could have been buried within this soft sand by the trampling of prehistoric people themselves. This was confirmed by a subsequent study made by two Peruvian archaeologists (Santiago Uceda and Carlos Deza) who found about 70 tools in an area of about 200 m² previously collected by Ossa.

THE CUPISNIQUE DESERT

Archaeological investigations in the Cupisnique desert have been undertaken by the present author since 1973. A doctoral dissertation ("*thèse de Doctorat d'Etat"*) was completed on this topic in 1982, and field work and analysis are still going on. Some particular aspects of this research have already been published (Chauchat 1976, 1977, 1979, Chauchat and Dricot 1979, Chauchat and Lacombe 1984, Dricot 1979), as well as a very brief and partial summary (Chauchat 1978).

It was in this area that Larco Hoyle, Bird, and Ubbelohde-Doering found the first remains of what became known as the Paiján complex. Paiján is a village just south of this zone on the northern margin of the Chicama Valley. Cupisnique is actually the name of a mountain and of the main gorge of this zone – the Quebrada de Cupisnique – and this name has been extended to the whole desert between Chicama and Jequetepeque.

Several groups of sites have been found: the Pampa de los Fósiles group is located west and north from the Cerro Yugo or Cerro Tres Puntas hills and about 15 km from the present shoreline. It was given this name because Larco's site Pampa de los Fósiles – now PV22-12 or Pampa de los Fósiles 12 – is situated there (see Fig. 2.3). The original place called Pampa de los Fósiles, however, is about 10 km from this site and on the plain. Other groups of sites are in the Quebrada de Cupisnique, in the Mócan area, and around the modern village of Ascope. So far, only the Pampa de los Fósiles and Ascope groups have been studied intensively.

All the archaeological material is found in open-air sites. We have called "units" discrete clusters of artifacts occurring on the surface and having areas around an average of 200 m². "Sites" are groups of units, which can be very large: Pampa de los Fósiles 12 has an area of about 0.8 km². Units can be separated readily into two broad classes. The first class is made up of quarries

Fig. 2.3 Campsites in Pampa de los Fósiles.

and workshops (Fig. 2.4), i.e., units devoted to the extraction of raw material and manufacture of particular kinds of tool. Two classes of tool were made in specialized workshops: projectile points for one part, and what we have called in French *unifaces* for the other. This term can be equated with Ossa's *slugs* (French *limace*), but there is considerably more variability in this class than in the mousterian *limaces*.

In contrast, the other class of units shows a great variety of artifacts and all the evidence points to their interpretation as living sites.

An elaborate stone technology

Bifaces and unifaces are made with carefully chosen stone and their workmanship is usually quite good. The unifaces are present in the Ascope area, with a small number of projectile points being present in the same workshops. Unifaces generally are made from volcanic tuff. Projectile points were made in considerable numbers in Pampa de los Fósiles and most often on rhyolite, with minor amounts of quartzite, quartz, and dacite. Unifaces are very scarce there. All these pieces occur in association with their chipping debris, a fact which allows for the conclusion that both classes were obtained by soft-

Fig. 2.4 Pampa de los Fósiles 12, unit 104, is one of the most important quarry sites in the region. A pink rhyolite outcrop has been extensively exploited by Paiján people. The material visible on the slopes consists mainly of flakes and Chivateros bifaces.

hammer percussion (probably wood). However, bifacial pieces were further worked into stemmed projectile points.

In Ascope, no special site for quarrying has been found; the raw material was extracted from the surface of alluvial fans. Blocks were chosen with a suitable flat face; one such face was formed by knapping off a large flake.

In Pampa de los Fósiles, workshops can be found by the dozen that are particularly rich in broken or defective pieces. The knapped material of these workshops is a kind of yellow and pink rhyolite, which has been found at several quarry units on nearby outcrops. Examination of the surface and a small test pit at the top of one of these quarries has shown the assemblage to be identical to the Chivateros assemblage (Chauchat 1976, 1979). Some of the last excavations made by prehistoric people in their search for material are still visible and show the outcropping rock with conspicuous traces of blows.

Most of the artifacts consist of flakes of all sizes and shapes and some very thick and long bifaces knapped with a stone hammer. There is also a small number of bifacial fragments knapped with a soft hammer, identical to those in the workshops, along with their characteristic biface chipping flakes (Chauchat 1979: 63–4).

The technological process of Paiján-point manufacture can then be summarized as follows: 1) extraction of a suitable block or a large flake; 2) the roughing out with hammerstone or sometimes directly with soft hammer – this last mostly on flakes; 3) the making of a long, comparatively thin, foliate piece by soft-hammer knapping; 4) the finishing of the projectile point by pressure flaking, first by shaping the stem and the tip, then regularizing the edges all around the piece. Phases 1, 2, and occasionally 3 were performed on the quarry site (Fig. 2.4), after which all pieces with desirable attributes were taken to the workshop, at a distance varying from 200 m to more than 1.5 km.

Campsites: versatile equipment

These units are associated with workshops in the same sites (Fig. 2.3) and can be assigned to the Paiján complex by the very frequent occurrence of some rhyolite biface chipping flakes and even actual bifaces or projectile points (Chauchat 1977: 19) (see Figs. 2.5, 2.6). However, these artifacts are always scarce and the assemblage is very different from the one observed in the workshops. Even the raw material is different. The other classes of tool already described by Ossa are present but several additions or modifications must be made. *A posteriori* tools are the most numerous class and comprise naturally backed knives (Fig. 2.7c), utilized flakes, flakes with dulled cutting edges (Fig. 2.7e), bruised flakes, etc.

A particular feature of the industry is the frequency of tools made by choosing or making two long, approximately parallel, abrupt facets with a cutting edge between them (Fig. 2.7d). This edge can be left without retouch

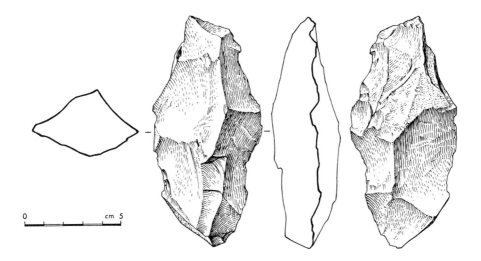

Fig. 2.5 Chivateros biface from the Pampa de los Fósiles. Drawings by Pierre Laurent.

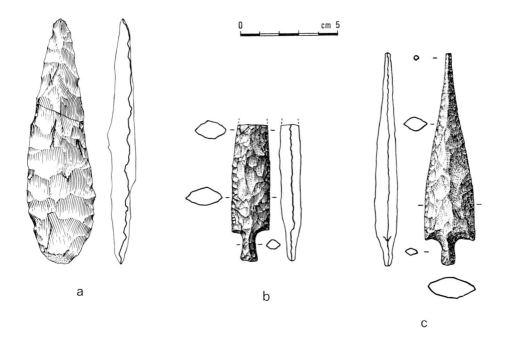

Fig. 2.6 Biface and projectile points from Pampa de los Fósiles. Drawing a by Claude Chauchat, b and c by Pierre Laurent.

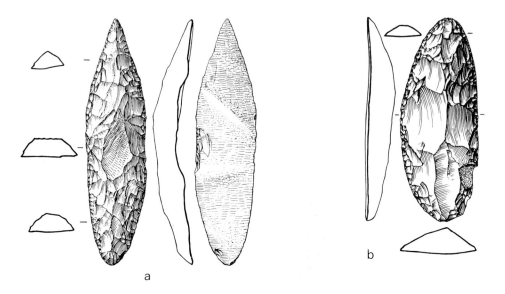

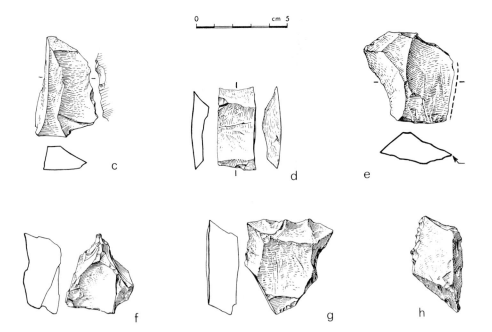

Fig. 2.7 a–b, unifaces from Pampa de los Fósiles and Ascope; c–h, other tools from Pampa de los Fósiles. Drawings by Pierre Laurent.

or bear a notch or a denticulation (Fig. 2.7g). Denticulates, also a numerous class, can be divided into massive, ordinary (Fig. 2.7g) and micro-denticulates (Fig. 2.7h). While the first two categories are separated on the basis of their size only, the third one can be of any size but denticulation is made by smaller notches. Notches, beaks, and composite tools made by combining these various types of retouch are also present. Pebble-tools are scarce and generally of the pebble-scraper type. This fact confirms that most of the pebble-tools in La Cumbre – where they are separated from pebble scrapers – belong to a later intrusive occupation, as suggested by their distribution within the site, completely at odds with the other tool distribution (Ossa 1973: fig. 115). Other miscellaneous artifacts are milling stones, hammerstones, rasps made of a common coral-like material, and very small round pebbles. Scrapers are rare, while endscrapers and burins are unknown. The scarcity of unifaces (slugs) reflects the same situation as with projectile points. These two implements, which are so numerous in workshop contexts, are not found in the living sites. This cursory description is based on the systematic, exhaustive collection of thirteen units having yielded several thousand artifacts, as well as on the examination of countless other campsites which are visible on the surface, but which were not collected or disturbed.

Subsistence patterns

During field work, several clues indicated that buried material could exist in these seemingly superficial sites. Already, landsnail concentrations had been shown to continue below the surface and in one instance were accompanied by abundant vertebrate micro-fauna. So, after the removal of all superficial artifacts, a shallow excavation was undertaken to an approximate depth of 10 cm. This led to the discovery of more artifacts, variable amounts of micro-fauna, and buried features such as hearths and pits.

The faunal remains deserve some description. Most conspicuous is the quantity of landsnails (*Scutalus*). Second in order of importance are fish and lizards, in variable proportions according to the units. Fish are indicated by an astonishing variety of sizes and species, while lizards are represented by two main genera, *Dicrodon* and *Callopistes*. There are some remains of the desert fox *Dusicyon sechurae*, as well as miscellaneous small birds, reptiles, and rodents. There is some amount of *vizcacha* (*Lagidium peruanum*) in Ascope. The present-day medium-sized wild fauna (deer, bear, puma) are absent. There are only two fragments of cervid bone. While fish is abundant, marine mollusks are absent – very unlike the later coastal preceramic.

Of course the absence of any remains of Pleistocene fauna is noteworthy in these middens, while the Cupisnique desert as a whole contains many palaeontological remains eroding out of the superficial layers. Edentates such as *Eremotherium*, *Scelidodon*, the giant armadillo *Pampatherium* as well as proboscideans *Haplomastodon*, equids such as *Equus* (*Amerhippus*), and camelids such as *Palaeolama* are the most frequently found of these animals, but there is no trace of human agency either on their bones or as cause of their death. What, then, was the function of the long Paiján points? Such a slender and acute tip would probably break, even before penetrating the tough hides of most of the Pleistocene fauna. On the other hand, such points would be very efficient on the soft flesh of large fish, allowing very deep penetration and avoiding the loss of the spear and the prey, which would certainly not be killed by the blow. Of course, this is pure speculation.

Strangely enough, the late date for the extinction of this Pleistocene megafauna is confirmed by a radiocarbon determination on rib bones from a *Scelidodon* excavated in collaboration with Professor Hoffstetter (Pampa de los Fósiles 19). This date (GIF 4116) is listed in Table 3 (p. 59). However, one would think that such a contemporaneity is unlikely, since such high-quality material as represented by these large bones does not appear to have been used by the Paiján people. We are left then with the distinct possibility that contamination on the order of several thousand years cannot be eliminated in bone samples, either on collagen or on apatite fraction.

Chronometric dating

That the utmost care must be given to sampling for radiocarbon dating is true for any kind of material. The first charcoal sample submitted for analysis gave a date strongly reminiscent of those obtained by Lanning on Luz sites (GIF 3565: Table 3). It was decided afterwards to take samples only from the bottom of the deposit and inside pits whenever possible. Landsnail samples were also tried but were abandoned after four results indicated that they are unreliable (these are not listed in Table 3). There are, finally, ten accepted dates on charcoal samples which fall within a period of 10,500 to 8,000 BP, approximately. Although these results are in general agreement with the Quirihuac dates, they are a little younger because of the less-protected nature of open-air middens.

When several samples from the same occupational unit have been analyzed, these results are widely dispersed, as shown by the Quirihuac Shelter and Pampa de los Fósiles 14, unit 2. This demonstrates that we cannot go further than a very general statement similar to the one that was made above on the chronology of the Paiján complex. More specifically, no relative position of the various sites can reasonably be inferred.

Some glimpses of the ecological setting

Direct evidence on climatic and other ecological data is scant in Cupisnique. Minute landsnails of the genus *Pupoides*, certainly too small for consumption,

Table 3 *Cupisnique early radiocarbon dates*

Site name	Nature of site	Nature of sample	Sample number	Age determination (BP)
P. de F.[a] 12, unit 7	Midden	Charcoal	GIF 3565	5,490 ± 140
P. de F. 13, unit 1	Campsite: midden	Charcoal	GIF 4161	9,810 ± 180
P. de F. 13, unit 2	Campsite: adult burial	Charcoal	GIF 3781	10,200 ± 180
P. de F. 13, unit 11	Workshop: hearth	Charcoal	GIF 4914	9,490 ± 170
P. de F. 13, unit 29	Campsite: hearth	Charcoal	GIF 4915	9,300 ± 170
P. de F. 14, unit 2	Campsite: hearth	Charcoal	GIF 5159	8,730 ± 160
P. de F. 14, unit 2	Campsite: hearth	Charcoal	GIF 5160	10,380 ± 170
P. de F. 14, unit 2	Campsite: hearth	Charcoal	GIF 5161	9,360 ± 170
P. de F. 14, unit 2	Campsite: hearth	Charcoal	GIF 5162	9,600 ± 170
P. de F. 27, unit 1	Campsite: midden	Charcoal	GIF 4162	8,260 ± 160
P. de F. 19	Palaeontological site: gen. *Scelidodon*	Bone Collagen	GIF 4116	8,910 ± 200
Ascope 5, unit 4	Campsite: midden	Charcoal	GIF 4912	9,670 ± 170

[a]Pampa de los Fósiles

are found on Pampa de los Fósiles 13, unit 1. Nowadays they are found only in the cultivated valley sand and in moist environments. Milling-stones are certainly clues to a denser vegetation. At such an early date it is highly unlikely to find an environment completely identical to that of the present. It is true that climatic conditions on the Peruvian coast are very stable, and there is no reason to infer that cold water upwelling should have disappeared during this period. The abundance of fish remains in the middens is a proof of this permanence of upwelling.

However, some factors have not been accounted for by the various authors who have tried to reconstruct past environments on the Pacific coast. The sea level during Pleistocene glaciations and especially during the last glacial phase was markedly lower than at present. Toward 10,000 BP it is reasonable to assume a depth of 35–40 m, from present-day sea level (Dillon and Oldale 1978, Oldale and O'Hara 1980). The shore then would have been at a minimum distance of about 10 km from the present shoreline, according to Peruvian naval charts. It must not be forgotten that the main factor affecting the climate and the vegetation in coastal Peru is the distance to the sea. With a farther seashore, influence from the Andes would have been stronger in the piedmont and more frequent rain discharges coming down during the summer could be expected. Moreover, this period coincides with a phase of deglaciation and increased humidity in the high Andes. Rain discharges coming down from the Cordillera during the rainy season should have been stronger than they are at present. Last but not least, it is quite possible, although not completely proven, that glacial phases should be characterized by a weakening of oceanic high-pressure cells. In this case, upwelling, though present, would have been weaker, so the influence of the sea would act on a shorter distance.

The net result of all these factors is that a substantial part of the coastal plain would have been under the influence of inland climate. As a consequence, life zones presently on the western slope of the Andes would have been lower, some invading the coastal plain. If we try to get a regional picture of this ecological setting we see that this means a desert more restricted to its present central part, with a coastal plain extending to areas that are now submerged, and more vegetation in the part of the coastal plain that still subsists. Thus the ecology of the higher part of the coastal plain may have been rather similar to those parts which today still benefit from underground or atmospheric water, such as more inland zones around 800–1,000 m high or in the wash of the Quebrada de Cupisnique.

For the Cupisnique sites this means that they were more inland than now, with distances of from 25 km for Pampa de los Fósiles to up to 50 km for the Ascope sites. This means also that plant resources and even running water were more abundant than now and that the ocean was probably as bountiful as it is or just slightly less.

The Paiján man

Human remains eroding out on the surface have been noted in the area of a campsite, Pampa de los Fósiles 13, unit 2. Two burials were excavated there by C. Chauchat and J. Dricot in 1975 (Chauchat and Dricot 1979, Dricot 1979). They are situated on top of a hillock overlooking the whole site. The anthropological study was made by Jean Paul Lacombe, MD, Laboratory of Physical Anthropology, Bordeaux University.

The first burial is that of a 12- to 13-year-old child, lying on its left side, head to the north-east, hands clasped near the face (Fig. 2.8). A perforated fish vertebra, possibly used as a button or pendant, was found near the sacrum.

The second burial lay less than 1 m from the first. It is of an adult, probably a young man, lying on his right side, head to the south-east, hands crossed on the pubis (Fig. 2.8). The bones are scored with brown lines due to the probable slow putrefaction of a mat. The corpse had been put on a layer of embers and partially covered by another layer of charcoal and ashes. A radiocarbon date was obtained on the inferior charcoal (Table 3: GIF 3781).

Both are primary burials: skeletons are complete and anatomical connection generally has been conserved. A slight displacement of the toe bones visible on the adult (Fig. 2.8) occurred during the excavation as the result of wind erosion of the underlying sand.

From an anthropological and anatomical point of view, the Paiján man is an original human type, with a very long head and a well-developed carinated dome (Fig. 2.9). The face is high and narrow and so is the nasal aperture; the orbits are circular with a slight tendency to be quadrangular. The skull capacity is 1,355 cm^3 for the adolescent and 1,422 cm^3 for the adult. The

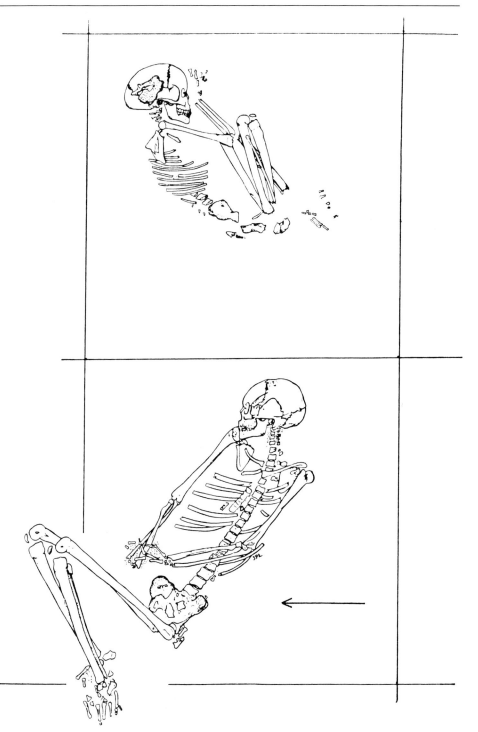

Fig. 2.8 Pampa de los Fósiles 13, unit 2: the burials. Above: the adolescent; below: the adult. The grid is 1 m wide. Drawings by Jean Paul Lacombe.

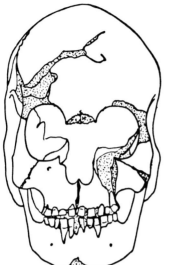
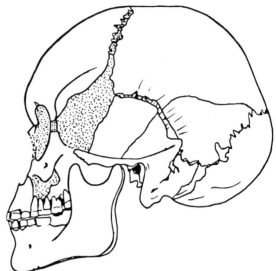
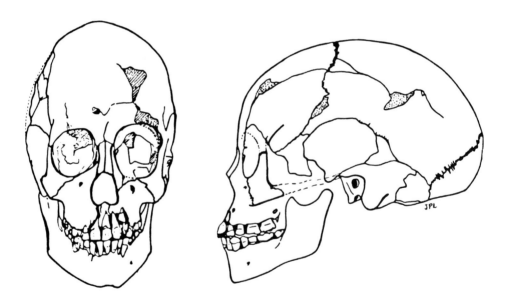

Fig. 2.9 Anthropometrical drawings of the Paiján crania. Above: the adult; below: the adolescent. Drawings by Jean Paul Lacombe.

stature is high: 140 cm for the adolescent and 168 cm for the adult (Chauchat and Lacombe 1984).

Interpretation of the Central Coast data

From the very brief description of the Piedras Gordas and Luz complexes we can see already that Lanning found in Ancón the same settlement pattern that is found at Pampa de los Fósiles and, to a lesser extent, at La Cumbre. Workshops are represented by the Luz sites proper while Piedras Gordas sites probably are living sites with just some trace of occasional chipping of projectile points. Piedras Gordas assemblage description (Lanning 1963a: 363) shows that most implements there are *a posteriori* tools and thick pieces equivalent to our massive denticulates. This description also depicts beaks or borers and milling-stones, all of which have their exact counterpart in the *Paijanense*.

The technological relationship between Chivateros and Luz complexes can be deduced also from the similar situation existing in Cupisnique sites where all intermediate pieces between Chivateros bifaces and stemmed projectile points can be found in close association. The disappearance of any workshop around the Chivateros quarry can be accounted for easily by later occupations or agricultural disturbance on the valley floor. The contemporaneity between the Chivateros and north-coast radiocarbon dates is thus explained by an identical cultural affiliation.

OTHER DATA

Outside the main area of study, the *Paijanense* is not well known. However, there is some evidence of its presence at several points along the coast.

South and north of the Cupisnique desert, Bird claimed to have found remains of the *Paijanense* between Moche and Virú and near Chiclayo airport (Paul Ossa, personal communication).

On the northern margin of Casma Valley, near Cerro Julia, the Peruvian archaeologist Carlos Deza found a fragment of a Paiján projectile point along with other lithic tools. Extensive middens with abundance of fish vertebra exist nearby. A small survey program carried out independently by M. Malpass, then of the University of Wisconsin, on the southern margin and the desert between Casma and the formative site of Las Haldas, led to the discovery of at least one surface lithic scatter at El Campanario (Lynch 1982: 212). In 1983, a more detailed survey and excavation program was undertaken by Santiago Uceda. Four *Paijanense* sites are now known. The activity facies already recognized in Cupisnique are present, with some modification. Minor changes in the shape of projectile points are also evident in comparison with the Cupisnique and Moche Valley collections. A test pit in one of the Cerro Julia middens disclosed an 80 cm-deep occupational sequence. Analyses of lithic and faunal material as well as charcoal samples, etc. are still in progress (S. Uceda, personal communication).

In Huarmey, Bonavia found at least two quarry sites with artifacts of the Chivateros assemblages (Bonavia 1979, 1982a). However, no other site has yet been discovered.

One of the more exciting discoveries was certainly made by F. Engel in the Ica desert, but has been mentioned very briefly by him, first with some description of the context but few details about the artifacts (Engel 1963), then as a very sketchy map giving the location of the sites, south of Pozo Santo (Engel 1966a). With F. Engel's kind permission, the author was able to study the lithic artifacts and later to visit the site, after a complicated translocation of the 1966 map to the modern geographical map of this zone. The assemblage comprises some large bifacial pieces and at least two stemmed projectile points, one similar to a Paiján point preform with wide, rounded stem, the other a fragment of a finished point. This last has a wide rectangular stem joined to the body by two wide notches and sharp barbs. This shape is completely unknown in the North Coast collections and could be a local development, given the distance.

The site is a low stone windbreak near a rhyolite outcrop. There are still many lithic artifacts on the surface and they bear strong resemblance to a part of Engel's collection. Particularly, there are many naturally backed pieces as well as pieces with a retouched back, the opposite side being the original edge of the flake or a denticulate. This kind of assemblage has not been defined yet from any other part of Peru, so it is not possible to assign it to a preceramic- or a ceramic-stage culture. There is no trace of a projectile point nor any bifacial chipping flake. There is not a single ceramic sherd on the surface. Despite all these contradictions, no other site fits better the location and description given by Engel in the whole area, and there seems to be a shallow depression that looks like an old test pit. At a distance of 3–5 km from this site we found several isolated biface fragments as well as a small workshop with biface chipping flakes and two broken foliate pieces. The raw material of these finds is mainly a local stone found in the tertiary beds, while the artifacts associated with ceramic-stage sites are all of obsidian from the Quispisisa quarry near Castrovirreyna.

The discovery of a fishtail point at La Cumbre by Ossa (1976) has already been mentioned. Another of these projectile points was recently reported from the extreme North Coast, but nothing is known about its context or actual circumstances of discovery (Chauchat and Zevallos Quiñones 1980). Unlike the La Cumbre point, this one is atypical within the fishtail-point class, having a more restricted stem than usual. This character, incidentally, would be very interesting if the fishtail-point complex was an antecedent of the Paiján complex, because this point could be representative of an intermediate stage.

CONCLUSIONS

The above-mentioned controversial finds, as well as the restricted area where the present description applies – from Lambayeque to Ica, to stretch it to a maximum – confirm that by no means can we pretend to know everything about this early part of coastal Peruvian prehistory. As a matter of fact, we have only just begun to understand a few facts.

The simpler chronological and cultural framework that is proposed here adjusts better to the technological nature of the material and puts an end to the proliferation of unnecessary cultural entities. As a consequence, early Peruvian prehistory appears considerably simplified. Two traditions are clearly documented, one on the coast, the other in the highlands, and all evidence suggests that they were independent from the very beginning.

There is no need to emphasize how much we have still to learn. Whole regions of the coast are absolutely unknown. If an origin to the *Paijanense* must be looked for in the far north, there is still no clue for it, although a development from the Ecuadorian El Inga fishtail-point complex has been proposed with some likelihood.

Later evolution of the *Paijanense* is equally obscure. It is true that surface-occurring artifacts are not good indicators of chronology, but there is absolutely no intersite variability liable of temporal interpretation. The only change of this sort is so far not continuous and is shown by the variation of projectile-point bases from Cupisnique to Casma, Ancón, and, finally, to Ica – if these last finds belong to the same tradition. On the North Coast and possibly on the Central Coast as well, there is no indication of contact or transition with later cultures. On the contrary, there is a rather wide gap between the latest Paiján dates and the beginning of the Late Preceramic Period.

Despite the visible progress in recognizing the lithic equipment of those early hunter-gatherers, it should be emphasized that this information is still preliminary. Several implement types may be completely unsuspected and others, presently accepted, may be rejected as the result of more refined investigation. Our classificatory scheme for lithic tools is still tentative. Nothing, in this regard, can replace careful and tedious examination of a large number of artifacts.

We are facing problems of an entirely different nature when we try to understand how this early adaptation to marine resource exploitation was acquired. If there was no big-game hunting on the Peruvian coast, it seems nevertheless that this elaborate technique of projectile-point manufacture was probably a relic of times when medium-sized terrestrial game was available. Projectile-point shape was then modified to fit to a new way of life with minimal change in technology. It can be suggested that the *Paijanense* pattern of subsistence is probably derived from a versatile but more terrestrially oriented hunting-and-gathering pattern, including also some amount of fishing. During migration from an equatorial environment to the then semi-arid coast of Peru, a shift had to occur from terrestrial to marine resources because the land supported less and less large game. But the other techniques for catching small animals remained effective.

The *Paijanense*, then, can be defined as the first adaptation to marine resources on the Peruvian coast during the Pleistocene–Holocene transition. This reliance on sea foods was to become a most important feature of subsistence among later coastal populations – but with different forms, according to sedentism, a larger number of people, and a different society.

The discovery of a different human type may also shed new light on the peopling of South America. At the beginning of the preceramic stage almost all the remains are dolichocephalic, while during the ceramic stage the skulls are short (brachycephalic) because of a massive contribution of mongoloid-type skulls. In spite of this sharp difference, without a trace of evolution, a racial differentiation exists already at the beginning of the peopling of the continent, the Paiján type being different from other known remains (Lauricocha, Lagoa Santa, etc.). But distance and habitat as well as dietary habits are certainly factors to account for this variability.

The Late Preceramic and
Initial Period

————————————— *ROSA FUNG PINEDA* —————————————
Translated by Margaret Brown

INTRODUCTION

The aim of this chapter is to present a synthesis of archaeological data from the central Andean region for the period between 3500 and 800 BC, covering the area's later preceramic phases until the emergence of the Chavín style.

This was a decisive period, in which the beginnings of more complex social organization become apparent and societies exhibit the progressive urbanization which was to engender, as the physical expression of Andean civilization, public architecture on a grand scale. The stylistic elements of the so-called Andean Co-Tradition (Bennett 1948) began to take form. Lumbreras (1979) has proposed a redefinition of this concept, and questioned its extent.

This chapter examines developments in social organization and their economic basis, as reflected in the architecture and its patterns. The usual subdivision of this period into Late Preceramic and Initial Ceramic stages, based on the appearance of pottery, offers a manifestly inadequate account of the interaction of parallel socio-cultural processes in the complicated course of their development. In a sense, each instance of accommodation within an area, region, or zone, or on an archaeological site, and its relationship to agriculture, herding, and acquisition of pottery, followed a particular historical course. Thus we find that there were peoples who did not adopt ceramics even though they were in contact with others in the northern Andes who were already accomplished potters. Moreover, while the subsistence economies of communities in the coastlands remained basically dependent on extractive industry, exploiting the rich potential of marine resources, the peoples of the intermontane valleys were practicing agriculture, herding, and pastoralism. Among the latter, a first group was responding to the chance to farm without irrigation, the others to early domestication of the native camelids, together with persistence of specialized hunting techniques on the high plateau. Settlement in the eastern Andean forests followed yet another course, arising from the constant need to shift villages for ecological or historical reasons. Natural routes following the network of waterways in the Amazon Basin made

Fig. 3.1 Sites relevant to the text.

1 Las Aldas
2 Alto Canal
3 Alto Salaverry
4 El Aspero
5 Aznapuquio
6 Bandurria
7 Barbacay
8 Caballo Muerto
9 Cerro Obrero
10 Cerro Prieto
11 Chilca
12 Chocas
13 Chupacigarro Grande A
14 Culebras
15 Erizo
16 La Florida
17 La Galgada
18 Garagay
19 Los Gavilanes
20 Gramalote
21 Hacha
22 Huaca de La Gallina
23 Huaca de Las Llamas
24 Huaca Prieta
25 Huacoy
26 Huaricoto
27 Kotosh
28 Manchay Bajo

29 Marcavalle
30 Mina Perdida
31 Monte Grande
32 El Olivar
33 Padre Aban
34 Pajillas
35 Pallka
36 La Paloma
37 La Pampa
38 Pandanche
39 Paracas 514
40 El Paraíso
41 Piedra Parada
42 Pikicallepata

43 El Pulpar
44 Qaluyo
45 Queneto
46 Rio Seco
47 Salinas de Chao
48 San Jacinto
49 Sechín Alto
50 Shillacoto
51 Valdivia (Real Alto)
52 Wairajirca
53 Waywaka

migration easy. The alluvial plains of these rivers were favorable to settlement and agriculture, which could be supplemented by hunting, fishing, and gathering.

Acknowledgement of pottery as a chronological indicator arose from its profusion in the archaeological record. Once adopted, furthermore, it has been represented as a novel vehicle for rapid communication between widespread communities.

Although the amount of evidence accumulated in the last decade is considerable, it remains inadequate for full description of the monuments and their associations. There is a shortage of absolute dates and of established local sequences. Other zones historically related to the Central Andes have not been studied systematically. The present study, therefore, stands subject to these limitations. It has been handicapped further because certain published, and unpublished, works by foreign scholars were not available to the author.

FROM EGALITARIAN TO
SOCIALLY DIFFERENTIATED VILLAGES

Organization of sedentary life in villages appeared precociously in the coastlands some 8,000 years ago, utilizing the seasonal "fog meadows" (*lomas*) which occur amid the arid landscape. Evidence shows that these early sites were not occupied permanently. The people were primarily dependent on gathering and on food from the sea, most of the time many kilometers away. Unfortunately, not all sites have been adequately published; and reports and illustrations occur dispersed among general texts.[1]

Prolonged occupation is documented in the Chilca Canyon and in the Iguanil *lomas*, where there are several sites that might be comparable in size with that of La Paloma (Engel 1973: pls. 1–3, 1976: 90–2). It is calculated that La Paloma encompasses some 4,000–5,000 huts, irregularly distributed in three superimposed settlements, apparently of short duration. The hut remains, which later served as graves, cover an area some 600 m across. A C14 reading of 4360 ± 340 BC has been obtained.[2] As yet, no comparable discoveries are known from other areas.

Domestication of plants introduced no notable social change. In the highlands, where evidence is earlier, the population continued to live in temporary encampments, which now occur frequently on the lower slopes.

Between 3500 and 3000 BC (classified as Period V by Lanning: 1967a) the number of village settlers near the coast increased. Squash, gourds, kidney and lima beans were cultivated, as well as cotton. These crops, and others such as maize, were not spread, or domesticated, simultaneously but occurred earlier at some coastal and mountain-valley sites than at others.[3] As a cultural phenomenon, farming of cotton was sufficiently significant to define a stage within the Late Preceramic Period. Intense industrial exploitation of this crop for textiles replaced earlier dependence on products made from cactus, cat's-tail reed, and junco-sedge fibers and skins. The few villages of this initial phase that have been studied are found scattered at Nasca, Paracas, Chilca, and Ventanilla-Ancon.[4] The last two sites are the later.

Although in Village 1 at Chilca and in Río Grande at Nasca houses of more developed plans – rectangular and with low wall-footings of stone – were built by people who had yet to acquire cotton (Engel 1966a: 87–8, 1966b: 34–6, 79), building patterns at La Paloma continued unchanged when cotton appeared in the Late Preceramic Period. The huts were small, circular or rounded in form and built from perishable materials. Hut no. 12 at Chilca is famous as a model of a conical form, preserved almost intact in the arid coastal climate, despite its fragility and the collapse it suffered before being abandoned. Its excavation and reconstruction (Donnan 1964) give a general idea of what houses were like in the central coastlands at this period. Over the floor, which was dug 35 cm below ground level to form an oval plan, rose a framework of willow (*Salix chilensis*), acacia (Inga sp. *Prosopis juliflora*), and bundles of cane (*Gynerium sagittatum*). Junco matting (*Cyperus* sp.) was attached to serve as walls. Additionally, three whale-ribs held the matting in position. The interior was reached, by stooping, through a small and well-fitting arched door. A quantity of shells, generally the gastropod *Concholepas concholepas*, was piled round the base of the walls to give maximum protection against wind and cold. Cooking activities were carried on outside, using heated stones (Engel 1966a: 87).

Some of the settlements of the late pre-cotton and cotton preceramic period indicate social differentiation. Distinctions are evident from location and size. In the earlier village 96 and in 514 at Paracas a larger building is surrounded by smaller ones (Engel 1970b: 8, 1976: 94–9). Such differentiation corresponds to a still-simple level of social organization. The principal building could have served either as the house of the chief of the group, or as a meeting-place for family headmen. The pattern of large round buildings surrounded by smaller ones is reminiscent of the much-later Valdivian village at Real Alto in Ecuador (Lathrap, Collier, and Chandra 1975, Lathrap, Marcos and Zeidler 1977, Marcos 1978).

With a basis in the internal differentiation visible in the relative sizes of the buildings, their forms, and the materials used in their construction, there began on the Peruvian littoral the phenomenon of increasing complexity of settlements. Population increase and its resultant pressures are manifest in the greater number, scale, and inter-connection of sites; and these now contain a variety of constructive units. The various stages in this process of urbanization are not yet understood clearly; but the innovations it introduced became evident in the linked concentrations of ambitious structures, comprising large and specialized buildings such as platforms, pyramids, or raised enclosures, designed for purposes other than domestic.

The settlements in the highlands are represented by those of the Mito tradition, which had been studied at the sites of Kotosh and La Galgada. Here we encounter regional differences in the pattern of ceremonial architecture, but with an active cultural exchange between different regions. Sites in the highlands and eastern slope frequently contain marine shells; and a necklace recovered from the earliest-occupation remains at Bandurria (Central Coast) was made from the seed of the *espingo*, a plant which grows on the eastern slopes of the Andes. A four-footed mortar found among a child's grave-goods in the upper part of the Huaca de los Sacrificios at the maritime site of El Aspero (Feldman 1980: 114–15) is similar to a find from the Central Highlands at Shillacoto, although at this site it was associated with Wairajirca occupation (Kano 1972b: 148–9). Since this kind of artifact is rare at both, the two sites must have been linked through a third center.

In this process of urbanization the Northern Highlands, the Central Highlands from the Mantaro Basin southwards, and the Southern Highlands and Coast show only marginal developments. In the Ayacucho highlands, for example, the earliest ceremonial architecture appeared only with Kichkapata pottery at about 700 BC (Lumbreras, personal communication). Public building appeared far earlier on the North Coast, although not until the end of the Late Preceramic Period. None the less, villages in this area increased, such as the ones as Huaca Prieta and El Pulpar in the Chicama Valley (Bird 1948, Engel 1958) and Cerro Prieto in the valley of the Virú (Strong and Evans 1952, Willey 1953). They are characterized by clusters of small, underground houses, walled with pebbles or, in the absence of stone, with rectangular, hand-made adobes set on end, or built from compacted mud. At Huaca Prieta communal labor was invested in the construction of containing walls (Moseley 1975a: 91–2); these, though, are on a modest scale and do not indicate differentiation.

In the southern Central Coast architecture at the end of the Late Preceramic Period shows a notable advance on earlier building. The site of Asia in the lower Omas Valley comprised a series of mounds, covering an area of some 30 hectares. Excavation of Unit 1 (Engel 1963) revealed a rectangular structure of 12 by 12.50 m, made up of rooms and passages. Wall foundations, of earth reinforced with rubble, are laid at right angles and the whole lies on a low platform of packed clay. Round about it are the stake-holes of supports for a number of flimsy shelters.

Judging from features of the architecture and the associated domestic remains, mounds such as this must represent residential units, surrounded by the huts of dependents. Had other and larger mounds been examined at the site before they disappeared, it might have been possible to determine whether there were hierarchical differences between the settlement units, or whether perhaps some religious structure was present. From his analysis of grave-goods, from each of the 49 burials reported, Moseley (1975a: 75–6) noted social distinctions based on age and sex.

Contemporary with the Asia site, a novel form of architecture emerged in the Chillón Valley. The building complex at El Paraíso (or Chuquitanta) has received much attention in recent publications about Peruvian archaeology, since it is the largest preceramic site known.[5] Lying about 2 km from the mouth of the Chillón river, it comprises thirteen or fourteen mounds, spaced out over an area of some 60 hectares. The mounds are between 3 m and 6 m high and are covered today by tonnes of sharp stones. The nuclear group of seven, south of the river, is set out in an approximately U-shaped configuration, with the largest mounds in the arms. Williams (1980a: 419) argues that the U-shaped plan of the Early Ceramic Period ceremonial centers would have evolved from patterns implicit at sites like El Paraíso, though here the arms of the U harbored multiple living-quarters, a feature which did not persist at the later centers.

Moseley (1975a: 26) concedes that El Paraíso presents a U-shaped plan, but considers it arose "more by chance than intention" (p. 99). It is, however, difficult to accept that such an arrangement is fortuitous, especially since it is the major site elements which are set together to define a vast free space, of regular outline, and open along one edge. The inhabitants would not have felt obliged to respect this area had it not served some purpose in the life or activities of the community. In answer to the question of what this function could have been, Williams (1980a: 419), on inferential evidence, proposes agricultural activity in the expanse of open ground.

One of the mounds lying at the foot of the U-shaped plan was excavated by Engel (1966c), and his reconstruction shows how it was built. To judge from the structural remains visible, which are remarkably homogeneous, the composition of other mounds should be similar. A solid structure 50 m square is ringed by three or four stepped platforms. There were five or six building stages in the construction, during which successive repairs and modifications were carried out. The final remodeling, which we can see today, achieved a complex of about 25 rooms of various sizes, inter-connected by doorways and passages with a central room. A stairway in the façade, overlying earlier ones, led up to this chamber, which served some special function: there was a rectangular depression in the middle, and at each corner a stone-lined pit containing traces of fire.

It is a matter of conjecture what activities took place in structures of this type (Moseley 1975a: 96–100). Very few everyday objects have been found in them; but close by there are refuse deposits that are principally vegetable. This association, taken with the evidence of pits found scattered in the interior which could have served for storage, lends support to belief in some domestic function – whatever other purpose, ceremonial or administrative, the sites might have served. Each unit, like that studied, could have been the abode of a family of importance. Absence of distinctions in the allocation of space and in the architectural form of the principal buildings, features in some way reminiscent of the Mito tradition, seems to reflect a social order free from conditions likely to enhance hierarchical differences, or the power struggle these would engender. But neither would such characteristics inspire territorial expansion, inasmuch as this would involve confronting other social systems, like that of the pyramid-builders we shall study below, supported and spurred on in their advance by an impressive religious superstructure. Consequently, in spite of their demographic potential, sites like El Paraiso died out as social entities in the Chillón Valley as abruptly as they had sprung up.

Mito tradition settlements

Buildings of the preceramic Mito tradition have been identified in the Huánuco region of the Northern Highlands, at Kotosh, Shillacoto, and Wairajirca.[6] The last sites seem to mark the limit of the distribution in the Huallaga Basin. A concentration of Mito remains is found in four groups of tell-like mounds lying on the narrow terraces of the Chuquicara (or Tablachaca) River, at an altitude of about 1,100 m. The largest site is Pajillas, on the river's right bank, in the Santiago de Chuco Province of the La Libertad Department. It contains eight mounds, the three largest disposed in a "U" which is reminiscent of El Paraiso. The other three sites are on the left bank, in the Pallasca Province of the Ancash Department. Of these, the La Galgada group has been excavated by Bueno Mendoza and Grieder (1979, 1980, 1981).

The so-called temples found in the composition of the mounds are in fact relatively small, four-sided enclosures. Along with square and rectangular ones at La Galgada there were others of curved outline, not recorded in the Huánuco region. Bueno Mendoza and Grieder (1980) interpret these as being older; one has furnished a corrected radiocarbon date of about 2400 BC,[7] which is thus assigned to this initial phase. Morphologically they are similar to the other enclosures, apart from the curvature of the walls and some differences apparent in the northern orientation of their entrances. The entrances of the squared enclosures, like those of curved ones from higher in the stratigraphy, face west. There is variation likewise at Kotosh, where the older enclosures face northwards and later ones southwards.

Yet despite variation in outline and constructive techniques among successive, and even contemporary, structures of this type, all are related by a constant basic form. The chambers or enclosures are provided with separate entrances, showing that each functioned independently. This distinguishes them from the building complexes of the coastlands, where the rooms are inter-connected and accessible only through a single entrance from the outside. In the coastal pattern interdependence of functions prevailed, since all interior inter-communication leads finally to one chamber or court, where special activities took place. Its importance is marked by strategic location, architectural or decorative detail, or the presence of unusual finds. A further

distinction of the Mito tradition is that its enclosures were not built expressly
to be filled in, as part of a process of constructing a rising series of platforms.
It is clear that the whole structure did gain height as a result of superimposition
of enclosures; but these were covered only after a period of use, probably
short, which possibly corresponded to a seasonal cycle. What were the functions for which the enclosures were used? There is no demonstrable answer,
except that they were essentially related to a central hearth. Surrounding walls
might be dispensed with, leaving only an open space, or niches and even the
usual peripheral benches omitted, but never the hearths. Whatever the nature
of the acts or rites, they were performed by the blaze and heat of the hearths.

Izumi and Terada (1972: 176) have designated this practice of building new
enclosures on top of disused ones as "temple burial." At Kotosh, moreover,
not only the enclosures but also stairways and passages were filled in, and
walls built to contain them. Some enclosures were intact up to the time they
were carefully covered, while others were first partially demolished. The
temple of Las Manos Cruzadas is an instance of the first type, and systematic
excavation has revealed the successive, almost ritual, stages in its interment.
Reliefs depicting the two pairs of crossed hands, one male and one female,
were protected by a thick deposit of fine black sand before filling of the
enclosure with boulders and smaller stones began (*ibid.*). The temple of Los
Nichitos was built on top, following exactly the earlier plan. Other structures
can be correlated by reference to this demonstrable sequence. Two belonging
to the earlier level were not enclosed, but functioned as open courts (*ibid.* pp.
146, 161–2). Similar buildings have been encountered recently by Richard
Burger at the site of Huaricoto, Marcará (Burger and Burger 1980), in the
highlands of Ancash. Finally, there is a third and older level to be described at
Kotosh, represented by the Templo Blanco and by a further temple lying below
Las Manos Cruzadas (Izumi and Terada 1972: 32, 35–40, 304). Its buildings
have certain features in common with the first phase at La Galgada: the
modest dimensions of the enclosures, use of white plaster, and absence of
niches in the walls of the peripheral benches. These similarities could be evidence of a roughly contemporary, historical relationship among the various
strands of a single tradition.

A corrected C14 reading suggests an initial date of *c.* 2400 BC for the Mito
period at Kotosh, while the latest readings obtained (but uncorrected) run up
to *c.* 1500 (Izumi and Terada 1972: 307).[8] The first date is in accord with the
first phase at La Galgada; the later readings would correspond to that site's
Pedregal phase (see below).

The mounds at La Galgada accumulated in the same way as those at Kotosh.
A succession of 23 floors was established in the southernmost mound. The
middle layers represent the Chuquicara phase, the second phase of the local
sequence, dated about 2300 BC. The third or Pedregal phase – *c.* 2200 to
1800 BC[9] – came to an end with the arrival of pottery, associated with a build-

ing of U-shaped plan constructed on top of enclosures in the mound on the northern edge of the site.

The Pedregal phase at La Galgada re-utilized enclosures of the Chuquicara phase to construct tombs of bottle-shaped outline, consisting of short covered galleries and rectangular burial chambers roofed with a false vault. Some similar structures have been described at Kotosh (Izumi and Terada 1972: 146). Motifs painted on cotton textiles and baskets denote a close stylistic relationship with textile art at Huaca Prieta (Bird 1963a, 1963b) and at Asia (Engel 1963).

Mito occupation at Shillacoto should relate to the Pedregal phase in that the walls of the later enclosure achieve a decoration in the setting of the stones, which have been shaped with extraordinary precision (Izumi, Cuculiza, and Kano 1972). Mural decoration is mentioned at Kotosh, but this is simple, painted or in relief (Izumi and Terada 1972: figs. 82, 94, pl. 29f). At La Galgada a combination of shaped-stone settings and niches, either inlaid or formed by corbel-like projections, decorate the outer face of the upper platforms. Structural decoration of subsequent architecture in the region between the Marañon and Huallaga basins would find antecedents in this final Mito tradition style.

It is stratigraphically established that enclosures grew larger as time passed. But apart from this chronological difference there are no differences in size, location, or other architectural feature to suggest any functional hierarchy between them. At La Galgada some distinctions can be seen between site complexes – in the size and number of the mounds and consequently in the density of the occupation. This, however, could have been a consequence of relative population numbers in the various communities involved. In the area adjacent to the mounds here lie foundations of the precarious dwellings of the people who built, and filled in, the enclosures, and who would have been in attendance when specialist functionaries gathered within them. Those who officiated also lived outside the mound area, since the enclosures are clear of any sign of activity or of domestic rubbish. Since no other residential centers have been identified, these people must have shared the same accommodation as the rest. Thus, social differentiation within the Mito tradition is not evident, either in architectural form or in the allocation of space. It would emerge in the ordering of the enclosures rites – that is, between those authorized to take part and those committed to support the system from without. Social distinctions would have been based on expertise, as well as age and sex, a pattern consistent with a simple level of tribal organization.

Among economic activities, hunting would have played an important role (Wing 1972: 331–2, 336). At La Galgada the less humid conditions have conserved evidence of cotton, peanuts, squash, beans, and maize. However, the rough terrain of the narrow river terraces on which sites such as this are concentrated is unsuited to agriculture. By contrast the location, within easy reach of the highlands of Ancash and La Libertad with their wealth of game animals, was highly favorable for hunting. In the uplands around the Calipuy range in Santiago de Chuco, the past abundance of guanaco is still talked about.

Thus it would seem probable that hunting would draw people to the mountains, while their agriculture was practiced principally in the valleys. When the scarcity of occupation remains, compared with the size of the mound complexes, is also taken into consideration, we are led to surmise that construction and use of the sites, with subsequent covering of the enclosures, took place only at recognized seasons, when different tribal groups came together.

Coastal settlements with pyramidal structures

From about 3000 to 2500 BC a series of striking stone buildings were being constructed in the area of the central coastlands. The earliest recognized are at Bandurria, Rio Seco, and Aspero. The site of Los Gavilanes, north of Huarmey,[10] is said to contain stone buildings of considerable size, which were occupied between 2850 and 2780 BC, immediately before the construction of a system of underground storage depots for housing harvests of grain.

Culebras is a hillside settlement complex one-and-a-half hectares in extent. Los Chinos in the Nepeña Valley to the north has similar architecture (Engel 1966a: 117–18). From the fuller information available about preceramic Mito buildings it is possible to recognize that these sites have certain important features in common, as the author Terada was first to observe (Izumi and Terada 1972: 300). It is difficult, however, to determine the exact nature of this relationship, given an absence of absolute dates and the relatively poor information available about coastal sites. The rooms built at Culebras were small, square or rectangular in outline, with rectangular niches in the walls. The floors were either paved or of compacted clay, probably several layers deep, since one is mentioned as being 5 cm thick (Engel 1957a: 88, 1957b: 66, 1965: 29). The rooms are clustered together on substantial platforms with rounded corners, reminiscent of those at La Galgada and in mound KM at Kotosh (Izumi and Terada 1972: 288–90). The whole complex is reached by a central stairway of monumental proportions, leading northwards: a further distinctive feature that relates specifically to La Galgada. In each room there is the narrow tunnel or roofed gutter which ran through each chamber, stone-lined like the subfloor ventilation ducts in Mito enclosures. According to Lanning (1967a: 67), these were guinea-pig hutches. There is no mention of benches or a central hearth at Culebras; but we do not know whether this should be ascribed to their absence, to restricted excavation (Engel 1957a: pl. XIVb), or to regional or functional differences.

Bandurria and Río Seco

At Bandurria, south of Huacho, two preceramic occupations have been identified (Fig. 3.2). The later one, which is not dated, is distinguished by its brachycephalic population and the use of baskets for infant burials (Fig. 3.3). Cultural remains from the earlier occupation are almost identical with those at Río Seco, which lies north of Chancay, although there is some discrepancy in the radiocarbon datings since readings from Río Seco seem several centuries later.[11] The most notable feature at Bandurria is a pyramid-mound. There are five or six of these at Río Seco, two of which measure about 10 m to 15 m in diameter and 3 m in height. They were built up by successive filling of rooms, all of which were inter-connected with a central unit. The room walls are embellished by a novel, structural, decoration (Engel 1957b: pls. XII–III,

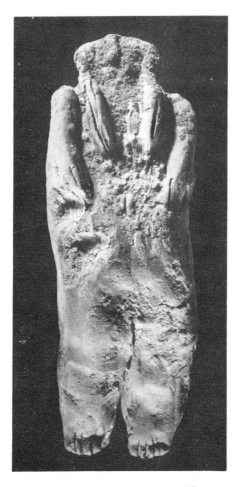

Fig. 3.2 Figurine of unbaked clay recovered at the base of first preceramic period deposits at Bandurria. Length 16 cm.

1966a: fig. 25–6, Wendt 1964: photo 6). The floors are free of refuse and show no sign of use or wear. For thresholds of the doorways use was made of the *Fourcroya*, which grows on the western slopes of the Andes between 1,450 m and 3,000 m (Weberbauer 1945: 154–5).

Río Seco is a good example of the earliest villages to contain evidence of social differentiation. There are distinctions both in the houses (Wendt 1964: photos 3–5, Engel 1966b: fig. 19) and in the size of the pyramidal structures. Once possible differences in date are allowed for, these could reflect role hierarchy. Occupation zones are integrated with the pyramids. At Bandurria remains of simpler buildings, which have not been excavated, lie near the pyramid-mound; there is an area with stone foundations, or low walls, 250 m away (Williams León 1980a: 384, fig. 1.7a). When this was partially cleared

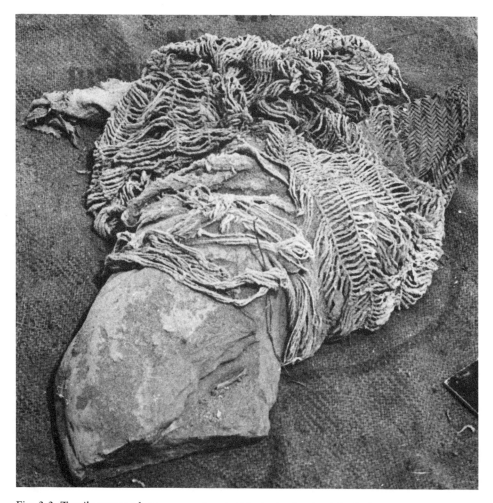

Fig. 3.3 Textile-wrapped stone, associated with the basket-burial of a boy. From the second preceramic period at Bandurria.

in 1977, stratigraphic evidence showed it belonged to the final occupation phase. Since the pyramid-mound also remains unexcavated, the inter-relationship is not known.

El Aspero

The settlement here covers an area of about 13.2 hectares. Differential assign-ment of space implies site-planning; and this may well mean that El Aspero is an example of "early urbanization of considerable formal complexity," as Williams León has claimed (1980a: 384). There are pyramid-mounds integrated with lines of large terraces, various residential groupings, and two kinds of underground structure which could have served for storage. Society and its organization on the scale implied would, of itself, require storage depots, larger or smaller according to need, for the distribution of foodstuffs and supplies during periods when the population was engaged on public projects.

Of the 17 standing mounds, 6 represent truncated pyramids, with heights of between 2 m and 10.7 m (Moseley and Willey 1973: table 2). The less-prominent mounds adjacent could contain structures like the ones excavated by Willey and Corbett (1954: 25–9). It has been thought that these might be dwellings for people who attended the temple activities (Moseley 1975a: 92). Possibly they also fulfilled other functions, of an administrative nature. Cruder houses were built on the northern edge of the site, on terracing in the hillsides. From corrected radiocarbon dates it appears that the pyramids were in existence by 2800 BC (Huaca de Los Sacrificios) or 2600 BC (Huaca de Los Idolos)[12] (Feldman 1980: 246–51).

The pyramids were built up by progressive in-filling of rooms. Feldman's excavation (1977a, 1977b, 1980) in three of the mounds – Huaca Alta, Huaca de Los Sacrificios, and Huaca de Los Idolos – established that the practice of depositing rubble during construction in containers of reed or cane came late in the sequence. The containers could represent measures in the unit of work assigned to each individual during the enterprise, as in the operation of the Andean *mit'a* (Feldman 1977a: 6–7). This idea is suggestive, if we note that the containers were used in the blocking of chambers, but not for retaining the filling on the sloping sides (Moseley and Willey 1973: 460–5). The wicker-work, too, was not strong enough for re-use in transporting the tonnes of rubble involved. At El Paraiso similar containers, one meter in diameter, were found with their contents intact on the floor of the rooms. This technique was used until Chavín times as an aid to effective organization of the super-abundant manpower available for construction of the imposing buildings of the central and north-central coastlands. Dumping of material was made easier; and a standard unit was maintained, which assisted in calculating the amounts required to fill up the chambers and construct platforms to the size desired. In this way, timing and assistance of thousands of participants were coordinated.

Social hierarchy can be discerned, not only in house remains but also in the pyramid-structures. Moseley (1975a: 94–5), after first allowing for temporal differences, cautiously interprets these distinctions as functional, corresponding to rank in the temple hierarchy. Each official would have had access to an altar or platform, for cult purposes. On Moseley's surmise the cult gods, too, were ordered on different levels, but he does not link this explanation to the process of social differentiation upon which civilization rests (Moseley and Feldman 1977). Accepting that the size and level of complexity or elaboration shown in a pyramid may well indicate the status of the associated gods, we postulate that their respective attendants (to avoid the term "priests," which caused difficulties for Moseley) could have functioned in a corresponding hierarchy. Charged with ministering to the terrestrial needs of their divine masters, they secured to themselves a privileged position, since they alone were entitled to dispose of the labor force of the majority. It is believed that hierarchy among this minority engendered the struggle for power, which, throughout Andean process, has measured success by ability to command sufficient manpower for ever-more striking enterprises, to maximize ascendancy and prestige. This ceaseless power struggle would have led to a dialectic process, whereby certain cults collapsed as they were integrated into, or dominated by, others. Such a process would account for the expansion of selected cult systems, which find reflection in the territorial demarcation of particular forms of "religious" architecture – an early indication of the Andean civilizations.

Settlements with circular pits

Little is yet known of the history of the circular pits or sunken plazas which were to develop to extraordinary elaboration at Chavín de Huántar (Lumbreras 1974e, 1977). Their distribution covers a vast and various territory, from the coast to the intermontane valleys. Williams León (1971, 1980a: 404–10, fig. 2.2) has propounded a typology based on stylistic analysis of the architecture. The first author to recognize these structures was Kosok (1965: 194, 221–5, fig. 18), who published aerial photographs of the coastal valleys of Supe and Santa.

On the North Coast the site of Alto Salaverry in the Moche Valley is of especial interest since it is here that a circular sunken pit, lined with masonry and clay mortar, first appears as a novel element in the architecture. It is relatively small and rudimentary, lying apart from other buildings and not associated with a pyramid (S. Pozorski 1976, Pozorski and Pozorski 1979a, 1979b). Similarly isolated examples are known in the Santa region at Cerro Obrero and Alto Canal (Kosok 1965, Cárdenas Martin 1977, 1979: 11, photo

42). At La Galgada an almost circular sunken structure, about 24 m in diameter, lies slightly north of the axis of the largest mound (Bueno Mendoza and Grieder 1981). Since it has not been excavated we do not know whether it belongs with the site's preceramic buildings or to the U-shaped structure. There are also two pits at Pajillas, albeit smaller in dimension, adjacent to the three principal mounds (Bueno Mendoza, personal communication).

Alto Salaverry remains undated. It has been assigned to final phases of the Late Preceramic Period on the basis of architectural features and the presence of twined-weft cotton textiles. If this conjectural dating is correct, and applicable to the other sites described, it would seem that circular sunken pits developed as independent functional units in the highlands, spreading from there until they reached the coast (Williams León 1972). This hypothesis would account for local variation more readily than would the theory of gradual diffusion from the south into the northern coastlands (Pozorski and Pozorski 1979b: 373–4, [opposed by] Williams León 1980a: 397).

Salinas de Chao is a further complex assigned, on slight evidence, to the Late Preceramic Period. One of the two circular sunken pits at the site lies at the foot of a structure standing on stepped platforms on the hillside, and in the line of its main axis. A new element is the great rectangular court, but this belongs with another stepped structure alongside. Thus the pits are not related to the courts – though this plan can be observed in certain Santa sites, such as Pampa Yolanda in Tanguche (Cárdenas Martin 1979: 10–12, photos 9, 14, 15, 37, 38).

The major concentration of complexes in which the sunken pits occur is found in the Supe Valley. There are about 30 sites, stretching some 40 km inland from the coastline (Williams León and Merino 1979). Williams León (1980a: 406) considers that Piedra Parada and Chupacigarro Grande A belong early in the series, before the design was standardized. The pit at the first site is located at the center of a square plaza and lies at the foot of a complex of rectangular enclosures built on two parallel platforms stepped into the hillside (*ibid.* fig. 2.3a, Feldman 1980: fig. 28). The Chupacigarro example is associated with a pyramid which has lateral wings (Williams León 1980a: fig. 2.3b).

The twined-weft textiles recovered suggest Piedra Parada should be broadly dated in the Late Preceramic. The formality and regularity of the site-plan, covering roughly 15 hectares, denotes progress towards urbanization far in advance of that at El Aspero. Reed containers were still utilized as a construction technique.

THE INITIAL CERAMIC PERIOD

Proliferation of large site complexes in the coastland valleys is characteristic of the whole of the Initial Ceramic Period. This must imply some mastery of irrigation techniques, since without these agriculture would scarcely have been possible in such arid surroundings. The evidence shows considerable increase in the currency of cultivated plants in comparison with the foregoing period. Site refuse incorporates a higher proportion of cultivars: cotton (*Gossypium barbadense*), gourds (*Lagenaria siceraria*), squash (*Cucurbita* sp.), peppers (*Capsicum* sp.), lima and kidney beans (*Phaseolus lunatus* and *vulgaris*), maize (*Zea mays*), peanuts (*Arachis hypogaea*), pacai (*Inga feuillei*), lucumo (*Lucuma abovata*), avocado (*Persea americana*), and guava (*Psidium guajava*). Faced with demand for larger harvests, land on the river plains would doubtless have become inadequate. Additionally, there was the hazard of flooding in the lower valleys. Some archaeologists think that transfer of settlements inland is attributable to changes due to a rise in sea levels (Feldman 1977b: 12–13). What actually is found on the Central Coast is evidence of eustatic transgression during the Holocene (Sébrier and Macharé 1980: 15–16), though even if certain preceramic sites were abandoned, the coastline continued to be inhabited. The new sites in the interior were selected for accessibility to land suitable for cultivation, and for locations which guaranteed short and easy leads into irrigation canals and ditches.

Although demand for cultivated crops increased, there was no reduction in the importance of sea-food (see Wilson 1981: 119). Maritime resources, on the contrary, remained so significant that a system of complementary economies appears to have grown up between inland settlements and coastal sites. Such a link can be illustrated, since the absolute contemporaneity of the sites is established, by analysis of the economies of Gramalote, on the Huanchaco coast, and mounds in the Moche Valley (Group I and Los Reyes). Gramalote exchanged maritime products – of the same species as those exploited by predecessors in the neighboring site of Padre Aban – for a range of agricultural products which would be difficult to grow locally (S. Pozorski 1976, Pozorski and Pozorski 1979c). A similar interchange developed between Las Aldas and Sechín Alto (Fung Pineda 1972a: 179, 1972b: 23–5). There must, too, have been contemporary settlements, like the littoral site of Tortugas (Fung Pineda 1972c), which supplied foodstuffs to centers in the Casma Valley. Comparable connections are implied between fishing villages, such as Curayacu, Chira-Villas and others along the shore from Mala to Ancón (Engel 1956, Lanning 1976b), and the large centers in the Lurín, Rimac and Chillón valleys, which include a surprising quantity of marine products among their débris.

Settlement in the highlands now begins to form part of the overall system, to judge by the spread into mountain areas of buildings of U-shaped plan, and use of llamas in the coastlands, for food (S. Pozorski 1976: 100–4) and ritual purposes. The Temple of the Llamas in the Virú Valley has revealed burials of these animals with their feet bound (Strong and Evans 1952: 27–34). Possibly they were also used as beasts of burden, allowing a greater volume of goods to be exchanged.

Evidence from the few sites which have been excavated in the northern highlands and coastlands does not show any major change in the pattern of the villages when pottery was introduced. Two such sites having certain pottery features in common will be noted: Pandanche, in the Cajamarca highlands (Kaulicke 1975), and Pampas, in the Ancash highlands (Terada 1979). At Virú, in the Llamas temple, the novelty is first documented by Middle Guañape ware which has a clear connection with ceramic traditions in the central and north-central coastlands (Fung 1972a: 170–6). T. Pozorski (1976a: 211–72), in a morphological survey of sites which could be related to the Caballo Muerto complex, showed that some in the Virú Valley like Huaca de La Gallina, Queneto, V-14 and Monte Grande in the Jequetepeque Valley could have been constructed during the Initial Ceramic Period, though possibly a site like Queneto was begun during the Late Preceramic.

The information available about forms of architecture on the southern coastlands and highlands is sporadic. Hacha in the Acarí Valley and Erizo in the valley of the Ica are coastal sites which have radiocarbon dates of about 1200 BC,[13] though a far higher chronology has been preferred (Gayton 1967: 1, Rowe 1963, 1967b). They are said to share the same style of pottery, though this has been neither described nor illustrated. This pottery has links with what is found at Marcavalle, where the earliest occupation was around 1300 BC (Chávez 1977: 163–60, 1145–7), at Pikicallepata (Cusco), at Qaluyo (Puno) (*ibid.* pp. 1038–41), and at Muyu Moqo on the site of Waywaka (Andahuaylas). The earliest-known beaten-gold work was discovered at this last site, from which there is a corrected C14 date of 1490 ± 100 BC.[14] Readings from Qaluyo, like those obtained at Chiripa and Wankarani in Bolivia, indicate that the *altiplano* plateau was occupied around 1450 BC by village communities using relatively evolved pottery with its own distinctive features. The Bolivian sites, moreover, produced evidence of copper-smelting (Chávez 1977: 157–60, 1020–6, 1144–5, Ponce Sanginés 1970).

Cotton textiles from Hacha have been described by Gayton (1967). In contrast to finds at the contemporary site of Gramalote (Conklin 1975), however, these are not twined-weft fabrics but exclusively plain-weave cloth, of fairly evolved technique, together with unknotted netting. From the Hacha midden, made up principally of marine residues, Rowe (1963: 5–6) has reported remains of various buildings with walling of compacted earth, which are apparently domestic. Notwithstanding the absence of archaeological excavation, he considers that they were public buildings and that housing would have been constructed in more flimsy materials, as in later periods. Plant remains recovered include squash, kidney beans, peanuts, guava, peppers, gourds, and cotton, though no maize.

At Marcavalle, as at Pikicallepata and Waywaka, the area, quantity, and density of the middens imply heavily populated villages. Excavation of the houses occupied during Phase A at Marcavalle, between 1000 and 900 BC, has produced only thin walls built from adobes (Chávez 1977: 152, 1088).

The early ceramic styles mentioned on the coast and in the highlands were related to each other and to those of the Alto Huallaga region (Wairajirca and Kotosh), Central Ucayali (Tutishcainyo), and the Cochabamba area (Chullpa Pampa). The relationship is especially clear in certain characteristic forms of small pot (Chávez 1977: 998–1068), notably a low and cylindrical double-spouted bottle, with a simple or divided bridge-handle. One from the Huánuco region is illustrated by Kano (1972b: fig. 4), another (termed "pre-Chavín"), from Disco Verde, Ica, by Engel (1966a: 152, 1976: 129), and, according to Chávez, others from Marcavalle may be similar to the latter. When we have sufficient information to define these relationships it is probable that a fourth pottery tradition will be recognized, represented by ware with decoration painted on before firing, a technique which was developing in the southern highlands and begins to be reflected in the Central Coast and Northern Highlands styles.

Across the Andes, regions south- and northeast of the Central Highlands exhibit an active response to current influences, reaching them via river systems feeding into the Amazon Basin, notably the Madre del Dios and the Ucayali, with its tributaries the Urubamba and Apurímac.

Other changes are associated with the arrival of pottery at Mito tradition sites. At Kotosh, alongside the appearance of a highly developed pottery in the Wairajirca style of 1500–1100 BC, new architectural practices are apparent in the scattered housing (Izumi 1971, Izumi and Sono 1963, Izumi and Terada 1972: 118–29). It is possible that the Shillacoto site harbors a highly stratified settlement, to judge from the find of an elaborate tomb containing exquisite pottery. The Wairajirca tradition continued into the following period, 1100 to 800 BC, at Kotosh, though knowledge of what the contemporary architecture was like is limited by the partial destruction of these levels in Chavín times. Shillacoto produced well-squared, quadrangular buildings, with both wall faces ashlar-finished and similar to one of the two structural types reported at Kotosh. They probably belong to the same phase as a tomb which contained bone objects with an incised feline design imitating the Chavín B Smiling God (*Dios Sonriente*) style, found at Chavín itself and at Garagay (Izumi, Cuculiza, and Kano 1972, Kano 1972b, 1979, Rowe 1967a, Ravines and Isbell 1976).

In addition to the Wairajirca and Kotosh ceramic styles which developed in areas subject to influences following Amazon tributaries like the Marañon, Huallaga, and Ucayali, there is a third, represented by Early and Late Tutishcainyo ware. It is associated with settlement patterns and other socio-cultural features adapted to conditions in the tropical forests (Lathrap 1958,

1968a, 1968b, 1970). Wairajirca and Early Tutishcainyo pottery share certain important features, though in others they differ.

Since the appearance of different pottery styles at widely separated points in the coastlands, highlands, and forests was virtually simultaneous, development of ceramics in the Central Andes was obviously a more complex process than one of gradual diffusion, either north–south out of Colombia and Ecuador, or westwards along the Marañon and Huallaga rivers (Lanning 1967a: 82–7). The possibility that pottery was invented independently at more than one center requires serious consideration – even though we concede that knowledge of pottery products spread early, before the practice of making them was taken up. The two small gourds from Huaca Prieta (Hill 1975, Lathrap, Collier, and Chandra 1975) incised with human faces characteristic of Valdivia Phases 3–5 are eloquent testimony that pottery from Ecuador, being more elaborate and attractive, was not particularly favored by the inhabitants.

Architecture of U-shaped plan

Of the archaeological features of the Initial Ceramic Period the U-shaped layout for buildings and ceremonial centers is pre-eminent. The extensive territory and period through which it prevailed gave rise to formal and stylistic variation. Differences in dating are not clearly understood since most examples remain unexcavated; this hampers definition of the whole phenomenon and analysis of the mutual, or external, influences at play.

At La Galgada it is established that a building of U-shaped plan overlies an enclosure complex of the Mito tradition. It has been assigned a date of c. 1800 BC on the basis of a radiocarbon reading from a wooden fragment found with a corpse lying recumbent on its back.[15] The burial was accompanied by twined-weft and looped textiles and a small black pot decorated with a snake motif in relief. This ware is still unmatched among known Central Andean ceramic styles of the period. It is in some way reminiscent of the Colombian–Venezuelan region pottery and could have been obtained by exchange across the river-network of the Amazon Basin. But the transmission of architectural form is another matter. Up to the present we know of no U-shaped temples along the upper reaches of the Ucayali, Huallaga, or Marañon rivers. There are, however, several examples in the coastlands. At La Galgada, the U-shaped plan is not the only novelty; there is also the masonry technique (Bueno Mendoza and Grieder 1980: 51, 53). This follows a style which is characteristic in coastal buildings of this period – at Las Aldas and the Temple of the Llamas, to name the best-known examples. The U-plan corresponds to Williams's Type (a2), as identified at Aznapuquio in the Chillón Valley. As this author notices, it also enhances "most of the pyramids of the archaic and formative phases" (Williams León 1980a: fig. 21 and p. 401).

The site of El Olivar in the middle of the Sechín Valley is similar to La Galgada in design. This comparison, and other architectural features, support ascription of the site to the Initial Ceramic Period (Fung Pineda and Williams León 1979).

It remains to define connections between the Central Coast (Aznapuquio), the North-Central Coast (El Olivar), and the North-Central Highlands (La Galgada), in order to determine the direction of those influences which, later, are found manifested in the Old Temple at Chavín de Huántar. There, the U-shaped plan of the pyramid encompassed, in the center of the court, a circular sunken plaza. This is a plan which has been recognized in the Mala Valley at Salitre (Williams León 1980a: 419); but its position in the expansion process cannot be determined without excavation.

Starting from such site-plans as El Paraiso and El Olivar, in the Chillón and Casma valleys, three traditions can be distinguished among the architectural schemes which emerged between 1800 and 1500 BC utilizing a U-shaped layout. The first, represented by Sechín Alto and Las Aldas, is found in the Casma Valley. Distribution of the second lies between the Huaura and Lurín rivers, where we shall describe the complexes of La Florida, Mina Perdida, and Garagay. The third has been studied in the Moche Valley, within the complex of Caballo Muerto. (We omit discussion of stylistic arguments prompted by the polychrome friezes at Garagay and Huaca de Los Reyes). The three architectural schemes were linked by a ceramic tradition which was developing on the Central Coast, characterized by particular forms such as wide-necked bottles, and cups of simple outline; and decoration by incision on a pre-polished surface is typical. Among pottery from the Caballo Muerto complex there are marked influences from another tradition, relating to styles in the northern Andes. This pottery could have arrived via the vast river-system of the north-western Amazon basin, which inter-connects an extensive area comprising forest, highland, and coastal regions.

U-shaped complexes in the Casma Valley

Moseley (1975a: 107) interpreted the architectural plan of Las Aldas as directly derivative from Piedra Parada. The matter is not, however, so simple as that, since the three characteristic components of the ground-plan – the pyramid, the plaza, and the pit – did not appear there all at one time. We know that at Las Aldas the pit came after the rest. Furthermore, compared with Piedra Parada and the homogeneous group of other sites containing ceremonial pits at Supe (Williams León and Merino 1979, Williams León 1980a: 406–7), the design of the great architecture of the Casma Valley stands out as a local creation (Williams León 1980a: 408–10). The question of its evolution will begin to be clarified when the history of the Las Aldas plazas is assessed; and there are studies afoot, especially at Sechín Alto, Huaca de Las Llamas, and El Olivar. Las Aldas and Sechín Alto share with El Olivar the U-shaped plan pyramid, and with Huaca de Las Llamas the rectangular plaza. We may recall that at Salinas de Chao one of the temples is made up of stepped platforms and there is no pit in the plaza they enclose.

Sechín Alto

Sechín Alto, in the Lower Casma Valley, is described by Tello, speaking solely of the site's principal pyramid, as "the largest monument of its kind surviving in Peru" (Tello 1956: 82). Present studies of aerial photographs reveal an overall plan of symmetrically ordered design, covering an elongated site of considerable size (see Fig. 3.4). In front of the main pyramid lie five large plazas, accounting together for an area of 400 by 1,400 m. The plazas second and fourth from the pyramid each contain a great pit, 50 m and 80 m in diameter, respectively. There is possibly a further one in the first court. A constellation of smaller buildings lies round the central pyramid and flanking the sequence of plazas, each oriented with respect to a principal site axis. It is estimated that the whole complex at Sechín Alto extends 300 or 400 hectares over the valley plain. The calculation derives from the observation that modern land boundaries retain the axial alignments of the monument, which extended to govern primitive division of the soil (Fung Pineda and Williams León 1979: 112–16, figs. 3–4, Williams León 1980a: 428).

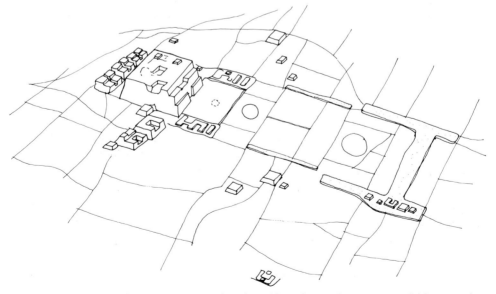

Fig. 3.4 Hypothetical reconstruction of Sechín Alto, drawn from an aerial photograph. Courtesy of Carlos Williams (see Williams León 1980: fig. 2.11).

The pyramid structures at the site are of two forms: either U-shaped or of corridor-type (Thompson 1962: 295, 1974: fig. 1). The principal pyramid is U-shaped. In contrast, Sechín Bajo and the majority of the minor pyramids have a central corridor. This second type would be the later. Thompson (1962: 297) assigns them to his Late Formative Period and U-shaped pyramids to his Middle Formative.

The different techniques and materials used in the construction of the Sechín Alto main pyramid are evidence of its protracted and complex history. The outer wall facings exhibit at least four methods of stone-bonding. In the upper platform there is walling and filling, using conical adobes (Tello 1956: 80–2, pl. VIII E–K, Thompson 1964a: 208, 238, Fung Pineda and Williams León 1979: photo 1).

Sechín Alto and Las Aldas are closely related by similarities in their architectural composition. The evidence is sufficient to allow the sequence established at Las Aldas to be valid for Sechín Alto as well. The start of building operations on the principal temple of Las Aldas is fixed by a series of radiocarbon dates obtained from reed containers in the fill of the lower access platform. These give (uncorrected) readings beginning at 1630 BC.[16] If we concede that the metropolitan center must have been built first and that Las Aldas, given its slighter dimensions, must have occupied a secondary position in the site-hierarchy, construction of the principal pyramid at Sechín Alto would thus have begun before 1650. Exploratory work by Collier (1962: 411–13) supports this, as do further absolute datings from radiocarbon readings (Berger, Ferguson and Libby 1965: 347) and thermoluminescent analysis (Mazess and Zimmerman 1966: 347–8). A subsequent level containing Gualaño pottery at Sechín Alto has been dated about 1500 BC; but this is certainly not the initial phase, since structures continue below the 5 m of section excavated.[17]

Las Aldas

Las Aldas is another settlement which has excited the attention of numerous archaeologists.[18] Lying on the shore south of Casma, it occupies an area of approximately 2 km². It comprises one major pyramid, with seventeen smaller ones at its side. Stretching out to the north-east from its base is a sequence of three great plazas, their alignment continued in a 2-km avenue, 60 m wide. In the first plaza is a large pit, or deep oval depression, with a smaller one in the western sector, opposite one of the smaller pyramids (Grieder 1975: pl. XXXVIII).

On the basis of radiocarbon dating, it has been assumed that Las Aldas was a preceramic complex (Rowe 1963: 5, Willey 1971: 109). There was indeed preceramic occupation at the site, and Engel's C14 reading of around 1850 (from a layer with cotton) could well be an appropriate date for it (Engel 1958: 3, 1963: 11, 1966b: 82). However, later excavations by Grieder (1975) and Matsuzawa (1974, 1978) have established that construction of the principal pyramid was begun by people who already used pottery.

At the same time (and contrary to Grieder's view of where a C14 reading of 1190 ± 80 belongs), stratigraphic evidence shows that the Great Pit was formed far later, since it cuts into a layer corresponding to the final phase of the Initial Ceramic Period (Fung Pineda 1972a: 58–9). It can be argued that the three plazas were also additions, possibly dating from the time of the pits. To judge by a heap of stones to one side, which were never set in position, one of these plazas was left unfinished. In this it is matched by the stairway of a temple of the second period, where Grieder (1975: 101, fig. 8) made the extraordinary discovery of a pegged line, abandoned even as the construction was proceeding.

U-shaped complexes on the North Coast

In the northern coastlands complexes of U-shaped plan appear with their own distinctive features; the site of Caballo Muerto is representative of this tradition. There are no clear antecedents locally. Willey (1953: 54) described an example in the lower valley of the Virú. The site stratigraphy showed preceramic occupation below layers with Guañape, Puerto Moorin, and Gallinazo style pottery. Relations between the Virú and Casma are evident from the Middle Guañape level, and seem to have been strong (Fung Pineda 1972a: 170–2). It appears probable that the tradition of U-plan architecture reached the North Coast at this time. The composition of the Pallka temple at Casma, with its stepped pyramid and projecting wings, recalls that at the Huaca de Los Reyes (see below), though we do not know what connections existed between the sites, since Pallka has not been studied systematically (Tello 1956: 32–48).

The Caballo Muerto complex lies in the Río Seco gorge in the Moche Valley, 17 km inland from the coast. Cultivable land in the vicinity is easy to irrigate. The site comprises seventeen mounds dispersed over an area of 2 km^2. The mounds fall into three groups, in series round the site boundaries, and are related by common spatial reference, entrance orientation, and configuration of the comparably sized principal mounds (T. Pozorski 1976a: 93–101).

The mounds of Group I – Herederos Grande and Chica (as named by Larco Hoyle 1938), Cortada, and Corredor de Los Nichos – are the oldest. Radiocarbon readings suggest the two Herederos mounds are contemporary, with a date (uncorrected) between 1500 and 1100 BC.[19] This is compatible with a range of readings obtained at Gramalote (where, however, the serial variation does not accord with the stratigraphic sequence).[20] This fishing village shared with the Group I and Los Reyes sites the use of various culturally diagnostic objects, such as jet mirrors, flat-rimmed stone cups, twined-weft textiles, and common pottery forms and decoration (T. Pozorski 1976a: 109–12, Pozorski and Pozorski 1979c: 420–1).

Huaca de Los Reyes

Huaca de Los Reyes is the best preserved of the Group II remains at Caballo Muerto and is considered the classic manifestation of religious architecture in the complex. First photographed from the air by George Johnson around 1929, it has been studied and excavated by Moseley and Watanabe (1974), Watanabe (1976, 1979), and T. Pozorski (1976a, 1976b). In all it covers 230 m by 240 m and is built from stone and clay. The façade is beautifully decorated with high-relief friezes, painted red, yellow, and white. There are two principal structures, contiguously aligned but lying at different levels. Lateral wings project from both, enclosing a sunken quadrangular court. The second of these leads into a third, larger than the others, where the mass of the participants could congregate. This differentiation of plans and levels characterizes the whole complex, with the courts becoming more elevated as they approach the pyramid summit which harbors its most secret chamber. There is a comparable rise in height between the lateral platforms which lead off the courts, with ascent by stairways and through pillared halls which have little compartments, also set to a U-plan. The restricted space between the columns and pilasters supporting the halls add a visual sense of confinement, to enhance the air of seclusion deriving from the semi-darkness. To reach the third court, and thence the upper guarded room, involves passage through further pillared chambers.

While restricting access to the summit by hampering approach, the level differences at the same time served to focus the vision. Peasants and fishermen congregated below might raise their eyes to contemplate the awesome figures in the friezes which crowned the edifice. Those radiocarbon readings from post-holes in the higher mound which are consistent suggest a period about 1300 to 1100 BC for the first of the construction phases at the site.[21]

When compared with the U-planned architecture of the Central Coast we are conscious that in the system of courts at Huaca de Los Reyes the formula is rendered in an almost intimate fashion, subjectively and to "strictly architectonic" ends (Williams León 1980a: 422).

U-shaped complexes on the Central Coast

From Lurín in the south northwards to Huaura the predominant form of U-plan comprises a major pyramid with projecting lateral wings, enclosing a plaza or open space of considerable dimensions. The complexes at La Florida, Garagay, and Mina Perdida cover 10, almost 9, and 7½ hectares, respectively.

Late in the series there are even larger examples, such as San Jacinto in Chancay, which covers 30 hectares. Leveling alone at this site, apart from the building, required movement of over two million cubic meters of material. Such size is one reason for Williams León's suggestion (1980b) that the spaces are more appropriate to agricultural or horticultural activity than for a congregation of people. He points out the likelihood that the population of the whole Central Andean region at the time could have been accommodated in areas of these dimensions. La Florida, for example, "could have held 100,000 people, allowing one person per square meter" (1980a: 415). His argument rests further on the observation that all the complexes open towards a source of water, and their orientation, between north and east and varying slightly from valley to valley, shows significant correlation with the course of the river (1980b: fig. 1). The complexes lie on cultivable land which easily could be irrigated, either by inundation or by digging canals. They all have an opening at one corner of the U, to allow the central area to be drained; and this can still be found in use on those sites which nowadays are under cultivation.

There are formal variations in the U-plans which distinguish the different valleys. Local modification would conform to details of social hierarchy, historical or chronological development, or adaptation to conditions at the particular site (Williams León 1980a: 411–12).

The formal site features are as follows. The major pyramid stands at the foot of the U. It has a central hollow, corresponding to an atrium, which opens onto the plaza. At certain sites there may be a square court, or vestibule, in front of the pyramid, also open to the plaza. Access to upper levels is through a single entrance from this court, via a stairway built along the main site axis. Use of the stairway was restricted: at Garagay, for example, there is no trace of wear on its fine coating of clay (Ravines and Isbell 1976: 259). In all, the marked symmetry of such complexes reveals a considered handling of space, aimed at controlling access to the sacred enclosures, through single entrances leading to areas which are increasingly elevated, restricted, and reserved.

The ranges of building flanking the complex, made up of a number of truncated pyramids, are not symmetrical; nor are the lateral wings of the principal pyramid. The smaller pyramids are composed of a series of superimposed platforms, amassed and rising as successive layers of chambers were filled in. The walls are built of hand-made adobes and/or of quarried or surface stones, held in a mud mortar and covered by several layers of clay plaster. Ravines and Isbell (1976: 262) report that the external wall of the atrium in the Middle Temple at Garagay was faced with four layers of plaster, the final and thinnest layer being of the finest clay. The smoothed surfaces carry relief-modeling of monstrous figures, painted in glowing colors. Black, white, yellow, blue-gray, red, pink, and green have been recorded at Garagay. Retouching and remodeling of the friezes was undertaken repeatedly: up to ten layers have been counted at this site, "almost without exception employing the same colors" (*ibid.*). Further mural decoration has been found in the Lurín complexes (Scheele 1970).

It has been suggested that the U-plan complexes on the Central Coast would have evolved from structures like El Paraiso or Chuquitanta, followed by still minor sites such as La Salina in the Rimac Valley, where there is a low pyramid overlooking a large and elongated sunken plaza. Here the related settlement lies near by, a remnant of older practices. The general site-plan would have spread quickly to the north, inspiring centers such as Salinas in the Chancay Valley, and Barbacay in the valley of Huarmey (Williams León 1980a). Experimentation within the nuclear area combined to achieve classical expression, at La Florida and Garagay in the Rimac valley, and at Mina Perdida in the Lurín. Such sites graduated to "head of a series" status, as a number of replicas were established around them as secondary complexes. By this time there is no settlement area in the vicinity.

To judge from their formal similarity, La Florida and Mina Perdida should be contemporary, and typologically they constitute a first generation. The published C14 datings, between 1800 and 1600 BC, from La Florida[22] support the inference that it came into being early in the Initial Ceramic Period. The samples came from layers with finds of dark incised pottery, including jars and bowls with thickened rims and a small two-spouted bottle with a bridge handle (Mejía Xesspe 1978). Despite its importance, Mina Perdida is another site which has not been studied adequately and there is no dating available for it (Bonavía 1965: 8–14, Scheele 1970: 135–40). In 1950 José Casafranca made some cuttings in the right-hand range of buildings, finding what he termed Chavín ware – though a similar identification has been supposed for the Initial Ceramic pottery from La Florida, and Scheele (1970) records that Casafranca compared his finds to this.

The complex of Garagay, together with Chocas and Huacoy (also known as San Humberto and Caudevilla) in the Chillón Valley, and Manchay Bajo at Lurín, belong to a second generation of sites (Williams León 1980b). If the calculated age of 1200 BC for the Garagay Middle Temple is valid (Ravines and Isbell 1976: 266) and we add a conservative estimate of 300 years for the Old Temple there, it would follow that Garagay must have been in existence alongside La Florida and Mina Perdida around 1500 BC.

The sunken circular pit reported in the main plaza at Garagay appears to have been an additional feature. It is located with reference to the line of the eastern range of buildings, not on the axis of the major pyramid. There are comparable marginal sitings elsewhere. At Cardal three pits were found on the flank of the right-hand building range, though here they were on the side away from the plaza (Williams León 1980a: 415–16). Excavation in the vicinity (Scheele 1970: 140–54) produced radiocarbon dates around 1000 or 900 BC,[23] though associated pottery was not of "Chavín" (or Patterson's

"Yanamanka": Patterson 1971a) style. At San Jacinto an oval pit lay at the edge, but away from the axis, of the plaza (Williams León 1980b: fig. 5). Therefore on the Central Coast it is implied that the pits were introductions, to satisfy some new demand of the cult; and in contrast to their position in the Casma complexes they were here a secondary feature.

SUMMARY

In the region of the Central Andes domestication of plants and animals was not a prerequisite for the adoption of settled life in villages. Such a development had been fostered already on the coast by the wealth and diversity of resources available, both in the fog meadows, or *lomas*, and along the seashores or around the mouths and banks of the rivers. In the mountains, specialized hunting on the high plains, with early domestication of the native camelids, and dry-farming in the intermontane valleys, produced no major changes in the social structure of groups practicing regular migration between different ecological levels, from the valleys to the punas. Information is lacking about the tropical forest, even though scholars such as Carl O. Sauer maintain that it was here that agricultural control of plant reproduction might have originated.

The first settlements to show evidence of social differentiation are encountered on the coast, in the preceramic sites of Río Seco, Bandurria, and El Aspero. Except at this last site, where it is relatively unimportant, there is no evidence of maize cultivation. By contrast, alongside food remains, cotton and gourds are prominent, destined for industrial use.

The catastrophe theory of Wilson (1981), overlooking precisely those ecological considerations it purports to assert, places too great an emphasis on the effect of "critical limiting factors" for marine resources when the coast suffered from temporary incursions of the warm sea countercurrent, *El Niño*, in contrast to the supposed persistence, at such times, of agricultural stability. The author has failed to appreciate, for example, that a short period of continuous frosts in the high mountains, consequent on even slight climatic oscillation, could – in the words of Dollfus (1981: 66) – "bring about the ruin of a local or agricultural economy." Similarly, as this writer has pointed out, persistent retardation of rainfall on the dry western slopes of the Andes would be an impediment to dry-farming; while mixed farming would be endangered by lack of sufficient pasture for livestock. Development of the circular-pit feature, which evolved, as has been argued, in highland-temple complexes, might reflect preoccupation with such climatic variation, since its function would seem to relate to the field of magic or astronomy.

Wilson has also made elaborate calculations to show that population density was sparse among the coastal communities of the Late Preceramic Period (Wilson 1981: 104–5), which in his view would not have advanced beyond a tribal status. Evidence from the burials excavated at Río Seco, however, shows a considerable population, of between 2,400 and 3,000 (Wendt 1964: 243–4). Probably about the same number were living at the contemporary site of Bandurria, while at El Aspero there must have been decidedly more.

It is a fact and not surmise that in the following Initial Ceramic Period the amount of cultivation increased. Large centers were constructed further inland along the coastal rivers and these reflect a variety of factors: population growth; mastery of irrigation techniques; and the establishment of a power structure which grew in strength alongside the religious organization connected to the pyramid-temples. Subsequently, along the coasts, it was not the intensification of agriculture which brought about a social organization which can be construed as hierarchical or stratified. Nor was it the teeming wealth of the biomass – although clearly systematic exploitation of its resources would contribute to the increase in population density which favors cultural advance. Meantime, inland, a mixed economy of farming and herding, in which hunting retained some importance, supported an increase in the population, whose organization becomes apparent in settlements of the Mito tradition. By contrast with the architectural patterns on the coast, however, these do not exhibit any hierarchy of function, either between different public buildings, or in the form and distribution of domestic groupings.

The point of departure for the process of social differentiation on which the civilizations of the Andes rested is to be found, as we understand it, in a politico-religious system. This was based on the economic power of a minority: the priesthood. In the name of the gods which its own members created and qualified as part of a powerfully repressive apparatus, the minority gained control of the labor force, thereby disposing of sufficient manpower to achieve increasingly grandiose public buildings. This served as a means of extending the sphere of subjugation it practiced. In this fashion the system would have expanded by the division of the cult into diverse local forms. This is manifested in the architectural traditions flourishing at Initial Period ceremonial centers.

Finally, the predominant role of the sea in the life of these ancestral societies, at the dawn of their civilization, is undeniable. Its shores fostered not only the growth of the fishing villages, but also the construction of temples.

Notes

1 Engel 1962: 32, 1963: 9–10, 1964, 1966a: 85–7, 1966b: 31–6, 1969, 1970a, 1973, 1976: 87–95.
2 I-2102:   4,360 ± 340 BC, Engel 1970a: 58.
3 Towle 1961, Lanning 1967a, 1967b, Patterson 1971c, S. Pozorski 1976, MacNeish 1977, Pickersgill and Heiser 1977, Cohen 1979, Smith 1980a.

4 Engel 1970a: 58, 1976: 94–100, Lanning 1963a, 1965, 1967b, Patterson and Moseley 1968, Moseley 1975a.

5 Engel 1966c, Lanning 1967a, Moseley 1975a, Patterson and Lanning 1964, Williams León 1980a.

6 Kotosh: Izumi and Sono 1963, Izumi 1971, Izumi and Terada 1972; Shillacoto: Izumi, Cuculiza, and Kano 1972, Kano 1972a, 1972b.

7 Tx 3167 $3,820 \pm 60$ bp: $2,380 \pm 164$ BC (corrected), Bueno Mendoza and Grieder 1980.

8 GaK-766b: $3,900 \pm 100$ BP: 2,480 BC (corrected)
   TK-42: $1,950 \pm 900$ BC (uncorrected)
   GaK-766a: $1,670 \pm 100$ BC (uncorrected)
   TK-110: $1,520 \pm 80$ BC (uncorrected)
   TK-109: $1,410 \pm 160$ BC (uncorrected)
   Two further dates are rejected, as being too late:
      TK-44: 240 ± 250 BC and GaK-764: 90 ± 100 BC.

9 Tx-2463: $2,260 \pm 187$ BC (corrected). Tx-3166: $3,660 \pm 80$ bp: $2,158 \pm 194$ BC (corrected), Bueno Mendoza and Grieder 1980.

10 Kelley and Bonavia 1963, Grobman *et al.* 1977, Grobman and Bonavia 1978, Bonavia and Grobman 1978, 1979, Castro de La Mata and Bonavia 1980, Bonavia 1982b.

11 Radiocarbon dates obtained in 1973 and 1974 during rescue work on early preceramic remains:
   1) Bandurria
      a) I-7448: $4,420 \pm 140$ BP, from matting in funerary wrappings (Courtesy of Dr Marvin Allison)
      b) V-3279: $4,530 \pm 80$ BP (from the base of deposits that contained the unique figurine)
      c) V-3277: $4,480 \pm 70$ BP (layer 4)
      d) V-3278: $4,300 \pm 90$ BP (layer 3)
      (Dates published for the first time, courtesy Dr F. Engel)
   2) a) NZ-209: $3,740 \pm 100$ BP, Fergusson and Rafter 1959
      b) NZ-210: $3,800 \pm 100$ BP, *ibid.*

12 1) Huaca de Los Sacrificios:
      a) UCR-242: $3,950 \pm 150$ BP: 2,533 BC (corrected)
      b) UCR-243: $4,060 \pm 150$ BP: 2,674 BC (corrected)
      c) UCR-244: $4,150 \pm 150$ BP: 2,790 BC (corrected)
      d) GX-3862: $4,260 \pm 150$ BP: 2,930 BC (corrected)
   2 Huaca de Los Idolos:
      a) GX-3861: $3,970 \pm 145$ BP: 2,558 BC (corrected)
      b) GX-3860: $4,360 \pm 175$ BP: 3,055 BC (corrected)
      c) GX-3859: $4,900 \pm 160$ BP: 3,702 BC (corrected)
      The second date from Los Idolos should be later than the first. The third is unacceptable, as being too early.

13 1) Hacha:
      a) UCLA-153: $2,960 \pm 90$ BP, Gayton 1967: 1
      b) UCLA-154: $1,297 \pm 80$ BC, Rowe, 1963: 5, 1967b: 19, 24–30.

2) Erizo:
   a) GX-0185:   3,890 ± 90 BP, Gayton 1967: 1
   b) GX-0186:   3,820 ± 85 BP, *ibid.*
   c) UCLA-969:   3,050 ± 80 BP, *ibid.*

14 UCLA-1808A: 3,440 ± 100 BP: 1,490 BC (corrected), Grossman 1972a: 131, 1972b.

15 Tx-2464:   1,867 ± 151 BC (corrected), Bueno Mendoza and Grieder 1980.

16 a) GaK-607:   3,580 ± 130 BP: 1,630 BC (uncorrected), Tokyo 1960: 518
   b) GaK-606:   3,590 ± 130 BP: 1,630 BC (uncorrected), Matsuzawa 1978: 666
   c) Tx-631:   3,430 ± 80 BP: 1,480 BC (uncorrected), from a burnt specimen of *Tillandsia* in Grieder's cut 1 (1975: 99–100); discovered 1 m above the floor dividing preceramic from ceramic layers

17 Gualaño ware is not associated with any particular class of architecture (Thompson 1964a: 206). C14 readings date it earlier than Cahuacucho pottery, but thermoluminescent data reverse their order. Neither has been illustrated. At the type site, Gualaño ware was described as similar to Early Guañape. Present through 3.75 m of section, it must comprise more than one phase and, from the brief description, might be linked to Phases 1 and 2 at Las Aldas (Fung Pineda 1972a: 66–90).

18 Engel 1957a, 1957b, 1963, 1970b, Fung Pineda 1969, 1972a, Grieder 1975, Tokyo 1960, Lanning 1958, 1962, 1967a, Matsuzawa 1974, 1978.

19 Huaca Herederos Chica:
   a) TX-1937:   3,040 ± 60 BP: 1,090 BC (uncorrected), T. Pozorski, 1976a: 112, 117
   b) TX-1938:   3,450 ± 70 BP: 1,500 BC (uncorrected), *ibid.*

20 Uncorrected dates from S. Pozorski 1976: 22, Pozorski and Pozorski 1979c: 418:
   a) Tx-1930:   1,100 ± 110 BC (upper layer 2)
   b) Tx-1929:   1,120 ± 90 BC (upper layer 3)
   c) Tx-1929:   1,300 ± 120 BC (upper layer 3)
   d) Tx-1931:   1,430 ± 60 BC (upper layer 1)
   e) Tx-1931:   1,580 ± 130 BC (upper layer 1)
   f) Tx-1930:   1,590 ± 80 BC (upper layer 2)

21 Uncorrected dates, T. Pozorski 1976a: 114–15:
   a) Tx-2180:   2,800 ± 60 BP: 850 BC
   b) Tx-1973:   3,140 ± 60 BP: 1,190 BC
   c) Tx-1972:   3,310 ± 80 BP: 1,360 BC
   d) Tx-1917:   3,680 ± 80 BP: 1,730 BC
Reading (a) is unexpectedly low and (d) is unduly high.

22 Uncorrected readings from La Florida; association of the samples unknown:
   a) N-44:   3,760 ± 170 BP: 1,810 BC, Ravines and Alvarez 1967: 25, Mejía Xesspe 1978: 512
   b) GX-1210:   1,730 ± 120 BC, Patterson and Moseley 1968: 129.
   c) N-87:   1,710 ± 170 BC, *ibid.*
   d) GX-0456:   1,695 ± 85 BC, *ibid.*

23 GX-1622:   900 ± 105 BC; GX-1623:   985 ± 110 BC, Scheele 1970: 140–54, table 3.

II
THE FLORESCENCE OF
COMPLEX SOCIETY

4

Unity and heterogeneity
within the Chavín horizon

RICHARD L. BURGER

A decisive change in Central Andean prehistory occurred during the Early Horizon when the multitude of distinctive local and regional cultures in central and northern Peru coalesced into the pan-Andean horizon usually referred to as the Chavín horizon or, more lyrically, Chavín civilization.[1] The nature of this occurrence remains poorly understood and even its chronological parameters are controversial. This chapter will focus on the Chavín horizon, examining the nature and degree of unity which characterized it, as well as the cultural diversity which this unity at times overshadowed. It will be shown that the unprecedented unification of previously unrelated units did not lead to total cultural homogenization. Despite changes in religious ideology, style, technology, and patterns of long-distance exchange, the societies which constituted Chavín civilization were still characterized by profound ideological, socio-political, and economic differences inherited from the Initial Period. The Chavín horizon, like the horizon of the Incas, appears to have been a significant, but short-lived, phenomenon, only partially successful in bringing about the radical restructuring of earlier regional Andean cultures.

PROBLEMS OF TERMINOLOGY AND CHRONOLOGY

Two intertwined terms, Early Horizon and the Chavín horizon, provide tools for this discussion, so a review of their definition and application is warranted before proceeding further.

"Chavín horizon" is the older of the terms and the definition of the Early Horizon is based on it. The idea of a Chavín horizon began with Julio C. Tello, the first archaeologist to expound convincingly the idea of a pan-regional Chavín culture (Tello 1930, 1939, 1943, 1960). Tello's definition of the Chavín culture incorporated a host of attributes found in architecture, ceramics, and sculpture. He derived his somewhat eclectic definition from a composite of firsthand observations of stylistic and technological attributes at Chavín de Huántar and other early sites in the highlands and on the coast (Figs. 4.2, 4.3). These other sites were initially designated as "Chavín" because they possessed one or more traits in common with Chavín de Huántar, but once this deter-

Fig. 4.1 Sites relevant to the text.

mination was made, their features, even when absent from Chavín de Huántar, were added to the general definition of Chavín culture. This intuitive and somewhat circular methodology produced a definition of Chavín so broad as to be almost meaningless. It eventually incorporated sites in Peru, Ecuador, and northwest Argentina whose dates spanned two millennia of Andean prehistory (Tello 1943, Carrión Cachot 1948: lam. XXVI).

Willey, drawing upon the critical insights of Kroeber (1944: 82, 111) and Bennett (1943: 326), attempted to clarify the situation by setting aside the problem of Chavín culture and concentrating on the notion of Chavín as a horizon style, an integrating mechanism for early Peruvian chronology (Willey 1945, 1951). To achieve this goal, Willey eliminated Tello's broad criteria for identifying Chavín architecture and ceramics, and focused on Chavín sculpture, with an emphasis on its style rather than its content. The sculpture at Chavín de Huántar was to serve as the standard of comparison for determining whether or not a site belonged to the Chavín horizon. It was assumed that the Chavín style was historically unique and would have spread with sufficient rapidity as to be considered approximately contemporary wherever it happened. The archaeological cultures or units linked together by the Chavín horizon style were defined as constituting the Chavín horizon.

Fig. 4.2 The New Temple built during the heyday of Chavín de Huántar.

The difficulty in applying this definition of the Chavín horizon style is evident even in Willey's 1951 article. Out of the large number of Chavín centers mentioned by Tello and Carrión Cachot, Willey pinpoints seventeen sites or areas where "indisputable Chavín stylistic affiliation" was manifested (Willey 1951: 125). A re-examination of these cases shows that few of them actually meet Willey's definition. Six of the seventeen sites produced iconography which is not closely related to any of the more than 150 published sculptures from Chavín de Huántar. For instance, the incised bottle from Morropón (Larco Hoyle 1941: fig. 209) which, according to Willey, was incised with a "repetitive stylization of a Chavín-like form" (Willey 1951: 115), is not similar to the style on any carving at the Chavín de Huántar temple. Despite this discrepancy, the Morropón bottle was used by Willey and others as the marker for the northernmost extension of Chavín influence (Willey 1951: 137).

Furthermore, over two-thirds of the sites with "indisputable Chavín stylistic affiliation" have only one or two examples of iconography which can be compared to the sculptures from Chavín de Huántar, and many of these pieces, in my opinion, would fail a rigorous comparison with specific Chavín sculptures.

Fig. 4.3 Stone frieze showing a procession of jaguars and anthropomorphic figures, Circular Plaza of the Old Temple at Chavín de Huántar.

Space does not permit a detailed treatment of each case, but the incised bone snuff tray from Supe, collected by Uhle in 1905 (Kroeber 1925, 1944: 40, 119), will be used to illustrate the kind of problems that occur. Representations of crabs have never been found at Chavín de Huántar, but the Supe tray (Fig. 4.4) clearly depicts an anthropomorphic crab with claws, antennae, legs, and a broad shell. The Supe crustacean does have two features associated with the iconography of Chavín de Huántar: eccentric eyes (i.e., eyes with the irises off-center) and a fanged mouth. However, the Supe image has irises in the lower half of its eyes, while Chavín de Huántar supernatural animals invariably have irises in the center or upper portion of their eyes. Similarly, the form of the fanged mouth of the crab has no analogue in the stone sculpture from Chavín de Huántar. Even the typical Chavín artistic convention of "kenning" is absent from the piece. Other differences could be enumerated but, I hope, the point has already been made. The Supe palette was considered an example of Chavín horizon style by Willey despite its distinctive style and content.

The supposition of Kroeber, Willey, and more recent scholars (e.g., Roe 1978, Keatinge 1981: 176) that a piece of art belongs to the Chavín horizon style if a number of generalized traits like fangs or eccentric eyes are present has led to the degradation of the concept of the Chavín horizon. These stylistic features, and even organizational conventions such as modular width or kenning, may have existed long before the Chavín horizon style and certainly existed after it. Unless this likelihood is kept in mind, a wide variety of art styles will be conflated and the dilemma encountered by Tello will continue to haunt us.

In 1979, four engraved shell disks were found attached to a cotton cloth in the patio of the north temple at Galgada. According to Grieder and Bueno Mendoza (1981: 50–1), one of these disks "is entirely in the Chavín style. The four heads are now of fanged feline monsters typical of Chavín art. The presence of this disk along with the others implies the existence of the mature Chavín style before 1800 BC." Needless to say, if this proved to be the case, the concept of a Chavín horizon style would have to be discarded since, by definition, a style which endures for 1,500 years is an artistic tradition rather than a horizon style (Willey and Phillips 1958: 31–40). However, photographs of the Galgada disk show that, while it does have certain traits in common with the Chavín horizon style, it is not decorated in the same style as the Chavín stone sculptures. The interpretation of the Galgada shell ornament as mature Chavín is, in my judgement, simply another example of the widespread practice of lumping Initial Period art with the Chavín horizon style. This tendency is not difficult to understand, since the Chavín style derives from these earlier iconographic systems.

If the Willey definition is strictly applied to his original sample, only about half of the cases discussed could be considered as manifesting the Chavín horizon style. The other examples might be better referred to as "Chavinoid,"

Fig. 4.4 Late Initial Period incised bone tray from Supe, depicting a supernatural crab.

in the sense that they hold some stylistic features in common with the sculpture at Chavín. These similarities are generic rather than specific, and frequently these Chavinoid artifacts portray the symbols of non-Chavín religious cults which flourished prior to or contemporary with the cult promoted by the Chavín de Huántar temple.

The interpretation of religious iconography is more familiar to art historians than anthropologically oriented archaeologists, and art historians have devoted considerable attention to the formation of the religious art styles of Judaism, Christianity, and Islam. Their studies suggest that religious ideologies cannot always be identified on purely stylistic grounds since new religions commonly adopt the style around them. Not only may the stylistic conventions of other cults be employed by newly emerging religions, but elements of the symbolic vocabulary of other groups may be absorbed and adapted, though sometimes with a concurrent shift in meaning (Kubler 1970). Elements of early Judaic art are sometimes difficult to distinguish from pagan antecedents and contemporary competitors in Canaan. Similarly, the early Christians borrowed and retained many elements of the secular and pagan Greco-Latin iconographic system used throughout the Mediterranean (Grabar 1968: xlv). The early Muslims likewise drew heavily upon the Christian painting tradition when decorating the Dome of the Mosque in the 7th century BC (Cruikshank Dodd 1969: 48–53).

These and other cases demonstrate that style and ideology should not be presumed to be coterminous. Emerging religions adopt familiar art styles as a means of expression in order to make their iconography comprehensible to their contemporaries (Grabar 1968) and, even if this was not a consideration, it would be unlikely that artisans of a new cult could innovate an entirely new stylistic or symbolic system on demand. In the Old World, it is the content, rather than the style, of religious art which can be used most effectively to differentiate between religious iconographies. This generalization holds true whether one is trying to distinguish between Jewish, Manichean, and Christian art on the Roman frontier (Grabar 1968: 30) or between pagan and Christian wall paintings in the catacombs of Rome (Kitzinger 1977: 20). These differences in content are produced by 1) the introduction of unprecedented symbols or themes, 2) the exclusion of important but irreconcilable symbols of competing cults, and 3) the relegation of major themes to positions of secondary importance.

In light of this discussion, it is significant that at least eight of the examples described by Willey from various parts of central and northern Peru do show indisputable similarities in both content and style to the sculpture from Chavín de Huántar. Moreover, since Willey's synthesis, archaeologists and looters have unearthed additional examples of art with the same style and themes as the Chavín de Huántar sculpture, thereby further documenting the empirical reality of a Chavín horizon style.

"Early Horizon," unlike Chavín horizon, is an exclusively chronological term. It was proposed by Rowe (1960, 1962a) in order to reduce the terminological ambiguity and imprecision so evident three or four decades ago (Ravines 1970b: 16–19). With the passage of time and the appearance of new evidence, its usage has, in some cases, become less than precise and occasionally even hindered archaeological synthesis rather than facilitated it. The Early Horizon was defined as the time beginning with the first appearance of Chavín influence in Ica and ending when polychrome slip painting replaced resin painting in that valley (Rowe 1962a: 49). This terminology, which functions only to delimit a block of time, intentionally eschews the assumption of widespread developmental stages implicit in alternatives like Cultist (Bennett 1948) or Formative (Strong 1948). The term Early Horizon, unlike Chavín horizon (Willey 1945), is free of any implication of stylistic or cultural homogeneity. Its definition is predicated on the archaeological identification of two hypothetical events in the prehistory of Ica: the arrival of a foreign, religiously charged art style and a change in the technology of local pottery decoration. These two events are dissimilar in character, and would certainly not have been of equivalent importance; none the less, they were presumed to serve equally well as chronological markers. While Rowe's definition (1962a) depends on when these events occurred in Ica, the block of time defined by them is considered to apply throughout the Central Andes, just as the convention BC can be employed in areas unaffected by the birth of Jesus. Consequently, a culture such as Chanapata in Cuzco, which was not directly impinged upon by the Chavín art style, can still fall within the bounds of the Early Horizon and, conversely, a sculpture in early Chavín style, such as the Lanzón, dates to the late Initial Period rather than the Early Horizon, since it was carved prior to the spread of Chavín influence to Ica. The Rowe definition of the Early Horizon is unambiguous although the criteria by which it is defined are admittedly arbitrary.

Nevertheless, sources of potential difficulty do exist with the Rowe nomenclature. What exactly is the "Chavín influence" referred to in the definition and how can it be recognized? Chavín has been used to denote a developmental stage of Andean culture history (Lumbreras 1971: 2), an archaeological period, a religious ideology, and an empire (Willey 1951: 103). But Rowe, following Willey, applies the term exclusively to the art style which is "substantially the same style as the sculpture at the highland site of Chavín de Huántar" (Rowe 1962b: 3). Consequently, in order to implement Rowe's definition, it is essential to know exactly when elements of the Chavín art style first appeared in Ica. Unfortunately, this precondition has yet to be achieved.

The Paracas Pottery of Ica (Menzel, Rowe, and Dawson 1964) is one of the few publications that addresses itself to this issue (see also Kroeber 1953). This volume describes the sequence of Early Horizon ceramics from Ica and notes the stylistic elements that have parallels with the iconography of the sculptures from Chavín de Huántar. Unfortunately, the first two phases of this ten-phase sequence are of limited utility, since they are based on a total of ten vessels. None of the pieces assigned to Phase 1 has reliable provenience, nor are they thought to have been associated with each other. Drawing on comparisons with ceramics excavated by Thomas Patterson at Ancón, at least one piece, an incised bottle (Menzel, Rowe, and Dawson 1964: fig. 9c, pl. 1b), is several centuries older than the other "Phase 1" vessels. Most of the other Phase 1 and 2 vessels bear a resemblance in form and decoration to Janabarriu-phase ceramics of Chavín de Huántar, as do the better-documented ceramics of Phases 3 and 4 of the Ocucaje sequence. The Janabarriu phase at Chavín de Huántar is believed to be coeval with phases D and possibly EF of the Rowe sculptural seriation (Burger 1984a: 244–6). It corresponds to the most active period of Temple activity at that highland center. Attributes like the convex-curved spouts, rounded exterior-thickened lips, and repeating circle-dot motifs are diagnostic of Janabarriu-phase ceramics (Fig. 4.5), and they appear also on the Phase 1 Olsen Bottle from Ocucaje (Fig. 4.6; Menzel, Rowe, and Dawson 1964: fig. 1a).

This correspondence suggests that the Ocucaje sequence may, in fact, begin midway through the Chavín sequence. Terence Grieder and Peter Roe (Roe 1974: 31–2) have reached a similar conclusion primarily on the basis of the

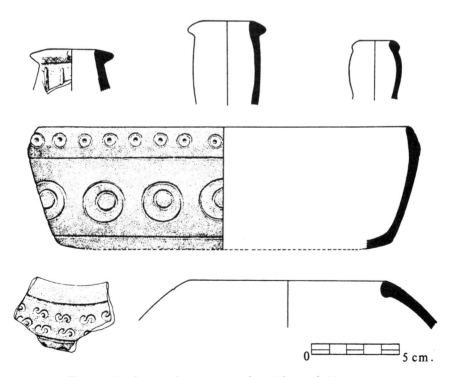

Fig. 4.5 Janabarriu-phase ceramics from Chavín de Huántar.

iconography of these vessels. Thus, while the influence of an art style related to the stone sculpture from Chavín de Huántar is present at the outset of the Ocucaje sequence, there is no reason to assume that these pieces represent its first occurrence in Ica. It is quite possible that the Chavín art style may have appeared on the South Coast prior to the Ocucaje sequence. In fact, unpublished excavations at Disco Verde in Paracas unearthed ceramics which apparently pre-date the earliest Ocucaje phases, and Chavín-related elements are reported to occur in association with these early local materials (Kauffman Doig 1971: 245). A study of the presence or absence of Chavín influence on the pre-Paracas and the early phases of the Paracas styles of Ica remains a prerequisite for drawing the dividing line between the Early Horizon and the Initial Period for Ica and, if one adheres strictly to the definition, for the entire Central Andes.

Many investigators have encountered additional difficulty with the Rowe terminology because they are unable to relate the materials from their research area to the "master sequence" of Ica (e.g., Pozorski and Pozorski 1979c). Trade ceramics would be ideal for such cross-dating (Patterson 1963), but early ceramics from Ica seem to have been exchanged infrequently with groups outside the South Coast. Paracas-style pottery has yet to be found at Chavín de Huántar and it is scarce at Ancón on the Central Coast. Judging from the Ocucaje gravelots and the ceramics from Dwight Wallace's excavations at Cerrillos (Wallace 1962), the inhabitants of Ica were likewise not importing

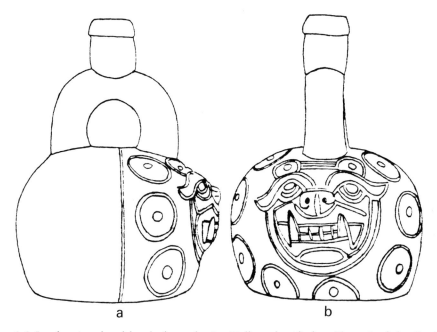

a　　　　　　　　　　　　　b

Fig. 4.6 Janabarriu-related bottle from the Ica Valley, classified as Phase 1 of the Ocujaje sequence. Height 16.75 cm. After Menzel, Rowe and Dawson 1964, fig. 1.

Table 1 *Selected radiocarbon measurements for Early Horizon samples from Ica and Paracas*

Site	Associations	Lab no.	Date BP (uncorrected)	Date BC (uncorrected)
Disco Verde	Disco Verde- and Chavín-style ceramics	NZ-685	2,715 ± 60	765
Disco Verde	Disco Verde-style ceramics, stratum 9	V-900	2,705	755
Puerto Neuvo	Disco Verde- and Chavín-style ceramics, stratum 2	V-899	2,609	659
Puerto Nuevo	Disco Verde- and Chavín-style ceramics	NZ-877	2,620 ± 60	670
Cerrillos	Ocucaje 3 ceramics; cut 2, pit C, stratum 3	P-516	2,408 ± 214	458
Cerrillos	Ocucaje 3 ceramics	P-517	2,302 ± 125	352
Cerrillos	Ocucaje 3 ceramics	P-518	2,195 ± 64	245
Cerrillos	Ocucaje 3 ceramics	GX-1345[a]	2,685 ± 140	735
Site 14A-VI-16	Paracas Cavernas I	NZ-1087	2,267 ± 91	317
Site 104-A1-14	Paracas Cavernas I	V-721	2,254	304
Cabezas Largas	Paracas Cavernas II (?)	NZ-1127-1	2,015 ± 70	65
Cabezas Largas	Tomb with Paracas Necropolis-style ceramics	NZ-1127-2	2,060 ± 170	110

[a] An unpublished measurement, provided by courtesy of Thomas C. Patterson. The other results presented here are taken from the compendium of radiocarbon measurements published by Ravines and Alvarez (1967: 28, 31–2, 34, 54–6).

quantities of exotic ceramics. A second approach to cross-dating, the comparison of constellations of stylistic attributes of pottery, can sometimes be applied as in the preceding discussion of the Olsen bottle. Unfortunately, in many cases, local styles outside of Ica are so plain or idiosyncratic as to render this technique useless.

Isolated styles can, of course, be related to the Ica sequence and the Rowe terminology by the comparison of absolute or chronometric dates. This approach has been attempted only with radiocarbon measurements and these efforts frequently were undermined by inconsistent laboratory results and the lack of a good comparative set of early measurements from Ica. The beginning of the Early Horizon was originally estimated as 600 to 700 BC (uncorrected radiocarbon years) but a subsequent study led Rowe to question this figure (Menzel, Rowe, and Dawson 1964: 4, Rowe 1967b). However, in those cases where other lines of evidence are insufficient, radiocarbon measurements may be able to provide a rough basis for cross-dating and for ascertaining whether a particular occupation falls within the Initial Period or Early Horizon. As can be seen in Table 1, samples from Disco Verde and Puerto Nuevo produced measurements ranging from 659 BC to 765 BC. Three of these samples are reported to come from strata containing very early Chavín elements mixed with the local ceramic style. On stylistic and stratigraphic grounds, these assemblages are said to precede the early phases of the Ocucaje sequence.

The three published samples analyzed from the Ocucaje 3 layers of Cerrillos (D. Wallace 1962) produced dates averaging 351 BC. Two samples said by Engel to have been associated with the earliest phases of the Paracas sequence yielded measurements of 317 BC and 304 BC (Ravines and Alvarez 1967). These results are consistent with two samples taken from Cabezas Largas and associated with later phases of the Paracas style; these samples dated to the 2nd and 1st centuries BC. It would seem that by the 4th century BC, Chavín iconography was being represented on Paracas-style ceramics of Ica and Chavín influence may have arrived several centuries earlier. These conclusions mesh well with the radiocarbon results from Chavín de Huántar, where the Janabarriu phase was estimated to have lasted from 390 BC to 200 BC, although the Chavín de Huántar temple was established at least four centuries earlier (Burger 1981). The similarity between the estimate for the Janabarriu phase and most of the measurements for the early Paracas samples is consonant with the stylistic similarities already noted between Ocucaje 1–4 and the Janabarriu phase.

It is understandable that, faced with the practical difficulties of utilizing the term Early Horizon, some investigators have abandoned the terminological distinction between the Initial Period and the Early Horizon, referring to them collectively as Early Ceramic, Formative, or, erroneously, Early Horizon. Other scholars have returned to the more simplistic Chavín/pre-Chavín dichotomy, sometimes incorrectly using the term Early Horizon as synonymous with Chavín horizon.

One prominent archaeologist, Luis Lumbreras, has sought to revive the use of quasi-evolutionary terminology. The Initial Period and Early Horizon are included within the Formative, which is divided into the following stages (Lumbreras 1974a: 49):

1 the Lower Formative, which includes pre-Chavín and non-Chavín complexes; the latter may be coeval with Chavín complexes elsewhere (e.g., Chanapata);
2 the Middle Formative, which corresponds to the diffusion of the Chavín complex;
3 the Upper Formative, which incorporates complexes derived from both Chavín and non-Chavín antecedents.

This system combines stylistic and temporal criteria with developmental factors and, consequently, the resultant nomenclature is not purely evolutionary, as was Lumbreras's earlier division of this timespan into Barbarie Media and Barbarie Superior (1974b: 214, republication of a 1968 article). The mixed character of the revised Lumbreras terminology makes its implementation imprecise and ambiguous.

The proliferation of chronological terms and the lack of consistency in their application should not, however, obscure an even more basic problem – the dating of the major complexes of monumental architecture from the Peruvian coast. There remains considerable disagreement on the age of Sechín Alto, Moxeke, Huaca de los Reyes, Garagay, and Haldas. These sites have frequently been described as Chavín horizon, Early Horizon, or Middle Formative centers (e.g., Lumbreras 1974a: 67–71, Kauffmann Doig 1978, Grieder 1975, Roe 1978). Others, including myself, believe these complexes were, in large part, constructed prior to the Chavín horizon during the late Initial Period (Burger 1981, Ravines and Isbell 1976).

REASSESSING THE FUNCTIONAL INTERPRETATION OF THE CHAVÍN HORIZON

A strictly defined Chavín horizon style would retain its original heuristic value as a temporal marker in central and northern Peru where it can be used to identify the first two or three centuries of the Early Horizon. Nevertheless, with the advent of radiocarbon dating and other chronometric techniques, this particular focus cannot but seem narrow alongside the more basic problems of what this horizon style represents and what factors were responsible for its sudden emergence and equally abrupt decline. The first of these questions has been addressed repeatedly from the outset of Chavín studies. There is a long-standing consensus that the Chavín horizon style is the symbolic expression of a religious ideology and that the Chavín horizon is the result of the diffusion of what may be referred to as the Chavín cult.

Rafael Larco Hoyle pioneered this mode of interpretation and even in his early writings he insisted that a set of beliefs centering around the feline spread over a wide area, profoundly influencing the diverse peoples who embraced this ideology. According to Larco Hoyle, these populations expressed their new religion through their art and the erection of temples, such as those in Casma, Nepeña, and Chavín de Huántar (Larco Hoyle 1938: 50, 1941: 8–9, 1946: 149). He explained the highland site of Chavín as a pilgrimage center, a mecca erected by members of the feline cult (Larco Hoyle 1941: 8). Wendell Bennett's explanation (1946: 92) of the distribution of the Chavín style was similar to Larco Hoyle's, and Gordon Willey, in his "functional" analysis of the Chavín horizon style, also concluded that "the diffusion of the Chavín art style can be explained most easily as the peaceful spread of religious concepts" autonomously manipulated by individual communities (Willey 1948: 10, 15). In the same year, Rebeca Carrión Cachot, elaborating upon Tello's view of a multi-faceted Chavín civilization, argued that the "Chavín empire" was religious, not political, and that this religion spread a homogenous art style, and a standardized set of rites over zones dissimilar in culture and environment (Carrión Cachot 1948: 169–72). This viewpoint remained unchallenged in the following decades and John Rowe, in a 1966 presentation at the Universidad Nacional del Cuzco, stated with uncharacteristic certitude that there

existed no doubt that the expansion of Chavín was a religious movement
(Rowe 1977: 9). Since then, despite an exponential increase in field work,
there has been virtually no dissent concerning this conclusion (Lanning 1967a:
98, 1974: 77–8, Lumbreras 1973: 90, 1974a: 46, 67, Lathrap 1973: 92,
Patterson 1971a: 41, 1973: 97–8, Moseley 1978b: 520, Cordy-Collins 1977:
353, Keatinge 1981).

Unfortunately, non-Andean concepts frequently have been injected into the
reconstructions of the hypothetical spread of Chavín ideology. There is a dis-
concertingly familiar cast to the popular model of proselytizing missionaries
converting an ever-widening number of groups at the expense of local cults
(e.g., Lanning 1967a: 98, 102). Cordy-Collins (1976) even has suggested that
the Chavín printed textiles of Karwa may have served as a kind of catechism
communicating the message of Chavín ideology to the peoples beyond the
Chavín heartland.

The consensus that Chavín was primarily an expansive religious movement
is in sharp contrast with the skepticism expressed concerning analogous
interpretations in Mesoamerican archaeology. While the Mesoamerican data
base is obviously distinctive and may call for alternative interpretations, the
theoretical orientation of archaeologists working in that area has at least
partially contributed to these interpretive differences. William Sanders, for
example, rejects this explanation for the appearance of the Central Mexican
Teotihuacan-style religious art and architecture at Kaminaljuyu, Guatemala,
on theoretical, rather than empirical, grounds. He writes:

> My major objection to this [missionizing] interpretation is that pro-
> selytizing religions are a relatively rare phenomenon in human his-
> tory, and they are associated primarily with Iron Age states in the
> Old World, which had political, social and economic institutions
> that were much more evolved than most Mesoamerican specialists
> believe such institutions could have been in pre-Hispanic Meso-
> america. Much more common among cultures at the institutional
> level of Teotihuacan are patron gods related to sociopolitical sys-
> tems and subsystems. Furthermore, overt missionization very rarely
> occurs outside of direct political control, and if it does occur outside
> of such control, it is usually a secondary objective. Sanders 1978: 40

Of course, the proselytizing religions in the Old World referred to by Sanders
are known from historic accounts rather than archaeological patterning. Does
the association of proselytizing religions with the states of the Old World
reflect anything more than the distribution of writing systems? What, if any,
configuration of archaeological remains left by a non-literate society would
constitute evidence for a proselytizing religion in the pre-Hispanic New World
or the preliterate Old World? Clearly, many Andeanists would differ with
Sanders on the criteria which should be applied in identifying these

phenomena. I believe that the question of prehistoric proselytizing religions must be investigated archaeologically, rather than being forced, along with iron, the state, and literacy, into a pre-packaged evolutionary stage.

Kent Flannery, in his early work on the Mesoamerican Formative, expressed skepticism about the existence of proselytizing expeditions by Olmec missionaries (Flannery 1968: 79). Acknowledging the wide distribution of similar religious art, he concluded that:

> the elite of a number of key highland regions came to emulate the behaviour of the Olmec elite, to borrow their symbolism, and adopt those aspects of Olmec religion which lent further prestige to their own position. Perhaps one superficial effect of this process was the spread of the Olmec art style through the highlands. I say "superficial" because I am confident that the spread of that style was not a primary cause of Formative Mesoamerica's unity, but one reflection of the fact that it was already unified in an economic sense.
> Flannery 1968: 108

Flannery, unlike Sanders, is willing to consider the peaceful spread of religious ideologies in the early pre-Hispanic world, but neither of these scholars is willing to consider models featuring a self-interested religious organization which promotes the spread of a universalist or ecumenical religion. Sanders and Flannery, at least in the latter's early work, also concur in the conviction that expansive religions are a secondary phenomenon, mirroring more important forces, such as economic unity or military conquest.

Sanders usefully differentiates between proselytizing religions and more localized patron gods tied to particular socio-political systems. He does not, however, consider religious phenomena which are intermediate in scale between these two extremes. Ethnographers working among the tribes and chiefdoms of Africa have documented the importance and widespread occurrence of religious phenomena which are more far-reaching than the parochial cults of the community but less inclusive than world religions like Christianity and Islam (Werbner 1977a: ix). These phenomena, sometimes referred to as regional cults, are often spread over thousands of square kilometers and incorporate groups differing in language, culture, and natural resources. The scale and configuration of these regional cults are comparable to the Chavín cult, and a closer look at this general phenomenon is warranted. Elizabeth Colson, in a study of the local cults and regional prophet cults of the Tonga of Zambia, makes the following general observation:

> No cult which primarily functions to serve the particular interests of a territorial community on a regular basis can serve a general public unless it radically alters its practice and its constituency: a cult

> serving a wider constituency on an ad hoc basis may well serve the
> special purposes of local communities. The two [regional and local
> cults] can co-exist and reinforce each other. The cult with universal
> claims then serves as a further court of appeals when a local cult
> does not satisfy its adherents . . . This was true in ancient Greece
> where each small city state had its own cult, associated with its fate
> as a human community but delegations went to consult the Oracle
> of Delphi, or perhaps Dodona, which served the entire classical
> world for many centuries. Colson 1977: 119

Local cults emphasize the exclusive domain, boundedness, and stability. They
are intimately tied to the land and the local system, and their rituals often have
a politico-jural focus. Regional cults, on the other hand, are non-congruent
with political and ethnic boundaries, and their ideology and rituals foster uni-
versalism and openness (Werbner 1977a: xxxiii, Turner 1974: 185). Each
regional cult has its own distinctive idiom, but they are similar in their formal
and hierarchic organizational structure, which maintains officials with the
authority to legitimize branches of the cult and limit deviance in local congre-
gations. Regional cults also usually resemble each other in their doctrines of
universality, theism, and moral responsibility; in order to survive and spread,
they must stress values of peacefulness based on recognition of the transcen-
dent interest of the macrocosm irrespective of long-standing differences,
hostilities, and competition between local communities (Werbner 1977b:
212). The right of free movement by religious functionaries and pilgrims
across communal borders is a basic feature of the "ritual fields" generated by
regional cults, and ultimately these "middle range" organizations provide networks for the flow of goods, services, information, and people. The potential
contradictions and conflicts created by the inter-penetration of regional and
local cults are often resolved by mutual affirmation and acceptance. Frequently, local cults acknowledge the legitimacy of the regional cult, and even
become formally affiliated with it, without necessarily modifying their own
ideology or rituals (e.g., Garbett 1977: 56–8).

A concrete example of a late-pre-Hispanic regional cult from the Andes is
known from Colonial accounts (Pizarro 1968, Estete 1968: 382–4, Cieza de
León 1967: 196, Rostworowski 1972, 1981, Patterson [n.d.]), and a number
of scholars have viewed its organization as possibly related to that of the
Chavín cult (Kaulicke 1976: 17–22, Patterson 1971a: 46, 1973: 97–8,
Keatinge 1981). The historical evidence on this 16th-century ceremonial network, whose primary center was located at Pachacamac, illustrates the way in
which religious networks could be organized in an Andean manner – one consistent with distinctively Andean concepts of community, reciprocity,
taxation, and kinship.

The center of the Pachacamac cult was a large ceremonial complex at the mouth of the Lurín River. It featured an oracle located within a chamber at the summit of one of the large adobe platforms but access to the oracle was restricted to specialists of the cult. There were also open plazas, where pilgrims fasted and participated in public ceremonies. The Pachacamac cult provided oracular predictions, favorable intervention with the elements, protection against disease, and, presumably, specialized knowledge concerning the favorable times for planting and harvesting. Divine sanctions, including earthquakes and crop destruction, were thought to be the consequences of antagonizing the god of Pachacamac.

A community interested in establishing a branch shrine had to petition Pachacamac and demonstrate its ability and willingness to support cult activities. If the request was accepted, a resident priest was supplied to the new branch by the center at Pachacamac (Patterson [n.d.]) and, in return, the supporting community set aside agricultural land and/or pasture for the cult and provided public labor for farming and herding (Rostworowski 1981: 167–8). Lands assigned to the cult were worked before the lands allotted to the local elite or the community members themselves and all segments of the society were expected, at least symbolically, to donate labor (Cobo 1892: bk XII, ch. XXVIII). A portion of the produce from the fields or herds supported the local branch of the cult, while the rest was sent as tribute to the principal ceremonial complex. Large quantities of cotton, corn, dried fish, llamas, and guinea pigs were brought to Pachacamac, as were scarce raw materials (e.g., gold) and manufactured goods (e.g., fine cloth).

By the time of the Spanish Conquest, Pachacamac had developed a network of shrines spanning the range of production zones. A branch oracle was established in the middle of the Rimac Valley, and the first leaves of the coca harvest from that area were brought to Pachacamac before the coca was chewed by members of the community (Rostworowski 1972: 39). Other secondary cult centers were located near the high-altitude pastures of llamas and alpacas, and also on the eastern slopes of the Andes. Branch oracles were reported from valleys throughout the coast of Peru and tribute was said to have been brought to Pachacamac from Ecuador. Rostworowski has described the ceremonial network of the Pachacamac regional cult as an archipelago of religious centers, stretching vertically across the diverse ecological zones of Central Peru and horizontally along the central and northern Peruvian coast (Rostworowski 1972: 43). The cult cut across a patchwork quilt of ethnicities and languages, forming a system parallel to and partially independent of the regional and national levels of political organization. The groups within this religious archipelago were linked ideologically by their shared belief in the oracle of Pachacamac, and the sense of supra-local and supra-national identity was expressed and reinforced through annual pilgrimages to Pachacamac by representatives of the participating communities.

The branches of the Pachacamac cult were conceptualized as the wives or children of Pachacamac, and each oracle had his or her own name and origin myth. The kinship said to exist between the secondary cult centers and the primary center was consonant with the reciprocal obligations and the sense of constituting a single ideological community.

The Pachacamac cult resembles many African regional cults in its multi-ethnic character, its maintenance of a formal and hierarchical organization, its funneling of tribute from branch centers into a primary center, and its binding together of a wide-ranging ritual field through pilgrimages. While it also shares these traits with some of the well-known proselytizing religions of the Old World, it more closely parallels African regional cults in its emphasis on oracles and its compatibility with older local cults. The "multiplication" of individualized but related branch oracles (Kaulicke 1976: 55) using the metaphor of kinship is perhaps the most distinctive aspect of this Andean regional cult. It is noteworthy that there is no historical evidence for the use of aggressive missionaries as a means of spreading the religious ideology of Pachacamac. This particular proselytizing stratagem is neither a necessary nor a common feature of non-Western religious movements. Moreover, the role of missionaries is difficult, if not impossible, to isolate archaeologically, and debate concerning their presence or absence in prehistory only blurs the broader issue of regional religious networks.

The dearth of investigation at Early Horizon ceremonial centers inhibits a critical evaluation of the degree to which the Pachacamac regional cult provides a viable model for the much older religious institutions of the Early Horizon. The major socio-political changes which occurred between Late Horizon and the Early Horizon make it likely that it will have to be modified on the basis of future field work. On the other hand, some aspects of it do appear to be consistent with the extant archaeological record.

If the growth of the Pachacamac cult followed older Andean traditions, some local religious centers of the Early Horizon would have remained relatively unaffected by the Chavín cult, even if they lay within its sphere of influence; in fact, they may even formally have recognized its legitimacy within certain specified realms. Huaricoto, in the Callejón de Huaylas, may be an example of this pattern. Established as a shrine in the final centuries of the Pre-ceramic Period, Huaricoto never attained more than local significance. The ritual activity at Huaricoto centered around the burning of offerings in small specialized chambers, a practice typical of the late Preceramic centers of the Kotosh Religious Tradition (Burger and Salazar-Burger 1980: 28–30). There is archaeological evidence for the continuation of these religious ceremonies at Huaricoto throughout the Initial Period and Early Horizon, and material evidence left from the rituals indicates that traditional local ceremonies continued to be carried out even at the apogee of the Chavín cult. In fact, the largest and most elaborate of the ritual chambers at Huaricoto was built during the Early Horizon. A carved Chavín spatula depicting the "Snarling God" of the Lanzón and pottery decorated with Chavín designs recovered from the edge of the central ritual precinct, provide evidence of the contemporaneity of the Chavín cult and of the apparent compatibility between the local cult of Huaricoto and the regional cult of Chavín (Burger and Salazar-Burger 1980: 31). It would have been expected that if the Chavín cult had spread at the expense of older cults, replacing the earlier religious systems with the new ideology, this pattern should have been evident in the Callejón de Huaylas, which is situated between the Callejón de Conchucos, in which Chavín de Huántar is located, and the coast.

Another instance of interpenetration of the Chavín cult with older local cults has been documented from the Jequetepeque Valley of the North Coast of Peru. This valley and the nearby Pampa de Cupisnique are justly famous for the Chavín-style pottery looted from cemeteries in the area (Larco Hoyle 1941: fig. 253, 1945: 17, Lapiner 1967: figs. 16, 39). However, a recent study of carved "Chavín" steatite bowls and cups from this area has demonstrated that although they are contemporary with the Chavín horizon style, their iconography often represents a supernatural spider associated with the taking of trophy heads (Fig. 4.7; Salazar-Burger and Burger 1983). The Rondon cup, said to be from the Chiclayo area (Kroeber 1944: 91), is similar stylistically and technologically to the other Early Horizon steatite vessels, but it depicts the two raptorial birds of the Black and White Portal rather than the local arachnid deity.

Many of the important centers during the Early Horizon already had emerged as central nodes of single or multi-valley polities during the late Initial Period and, in that capacity, they were the focus of religious activity dedicated to patron gods associated with their particular territorial interests. The diffusion of the Chavín cult during the Early Horizon may have implied no more than the addition of a branch oracle of Chavín alongside the local shrine, just as the Incas established a branch of the Sun cult alongside the Pachacamac oracle without disrupting its activities.

The discoveries which most clearly illuminate the distinctive regional organization of the Chavín cult were illegally made by looters at the site of Karwa. A short description of this unfortunate incident and the materials resulting from it will be presented before considering the implications. The Karwa cemetery lies 8 km south of the Paracas Necropolis and its location was noted by Tello (1959: fig. 1), but the site did not attract the attention of archaeologists until 1970 when *huaqueros* uncovered a large rectangular tomb which differed in shape, size, and construction from the surrounding interments. The unusual tomb reportedly contained the bodies of several individuals and an abundance of grave goods (José Pinilla, personal communication). Over 200 fragments of decorated cloth were recovered from the tomb, along with Paracas ceramics dated to the early phases of the Ocucaje sequence (Cordy-Collins 1977: 11). A small number of sherds said to have been

associated with the Chavín textiles of Karwa, are currently stored in the
Museo Amano. These fragments are closely related in form and decoration to
the Janabarriu-phase ceramics of Chavín de Huántar.

Most of the textiles from the Karwa tomb were not decorated according to
local Paracas tradition. Instead, vivid depictions of the symbols of Chavín de
Huántar were painted in red-orange, tan, brown, olive-green(?), and blue pigments; on some pieces, a resist technique was used to form white Chavín
motifs on a colored field. The textiles were made of loosely woven cotton
thread and were painted in the style of phase D Chavín de Huántar sculptures
(Roe 1974: 31).

Individual design elements, such as eyes and ears, have counterparts on the
sculpture from Chavín de Huántar, and the painting adheres to the rules of
Chavín composition (Fig. 4.8). The best-known Chavín compositional canons
are 1) kenning and 2) approximate bilateral symmetry, but also important are
3) anatropic organization, which allows a composition to be inverted yet still

Fig. 4.7 Steatite dish depicting a supernatural being with spider attributes holding trophy
heads. Diameter 14.6 cm. Courtesy Dumbarton Oaks Collection, Washington, D.C.

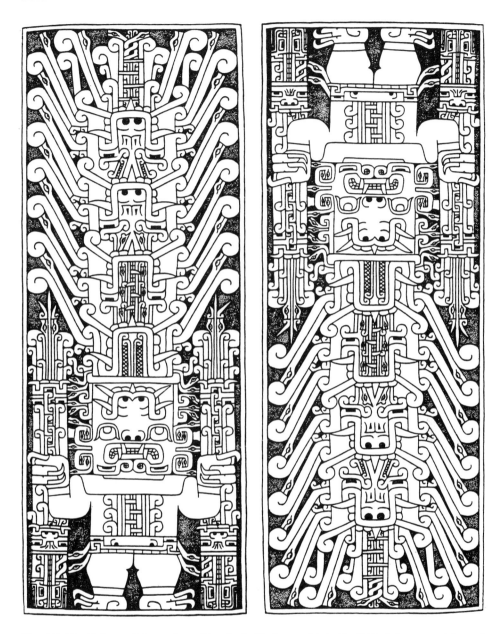

Fig. 4.8 The Raimondi Stone from Chavín de Huántar with its Staff God shown upright and inverted to illustrate the anatropic design. Granite, 195 cm × 74 cm. Courtesy Dr John Rowe.

present upright images, 4) reversible organization, which allows a compotion to be rotated on its side by 90° or 270° and still contain upright images, and 5) double-profile composition, in which profile heads are doubled and joined so they can be understood as a single face (Rowe 1962b, Kubler 1975: 253–4). All five of these complex and somewhat idiosyncratic artistic conventions are followed at Karwa in an orthodox Chavín de Huántar manner.

As already noted, the iconographic content of the Karwa textiles is closely linked to that of the Chavín de Huántar sculptures. The common subsidiary supernaturals at Chavín de Huántar are felines or raptorial birds shown in profile. Examples of both animals appear on the Karwa textiles (Sawyer 1972: figs. 3, 4), in borders surrounding the primary figure (Cordy-Collins 1976: figs. 96a–c, 117, 118). The Staff God, or a supernatural resembling it, is the most frequent primary figure on the Karwa textiles, a fact consistent with Rowe's reconstruction of the phase D Chavín de Huántar pantheon (Rowe 1962b: 20). Twenty-five representations of "Staff God" figures appear in the Karwa collection studied by Cordy-Collins and at least 23 other similar representations occur on textiles from the same tomb.

The cayman is the most important of the animal representations in the corpus of Chavín sculpture (Rowe 1962b: 18, Lathrap 1973), and it generally is acknowledged to be one of the principal deities in the Chavín pantheon. However, its representation in art is rare and generally utilizes the usual convention of split representation or "flayed-pelt convention" in which the animal is split down the middle so that mirror-images are formed by its sides (Roe 1974: 22). The best-known examples of Chavín caymans are found on the Tello Obelisk and the Yauya Stela (Rowe 1962b: figs. 3, 6). Three representations of this deity are known from the Karwa tomb (Roe 1974: fig. 12, Lavalle and Lang 1979: 55), two of which are shown by split representation.

The content and style of the Karwa textiles leave little doubt that a variant of the religious ideology of Chavín was being propounded on the South Coast during the middle of the Early Horizon. Despite the 530 km separating Karwa from Chavín de Huántar, the complex body of information which constituted this ideology appears to have been transmitted intact, without simplification or unintended distortion. The replication of Chavín motifs on early Paracas pottery and pyroengraved gourds provides some indication of the successful penetration of the Chavín cult into local coastal society.

However, the Karwa textiles are not simply painted copies of the Chavín de Huántar sculpture. Rows of conventionalized eyes, concentric circles, S's, and double-profile snake heads were used as borders on the Karwa cloths (Cordy-Collins 1979b: fig. 18, Lumbreras 1974a: fig. 86, Roe 1974: fig. 18), but rows of them are absent from Chavín sculpture. These same symbols do occur at Chavín de Huántar on Janabarriu-phase ceramics (Burger 1979: 141–3, lam. C. Tello 1960: lam. 167). The use of these symbols and the circular format on many of the Karwa textiles may represent a coastal adaptation of the highland style. Alternatively, these pieces could mirror the unknown textile style from Chavín de Huántar.

If the branches of the Chavín cult were integrated along in the same fashion as those of the Pachacamac cult, we would not expect them to be smaller versions of Chavín de Huántar, since each one would have been dedicated to a wife or child of the main deity, in this case the "Staff God." This principle of cult organization may help to explain some of the anomalous elements in the iconography of the Karwa textiles. For instance, several iconographic themes at Karwa are absent from the Chavín de Huántar sculpture. Among the most important of these is the frequent representation of the Staff Deity as female (Fig. 4.9), with breasts kenned as eyes and vagina kenned as a vertically oriented set of teeth and crossed fangs (Lyon 1979: 98–103). In some of the frontal representations of this deity gender is not specified, but at no time is the deity explicitly shown as male. The Karwa Staff Goddess is sometimes shown with cotton bolls emerging from her headdress and staffs. It is reasonable to suggest that the Karwa Staff Goddess is the patron and/or donor of cotton, the quintessential coastal cultigen (Cordy-Collins 1979a). Zoomorphized representations of the cotton plant and stylized cotton bolls also occur as repetitive motifs on several other textiles.

Rayed circles, also unknown from Chavín de Huántar, appear on the Karwa textiles as minor elements in between secondary supernaturals and, in one instance, the symbol appears prominently on the torso of the Staff Goddess (Lavalle and Lang 1979: 51, 52, Lumbreras 1974a: 79, Cordy-Collins 1976: 49). Cordy-Collins has identified the rayed circle as a sliced section of the hallucinogenic San Pedro cactus (*Trichocereus pachanoi*); representations of more naturalistic cacti, also interpreted as San Pedro, appear on another Karwa textile (Cordy-Collins 1977: 184, fig. 6, Sharon and Donnan 1977: 387). The San Pedro cactus was occasionally depicted on sculptures at the Chavín de Huántar temple (Tello 1960: fig. 50, Lumbreras 1977: fig. 26), but it was not a frequent theme. It is noteworthy that although the Tello Obelisk depicts the cayman as the donor of manioc, the bottle gourd, capiscum pepper, and other cultigens, it does not represent cotton or the San Pedro cactus (Lathrap 1971a, 1973).

As already noted, the frontal Staff Deity at Karwa is shown as unmistakably female or without indication of gender. This strongly suggests that the Karwa deity is female (Lyon 1979: 102–3). Since the specification of female gender and the secondary associations of the deity are distinct from the Staff God or Smiling God representations at Chavín de Huántar, it is a plausible interpretation that a local female supernatural is being represented. Perhaps, drawing upon the Pachacamac model, these textiles depict the wife or the daughter of the Chavín de Huántar Staff God shown on the Raimondi Stone. An analogous interpretation could be applied to the distinctive Staff Goddess carved on the monolith from the northern highland center of Pacopampa (Lyon 1979: 98–9, pl. XXVII). An alternative to this interpretation, proposed by Cordy-Collins (1980), is that the Staff Deity is dualistic and the Staff Goddess of Karwa simply represents its female aspect. Whatever explanation is provided for the differences between the iconography of Chavín de Huántar and Karwa, the contrasts document the inherent flexibility of the Chavín cult and its willingness to focus on themes and symbols meaningful to populations living within coastal environments.

Some of the decorated Karwa textiles are said to have been used as mummy-wrappings (José Pinilla, personal communication), but the original function of

Fig. 4.9 Painted cotton textile fragment from Karwa, Ica, depicting a Chavín-style Staff Goddess and her association with vegetation. After Roe 1974, Fig. 14.

the large painted Karwa textiles remains problematic. They may have been analogous to the stone sculptures at Chavín de Huántar or the adobe friezes at Cerro Blanco, decorating the exterior or interior walls of a Chavín shrine somewhere in Ica before they were finally interred. In the dry climate of the coast, textile hangings would be a practical alternative to other media of public display. One painted textile from Karwa is calculated to have been 4.2 m wide by 2.7 m high (Cordy-Collins 1976: 52). This textile would have had a total surface area roughly eight times larger than that of the Raimondi Stone, and many of the other textiles are comparable in size to stone and clay sculptures of the Initial Period and Early Horizon.

The Karwa tomb has no known parallel, but the Chavín painted textiles that were extracted from it are not unprecedented. Two textiles painted with Chavín motifs appeared on the New York art market in 1960 and were said to have come from the Callango section of the Ica Valley (Sawyer 1972: 92, figs. 1, 8); the style and technology of these pieces are almost identical to those of the Karwa samples. Another painted Chavín textile was reported to have been looted from a deep tomb 15 km inland from the coast of Chincha. This piece featured a late Chavín motif painted in yellow, white, rose, and brown, but it differed in construction technique from most of the Karwa textiles (Conklin 1971).

At present, the Chavín horizon style can be documented unevenly on the coast from Ica to Lambayeque and in the highlands from Huanuco to Pacopampa (Cajamarca Department). The themes represented on these objects are conspicuously lacking in explicit political content. Unlike Olmec art, the Chavín style does not portray historical personages, scenes of conquest and submission, or the explicit confirmation of royal authority by supernaturals (Coe 1972). The "wholly other" concerns of Chavín iconography are likewise in sharp contrast with the significant socio-political content of the Peruvian art style of the Early Intermediate Period.

In the northern highlands, where textiles and pyroengraved gourds have little chance of survival, stone sculptures provide prima-facie evidence of the spread of the Chavín cult. Chavín-related sculptures have been known for several decades from the sites of Kuntur Wasi and Pacopampa. The Chavinoid sculptures at both sites utilize a style similar to that of the final phases of the sculptural sequence at Chavín de Huántar (Roe 1974: 26–7), but their size and some of the design elements indicate that they were produced locally. The most notable sculptures from Pacopampa are two standing jaguars (Larco Hoyle 1966: fig. 37, Rosas and Shady 1974: photos 12–13) and the stela of the Staff Goddess mentioned in the preceding discussion (Larco Hoyle 1945: 3, Lyon 1979: 98–9). At Kuntur Wasi, the only published examples of sculpture that display strong Chavín influence are a modeled head, reminiscent of a tenon head, and a low relief of a face formed by double-profile composition (Carrión Cachot 1948: figs. 16, 17). While the sculptures themselves are probably the most compelling evidence for the spread of the Chavín cult to these older northern centers, the complexes also shared numerous architectural elements with Chavín de Huántar, such as the use of cut stone, stone columns, sunken rectangular plazas, and so forth. The question of whether the layout of these centers was substantially modified during the Early Horizon remains to be determined.

In the upper reaches of the Zaña Valley, explorations encountered seventeen paintings on the cliffs of Monte Calavario. One painting depicted a Staff God in yellow, white, green, and brown. The painting measures 2 m in height and 1.4 m in width. Felines, birds, and another anthropomorphic figure resembling the Staff God, but lacking staffs, were also noted (Mejía Xesspe 1968: 18–22).

Monumental examples of the Chavín horizon style rarely have been encountered along the coastal plain, but, as Tello vividly demonstrated in his 1933 excavations in Nepeña and his 1937 excavations in Casma, apparently insignificant adobe mounds frequently encapsulate remarkable adobe Initial Period and Early Horizon temples. The friezes covering the shrine of Cerro Blanco remain the earliest clear-cut evidence for appearance of the Chavín horizon style on the coast (Tello 1943: 136–9). A poorly documented Early Horizon site within the Cooperativa Casa Grande in the Chicama Valley had painted adobe columns, one of which displays a bird motif reminiscent of the decoration on the columns of the Black and White Portal at Chavín de Huántar (Kosok 1965: 109, fig. 32). The Early Horizon representation of Chavín motifs in painted clay is part of the coastal tradition of decorated temples, exemplified by Initial Period centers such as Moxeke, Garagay, and Huaca de los Reyes.

Portable objects bearing Chavín iconography have been recovered on the coast and in the highlands. These objects, judging from their form and decoration, appear to have functioned in ceremonial contexts as ritual paraphernalia or as part of the costumes of the officiants. Several classes of portable item are believed to be involved in the preparation and ingestion of hallucinogens. Among the most common items are the elaborately carved mortars, too small to have been used for grinding corn or other staples. It has been suggested that these mortars are the forerunners of the *vilcanas* of the 16th century (Kaulicke 1976: 44). *Vilcanas*, according to the 16th-century Spanish chronicler Cristóbal de Albornoz (Duviols 1967: 22), were small stone or hard wood mortars carved in animal forms and used by sorcerers to grind *vilca*, a term sometimes applied to a snuff made from a hallucinogen in the Leguminosa family (von Reiss Altschul 1967: 304, cf. Rowe 1946: 292). Among the finest examples of these Chavín mortars are the pair collected by Larco Hoyle at Pacopampa: one mortar is carved in the form of a raptorial bird, the other in the form of a feline, and the pestles are given the shape of a serpent (Larco Hoyle 1946: pl. 65). Engraved bone tubes, bone and metal spatulas, and small spoons were also probably designed for inhaling snuff (Wassén 1967, Cordy-Collins 1980).[2] Like the small mortars, these items are decorated with familiar Chavín themes, especially animals that are associated in South America with shamanistic transformation (Fig. 4.10). It is plausible that some of the elaborate pottery with Chavín motifs may have been used also in ritual drinking, votive offerings, and food consumption in ritual contexts. Residue and contextual studies will be critical in evaluating the hypothetical functions of all of these classes of artifact.

This brief review of the existing evidence for the Chavín horizon style reveals that it consists of a small number of items, most of which are probably related to the rituals of the Chavín cult.[3] While this evidence supports the empirical reality of a Chavín horizon style, this style may not have been the only, or even the dominant, iconographic style at most sites in central and northern Peru during the Early Horizon. Its preeminence has been exaggerated because of: 1) the misidentification of Initial Period and non-Chavín Early Horizon iconographies as Chavín, 2) the use of stone sculpture by the Chavín cult as a favored medium of expression in the highlands, and 3) the influence that the order of discovery has had on the interpretations favored by Andean

Fig. 4.10 Chavín-style snuff spoon of gold and silver. Courtesy Dumbarton Oaks Collection, Washington, D.C.

archaeology. The first of these factors has already been discussed but the other two deserve further consideration.

Chavín de Huántar, in addition to its other attributes, was a center for the production and display of fine stone sculpture. Tello recovered over 100 pieces of Early Horizon sculpture at the site (Tello 1960: 158–304), and Marino Gonzales, Luis Lumbreras, and Hernán Amat subsequently discovered dozens of additional stone sculptures in the New Temple, the New South Wing, and the Circular Plaza (Lumbreras 1977, Kaufmann Doig 1978). The high frequency of early stone sculpture at Chavín de Huántar is echoed at secondary sites near the Temple. These archaeological sites, usually only one or two hectares in size, have received only slight attention, but they are presumed to be hamlets of the scattered rural population which provided labor and agricultural produce to the ceremonial center (Burger 1983: 21–3, 1984a: 248–50). Espejo and Tello reported finds of sculpture at Gotush (Espejo Nuñez 1955, Tello 1960: lams. XLII, XLIII), Waman Wain (Espejo Nuñez 1951, Tello 1960: fig. 48), Runtu (Tello 1960: figs. 40, 83, 84), and Yura-yako (Tello 1960: fig. 81). During field work in the Chavín de Huántar area, I documented fragments of sculpture from Pojoc and additional pieces of sculpture from Waman Wain (Fiog. 4.11). All five of these small sites with sculpture are located within a 10 km radius of Chavín de Huántar.

The quantity of stone sculpture in the Chavín de Huántar area appears to be substantially greater than at contemporary ceremonial centers elsewhere in Peru. During three seasons of excavations at Kotosh, 70 km southeast of Chavín de Huántar, the University of Tokyo Expedition failed to uncover a single stone sculpture, despite the strong similarities between Chavín de Huántar and Kotosh in ceramics and architectural technique (Izumi 1971: 66–7, Izumi and Terada 1972). Sculpture was likewise not encountered during the explorations and excavations at other Early Horizon sites in Huánuco (Paucarabamba, Piquimina and Sajarapatac). The excavations at Huaricoto, 55 km northwest of Chavín, have not revealed sculpture in the Early Horizon or pre-Early Horizon layers (Burger and Salazar-Burger 1980: 28–9). At La Pampa, a large site with a major Early Horizon occupation located 125 km north of Chavín de Huántar, one piece of early sculpture was found next to the local church, but the excavations of the Japanese Expedition to Nuclear America did not unearth additional examples during the two seasons of field work (Terada 1979: pl. 129). The initial visit and exploration at Pacopampa brought to light several stone sculptures, but the recent excavations by Rosas and Shady, Fung Pineda, Flores, Kaulicke, Santillana, and Morales did not encounter sculpture in archaeological strata and only two additional pieces have been recorded during extensive surface explorations.

It would seem that stone sculpture was produced only on rare occasions outside of the Chavín de Huántar heartland during the Early Horizon. Moreover,

Fig. 4.11. Rustic rendition of a Chavín-style jaguar, 33 by 15 cm. Sculpture discovered at the high altitude village site of Waman Wain, Ancash.

sites like Pacopampa, La Pampa, and Kotosh, which were important ritual centers during the Initial Period, centuries before Chavín de Huántar was founded, have not produced any indication of a pre-Chavín tradition of stone sculpture. It would appear that stone sculpture was not characteristic of pre-Chavín or non-Chavín ceremonial centers in the highlands and, therefore, a heuristic device which puts an arbitrary emphasis on the iconography of stone sculpture inevitably produces syntheses which stress the homogeneity of the far-reaching Chavín cult during the Early Horizon, while ignoring or understating the importance of Initial Period or Early Horizon cults which did not choose to make public displays of religious symbolism on imperishable materials.[4]

The sequence in which scientific discoveries were made has also played an important role both in shaping the priorities of research and in interpreting the results stemming from those investigations. Chavín de Huántar and its remarkable art style were thrust into the academic limelight at a time when most of the other coeval sites had received little or no attention. The Raimondi Stone was brought to Lima from Chavín de Huántar in 1874, and its presence in the capital sparked a lively and prolonged debate about its age and style, even among investigators unable or unwilling to journey to the highlands (e.g., Uhle 1910, Markham 1910, cf. Polo 1899). Raimondi, Wiener, and other early travelers wrote popular accounts about the Castillo of Chavín de Huántar before the turn of the century (Kauffman Doig 1964), and one of them, Ernst Middendorf, even postulated a pre-Inca Chavín empire that included part of the highlands and adjacent coast (Middendorf 1895: 94–104). When Julio C. Tello finally visited Chavín de Huántar in 1919, he was predisposed to consider it as a crucial early center, and his discovery of the Tello Obelisk and dozens of other impressive stone sculptures only strengthened this inclination. Though the sequence of archaeological finds was, to a large degree, fortuitous, the impact they made colored the perception of later discoveries at sites like Punkurí, Moxeke, and Cerro Blanco. Larco Hoyle's proposal (1941: 19) that these related early cultural manifestations be called Nepeña rather than Chavín undoubtedly would have had more acceptance if Cerro Blanco and Punkurí had been discovered in 1883 rather than a half a century later.

It should be recalled also that the elaborate iconographic system discovered at Chavín de Huántar had particular appeal because of the theoretical orientation of scholars like Tello and Kroeber. A fascination with style and iconography was one aspect of their concern with culture history. If they had owed their allegiance to a materialist paradigm, they would probably have minimized the significance of Chavín de Huántar art style and instead have emphasized the importance of sites like Sechín Alto, whose sheer volume implies an enormous expenditure of energy.

RELIGION, INNOVATION, AND DIFFUSION

The broader significance of the Chavín horizon in Peruvian prehistory may be better appreciated if focus is temporarily shifted from the spread of a horizon style to other, ostensibly unrelated, spheres of human activity, such as technology. Studies of material culture and ancient technology generally have lagged behind those of style, but recent investigations have produced conclusions which, in a sense, justify Tello's insistence on the concept of a multifaceted Chavín civilization. In both metallurgy and textile production, numerous innovations appear suddenly and diffuse over an extensive area, laying the basis for later regional technological developments. The introduction and diffusion of this new technology appears to be intimately involved with the spread of the Chavín cult.

William Conklin has proposed that textile production was truly revolutionized during the Chavín horizon by an

> astonishing range of new techniques and materials first utilized as carriers of the Chavín designs. In fact, a set of inventions was promulgated whose influence obliterated most of the older textile traditions in the coastal areas, and which became the foundation for later Peruvian textile evolution. Conklin 1978: 1

These textile innovations included 1) the use of camelid hair in cotton textiles, 2) textile painting, 3) supplemental discontinuous warps, including various types of tapestry, 4) the dying of camelid hair, 5) warp wrapping, 6) negative or "resist" painting techniques (i.e., tie-dye and batik), and 7) the replacement of finger manipulation by the heddle loom (Conklin 1971: 15). After studying collections of Early Horizon textiles from the South, Central, and North Coast, Conklin concluded that

> There are no regional distinctions in these textile techniques or in their associated art styles such as are characteristically found in ceramics. Indeed, the purest expression of the "horizon" concept may be found in these textiles, and Chavín cultural expansion may now be defined in terms of textile technology. Conklin 1978: 4

Technological advances of a comparable magnitude also occurred in metallurgy at roughly the same time. Only small sheets of hammered gold are known from the Initial Period (Grossman 1972b), but, during the Early Horizon, large objects of hammered gold with complex Chavín-style motifs were produced by a suite of techniques which have no known antecedents. According to Heather Lechtman (1980: 279), the production of three-dimensional forms by metallurgically joining pieces of preshaped metal sheet is one of the important traditions in Peruvian metallurgy, and it appears for the first time during the Early Horizon. Soldering, sweat welding, repoussé decoration, and the creation of silver-gold alloys were all utilized in the production of Chavín-style objects. Furthermore, there are examples of gold artifacts which have been excavated or looted from a large part of the sphere of Chavín influence. This pattern contrasts with the single isolated example of Initial Period gold-working in Andahuaylas. How can we explain this sudden quantum jump in the development and distribution of gold-oriented metallurgy during the Chavín horizon? Lechtman writes:

> It may be that in the Central Andes gold was used earlier than any other metal and that its prominence in the archaeological record during the period of spread and influence of the Chavín cult . . . reflects a religious and ceremonial bias of the cult for that metal . . . My feeling is that gold may have had special symbolic significance for the cult and that certain religious values or doctrine were expressed through its use. Lechtman 1980: 275

Both Conklin and Lechtman propose a link between the Chavín cult and the introduction of new technology. But what is the nature of this link? Like all religions, the Chavín cult was faced with the paradox of trying to describe the undescribable and trying to evoke an experience not of this world while relying on materials, techniques, and symbols drawn from the familiar environment and the people who inhabit it. All religious art is based ultimately on analogy and metaphor, but Chavín artists made this principle the cornerstone of their style, spinning visual metaphors into a web so complex that many find the end product incomprehensible. Yet even modern viewers find that the best of Chavín art succeeds in evoking the sensation of being in the presence of something extraordinary. The artistry of Chavín was considered by Alfred Kroeber (1947: 429) to be the pinnacle of prehistoric South American art, and it has been presumed to be the work of full-time specialists who could dedicate themselves to developing an artistic style capable of communicating the power of Chavín religious ideology.

The materials used as the medium of this religious art style also may have been expected to convey the sensation of the "wholly other" to the viewer. This objective could have provided, in part, the stimulus for the sudden burst of invention which provided artisans with new mediums (such as three-dimensional metal or polished granite), and innovative ways of transforming old media into the equivalent of new media (such as the brightly painted polychrome textiles). Most of these Early Horizon technological innovations did not produce any clearcut saving of energy. On the contrary, surpluses would have been required just to allow these technologies to exist. However, the inventions did provide the means of manufacturing objects which were distinguishable immediately from other items and therefore especially suitable and effective as symbols or emblems of religious authority. The images in polished granite or breastplates in hammered gold must have been awe-inspiring when viewed by those unfamiliar with the new technology. This phenomenon brings to mind the calculated use of mechanical lions and birds in the reception room where the Byzantine emperor received foreign dignitaries. The ability of a cult to convey or evoke religious awe through artistic or technological devices would have helped to validate its sacred propositions and the authority of its representatives. The success of the Chavín cult and the extension of its ritual field into new zones would have produced additional resources and demand for the further development and production of religious paraphernalia. In this view, the maintenance of full- or part-time artisans could have been motivated by pragmatic as well as theological considerations, and the "early great art style" of Chavín (Willey 1962) may have contributed actively to the prestige and success of the Chavín cult.

The network established by the spread of the cult permitted contact between distant zones and would have facilitated the sharing and borrowing of innovations, allowing a more rapid accumulation of technology than would have been possible if these regions had been isolated from each other. It is also widely recognized that larger, more compact settlements provide a better matrix for scientific and artistic development than does a dispersed settlement pattern (e.g., Flannery 1968: 99). This milieu would have existed in the nucleated "urban towns" of the Early Horizon, such as those that grew up around the religious centers of Chavín de Huántar, Pallka, and Pacopampa (Burger 1981, Tello 1956: 33, Kaulicke 1976: 26). The size and composition of these towns is poorly understood but the Janabarriu-phase population of Chavín de Huántar has been estimated to be between 2,000 and 3,000 individuals (Burger 1984a: 247). As in Mesoamerica, new technology may have been stimulated also by increasing social differentiation and the consequent demand for new prestige or luxury goods to serve as indicators of social status (Flannery 1968). Whatever the cause, technological innovation unquestionably was a significant and integral part of the spread of the Chavín horizon style.

INTERACTION, CERAMIC STYLE, AND SOCIAL IDENTITY

The spread of technological information about metal-working and cloth production through the network of the Chavín cult may not, in itself, have greatly transformed Early Horizon society, but the processes involved in their diffusion presuppose the opening of channels of communication between small-scale polities with a prior history of only limited interaction beyond immediately adjacent units. The intensification of this "peer polity interaction" (Renfrew 1982: 287) seems to have been made possible by the existence of a shared religious ideology which linked ethnically and probably linguistically distinct groups into a single supra-political entity, which may be referred to as Chavín civilization.

The most tangible evidence of a new scale of interaction between local territorial units is seen in the sharp increase in exotic goods at primary and secondary settlements. Edward Lanning wrote (1967a: 102–3):

> Just as the Initial Period was a time of regional isolation and restricted trade, so the early part of the Early Horizon – the time of the Chavín diffusion – was a period when all of the old barriers fell, when goods and ideas were exchanged through much of ancient Peru.

While this pattern has been acknowledged repeatedly, quantitative evidence rarely has been presented either to support or to refute it. Recent studies have documented considerable amounts of exchange in late Preceramic and Initial Period times between ecologically complementary zones; coastal shell, a piranha mandible, pottery from the eastern lowlands in the intermontane highland valleys, permit the inference of east–west trade networks in pre-Chavín times (Lathrap 1971a, Matos Mendieta 1968a, Wing 1972: 331, 333, Shady and Rosas 1980, Burger and Salazar-Burger 1980). Exchange between regions with similar environments, however, seems to have been substantially less. The techniques of provenience analysis, widely utilized elsewhere in world archaeology during the last two decades, offer a new source of information on patterns of exchange. Thus far, the only material from Peru to be studied using techniques such as neutron activation (NAA) and X-ray fluorescence (XRF) is obsidian. The results thus far support the view that there was a sharp increase in long-distance trade during the period of the Chavín horizon. Virtually all of the obsidian used within the Chavín interaction sphere was obtained from Quispisisa, a natural deposit located near Castro-virreyna, Huancavelica. This area of the south-central highlands was isolated from the developments in north-central and northern Peru during the Initial Period, and during the 2nd millennium BC obsidian from the Quispisisa mine rarely was utilized outside Ayacucho, Huancayo, and the adjacent South Coast (Burger and Asaro 1979: 300–6).

A change in this pattern of distribution is best documented at Chavín de Huántar, where excavations in the settlement around the Temple produced a total of five obsidian flakes from late Initial Period and early Early Horizon contexts, but over 500 pieces from Janabarriu-phase contexts (Burger, Asaro, and Michel 1984: 263–7); even small hamlets like Pojoc and Waman Wain seem to have had limited access to Quispisisa obisdian during this time (Burger 1983, cf. Burger 1980). Of the 88 pieces of obsidian from the Chavín de Huántar area tested using XRF and NAA, 96% were shown to come from Quispisisa, some 470 air km to the south. There is evidence that other centers including Kotosh, Pacopampa, Huaricoto, and Ancón also began to utilize obsidian during the Chavín horizon, and samples analyzed from three of those sites also came from Quispisisa. It is unlikely that obsidian exchange was a particularly important element within the Early Horizon exchange network, but the ease with which it can be recognized and studied provides a useful index of the heightened intensity of the north–south trade.

Ceramic style has been studied frequently also in order to gauge the degree of interaction between groups, and the traditional assumption has been that degree of contact would be directly reflected in the sharing or similarity of ceramic attributes (e.g., Lathrap 1977a: 1320). This approach has been criticized recently from a number of perspectives but perhaps the most telling critique has grown out of Ian Hodder's ethnographic studies on the articulation between style, material culture, and ethnicity in traditional African societies. He observes:

> The distribution of material culture traits, and the maintenance of group identity in terms of material culture, are not necessarily and wholly structured by patterns of interaction. It is quite possible to have distinct groups with distinct material cultures, but who have very strong and frequent interactions. Hodder 1977: 269

The styles of pottery, like other items of material culture, are portrayed in his studies as transmitters of social and personal identity, which can be actively manipulated to reinforce boundaries or, when convenient, to blur pre-existing divisions in order to express an ideology of complementarity rather than competition and conflict (Hodder 1982: 55, 63). Thus, the nature of interaction and the level of competition between groups may be more important than the degree of interaction in determining patterns of material culture (*Ibid.* p. 35). The decision of a household to acquire or produce pottery which closely resembles that of a neighboring group is a conscious decision which expresses their world view at a specific time. From this perspective, it is intriguing to review the ceramic styles of the late Initial Period and Early Horizon as a possible indicator of changing social identity, rather than as an index of interaction intensity. Changes in pottery style need not, theoretically, mirror the diffusion of the Chavín cult or the increase in the long-distance exchange of ritual paraphernalia or utilitarian items such as obsidian.

It is significant therefore that a constellation of ceramic traits diffused throughout much of the Peruvian coast and highlands during the Early Horizon (Fig. 4.12). These ceramic features include 1) stirrup-spouted bottles with flat bases, convex curved or straight spouts, and thickened flanged rims with flattened or rounded lips, 2) bowls with externally beveled rims and flat bottoms, 3) neckless ollas with thickened and rounded or flattened lips, 4) rows of repetitive designs made by stamps, seals, or incision; circles, circles with central dots, concentric circles, S's, and eccentric eyes are most common, 5) decoration made by broad incisions in leather-hard paste, 6) a broad spec-

Fig. 4.12 Map showing the distribution of Janabarriu-related ceramic styles of the Early Horizon. After Burger 1984b, Map 2.

trum of texturing devices including rocker-stamping, dentate rocker-stamping, dentate impressions, *appliqué* nubbins, and combing, 7) the use of graphite paint within broad incisions on red-slipped vessels. This complex of attributes is best known from Chavín de Huántar, where it is characteristic of the Janabarriu phase, the ceramic phase coeval with D/EF of the Rowe sculptural sequence (Burger 1984a: 244–6). The diffusion of this constellation of ceramic traits over a broad area is an unprecedented aspect of the Early Horizon. Some of these features appeared individually at an earlier date in other areas, but the intrusion of a complex of new ceramic features drawn from the above list can be recognized easily, and Table 2 lists some of the possible instances of this diffusion. In many cases, the local Initial Period sequences and even the Early Horizon ceramic component are not known in detail and, until they are, the assumption that these ceramic traits are intrusive must remain a tentative one.

The diffusion of Janabarriu-related ceramic traits can be considered in more detail using examples taken from near the northern and southern limits of their distribution: Pacopampa and Ica. At Pacopampa, the Pacopampa Chavín style of the Early Horizon is characterized by stamped circles, concentric circles, circles with central dots, S's, and crescent-shaped eyes. These motifs partially replaced the earlier incised geometric and figurative designs of the Pacopampa Pacopampa phase (Rosas and Shady 1970: lams. 11, 12, Rosas and Shady 1974: photo 23). In some cases, stamped circles were combined with earlier decorative techniques by placing stamped circles within or surrounding volutes or steps, a combination which never appears at Chavín de Huántar. The Pacopampa Chavín phase is also typified by broad lustrous incisions rather than the matte and irregular "inciso cortante" of the previous phase, which were usually made in dry paste (Rosas and Shady 1970: 88). On the other hand, many Pacopampa Chavín bowls have carved rims and interior pattern burnishing, techniques which continued from the local ceramic tradition. Stirrup-spouted bottles, neckless ollas, graphite-filled incisions, and various surface-texturing techniques were introduced in the Pacopampa Chavín phase, but they remained unpopular. The Pacopampa Chavín style is, quite simply, an independent style which incorporates motifs, decorative techniques, and forms drawn from an outside source and synthesizes them with the local ceramic tradition.

On the South Coast of Peru, intrusive Janabarriu-like traits were combined with non-Chavín features to produce the distinctive local style known as Paracas. As noted earlier, phases 3 and 4 of the Paracas sequence show marked similarities to the Janabarriu phase of Chavín de Huántar. However, zoned polychrome resin painting and resist painting are more common decorative techniques than the Chavín-related rows of stamped or incised concentric circles, which also occur. Although stirrup-spouted bottles with convex curved spouts were produced, they seem to be less frequent than the double-

Table 2 *Janabarriu-related ceramic assemblages of the Early Horizon*

Site	Location	Cultural phase	Reference
Pacopampa	Chotano Basin, Cajamarca	Pacopampa Chavín	Rosas and Shady 1970: lams. 11, 12, 1974: 20–3
Pandanche	Chotano Basin, Cajamarca	Pandanche CI	Kaulicke 1975, 1976
Kuntur Wasi	Jequetepeque Valley, Cajamarca	Chavín Clasico	Carrión Cachot 1948: 61–4, Ishida *et al.* 1960: 316
La Pampa	Manta River, Ancash	La Pampa Period	Onuki and Fuji 1974: pls. XIV–XIV, Terada 1979: pl. 63a
Chupacoto	Huaylas, Ancash	(Unspecified)	Ishida *et al.* 1960
Huaricoto	Callejon de Huaylas, Ancash	Capilla Phase	Burger and Salazar-Burger 1980
Chavín de Huántar	Mosna Valley, Ancash	Janabarriu Phase	Burger 1979: 147, 1984a: 368–87
Kotosh	Upper Huallaga Valley,	Kotosh Chavín	Izumi and Sono 1963: pls. 126–9, Izumi and Terada 1972: pl. 111
San Blas	Lake Junín, Junín	Middle Formative	Nomland 1939, Morales 1977
Ataura	Mantaro Valley, Junín	(Unspecified)	Matos Mendieta 1973
Atalla	Ichu River, Huancavelica	Chavinoid	Matos Mendieta 1959a, 1972: fig. 7, upper row, Browman 1977: 23
Wichqana	Huamanga River, Ayacucho	Kishka Pata Period	Flores Espinoza 1960: figs. p–w, Lumbreras 1974c: 55–9
Chupas (Usno Era)	Huatatas River, Ayacucho	Kishka Pata Period	Casafranca 1960, Lumbreras 1974c: 65–9
Chongoyape	Lambayeque drainage	(Unspecified)	Lothrop 1941: pl. XIX
Morro de Eten	Lambayeque drainage	(Unspecified)	Alva and Elera 1980: 2
Huaca de los Chinos	Moche Valley, La Libertad	(Unspecified)	Watanabe 1976: 163–4
Huaca Herederos, Chica	Moche Valley, La Libertad	(Unspecified)	Watanabe 1976: 73–6
PV31-175W	Nepeña Valley, Ancash	(Unspecified)	Proulx 1973b: 194–9, pl. 25
Pallka	Casma Valley, Ancash	(Unspecified)	Tello 1956: lams. IIG, IIIA
Bermejo	Between Rio Seco and Rio Fortaleza, Ancash	(Unspecified)	Silva 1975: lams. 10–15, 1978
Supe Lighthouse Site	Puerto de Supe, Lima	(Unspecified)	Willey and Corbett 1954: figs. 5i, 8j
Ancón	Between Rio Chancay and Rio Chillon	Phases 5 and 6	Scheele 1970
Cerrillos	Ica Valley	Ocucaje 3 layers	Wallace 1962

spout and bridge bottles (Menzel, Rowe, and Dawson 1964: figs. 10a, 11a, 11b, D. Wallace 1962: fig. 37), which can be traced to the Initial Period styles of the South Coast. Many of the heavily decorated bowls and bottles in the early Paracas style incorporate Chavín themes and symbols, but the emphasis on modular width in the composition is a local characteristic, as are most of the forms and decorative techniques.

The northern limit of Janabarriu-related ceramic assemblages can be placed tentatively at Pacopampa in the highlands and at Puerto de Eten and Chongoyape in the Lambayeque–La Leche drainage on the coast. The apparent absence of Janabarriu-related features in the Paita style of Piura (Lanning 1963b: 206) or the Pechiche style of Tumbes (Izumi and Terada 1966: 83–5, 88) strengthens the possibility that the instances cited actually do approximate the northernmost extent of the diffusion. The Morropón bottle, whose form has strong Janabarriu-related traits, was found further to the north, in Piura, but Lanning (1963b: 205) believes it may be a trade piece because it is alien to the local early ceramic styles.

The northern limit of Janabarriu-related ceramic features may correspond to some sort of frontier beyond which the nature of interaction was reduced or was of a fundamentally different sort. Chavín iconography never has been found beyond this hypothetical frontier, so this imaginary line may delimit the northern extent of the expansion of the Chavín cult as well. This hypothetical northern frontier during the Early Horizon is also coterminous with northern distribution of known monumental ceremonial centers from the late Initial Period and Early Horizon (Burger 1984b).

The southern limit of the diffusion of Janabarriu features on the coast is Ica, but further research probably will document their presence in the Nazca area. Paracas-style ceramics and petroglyphs with Chavinoid features are known already from the Palpa area (Mejía Xesspe 1972, Menzel, Rowe, and Dawson 1964: 1, Cordy-Collins 1976:40). In the highlands, Janabarriu-like ceramic traits spread up to the southern limit of the Mantaro drainage. This diffusion is evidenced by the ceramics from Atalla, located 15 km south of Huancavelica, and from Chupas, located 7 km south of Ayacucho (Matos Mendieta 1959a, Browman 1977, Casafranca 1960).

The southernmost limit of recorded Initial Period ceremonial centers is the Mala Valley on the coast and Huanuco in the highlands. It would seem, then, that the Chavín sphere of influence in the south extended considerably beyond the area of earlier large ceremonial centers, linking regions of lesser socio-political development with the more advanced northern regions. Browman (1974b) has suggested that the linkage in the highlands may have been purely economic in scope, and that the Chavín cult never may have penetrated the Central Highlands. However, the evidence from mounds like Ataura, Atalla, and Chupas is so scanty that it is premature to rule out the presence of the Chavín cult. After all, the cult was operating on the South Coast, the region immediately west of Huancavelica and Ayacucho.

The establishment of monumental centers like Atalla in the Central Highlands could reflect the organizational skills and religious ideology, as well as the socio-economic stimulus, provided by intensified contacts with the north. The asymmetric relationship which existed between the Chavín de Huántar heartland and the Central Highlands during the Early Horizon would have been fundamentally different from that with the advanced Northern Highlands and Central and North Coast. As in Mesoamerica, comparatively marginal regions such as the Central Highlands offered rare raw materials which could not be obtained from other developed regions. Obsidian, which has been discussed already, and cinnabar are two documented instances of scarce materials brought to the northern centers from the Central Highlands.

Cinnabar was widely used for rituals and personal adornment in ancient Peru. The only major source of cinnabar known to have been exploited before the Spanish is found in the Central Highlands, near the modern city of Huancavelica (Petersen 1970: 6–7). The cinnabar (mercuric sulphate) deposit there and the traditional methods of mining it are described in numerous ethnohistoric documents (Ravines 1970a: 234, 251). Cinnabar is believed to have been used widely during the Early Horizon, but this presumption rarely has been tested. The presence of cinnabar on an earspool recovered from a Janabarriu-phase house in Chavín de Huántar was verified chemically (Burger 1984a: 198). Chuncuimarca, a site near Huancavelica, produced an unusual number of grinding implements, all of which had residues of red pigment, presumably cinnabar (Ravines 1970a: 250). The ceramics associated with these tools date to the end of the Initial Period or the beginning of the Early Horizon; they bear some resemblance to pottery from Atalla (Ravines 1970a: 254). The Chuncuimarca investigation would seem to confirm that cinnabar was being mined and processed for export in the Huancavelica area prior to or during the Early Horizon.

Studies further to the south provide support for the proposed southern limit of the Chavín horizon. Exploration and excavation in the Andahuaylas area of Apurimac failed to encounter Chavín-related ceramics, even though an excellent sequence of early pottery was obtained at Waywaka (Grossman 1972a). Similarly, the Marcavalle- and Chanapata-style ceramics of Cuzco lack any indication of close ties with the Janabarriu-related pottery of the Central and Northern Highlands (Chávez 1977: 1063, Rowe 1944: 55, Yabar 1972), although these styles are believed to span the Early Horizon.

It would seem that a wide range of Peruvian cultures in the mid Early Horizon chose to modify their traditional ceramic styles in order to emulate more closely the pottery of groups beyond their territory. In a sense, this constitutes a sort of horizon phenomenon like that described for the Chavín art style or noted by Conklin for the technology of textiles. Unlike those, however, the changes in ceramics were probably not initiated by a centralized religious authority. Even during the Late Horizon, most ethnic groups continued to produce their ceramic styles without imitating the Imperial style of the Incas. It can be suggested that the emergence of these Chavinoid pottery styles may mirror the adoption of a more universalist ideology and reflect a desire to manifest this sense of supra-group identity. This interpretation draws support from the decoration of utilitarian ceramics with simplified Chavín elements

(S's, concentric circles), which also are used in Chavín religious art. The new pottery styles are an expression of a changing ideology. The move towards a broader, more universal social identity, however, may have been more of an ideal than a social reality. In any case, this world view would seem to be a significant departure from the patterns of the Initial Period.

THE ISSUE OF CAUSALITY – SOME SPECULATIONS

Establishing the general nature of the Chavín horizon is a minimal precondition for considering the factors which may ultimately account for its appearance. In light of the foregoing discussion, an explanation of this kind ideally should concern itself with isolating the determining conditions for the spread of the Chavín cult and showing how these were sufficient to cause it to take place (Trigger 1978: 39–40). The problem at hand is not equivalent to the explanation of the "emergence of complex societies" or "state formation" in Peru, although frequently it has been lumped together with them.

Ultimately, discussion of the ebb and flow of prehistoric regional cults must draw upon the knowledge of those religious movements which have been studied historically and ethnographically. In spite of the bewildering diversity of cults which have been documented, there seems to be a consensus that, regardless of their particular features, they appear to be called forth by crises. Cargo cults, millenarian movements, and vitalization cults can all be considered as subclasses of the more general phenomenon referred to as "crisis cults" by Weston La Barre and as "revitalization movements" by Anthony Wallace (La Barre 1971: 11, A. Wallace 1956: 267); even widespread religions such as Christianity can be considered as relics of crisis cults surviving in routinized form (A. Wallace 1956: 268, La Barre 1971: 11).

Religious ideology, of any sort, must provide a coherent description and explanation of the nature of the social universe, and at the same time supply a means for manipulating it (Moore 1969). By satisfying the existential and interpretive needs of its adherents, religious ideology reduces psychological stress and gives meaning to the life cycle of the individual members of a society. Religion and its ritual expression can be a powerful force in regulating and maintaining the stability of cultural systems (Rappaport 1967), but when a religious ideology is perceived as insufficient, the ultimate basis of authority is undermined. Even in a relatively stable society, the religious ideology is congruent only approximately with social structure; there inevitably exists imperfection in the fit, and some tension always will be present between a set of symbolic conceptions and the social reality. The continually changing conditions and the flawed understanding that all humans have concerning the world in which they live are, in part, responsible for this discrepancy, but frequently there also may be a conscious misrepresentation of social reality in order to legitimize dominance relations by particular segments of the society who wish to represent the status quo as an expression of natural or constant universal laws (O'Laughlin 1975: 348–51).

A two-way interaction exists between belief systems and social reality (Eickelman 1977: 4) but, in periods of accelerated change, the established ideology may not prove flexible enough to prevent a widening gap between the metaphysical and the experiential world. The growing consciousness among populations of this inconsistency results in psychological stress on an individual level and a widespread sense of crisis on a societal level (La Barre 1971: 23), frequently coupled with a sense of "negative deprivation," the perception that the spiritual and material condition has declined relative to a level enjoyed in the past (Nicholas 1973: 72, La Barre 1971: 24). In such troubled times, a number of directions may be taken, including avoidance migration and violent revolt, but perhaps the most frequent course is the adoption or innovation of religious ideology better suited to explaining the new social reality. Both Wallace and La Barre emphasize that while this process is based on the natural response to psychological stress, the decisions involved are deliberate efforts to bring beliefs and reality into congruence, sometimes provoking a marked cultural revitalization (A. Wallace 1956: 267).

La Barre, after a comprehensive review of the literature, concluded that many different factors are capable of producing the crises which serve as catalysts for the appearance and spread of these cults. Ecological, economic, political, and military forces may singly or in combination produce the necessary condition (La Barre 1971: 26, A. Wallace 1956, cf. Van Binsbergen 1977: 144, Schoffeleers 1977: 237). The process of cult expansion is associated almost invariably with charismatic figures, but the appeal of their message is ultimately dependent on the conscious or unconscious wishes of the believer (La Barre 1971: 20).

Can the Chavín cult profitably be viewed as a crisis cult or revitalization movement? The general observation of Jones and Kautz (1981: 28) is relevant in this regard:

> Research in the Americas, in particular, has tended to associate signs of early civilization and political centralization as a process of stabilization rather than a symptom of overwhelming dislocating change. Ideological continuity has often been stressed as opposed to ideological revolution, early civilization has been viewed as the harbinger of panregional cosmological codification instead of a moment of cultural distress in an ongoing series of transformations in which the political stakes in sanctified leadership were increasing at geometric rates.

In the case of the Chavín horizon, the revolutionary aspect of this intrusive ideological force has received its due recognition and there is widespread acceptance of the likelihood that radical cultural changes may be associated with it, but, paradoxically, the teleologically skewed perspective of recent scholarship has emphasized this process as part of a gradualistic and almost irreversible trend toward greater complexity, and little serious consideration has been given to the special conditions that would have undermined the viability of the belief systems associated with the Initial Period polities. What motivated members of these highly conservative societies to embrace the alien Chavín cult?

The possibility that an unspecified crisis may have been responsible for the increasing importance of Chavín de Huántar and the spread of the Chavín cult was raised by a comparison of the radiocarbon measurements of Chavín de Huántar and several well-known coastal centers (Haldas, Garagay, Huaca de los Reyes). I observed that most of these centers were abandoned or in decline before the spread of the Chavín cult, and suggested that the expansion of the Chavín cult might have been intimately related to the decline of traditional Initial Period ceremonial networks along the coast (Burger 1981: 600). Subsequent research by Thomas and Shelia Pozorski in Casma has indicated that the apogee of mound construction in that valley occurred prior to the expansion of the Chavín cult and that a radically different cultural pattern emerged during the Early Horizon (S. and T. Pozorski, personal communication). A similar pattern has been documented for the Lurín Valley (Patterson 1983).

In recent years, Moseley and his colleagues have begun an ambitious investigation of the history of the recurrent El Niño disasters and the long-term radical environmental alteration cycles on the coast of Peru. The largest recorded El Niño since Colonial times occurred in 1925 and was associated with massive flooding, and destructive inundations also have resulted from the more modest El Niño events of recent decades. Moseley's research produced evidence that rare floods of a magnitude even greater than that of 1925 occurred in pre-Hispanic times. The best documented of these was a flood during the Later Intermediate Period whose peak flow was at least two to four times the size of the 1925 episode (Nials *et al.* 1979b: 6). There is also evidence of a flood of a very large magnitude at approximately 500 BC (Nials *et al.* 1979b: 10). Robert Bird (personal communication), using a different methodology and a different data set, has concluded that a tidal wave struck the North Coast in approximately 500 BC. The massive flooding adduced by Moseley and Bird apparently was followed by a lengthy period of climatic deterioration along the coast.

> By about 500 BC, a major cycle of landscape deflation began. Previously occupied surfaces were stripped by desert rains and wind action, creating a very fragmentary archaeological record. Moseley, Feldman, and Ortloff 1981: 248

If verified by further research, the El Niño disaster and subsequent prolonged environmental difficulties would provide a convenient *deus ex machina,* partially accounting for the destabilization of the polities on the coast just prior to the expansion of the Chavín cult. Since the Initial Period coastal polities were closely linked to adjacent highland polities through trade and exchange, any disruption of coastal socio-political systems would have ramified into areas not directly affected by those climatic conditions. One could imagine a scenario in which the inability of traditional politico-religious leaders to cope with environmental deterioration could have called into question their authority and the belief system which provided its validation. The appeal of a more universalist religious ideology for the populace under such circumstances would be understandable, as would be the desire of existing leaders to co-opt such an ideology in order to maintain the old dominance relations within a modified ideological framework. In this scenario, the introduction and promotion of an innovative religious system like the Chavín cult could have had multiple functions: for the populace, it may have provided a more coherent explanation of the changing social reality and offered the hope that these conditions could be dealt with more effectively by a religious system whose realm extended beyond the provincial boundaries of local systems; for traditional authorities, the adoption of a branch of the cult may have been one of the few options available to prevent a complete collapse of the socio-political system. For both groups, it may have provided access to an exchange network and a host of new economic options.

However, even if these environmental reconstructions are verified, it is unlikely that they alone would account for the special conditions leading to a revitalization movement on the scale of Chavín. Forces generated by the contradictions within Initial Period societies also may have been significant part-causes for the unprecedented spread of a regional cult. Patterson has noted that the development of new forms of labor and new ways of appropriating or extracting surplus social product could in themselves precipitate sudden changes and, in his analysis of early social formations on the Central Coast, he concludes that a system of social classes was consolidated at the end of the Initial Period. He hypothesizes that this important social transformation was responsible for the cessation in public construction of monumental platform complexes (Patterson 1983). Needless to say, a radical change of this sort might call forth a new ideology, better equipped to mask these new social relations. Such an ideology would have to be shared by the elite and the populace if it was to provide an adequate basis of authority for the former. Patterson's conclusions, though consistent with the dearth of elaborate Initial Period interments and the occasional discovery of rich Early Horizon burials such as that at Karwa or Chongoyape, are far from being substantiated. Other factors, especially changes in the intensity of trade, agricultural production, and the possibility of military conquest, deserve to be considered as possible contributing factors.

Crisis cults often have been described as over-determined, which is to say that there are usually multiple part-causes responsible for their appearance (La Barre 1971: 27). Trade and warfare have been especially important precipitating factors in the last two centuries of international conquest, colonialism, and capitalist expansion. The role of trade in this process is suddenly to force relatively isolated communities into a much larger system, thereby creating existential needs to incorporate the enlarged reality into the ideological framework; this response was reinforced, no doubt, by the practical social and economic advantages of adopting a more universalist ideology (Thoden van Velzen 1977: 114, Flannery 1968). Similarly, military defeat and subjugation may be inconsistent with the sacred propositions supporting the rights of the ruling authorities and, as in the case of the Late Horizon in Peru, this unresolvable contradiction may lead to the rapid collapse of the ideological armature of the defeated rulers. While conquest is prominent in the minds of many archaeologists as an explanation for the rapid spread of a religious cult (e.g., Sanders 1978, Rowe 1977), it is only one of many factors capable of stimulating such cult activity.

To recapitulate, the adoption of the Chavín cult actually could have been a means of resolving the strains within regional systems which had developed by the Early Horizon and thus, in a sense, the initial function of the unprecedented adoption of the Chavín cult would have been conservative in that it would have helped to maintain a traditional way of life in the face of changed circumstances (Jones and Kautz 1981: 27). Once introduced, however, it was likely that affiliation with the Chavín cult brought with it unintended consequences, some of which may have played an important role in transforming the way of life that it was designed to salvage.

It is appropriate to end this chapter with the question posed by Weston La Barre (1971: 10): "Is a cult a success or a failure if it succeeds in becoming increasingly institutionalized but fails to have any resolving effect on the secular problems that engendered it?" The conspicuous success of the Chavín cult as an expansive religious movement and the indelible impact it left on early Peruvian society tends to draw attention away from its relatively short duration, which in most areas probably did not exceed two centuries. From this vantage point, the Chavín cult could be considered a failure since it did not prevent the complete systems collapse which occurred at the end of the Early Horizon. Those societies which finally emerged from the ashes of Chavín civilization appear to have been organized in a fundamentally different manner than were the "formative" polities of the Initial Period and Early Horizon.

Notes

1 A horizon, according to Willey and Phillips (1958: 33), is primarily a spatial continuity represented by cultural traits and assemblages whose nature and mode of

occurrence permit the assumption of a broad and rapid spread. "Horizon," when used in this context, is written in lower case (e.g., Chavín horizon) in order to avoid confusion with Rowe's relative chronological terms, such as Early Horizon.

2 Snuffing equipment pre-dating the Early Horizon was recovered by Junius Bird at Huaca Prieta (Wassén 1967: 256–7), and Middle Horizon artifacts for inhaling snuff are quite numerous (*Ibid.*: 24–6, fig. 30). The similarity between these artifacts and ethnographically collected specimens leaves little doubt as to their function, although the composition of pre-Hispanic snuff is unknown. The Supe spatula (Fig. 4.4) strongly resembles ethnographic snuff trays.

3 Although a bone carved in Chavín style was discovered at Huaricoto (Burger and Salazar-Burger 1980: 31), the Early Horizon shrine there proved it to be non-Chavín in architecture, organization, and ritual. This example underscores the danger of identifying a site as "Chavín" on the basis of one or two diagnostic artifacts.

4 The temple of Cerro Sechín appears to be an exception to the general absence of pre-Chavín sculpture. The stone façade of one of its late renovations incorporates some 400 sculptures of victorious warriors and dismembered and mutilated victims. Though its age has been the subject of considerable debate, recent excavations have recovered carbon samples from a context coeval to the carvings, and the resulting measurements strongly suggest a late Initial Period date for the sculptures (Sanmaniego, Vergara and Bischof 1985).

5

The patterns of art and power in the Early Intermediate Period

WILLIAM J. CONKLIN
&
MICHAEL EDWARD MOSELEY

The term "Early Intermediate Period" (EIP) designates a unit of time estimated as beginning in approximately 300 to 400 BC and ending in about AD 500 to 600. Intermediate periods in the Max Uhle/John Rowe chronology for Peruvian prehistory tend to be the "leftovers" between the horizons, and it could be argued that as such they do not necessarily constitute a coherent and intelligible unit of study. They certainly were not thought of by Uhle as having the coherence which he believed characterized the horizon time periods, and Rowe's purpose in providing the name "Early Intermediate Period" was to create a non-interpretive framework. Nevertheless, several efforts have been made to provide descriptive titles which would be indicative of the EIP's general characteristics.

Bennett (Bennett and Bird 1960), seeing art history as the central discipline of archaeology and in an effort to provide identity for the EIP, coined the term "Mastercraftsman Period," which was obviously a reference to the highly developed pottery styles of Nasca and Moche, which occur between the Early and Middle Horizons. Lumbreras (1974a) utilized the term "Regional Development Period" for approximately the same time slot, seeing orderly cultural evolution as the central framework for the structuring of archaeological evidence. While both of these descriptive titles accurately describe certain aspects of the archaeological record, the unique and idiosyncratic are obscured in the attempt to generalize about the salient cultural features. Nasca ceramics in a museum display case are indeed quite comparable to Moche ceramics, but the broader evidence suggests that these two cultures had entirely different societal structures and power bases, and also had entirely divergent destinies. Perhaps it is time in the evolution of Peruvian archaeology for interest in cultural individualism, with less demand for coherence to political and historical schemata.

The analytical tool used in this effort at understanding the individualities as well as the similarities of regional cultures is the notion of "patterning," which is defined as the formal configuration of material culture at any given scale. Comparative pattern analysis theoretically could be made on a wide range of the remaining formal configurations of the EIP cultures, but archaeological

Fig. 5.1 Sites relevant to the text.

work in Peru has by no means been extensive enough for such a complete review. Patterns, if they were available, could provide complete comparative scalar sequences: settlement distributions, road patterning, irrigation networks, earth-art patterning, settlement-site planning and urban design, characteristic pyramid form and distribution, house-plan types, characteristic ceramic forms, characteristic textile structures and fiber-spinning patterns, etc. Such comparative data are not often available, however, because different Andean areas are understood in terms of very different types of archaeological data as a result of preservational differences and as a result of the changing interests of archaeologists. For example, inferences about the south coastal Nasca Valley rest primarily upon seriated mortuary goods, while those about the north coastal Virú Valley rest upon surface ceramics and settlement analysis.

Pattern analysis is actually a common, though perhaps somewhat unconscious, tool of the analytic archaeologist. Where pattern configurations can be related to earlier or later ones, they are presumed to reveal cultural continuity. Where similar sets are synchronic, cultural coherence is suspected. Analyzing the quality and symbolic meaning of patterning is the proper work of the art historian, but analyzing the societal implications of patterning is indeed the central work of the archaeologist.

The beginning of the Early Intermediate Period is also, by definition, the time of fading for the Early Horizon. The unity of the Chavín cult, whose characteristic art patterns had become so widespread through ancient Peru and were seemingly the hallmark of high culture, dissolved. The great coastal architectural complexes which were associated with the Chavín cult – Caballo Muerto in the Moche Valley, Cerro Sechín in the Casma Valley, Garagay in the Rimac Valley, Mina Perdida in the Lurín Valley, and others – all were gradually abandoned. The late highland focal center of the cult at Chavín de Huántar apparently was not abandoned, but new construction stopped and it became a pilgrimage ruin. But no direct evidence of the Chavín cult, neither art nor architecture, has been discovered in the southern highlands – in the great *altiplano* which extends north and south from Lake Titicaca. This independence of the Southern Sierra is highly predictive of its EIP future. It is also important to note that the patterns of distribution of architecture marked with Chavín designs and the patterns of the distribution of pottery and textiles marked with Chavín designs are not identical. Major differences occur in the south, where the southernmost evidence of monumental Chavín architecture is in the gigantic U-shaped pyramids of Garagay in the Rimac Valley and Mina Perdida in the Lurín Valley, and yet 200 kilometers further south extensive evidence of Chavín textiles and other portable Chavín art has been reported.

These patterns of distribution would tend to suggest that the South Coast of Peru was far more influenced by the art of the Chavín cult than by its organizational power. Specifically, the Nasca Valley has no Chavín-marked pyramidal structure, no evidence of constructions which would indicate large-scale organized labor during the Early Horizon. The absence of a tradition of organized power in the Nasca Valley during the Early Horizon is an important clue to the understanding of the succeeding Early Intermediate Period in the Nasca Valley. Cults and religious traditions other than Chavín no doubt also existed during the Early Horizon, but because they were not the sponsors of such elegant art, their patterns cannot be traced.

A review of the Early Intermediate Period evidence can be organized on a coastal area basis, followed by a discussion of the sierra.

THE NORTHERN COASTAL AREA

By the beginning of the Early Intermediate Period, the agricultural basis of Andean society essentially had been established. All of the characteristic food crops had been domesticated, cotton had replaced other vegetable fibers for textiles, ceramic techniques were evolving rapidly, and camelids were beginning to be evident, even on the coast.

The Moche Valley, which became the focus of the north coastal area during the EIP, probably has been occupied continuously from the time of the Early Horizon up to this very day, but the actual archaeological remains do not provide complete evidence of that continuity.

These gaps in the archaeological record in part may be explained by preservational factors. It is likely (Moseley 1983) that tectonic movement of the coastal plain caused changes in deposition and erosion which buried or destroyed much of the relevant archaeological evidence. However, a most impressive architectural grouping – the Caballo Muerto complex (Pozorski 1976a, 1982) – survives from the Early Horizon in the Moche Valley. One of the main structures of this capital was the multi-stage, U-shaped Huaca los Reyes (Conklin 1985a). Such structures already had a long history in the Moche Valley, with the central and upper valley dotted with pyramids and mounds from earlier times. But there is a hiatus in the preserved architectural record of the Moche Valley after the abandonment of Huaca los Reyes. The adjacent valleys, Virú to the south and Chicama to the north, provide supporting evidence, though, for continuity of the cultural tradition. Salinar-style ceramics provide not only an evident artistic transition between the early Horizon and the forthcoming Moche culture, but also many realistic images of life, such as vessels showing pitched-roof houses. The Gallinazo culture, which had as a focus the Virú Valley (although its characteristic ceramics also are found from the Chicama to the Santa valleys), is somewhat more fully understood than Salinar. The first fortified adobe monument in the Virú Valley, Tomoval (Fig. 5.2), is associated with Gallinazo ceramics, and villages with plazas and small pyramids have been identified. The earliest recorded use of camelid hair (probably alpaca) in textiles on the North Coast occurs in a

Gallinazo textile fragment (Conklin 1974a), where the alpaca is dyed in colors resembling the colors used in cotton Chavín warp-wrapping and later Moche full tapestry.

It seems likely that the Moche Valley itself went through a closely related evolution during the early portion of the Early Intermediate Period, though most of the supporting evidence is missing today. Most intriguing of all the remains from this time period in the Moche Valley are the very fragmentary remains of major canals high above the valley bottom, suggesting the establishment of large-scale water distribution systems and their necessarily correlative governmental organizations (Moseley 1983).

The central monumental constructions of the Moche Valley during the Early Intermediate Period are the closely related structures known as Huaca del Sol and Huaca de la Luna, the largest adobe monumental construction in ancient Peru. Huaca del Sol was about 40 m high and 340 m long (Fig. 5.3). Building was done in multiple stages interspersed with periods of use, and a corvée labor system was used to mobilize workmen from communities scattered over a broad area (Hastings and Moseley 1975). Huaca del Sol seems at all stages to have had activities associated with refuse (mundane activity);

Fig. 5.2 Tomoval, Virú Valley. Courtesy R. Feldman.

Huaca de la Luna, however, was kept clean and was decorated with murals (sacrosanct activity).

The pyramids are associated with the well-defined Moche art style that found expression in ceramics, textiles, and murals. The ceramic artwork has been divided into five phases, the first of which was borrowed or imported from an outside source. This derivation is evident in the lack of local antecedents and origins for the formal style. By contrast, domestic pottery appears to be an uninterrupted outgrowth of the preceding Gallinazo phase, as are most elements of Moche subsistence, settlement, and architectural patterns.

During the third and fourth phase of the Moche ceramic sequence, each valley from the Chicama to Nepeña contained at least one sizeable monument built in the architectural canons expressed at Sol and Luna. Although the monuments do not approach Sol in scope, each is generally the largest construction in its valley for the period. Moche architectural and cultural hegemony clearly stopped in the Nepeña Valley, but its political frontiers probably extended further south. This cultural break predictably coincides with the Casma Valley, whose great former center of Sechín Alto certainly

Fig. 5.3 Huaca del Sol, Moche Valley. Courtesy Shippee-Johnson expedition.

must have imbued the area with a strong on-going social tradition, even if its political fortunes had waned.

North of the Chicama Valley, Early Intermediate Period events are less clearly understood, with virtually no evidence for the early portions of the EIP. The very end of the EIP is denoted by the earliest levels of occupation at Pacatnamú, a monumental grouping of pyramids and compounds overlooking the river mouth of the Jequetepeque Valley and containing late Moche ceramics and textiles (Conklin 1974a). Still further north, in the Lambayeque Valley, late Moche pottery and other even later evidence associated with the vast architectural complex of Pampa Grande suggest that it must have become the late capital of a transposed Moche empire.

Even further north, beyond the Sechura desert peninsula, appears the evidence of the Vicus culture. There, in the Piura Valley, many undocumented tombs have yielded copper work, gold, and ceramics which have strong affinities with Moche art, and which date to the EIP. On a comparative art-style basis, the Vicus culture seems to have had a long history, beginning in the Early Horizon with several villages, two pyramids – one quite large – and two heavily fortified hilltops preserved (Richardson 1978).

Another late administrative center of the Moche culture, though, occurs back in the Moche Valley, somewhat upstream from but still within view of the old great pyramids of Sol and Luna – the site of Galindo. Here a new, small pyramid and associated compound were constructed, together with other administrative facilities and impressive, though incomplete, canals or dry moats (Bawden 1977, 1982). The town ruins have a wall and moat through their center dividing lower-class dwellings from the more elaborate ones, with that pattern suggesting a radically divided society.

By the end of the Early Intermediate Period Galindo had been abandoned, and after that Pampa Grande. The focus of the tradition, though, came back to the Moche Valley after the Middle Horizon in a reorganized form as the Chimú culture. Moche cultural traditions, then, must have been ones that respected power, with the art distribution and population distribution shifting obediently as the regional rulers, with their pyramids, rose and fell.

The Santa Valley, 110 km south of the Moche Valley, is unique amongst the family of valleys that mark the North Coast of Peru. The lower portion of the Santa is perpendicular to the coast, like all other Peruvian coastal rivers, but the upper section of the Santa turns 90 degrees and forms a long highland valley called the Callejón de Huaylas, which runs parallel to the coast. The cultural history of the Santa during the Early Intermediate Period is fully as unique as the pattern of the river.

Along the ridges which run on either side of the lower valley are a series of ruins that date from the end of the Early Horizon and the beginning of the Early Intermediate Period – ruins which have all the forms and patterns of European castles: moats, keeps, redouts, lookouts, and concentric surrounding walls (Fig. 5.4). Often between the closely spaced castles are dividing walls which run down to the valley bottom and seem to demarcate property and agricultural areas. The pattern speaks of dozens of small fiefdoms, separate and at least roughly equal, though the latest of these castles seem to control larger territories and trade routes (Topic and Topic 1982). The upper Santa has a somewhat similar pattern of hilltop castles, though they are not as elaborate and seem to be somewhat later. But also in the upper valley are two other types of architectural complex – valley ceremonial centers and hilltop shrines. One of the valley ceremonial centers, Huaricoto, had a continuous religious tradition running from the Chavín cult (and other cults) during the Early Horizon through the Early Intermediate Period and perhaps even later (Burger and Burger 1980). The valley also had a rich history of burial-vault forms, beginning with rude, small, below-ground rectangular structures in the Early Horizon, through larger, cut-stone, below-ground structures during the Early Intermediate Period, to very impressive above-ground structures with elaborate internal burial-vaults, such as Willka Wain, which dates to the

Fig. 5.4 Moche-Phase hilltop fortification, Santa Valley.
Courtesy Shippee-Johnson expedition.

Middle Horizon and has associated Huari ceramics (Gary Vescelius, personal communication).

Just off the elbow of the Santa Valley is a site which has still another independent history – La Galgada (Grieder and Bueno Mendoza 1981). Initial Period burials, found at the lower levels of La Galgada, have well-preserved textiles as well as ceramics that show ties to widespread cultural traditions. In later phases the elaborate figurative ceramics of Recuay are evidence of a more localized development. The architecture is elaborate and unique to Peru, with cantilevered stonework.

The architectural and developmental patterns of the Santa during the Early Intermediate Period thus form an almost total contrast to those occurring in the Moche Valley to the north. Where centralized power is seemingly always in evidence in Moche, it is never in evidence in the Santa. Power in the Santa is balanced among many small centers. In the Moche Valley, the center of power seems to shift location, whereas in the Santa, the multiple small centers of power seem to have extraordinary longevity. In the Moche Valley, elaborate water distribution systems evolved, but nothing comparable evolved in the Santa Valley. Power based on such total control over water resources must have been more concentrated and hence transportable than power based simply on territoriality.

THE CENTRAL COASTAL AREA

The central section of the Peruvian coast, as it is usually defined, contains a dozen river valleys which interdigitate with the coastal desert. The river valleys of this coastal section contain many of Peru's most impressive early constructions – monuments and extensive architecture which date from the preceramic, Initial Period and Early Horizon – periods before that with which this chapter is concerned. In the northern portion of the Central Coast, Aspero (on the north side of the Supe Valley) and Piedra Parada (on the south side of the valley), because of their scale, platform mounds, symmetrically arranged terraces, and sunken courts, strongly suggest corporate labor organization during their construction in the preceramic period (Feldman 1980).

The evidence for early, well-organized construction power in the middle portion of the Central Coast is even more extensive. On the south bank of the Chillón River, the largest known preceramic site, El Paraiso, extends over 50 to 60 hectares, and contains vast areas of agglutinated, stone-walled rectangular rooms, some suggesting communal use. An irregular U-shaped form exists for the main complex, which has many indications of repeated rebuilding.

In the Rimac Valley, on the other hand, Huaca La Florida (dated to the Initial Period) consists primarily of a single large U-shaped platform mound with no associated concentration of possible residential development. Garagay, another U-shaped platform mound in the Rimac Valley, apparently received major formal configuration during the Early Horizon, though it probably also has Initial Period origins. Extensive murals with Chavín-like art have been found on parts of Garagay (Ravines and Isbell 1975). The many additional U-shaped early mounds that have been found within this group of Central Coast valleys (Williams León 1980b) further attest to its early emergence as an important power center.

Thus within the Central Coast, there was a strong pattern of architectural evidence for organized communal and cultural activity during the Preceramic Period and Early Horizon, establishing a tradition of a powerful commonality which would presumably be precedent-setting for the events of the Early Intermediate Period. However, in the peripheral portions of the Central Coast, there is little evidence of life during the EIP, but there is strong evidence associated with one middle group of rivers which flows through what is now metropolitan Lima – the Chillón, the Rimac and the Lurín. Their valleys, together with the Chancay to the north, probably had an inter-related and complex cultural history during the Early Intermediate Period. Several sites within these valleys (which date from the beginnings of the EIP) have a pottery style called Miramar (Patterson 1966), and have small, village-scale pyramids which suggest a remembrance of the earlier giant constructions. However, near the end of the Early Intermediate Period, a well-organized focus of a successive culture (which is called the Lima culture) existed under the present-day city of the same name, with many pyramid ruins still existing though now surrounded by modern urban development. Probably the urban heart of this culture was the vast near-Lima ruin called Cajamarquilla, and the ceremonial heart was the pyramid complex called Pachacamac, located near the ocean at the mouth of the Lurín Valley.

But evidence of the Lima style in ceramics and textiles is also found in nearby valleys. The expansion of the Lima culture has been examined carefully in the upper Lurín Valley just south of Lima (Earle 1972). At the beginning of the Early Intermediate Period, population was focused in the upper portion of the valley, with isolated free-standing houses characteristic, and with evidence of short irrigation canals. Gradually the population expanded, moved down the valley, and utilized longer irrigation canals to agglutinated dwellings. Elite structures on hilltops also began to occur. Near the end of the Early Intermediate Period, after intermittent influences from the nearby Rimac Valley, the Lima culture became completely dominant. Perhaps the local Lurín Valley administrative center of the Lima culture was the habitation complex associated with the pyramid of Pachacamac. The Lima-culture religious center of Pachacamac continued to be important for another thousand years, until it was ransacked by the Spaniards.

In summary, after the impressive constructions of the Initial Period and Early Horizon, with their connotations of great power and religion, the Central Coast's cultural energy for a time went into decline, with hundreds of years of village life once again in the beginning of the Early Intermediate Period in many portions of the Central Coast. Highly organized society reappears in the form of the Lima culture in the latter part of the EIP.

THE SOUTHERN COASTAL AREA

The Ica Valley has the special distinction for Peruvian archaeologists of being the valley whose ceramics were selected for the formation of a master sequence of periods and epochs by Rowe (1967c). This effort was directed at providing an objective time framework for the placement of archaeological data, without the interpretation of the data's being prejudiced by preconceptions about evolutionary stages. The Early Intermediate Period is defined in simple technological/stylistic terms as beginning at the time when ceramic polychrome slip painting replaces resin painting in the Ica Valley; there were to be no cultural or evolutionary implications associated with the definition. The Early Intermediate Period was then subdivided into eight epochs that corresponded to eight sequential styles of Nasca pottery. These epochs and periods were to be used throughout Peru, with correlations determined by a variety of means, among them stylistic comparisons and radiocarbon dating. It is fair to say that the division into periods has been extraordinarily helpful in the organization of data, but that the smaller division into epochs has found only occasional usefulness in cross-dating and thus in organizing non-Nasca data.

While the division of Nasca pottery into eight successive ceramic phases may be a tight system for the organization of the ceramic data from the area, the purpose of the system was to provide clues for the organization of settlement patterns, irrigation data, architectural studies, agricultural patterning studies, etc. Unfortunately, little of this pattern analysis has been done for the Nasca Valley. The types of patterning data which are available for cultural interpretation from the Nasca Valley differ greatly from the types of data available from other areas of Peru.

The Nasca data consist almost exclusively of art in the form of textiles, ceramics, and desert markings. More Early Intermediate Period textiles have been preserved from the Nasca and associated valleys than from any other location in Peru. The technical characteristics of Nasca textiles during all epochs are more advanced than those occurring in other coastal areas of Peru during the same period. This advanced development began during the Early Horizon when camelid hair from the alpaca began to be used in the textiles, which still contained Chavín figurative elements. By the beginning of the Early Intermediate Period, massive quantities of alpaca were used in the elaborate mummy-wrappings found in the Paracas Necropolis. The design motifs characteristic of Paracas and the ensuing Nasca culture have their first expression in textiles. The presence of alpaca clearly implies excellent trading relations with highland areas at a very early time period. On the North Coast of Peru, alpaca was not available in such quantities until nearly a thousand years later (Conklin 1974a). This southern head start in textile development continued throughout the Early Intermediate period, and the technical variety, the invention, and the diversity of design ideas are unequalled in other areas of Peru.

Some of the Paracas Necropolis pottery associated with the elaborate textiles was white-slipped plain ware – the Topará style; subsequently, Nasca pottery became elaborately painted and modeled. Dawson has established the characteristics of the various phases based on these changes (Menzel, Rowe, and Dawson 1964). Nasca 1 pottery continues the mythical themes of the Paracas textiles but also introduces a fresh variety of non-mythical animals, including birds and fish, and many kinds of fruit. If it is possible to read cultural characteristics directly from art patterns, then this clearly suggests a gradual secularization of the culture, a movement away from the demonic terrors represented in Paracas art. Nasca 2, 3, and 4 are called "Monumental" because of the simple power of the art – its lack of unnecessary detail, with bold figures of demons or animals against plain white or dark red backgrounds.

In Nasca 5, bodiless human and demon heads appeared and new ceramic forms were introduced. Nasca 6 and 7 pottery designs have similar themes, which are now elaborated, filling in the background space; the style has been called "Proliferous." Dawson has suggested the possible presence of North Coast influence during this phase because some of the vessels contain design ideas resembling Moche ones, which were contemporaneous. Such influence has not been detected in the Lima culture, which was also contemporary and geographically between the two, which suggests that the influence may have come by sea. Nasca 8 sees still further break-up of the design motifs, with disjointed human and demon figures appearing. Throughout the sequence, a gradual loosening of the religious imagery occurs, with the art heading toward elaboration and complexity. However, this sequence was interrupted by influence from a highland culture at the beginning of the Middle Horizon.

Few extensive architectural remains are known from the Nasca culture. Most of these, which date from Phases 2, 3, and 4 of the ceramic sequence, have been reviewed by Rowe (Rowe 1967d).

Dos Palmos, one of these sites in the adjacent Pisco Valley, consists of extensive, agglutinated, rectangular dwellings with occasional open plazas. Another site is Tambo Viejo in the Acari Valley, which contains Early Intermediate Period 2 local-style pottery and Early Intermediate Period Nasca-style pottery. Tambo Viejo was abandoned at the end of Early Intermediate Period 3.

The most impressive site of this complex of southern valleys, though, is Cahuachi in the Nasca Valley, which dates to Nasca 2–4. The ruins of Cahuachi contain a series of terraced hills, pyramids, burial areas, and walled enclosures. One of these pyramids is called the Great Temple (Strong 1957), and is some 20 m high. The ruins, overlooking the valley of the Nasca and just below the great Pampa de Nasca, give the impression of being a ceremonial or power center of some importance. The coincidence of the rise and fall in three adjacent valleys of these urban centers with their common ceramic styles caused Rowe to postulate a brief Nasca empire.

The most famous patternings of the Nasca culture, however, are the Nasca lines, which occur for the most part on the Pampa de Nasca, the desert plain above and to the north of the Nasca river valley (see Fig. 5.5). These markings on the desert were created by brushing away the upper, dark oxidized desert surface, revealing lower, light-colored sediments beneath. The lines have some conceptual coherence with the incised patterning on the ceramics of the Nasca Valley prevalent during the Early Horizon. The desert markings occur in several pattern types, which are probably chronological. The earliest are figurative drawings representing, in many cases, the demons and animals shown on Paracas and Early Nasca textiles, especially those created by cross-knit looping, a process commonly referred to as needle knitting. Cross-knit looping uses a single thread for the creation of the textile. The desert figures

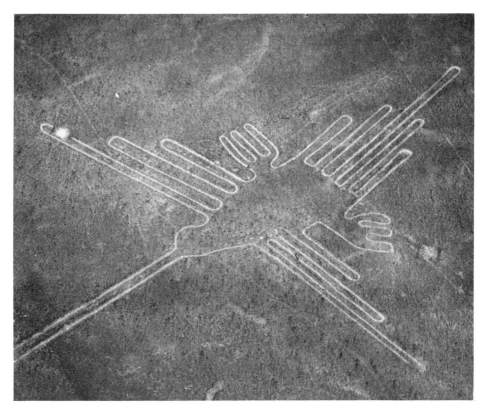

Fig. 5.5 Line drawing in the form of a bird, Nasca plains. Courtesy R. Feldman.

are drawn with a single continuous line, and thus they have some conceptual unity with their correlative textiles. Somewhat later drawings consist of straight lines – that is, lines which are straight in the two horizontal dimensions but which go up and down the hills and contours which are encountered. These lines in some cases proceed for many tens of kilometers across the desert with amazing straightness and seemingly with an horizon obsession. Still later markings consist of long thin triangles or trapezoids – in effect, incised lines which have undergone a slight radial movement. In places, many of the lines seem to be organized around focal points (Anthony Aveni, personal communication). These three types of line may well coincide with the three ceramic art styles of Nasca 1, Monumental (2, 3, and 4), and Proliferous (6 and 7).

Without doubt, understanding the lines is important to understanding the whole Nasca culture, for they represent by far the largest artifacts of the culture. Although the lines are all technically similar, each seems to have been created separately and not as a part of a larger conception planned by one mind at one time. Nevertheless, over time the individual marks adhere to a broad stylistic sequence. One explanation of their function would be that they were memorial markers for individuals, and thus differ somewhat from one another in widths, orientation to huacas, to horizon points, and to settlements. Calendrical significance for the lines has been suspected, but not yet demonstrated. Ground markings are known in other parts of Peru, and hence Nasca lines are not without relatives in ancient Peruvian art. In summary, their unique characteristics are the purity of their conception and the quality and scale of their construction. Thus individuality – with cultural coherence but without evidence of large-scale power – marks all of the types of patterning that occur in the Nasca Valley in the EIP. The absence of large-scale power must also explain why the Nasca culture, unlike the Moche culture, did not survive the Middle Horizon.

THE CENTRAL AND SOUTHERN SIERRA

In contrast to the coastal areas where multi-valley cultures such as Moche, Lima, and Nasca arose, the Peruvian sierra during the Early Intermediate Period was primarily the setting for the development of many small, independent cultural groups. Montane valley basins are characteristically smaller than coastal valleys, and cultural identity during the Early Intermediate Period was usually defined by the visible horizons, even though resources from other zones were utilized. Study of the patterns of sierra architecture and ceramics permits something of the resource-utilization patterns and cultural spheres to be understood. Four sierra areas can be considered: the Ayacucho Valley, the Andahuaylas Valley, the Urubamba Valley, and the Titicaca Basin.

Settlements within the Ayacucho/Huanta basin at the beginning of the Early Intermediate Period were extremely small, but they seem to coalesce into more distinct village patterns at the end of the period. This slight movement toward urbanization occurs, interestingly enough, prior to any evidence of the oncoming Huari culture, which is usually credited with being the local urbanizing influence (MacNeish, Patterson, and Browman 1975).

The most important of the local cultures in the Ayacucho Basin during this period is called the Huarpa culture, named for the local river with which its sites are associated. Some Huarpa sites have been identified by their characteristic ceramics (Lumbreras 1974a). All of them are small and irregular, except for the site of Nawimpuko, which is on a hilltop overlooking the modern town of Ayacucho. Nawimpuko seems to have been a real city, with rectangular houses, streets, and associated terraces. Several forms of small canals and water-control devices, as well as extensive agricultural terraces, are associated with Huarpa ceramics, suggesting a well-developed local hegemony. The ceramics of the Huarpa culture show artistic influence from the ceramic art of the nearby and contemporary Nasca Valley culture. Evidence of this developed local culture disappears with the advent of the Middle Horizon.

Further south is another of the major intermontane valley basins that are characteristic of the Central Highlands of Peru – Andahuaylas. Projecting into and overlooking the lush Andahuaylas Valley bottom are a series of ridges or spurs from the towering mountains above, which always ring the sierra horizon. These ridges were favorite locations for settlements in this area during the Early Intermediate Period. In terms of altitude, these sites are intermediate between the zone where maize is grown and the upper zone where tubers are grown (Grossman 1976). Camelid domestication was fully developed, as is evidenced by both camelid burials and clay models of camelids.

The special overlook locations no doubt had a certain control function, though there is no evidence of defensive walls or of warfare in Andahuaylas during this seemingly tranquil period of small villages without large-scale political control.

Still further south along the Andean chain is the spacious Urubamba Valley, which was destined later to contain the Inca capital of Cuzco. The Chanapata ceramic style is a local style that dates from the Early Intermediate Period, and is associated with stone-faced terraces and below-ground dwellings. Chanapata ceramics have been found on sites that overlook the valley below, in contrast to the Initial Period site of Marcavalle, which was in the middle of the valley bottom (Mohr Chavez 1981). The scanty evidence available for Chanapata culture suggests that the occupational patterning and ecological posture of the occupants was not inconsistent with those of the preceding Marcavalle, which was based primarily on camelid herding.

The far southern portion of the Peruvian sierra contains a unique geographical and ecological event – a mountaintop sea called Lake Titicaca. The presence of this lake and its associated valleys permitted a special resource-utilization pattern, and was, within the context of sierra valleys, a unique, large-scale, visible, and accessible development area. Evolving from the region surrounding this amazing water body was a Southern Sierra cultural tradition which, in its final manifestation in the Late Horizon as the Inca culture, conquered all of Peru. The Inca claimed mystical origins on the islands of the magic lake, and their textiles, their architecture, and no doubt their under-standing of political power structures came from a long Southern Sierra tra-dition – a sequential though overlapping evolution connecting the sites and cultures of Chiripa, Pucará, Tiwanaku, Huari, and finally Inca Cuzco. The major artifactual definitions of this cultural tradition – the importance and precision of its architecture, the graphic brilliance of its interlocked tapestry patterning, the carved stone stelae of its religions – all point to a well-kept tradition of organized power, which the evidence indicates had its initial focus during the Early Intermediate Period at sites very close to the great lake.

Lake Titicaca, the focus of this cultural history, occurs at an elevation of some 3,800 m. It is the largest lake in the world at such a height – a kind of ocean in the sky. The waters of the lake carry an array of aquatic species including Suche, Carawi, and lake snails. The lake edge, with its marshy shallow waters, provides a very special and valuable ecological zone for a variety of reeds and other water-edge agricultural products. The setting thus provides a lacustrine base for the evolution of culture: a base which in many ways was comparable to the maritime foundations of the coastal cultures of Peru (Moseley 1975a, 1978c).

The evolution of the Early Intermediate Period site of Chiripa illustrates the cultural history of the Titicaca Basin. Though there may have been other similar local cultural foci, Chiripa appears to have been a highly important ceremonial center. Only some 500 m from the edge of the lake, the now rounded mound overlooks the lake and its islands to the north. The lowest and hence earliest levels of the Chiripa site date to about 1350 to 850 BC, accord-ing to Browman (1980). The evidence of the relative importance of the lake during this early period includes snail shells, bones from several local varieties of fish and birds, and totora reeds. Also, within the refuse from this early period, textile instruments were found, as well as evidence of llama, alpaca, guanaco, and vicuña.

Shortly after 900 BC, the first architectural statement of the temple appeared in the form of stone walls around the mound, forming a square with subterranean houses in the interior. The most notable architectural structures of Chiripa occurred, however, at the very beginning of the Early Intermediate Period, dated from 600 to 100 BC. They consist of a group of sixteen sym-metrically arranged houses, three on each side of a square with an additional house placed diagonally at each corner (Fig. 5.6). The architecture of these houses is highly developed and specialized. The exterior walls consist of rectangular cells, placed side by side, accessible from the inner room through "windows" or niches, which apparently formed carefully protected storage. The opening into the house was fitted with sliding doors, with the lower and upper halves separately operable. Door jambs were constructed of rectangular adobe blocks, though the walls themselves were of rubble. The formed adobe blocks permitted special accuracy in the construction of door jambs, which were finally plastered over with a two-tiered stepped jamb design. The walls also were stuccoed and then painted with terracotta and green paints, occasionally with use of a chevron design (Alan Sawyer, personal communication). The focus of this carefully constructed, protective house compound was a sunken, sacred plaza, which probably contained one or more vertical stone stelae in the center (David Browman, personal communication).

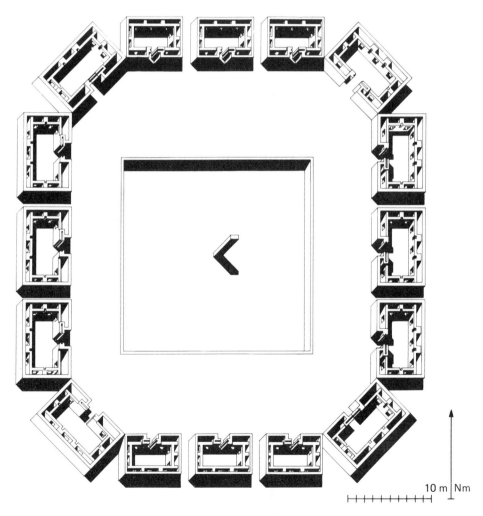

Fig. 5.6 Reconstruction of Chiripa at the beginning of the Early Intermediate Period.
Courtesy W. Conklin.

This elaborate construction provides a key to the understanding of the patterns of all later architecture of the Southern Sierra tradition: the stepped frame doorways of Tiwanaku, the incised niches of the Gate of the Sun, the ubiquitous stone niches of all Inca architecture, and the stepped jambs of Inca entrance doors. In a larger sense, the Chiripa houses are the didactic prototype for all Inca structures which characteristically surround a plaza. Clearly the beginnings of the architectural and sculptural traditions of the Southern Sierra are in evidence at the beginning of the Early Intermediate Period in Chiripa.

The presence of camelids and weaving instruments and the absence of cotton combine to suggest that the camelid-hair textiles of Pucará and Tiwanaku may well have had an early focus in Chiripa. The blue-green paint color occurring on the stucco became a prominent color of the painted statuary of Tiwanaku, and the predominant background color of Tiwanaku tapestry. But Chiripa is no doubt not a unique site, though it does illustrate this phase of Southern Sierra history. Tiwanaku itself must have had an overlapping history with Chiripa and have been growing and evolving parallel to, but independent of, Chiripa, for near the end of the Early Intermediate Period Chiripa was abandoned (David Browman, personal communication) or destroyed (Junius Bird, personal communication). Directly on top of the ruins, a Tiwanaku subterranean temple was constructed, one which closely resembles the Subterranean Temple of Tiwanaku itself.

On the north side of Lake Titicaca, but not so closely related to the lake as Chiripa, was the Early Intermediate Period culture center of Pucará. This site contains a major stone-walled court with semi-subterranean burial vaults built of carefully dressed stone blocks and slabs. The court itself is at a lower level than the surrounding constructions, which have compartments with doors facing the inner court (Bennett 1936). Earlier levels of temples are also reported to exist (Mujica Barreda 1978).

The ceramics of Pucará are elaborate, with incised patterning, added modeled figures, and brilliant colors. A ceramic trumpet in the Pucará style exists, and is presumably from the site; a very similar ceramic trumpet was found at Chiripa. Pucará textiles which have been preserved on the desert coast of southern Peru and northern Chile are of interlocked tapestry and utilize the colors and designs of Pucará ceramics (Conklin 1985b). Much of the art of Pucará, in addition to feline images, is concerned with frogs and fish, the latter occurring most commonly on the stone art. Flying figures carrying staffs are portrayed on the ceramics. As a whole, the art style of Pucará is clearly precedent to Tiwanaku, and seems more elaborate and more developed than the art of Chiripa.

Tiwanaku itself, which as noted above must have had its origins in the Early Intermediate Period, had its time of greatest power and expansion during the Peruvian Middle Horizon. The ruins suggest a ceremonial city of impressive grandeur. Lake Titicaca just can be seen in the hazy horizon to the northwest, though the ceremonial mounds and sunken temples of the site seem to relate as well to the surrounding *altiplano* and mountainous horizons. The surrounding valleys show evidence of ridged field agriculture, some of which have associated Tiwanaku ceramics (Alan Kolata, personal communication). Without doubt, Tiwanaku was a major population center as well as a place of temples and ritual. Thus the focus of Southern Sierra culture, during the Early Intermediate Period, moved away from the lake and "up valley", as did so many other contemporary Peruvian population centers.

Slowly, after decades of archaeological work, the form of the temples and the culture of Tiwanaku are beginning to emerge. From this site emanated that phenomenon which became a time marker for all Peruvian cultural history – the Middle Horizon. Within its brief time span most of the richly individualized valley and basin cultures of the Andes were upset. The Middle Horizon brought at least the appearance of a kind of national unity, but at the expense of the valley cultural vitality which characterized the patterns of art and power during the Early Intermediate Period in the ancient Andes.

6

City and state in Middle Horizon Huari

WILLIAM H. ISBELL

The form and development of the indigenous Andean state and city continue to be topics of research and debate. Questions still to be resolved include satisfactory definitions of crucial concepts and categories and their archaeological correlates. Equally critical is the lack of archaeological research: interpretations of Andean prehistory cannot help but reflect bias from incomplete information. Cultures which have been well investigated can be evaluated with accuracy, but scarcity of information promotes speculation. Sometimes the speculation leads to overestimation of prehistoric complexity and development, sometimes the reverse. Huari is an excellent case in point. It has been called a huge city by some, a ceremonial center by others. It has been considered the capital of a pan-Andean empire, spread by conquest and held together by a marvelous administrative sophistication. It has also been thought to be one of many equivalent, small polities participating in trade as well as intellectual exchange during the rise of urbanism and states. It has even been considered a dependent provincial capital established during expansion from the *altiplano* center of Tiwanaku.

Recent research of Huari and related sites makes it possible to offer a new description of the prehistoric city, to re-evaluate its rise and relations with Tiwanaku, and to examine the organization and structure of its sphere of political influence. It is also possible to offer several explanatory interpretations of Huari's evolutionary transformations and to identify some of its major contributions to Andean culture. Until more research has been carried out, and several theoretical and methodological issues have been resolved, we cannot determine even the place and time of origin for the Andean city and state, to say nothing of explaining this evolutionary change. However, the study of Huari does tend to confirm its urban status and its manipulation of a state administrative apparatus. Furthermore, it appears that Huari rulers invented a system of administration and revenue collection unique among the world's archaic states. This invention set Andean civilization on a course all its own among the pristine civilizations of the world.

In the middle of the 16th century, Cieza de León (1947: ch. 87) visited the

Central Highlands of Peru and the Ayacucho Valley where Huari is located. He described a ruin with huge, deteriorating buildings that had square ground plans. Since this form contrasted with the elongated constructions characteristic of the Incas, and the buildings appeared to have been abandoned for a very long time, Cieza concluded that they belonged to an ancient, vanished civilization that preceded the Incas in the Andes. Cieza referred to the ruin with the name Viñaque, the name of the major river of the Ayacucho Valley drainage where the ruins were to be found. Over subsequent centuries, many amateur archaeologists searched for Cieza's Viñaque, but since the discovery of Huari, with its stone monoliths and huge buildings, no one has doubted that Cieza's visit took him to Huari.

In Ayacucho, the name of the main river changes many times. The name Viñaque is preserved in the modern community of Simpapata, which lies on one of the finest fords of the river. Immediately behind the Simpapata plaza and the single row of modern buildings, are archaeological remains that include large, square enclosures dating from the Middle Horizon. This archaeological zone, named Simpapata for the modern community, covers about 48 hectares (see site no. 90, Isbell and Schreiber 1978: fig. 3, table 2). In addition to square enclosures, there are remains of circular constructions, terrace walls, and abundant pottery from the early Middle Horizon. However, one diagnostic sherd of Cuzco Polychrome B was also recovered, showing that the settlement was at least visited on occasions during the Late Horizon and/or early Colonial period. It seems likely that the colonial road crossed the main river at Viñaque and that Cieza witnessed the square ruins of Simpapata when he passed next to them.

Huari lies high on the eastern edge of the Ayacucho Valley, between 2,700 m and and 3,100 m above sea level in the headwaters of the little Ocopa River. This tributary of the main stream merges with it about 3 km above Simpapata. If Cieza de León did not visit Huari, then its first popular description can be attributed to Julio Tello (1970), who discussed Huari's monumental ruins and its influential art style in a 1931 Lima newspaper article following his archaeological expedition to the Ayacucho Valley site.

Huari was still virtually unknown when Kroeber (1944) synthesized Andean prehistory. Its first scholarly interpretations can be attributed to Larco Hoyle (1948), Rowe, Collier, and Willey (1950), and Schaedel (1948), whose writings revealed enough of its importance to attract an exploratory expedition directed by Wendell Bennett (1953). Bennett was concerned primarily with defining the Huari ceramic style, and determining its relationships to both the Bolivian Tiahuanaco and Coast Tiahuanaco styles. He did observe that the core of Huari covered at least 1.5 km^2, where walls of angular stone set in mud were common, and occasional dressed stone constructions could also be found. However, Bennett could make no sense of the architec-

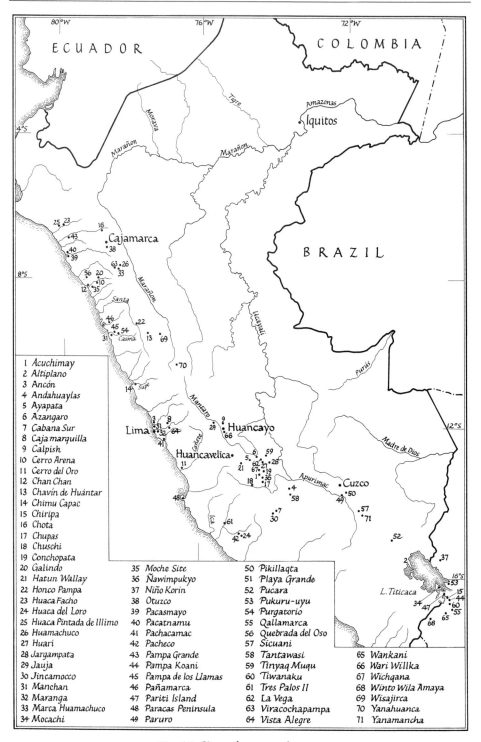

1	Acuchimay	
2	Altiplano	
3	Ancón	
4	Andahuaylas	
5	Ayapata	
6	Azangaro	
7	Cabana Sur	
8	Caja marquilla	
9	Calpish	
10	Cerro Arena	
11	Cerro del Oro	
12	Chan Chan	
13	Chavín de Huántar	
14	Chimu Capac	
15	Chiripa	
16	Chota	
17	Chupas	
18	Chuschi	
19	Conchopata	
20	Galindo	

35	Moche Site	50	Pikillaqta		
21	Hatun Wallay	36	Ñawimpukyo	51	Playa Grande
22	Honco Pampa	37	Niño Korin	52	Pucara
23	Huaca Facho	38	Otuzco	53	Pukuru-uyu
24	Huaca del Loro	39	Pacasmayo	54	Purgatorio
25	Huaca Pintada de Illimo	40	Pacatnamu	55	Qallamarca
26	Huamachuco	41	Pachacamac	56	Quebrada del Oso
27	Huari	42	Pacheco	57	Sicuani
28	Jargampata	43	Pampa Grande	58	Tantawasi
29	Jauja	44	Pampa Koani	59	Tinyaq Muqu
30	Jincamocco	45	Pampa de los Llamas	60	Tiwanaku
31	Manchan	46	Pañamarca	61	Tres Palos II
32	Maranga	47	Pariti Island	62	La Vega
33	Marca Huamachuco	48	Paracas Peninsula	63	Viracochapampa
34	Mocachi	49	Paruro	64	Vista Alegre

65	Wankani
66	Wari Willka
67	Wichqana
68	Winto Wila Amaya
69	Wisajirra
70	Yanahuanca
71	Yanamancha

Fig. 6.1 Sites relevant to the text.

tural remains. He stated that most of the walls were defense walls, division walls, or terraces which were not oriented to any fixed plan. Rather, they presented a pattern of haphazard confusion.

Luis Lumbreras (1974a: 159–62) provides a recent description of Huari based on several seasons of his own research. However, he focuses on three of the better-preserved architectural complexes, adding little to what Bennett had to say about Huari's total area, overall form and organization, or prehistoric population size. Only MacNeish, Patterson, and Browman (1975: 61) offer a bold new interpretation of Huari. They suggest that the site was composed of 70 to 80 walled compounds with rectangular or square outline that ranged in size from 100 m to 400 m on a side. Rectangular rooms were nested around D-shaped or circular central courts. Each large compound was the residence of a distinct group of occupational specialists, including artisans who converted imported raw materials into manufactured goods for export. The population of the ancient city is placed at a minimum of 50,000 and perhaps more than 100,000 persons. This interpretation incorporates data from unreported, albeit limited, research at Huari conducted by the Ayacucho Archaeological-Botanical Project. We must await a full description of these findings in order to evaluate the tentative interpretation, but it is not entirely consistent with field data collected by the Huari Urban Prehistory Project since 1977.

The complexity and poor preservation of Huari's architectural remains account for much difficulty interpreting the settlement's form and organization. Four factors are responsible. First, the architecture at Huari belongs to several different construction periods which cannot be differentiated easily without excavation. Second, walls with distinct prehistoric functions – retaining walls and room enclosure walls for example – are indistinguishable in surface remains. Third, Huari has been subjected to a great deal of looting which has destroyed some architectural remains, covered others, and exposed still others on the artificial surface. Looting had begun in the final years of the city's life, as its authority collapsed and the residents took flight, but it has continued until today so that the volume of earth and stone that has been moved is awesome. Fourth, and perhaps most devastating to Huari, is the impact of cultivation. Today, virtually all of Huari is dry farmed with a combination of perennial *Opuntia* cactus and annual crops that require regular plowing. This has certainly been the case for more than a thousand years and farmers have slowly altered the face of the site by picking up rocks and piling them into field boundary walls. Many ancient walls have been obliterated to the bottom of the plow zone – perhaps 50 cm – and they can be encountered only by excavation. New, dry-laid walls have been constructed. In some cases they cover old walls, but in other cases they bear no resemblance to ancient wall positions. Some long walls that seem to divide Huari into sectors can now be recognized as walled trails or roads constructed since the city was abandoned.

Sections of them are built against, or on top of, ancient walls while other sections are totally recent. All in all, the pattern which meets the eye is that described by Bennett (1953) – a haphazard pattern of confusion.

It is clear that Huari grew continuously and gradually, changing its form with each new period of construction. In some cases, old buildings were leveled and the new constructions could express neat, orderly plans. In other cases, new buildings were wedged into existing spaces so that their form had to be accommodated to existing walls, contours, and shapes that obscured the underlying plans. Certainly the organization of Huari is disorderly and complex, but it is not haphazard. The plan of the city remains to be discovered by careful study of the surface walls and extensive removal of the plow zone to reveal ancient wall tops. Perhaps an advanced form of remote sensing can provide enough information about buried walls to determine the overall order at Huari. Until this research is carried out, interpretations must remain general and somewhat speculative.

Huari possesses a heavily built-up architectural core located on the undulating and irregular top of a steep-sided ridge. This urban nucleus includes a roughly circular area of about 300 hectares that is covered by the remains of field stone walls which employed clay mortar as well as clay and lime plaster finishes. Most of this area was terraced into huge steps with more or less level surfaces. The shape of each terrace probably reflects earlier contour lines which were regularized during construction. In some cases, the stone retaining walls of the major terraces were double walls with a corridor about 2 m wide between them. None has been excavated, but the double walls may have enclosed narrow streets running in concentric patterns around a more or less circular city. Two trails of similar width, with rubble walls on either side, descend from the high center of the settlement crossing the concentric pattern streets at right angles. These also may be remnants of old streets, or they may be strictly modern.

Some very massive walls divide Huari into irregular sectors. They run parallel and perpendicular to the contours and are several meters wide; the largest is five meters thick. These field stone constructions could have served as bases for roads, or they may have separated groups or classes of people within the city. However, they do not fortify the outer edge of the community, nor are ascending steps, parapets, or other indicators of fortifications preserved on walls anywhere in Huari.

Within the city sections there were numerous building compounds defined by walled enclosures which appear to have been trapezoidal, rectangular, or square. In some cases they are located within the area of one large terrace, but in other cases the enclosures cross terrace levels to include several horizontal surfaces. Multi-level building sites must have been viewed as normal at Huari since even plastered floors of patios and rooms may have a step or two which change the surface level all the way across them.

The enclosure compounds seem to range in size from about 40 m on a side to some which are much more than 100 m in length. However, there are only a few examples with all four sides preserved, so generalizations about size and form will have to await further excavation.

Within the walled enclosures, buildings were two or three stories high. Several patterns of floor plan seem to have existed. One consists of tightly nested rooms arranged around a circular or D-shaped courtyard (MacNeish, Patterson, and Browman 1975: 61, Vescelius, personal communication). This plan has not been described in detail, and maps of such compounds have not been published. The antiquity of the pattern in Ayacucho is unknown, and its origin remains strictly hypothetical. However, the similarity of the layout to the D-shaped arrangement of rooms around sunken courts at Pucara, in the *altiplano*, seems more than coincidental. The second pattern, which may be later than the former, divides rectangular enclosures into square or rectangular patios with elongated, hall-like rooms around three or four of the patio sides. Fig. 6.2 is a map of the Moraduchayuq compound, which is now partially excavated. The plan of patio with surrounding elongated rooms is especially apparent in the north-central portion of the compound where four patios were completed with stone partition walls about 2 m inside the dividing walls on three or four of their sides. Rows of projecting stones, or corbels, set into the partitions and dividing walls were used to support upper floors in the narrow rooms arranged around open patios which measured about 8 m to 10 m on each side. The patio floors were finished with tamped earth and a layer of white plaster. At the edges were raised platforms or benches parallel to the long, narrow rooms and onto which their doors opened. The benches were usually 25 to 30 cm high and from 50 cm to 2 m wide. They were probably roofed with broad eaves which projected into the patio from the multi-storied rooms, protecting the benches from sun and rain, but leaving an ample area open for light, fresh air, and drainage. Each patio was equipped with an underground canal about 30 cm to 60 cm in height and width. The canals had small, tubular access holes that were capped with circular stones with central perforations. Rather than branching dendritically as they flowed downhill, the canals converge, which suggests a system of drains rather than a plumbing system for water distribution. However, the drains may have carried water into central cisterns for storage and eventual consumption.

The origin and antiquity of the checkerboard arrangement of patios with elongated rooms is unknown. It may not have been present at Huari before Middle Horizon 1B, when it is clearly documented. However, the similarity of this modular unit design to the patios and halls of settlements such as Viracochapampa, Pikillaqta, Jincamocco, and Jargampata is especially clear (Isbell and Schreiber 1978). It also is interesting to observe that a comparable plan may have characterized the Putuni and Kherikala at Tiwanaku, which were open patios surrounded by four halls of inter-connected rooms.

Remains from the elongated hall-like rooms around patios indicate that they were residential. Some of these narrow halls had large niches and abundant kitchen refuse while others contained few domestic remains, lacked large niches, and had caches of valuables and perhaps human burials under their carefully plastered floors. Small niches occurred in both kinds of rooms. They probably held lamps or some other burning material which helped to light the halls that generally had only two small doorways onto the patio.

Communal kitchens or recurrent facilities which might have been barrack-like dormitories are absent in the ground-floor rooms which are preserved. Consequently, it seems unlikely that the Moraduchayuq compound housed unisex, special-function groups such as soldiers or *acllas*. Rather, several small kitchens and private rooms where valuables were hidden imply that families were living in a building similar to an apartment house.

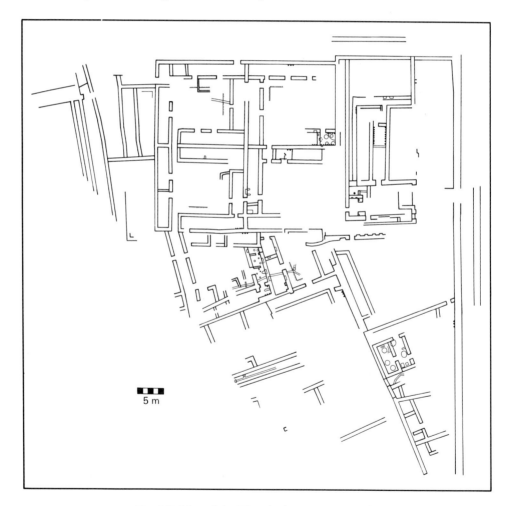

Fig. 6.2 Map of the Moraduchayuq compound.

At Moraduchayuq there is no indication of agricultural pursuits or craft specialities, although a high frequency of serving-bowls, as well as elaborate cups in one section, may reveal that the residents hosted feasts and drinking bouts. Generosity expressed through giving gifts and sponsorship of feasts and drinking bouts was expected of elite Andean administrators, so it may be that Moraduchayuq was the residence of administrative specialists. Another compound studied by Vescelius (personal communication) contained remains from ceramic production, and several unexcavated areas of Huari are known to have a high frequency of particular artifacts on the surface – for example, small quartzite projectile points, or waste "turquoise" from manufacturing.

These data could be interpreted as an indication of a high degree of occupational specialization at Huari, including both administrative specialists and craftsmen who were not involved in agriculture. However, such a conclusion is not fully justified. Stone (1978, 1979, 1981) has studied the lithic remains from about 100 collection units whose surface area totals about 40 hectares of the southern and western portion of greater Huari. She has found standardization in stone tools – which might suggest production by specialists. Furthermore, there is a heterogeneous spatial distribution of artifacts and raw material classes which also might support the notion of craft specialization. What is absent is any indication of lithic workshops, as evidenced by high concentrations of debitage. At many other ancient centers, lithic workshops are among the most common and easily identified crafts. The lack of them at Huari raises serious questions, and the general distribution of waste flakes across the site implies that at least a fair amount of stone-working was going on at the domestic level.

The size and aggregate population of prehistoric Huari is still unknown, but some data can be brought to bear on the subject. Surface surveys conducted by the Huari Urban Prehistory Project in 1977 revealed that sherds and other refuse extend far beyond the area of approximately 300 hectares which has been designated as Huari's architectural core. From the center of the core, refuse can be traced, essentially uninterrupted, for 3 km to the south and the east, about 1 km to the north, and ¾ km to the west. This implies that the Huari archaeological zone includes an area of 1,000 to 1,500 hectares.

Stylistic seriation of Huari ceramics, and other means of chronological control, are not developed sufficiently to permit determination of the relative frequency of refuse by periods in the Huari surface collections. Only a small proportion of diagnostic sherds can be assigned to brief time periods. Stratigraphic excavations in trash middens have begun to correct the situation but many problems remain to be solved. This means that it is still impossible to make accurate evaluations of what areas of Huari were occupied at what times. In very general terms, the eastern extreme of Huari was occupied in the Early Horizon, and more intensively in the Early Intermediate Period. However, little trash accumulated there during the Middle Horizon. One section in

Table 1 *Huari surface collections*

Sherds per m^2	Population per hectare	Sample area in hectares	Estimated population (minimum–maximum no. persons)
.2–2	2–10	4.98	10–50
2–20	10–25	17.71	177–443
20–100	25–50	12.32	308–616
100–200	50–100	1.45	73–145
200+	100–200	1.75	175–350
		Total 38.21	743–1,604

the southeast has only Early Intermediate Period refuse, while in the west, Early Intermediate Period trash underlies pottery of Middle Horizon 1, but Epoch 2 pottery is not abundantly represented. Along the northern margin of Huari, pottery of Epochs 1 and 2 lies stratified above bedrock, although Bennett found Early Intermediate Period ceramics underlying similar pottery in his excavation number 4 (Bennett 1953). Most of the architectural core of Huari yields scarce Early Intermediate Period pottery and much more abundant sherds of Middle Horizon 1 and 2.

If there is a direct relationship between the density of sherds on the surface of a prehistoric settlement, and its past population density, as proposed by surveyors of the Valley of Mexico (Blanton 1972, Parsons 1971, Sanders 1965), then some very tentative estimates of Huari's prehistoric population can be made. It seems reasonable to suppose that at least one-half to one-third of the site was occupied during the Middle Horizon when the city was at its peak. An estimate of 500 occupied hectares is certainly not excessive.

Sherds have been collected from about 100 surface units on the southern margin of Huari, outside the architectural core of the site. Ceramic densities have been calculated, and if population conversion figures employed in the Valley of Mexico survey are modified as indicated on Table 1 to reflect the fact that Huari was an intensely occupied urban area, a summary of the resident population on a 38.21 hectare sample of the site is available.

Table 1 indicates an average density of between 19.5 and 42 persons per hectare in the southern margin of greater Huari. If this average is attributed to all of Huari during its population peak, the city of 500 hectares should have had a population of between 9,715 and 20,985 persons.

This figure of 10,000 to 20,000 inhabitants at Huari is acceptable, although it may be quite conservative. It is likely that the architectural core of the city was more densely occupied than the outer margins – although the core must also have included unoccupied public spaces. Data from the Moraduchayuq compound and the Cheqo Wasi sector may be instructive. Moraduchayuq covers about half a hectare, so it could be considered to have had between ten and twenty residents by the density average established above. However, this seems extremely low in view of the fact that the compound includes at least six patios with multi-storied elongated rooms around each side. For the sake of this discussion, let us assume that the long, narrow rooms around patios were residential, and only residential, and that they were only two stories high. Let us also assume that all the other rooms and enclosures at Moraduchayuq possessed non-residential functions. In that case, the floor space of roofed, residential rooms was about 1,200 m^2. If 10 m^2 are allowed per person, the floor area suggests a population in the neighborhood of 120 inhabitants in .5 hectares. On the other hand, excavations at Cheqo Wasi by Mario Benavides (1979) have revealed an area of architectural remains comparable to Moraduchayuq in size but there are no patios surrounded by elongated rooms, and little evidence of occupation. Rather, Benavides found a series of dressed stone boxes enclosed by field-stone walls. Surely this area had few residents and its principal function was ceremonial, most likely some sort of mortuary monument.

If the residential density of multi-story habitation compounds was about 240 persons per hectare and the architectural core of the city was evenly divided between residential and public space, the population density of the core was about 120 persons per hectare. If, at its peak, one-third of Huari's 500 hectares was architectural core, and two-thirds was residential margin, and a density of 120 persons per hectare is presumed in the core, as compared with 19.5 to 42 persons per hectare in the periphery, the population of Huari may have ranged between 20,650 and 34,000 inhabitants.

These two estimates show that Huari is a huge archaeological zone, and that in the past it possessed a large resident population. Although the MacNeish, Patterson, and Browman (1975: 61) estimate of 50,000 to 100,000 inhabitants cannot be accepted, and it appears that they also overestimated the degree of occupational specialization, Huari was a large city whose citizens carried out a range of administrative and ceremonial activities as well as crafts.

Carlos Ponce Sanginés (1969, 1971, 1972, 1979) has stated that Tiwanaku possessed an inhabited area of 420 hectares, but he has not discussed his data base, or attempted to determine how much of the site was occupied at one time. He has simply estimated the prehistoric population of Tiwanaku at about 100,000 and claimed a high degree of occupational specialization for the residents. Since these interpretations lack supporting evidence from surface collections or excavations in residential areas, they cannot be given a great deal of credence. Authors who have considered Tiwanaku to have been larger, more populous, more advanced, and more influential than Huari during the Middle Horizon must re-examine the information available from both sites.

There can be no doubt that Huari and Tiwanaku share common cultural attributes and that some kind of interaction took place between the two. Several lines of evidence indicate that the first exchange occurred at the end of Tiwanaku III or the beginning of Tiwanaku IV in the Tiwanaku chronological scheme proposed by Ponce Sanginés (1971, 1972) and at the beginning of Middle Horizon 1 in the Huari chronological scheme employed by Menzel (1964, 1968, 1977). However, significantly complex socio-political adaptations had been achieved in both areas before the exchange, and it is essential that we understand these antecedent cultural systems if we are to understand the exchange.

Little is known about Tiwanaku and the southern *altiplano* cultures during the Tiwanaku I and II periods. However, Tiwanaku III, best dated between AD 100 and 500, witnessed the growth of a centralized and hierarchical theocracy with its capital at the Tiwanaku site. At least two lines of evidence support this interpretation.

At the end of Tiwanaku II, or beginning of Tiwanaku III, a semi-subterranean temple was constructed in what was to become the northeast corner of Tiwanaku's monumental civic center. This temple was dedicated with a stylistically early statue, stele 15, which Bennett (1934: figs. 31–2) called the "Bearded Statue." Within the same Tiwanaku III period, but probably subsequent to the construction of the semi-subterranean temple, three other monuments were erected at Tiwanaku. The Kalasasaya and Pumapuncu were both stone-faced earthern mounds, each covering more than a hectare. They possessed rectangular outlines and flat tops. Access to the top was through one or more megalithic gateways placed in the east wall of the platform. Immediately behind the gateway was a rectangular court sunken into the elevated surface of the mound. Like the semi-subterranean temple, each court probably was dedicated with a monolithic statue. Considering the sunken courts in the east-central end of both the Kalasasaya and Pumapuncu, their form can best be described as U-shaped platforms with the open ends toward the east. The third monument which completed the major buildings in Tiwanaku's civic center was the Akapana, another earthen mound covering almost three hectares that rose in a series of stone-faced steps to an elevation of 15 m above its base.

The labor invested in Tiwanaku's civic center monuments during Period III was immense. However, Period III pottery does not appear in all the excavations reported from Tiwanaku so it is unlikely that the residential area exceeded 30 hectares, a community which probably did not surpass a total population of about 3,000 individuals. Consequently, the labor pool available for construction must have included the inhabitants of many other settlements.

The second line of evidence for a centralized, hierarchical theocracy at Tiwanaku comes from the distribution and size of other temple monuments in the southern *altiplano*. Tiwanaku possessed at least four ceremonial buildings of great size. Only 12 km from Tiwanaku, at Qallamarca, a smaller temple similar to the Kalasasaya was built during Tiwanaku III. On the shores of Lake Titicaca, 20 km away, another ceremonial building similar to Tiwanaku's semi-subterranean temple has been described at Chiripa, and a third example of Period III ceremonial architecture may be the Kalasasaya-like platform at Wankani (Ponce Sanginés 1972). These seem to represent second-order ceremonial centers, smaller than and dependent on the supreme religious authority and the ceremonial splendor of Tiwanaku. Both Mujica Barreda (1981) and Ponce Sanginés (1972) list what may be smaller ceremonial centers at Pukuru-uyu and Mocachi, still farther from Tiwanaku. There might be third-order ceremonial centers in a hierarchical structure whose solar locational pattern suggests a three-level administrative structure focused on Tiwanaku. Secondary centers surrounded the capital at a distance of 10 km to 20 km and controlled the flow of information, and perhaps goods, services, and personnel between the capital and the minimal communities. However, it is unlikely that Tiwanaku's theocracy concerned itself with many domains of life since there is no evidence for a large bureaucracy. During Tiwanaku III there were no palaces or comparable residential facilities at the capital site that could have housed great numbers of administrators. Small rooms have been found on the terraces of the Akapana, and there is a row of rooms about 2 m square along both sides of the sunken court of the Kalasasaya. These might have been the quarters, and/or offices, of priestly administrators, but the small number and size of these rooms makes it unlikely that there were more than a few dozen individuals occupying such positions of authority, even at the Tiwanaku capital itself.

Political and religious organization in the Ayacucho Valley appears to have followed an evolutionary trajectory very different from that of the *altiplano* and Tiwanaku. In the Early Horizon several temple platforms were constructed and the distribution of settlements suggests a simple theocratic organization which may not have exceeded two structural levels.

Settlement studies conducted in the Ayacucho Valley by R. S. MacNeish (1981) divide the Early Intermediate Period into only two phases. The earlier one, Huarpa, is dated from 200 BC until AD 200, while the second, the Ocros Phase, is dated from AD 200 to 700 (see Benavides 1965).

Studies at Huari show that the black-on-white pottery characteristic of the Huarpa Phase continued in use into the beginning of the Middle Horizon – at least until AD 600 in absolute time. Conversely, Ocros pottery, an orange slipped ware often decorated with polychrome designs, probably did not appear until Early Intermediate Period 7–8, which would place its earliest manifestation at around AD 400 to 450. This means that the Huarpa period was really much longer than the MacNeish (1981) chronology allows, and that some sites from the beginning of the Middle Horizon probably have been mistaken for two component occupations because of the co-occurrence of Huarpa and Ocros pottery. Consequently, the seemingly vast number of sites and large population indicated for the Ayacucho Valley during Huarpa times may be an artifact of the abbreviated timespan assigned to the phase and the incorrect inclusion of some sites. Furthermore, marked population growth at the end of the Early Intermediate Period is probably obscured by allowing 500 years for the Ocros Phase rather than 250 to 300 years.

The settlement system of Early Intermediate Period Ayacucho reveals some fascinating features. The most surprising is the virtual disappearance of plat-form pyramids. The second is the lack of complexity in the settlement hier-archy. While Tiwanaku and other areas such as the North Coast built more monumental ceremonial centers, and moved progressively toward a three-level ritual hierarchy, Ayacucho embarked upon a different organizational direction. It may be that Ayacucho was experimenting with indigenous non-Chavín organizational potentials.

During the Huarpa and Ocros phases, no single settlement in Ayacucho dis-tinguished itself as the capital of a valley-wide state. None possesses enough public architecture to imply control of all the labor in the valley. None had a population so large that a valley-wide tribute base would be indicated. Rather, there were numerous settlements of similarly large size and relatively few small ones. Isbell and Schreiber (1978: fig. 4) document only two settlement-size modes for Ayacucho during the Early Intermediate Period, and large settlements are actually more common than small ones. This situation might be explained as a balance achieved among a number of chiefdoms which were held in check by endemic warfare. The small communities would have been dependent on chiefs in larger settlements but their relative scarcity would reflect the strong selective pressures of warfare. However, Early Intermediate Period communities were not fortified. They were not located in highly defens-ible positions; nor are there other indices of conflict. In fact, many of the largest settlements are located in clusters, within a few kilometers of one another, so peaceful conditions must have been the norm.

The largest communities in Ayacucho were located in the most productive portions of the valley. However, the concentration of towns makes it very unlikely that such large populations could be supported on the limited acreage surrounding each settlement. Rather, the inhabitants of the towns must have received products from more distant areas of production, but without the benefits of monumental temples that might have served as nodes in an exchange network, and without a regional administrative hierarchy which controlled all the resource zones. A collaborative, relatively peaceful economic adaptation seems to have been achieved with a minimum of political cen-trality, not exceeding that of a complex chiefdom.

Improbable as this reconstruction of Early Intermediate Ayacucho society seems, it sounds like the pre-state antecedent of vertical archipelago economics which Murra (1972) has identified as a uniquely Andean pattern of organization and resource exploitation, although Murra's description of the 16th-century highland Chupaychu and Lupaqa economic pattern is based on the organization of these polities during Inca times. It is clear that neither monumental ceremonial centers nor an ultimate state authority was necessary for the system to function. The principal feature of the system was the existence of an ethnic capital with exclusive resources in its immediate area, whose members also employed more distant resource zones. Access to the various resources was shared and exploitation of distant areas was achieved by colonists from many capitals who often resided and worked in multi-ethnic, special-function settlements. Somehow, the products of the various resource zones were pooled and redistributed within each ethnic group without the territorial organization or compulsory powers of a state administration. By an ill-understood mechanism, which probably involved more or less symmetrical exchange of colonists, relative peace was maintained among complementary ethnicities.

Early Intermediate Period sites in Ayacucho may represent ethnic capitals as well as special resource exploitation communities in particular environmental zones. Multi-ethnic communities would help to explain the relative homogeneity of Ayacucho ceramics in the absence of valley unification under a single authority. The large and almost adjacent communities in peaceful contexts can be explained, although colonies of Ayacucho groups in more distant locations should be identified.

The strongest candidate for an Ayacucho colony in a distant and distinct ecological zone comes from the coastal Nasca Valley during Early Intermediate Period 7 and 8 – the final epochs of the period. Paulsen (1980) has shown that circular stone buildings reported by Strong (1957) at Huaca del Loro and Tres Palos II, as well as Pacheco, are derived from Ayacucho, and that the Nasca pottery of late Epoch 7 and Epoch 8 found at Huaca del Loro was coming under Ayacucho influence as well. These three settlements are located on major tributaries of the Nasca drainage, forming a straight line parallel to the coast near the 500 m contour. It is likely that all were on upper-to-lower-valley roads, but also at the point where they were crossed by a north–south coastal highway. Selection of such strategic locations by the Ayacucho colonists shows that their interest may have been extending beyond the peaceful exploitation of coastal lands by migrants. A step already may have been taken toward converting cooperative colonization into empire.

This reconstruction suggests that by AD 400 Tiwanaku had developed a centralized, hierarchical, and theocratic organization with continuous territory extending at least 50 to 60 km from the capital city. On the other hand, the Ayacucho Valley was organized into several secularly administered, multi-ethnic, special-resource exploitation communities in a number of distinct ecological zones. It would seem that a system of colonization in distant areas had been developed at least by Early Intermediate Period 7 and that by that time the Ayacucho colonies in the Nasca Valley might have anticipated the kind of control of periphery resource areas that characterizes empires.

At the end of Tiwanaku III, or beginning of Tiwanaku IV, a new set of religious icons appeared at Tiwanaku (D. Wallace 1957). At roughly the same time, the same set of figures appeared at Conchopata, an Ayacucho Valley settlement only 10 km from Huari (Menzel 1964). In its full expression, this new iconography, which I shall refer to as Tiahuanacoid iconography, included a number of themes. The principal theme is a standing human figure viewed front-face. The arms are raised to shoulder height and spread widely. Each hand grasps a staff or similar object. The head is adorned with an elaborate headdress which includes two or more stalk-like projections that terminate in animal heads. An elegant necklace or collar also adorns the front-face deity, and it seems that there are two variants of this mythical being. One wears a long shirt which is belted at the waist while the second wears an unbelted garment (Cook 1979). Menzel (1964, 1968, 1977) described this deity and discussed the belted and unbelted variants found at Pacheco as male and female.

In especially elaborate scenes the front-face deity is shown in its full or abbreviated form with an angel, or one or more rows of angels, to its right and to its left. Generally, the angels face the deity. In the most simplified examples of Middle Horizon iconography one or two elements, such as a geometricized version of the angel's profile head, appear alone or as repeated figures in band or panel decorations.

Several other icons occur in Tiahuanacoid styles along with the front-face deity and attendant angels. They include a feline which is sometimes depicted in a very realistic manner. Another is a mythical animal with the head and body of a bird but which may have two or four legs with human or feline characteristics. Third is a staff or band with head and other animal features. In some cases it has a head at each end while in others it has a head, tail, and legs which make it so similar to the feline or bird that it may not be a separate icon at all.

A large number of specific features, or minimal iconographic units, also distinguishes the Tiahuanacoid style. One of the most frequent is the interlocking meander band which generally surrounds the head of the front-face deity. Depictions of eyes usually have circular or geometric shapes. They are divided vertically into two color zones which are typically black and white. A design which may be quite elaborate encircles and hangs from eyes of mythical creatures. Zoomorphic heads project from the headdresses of the principal icons but also from the feet and wings of the angels. Generally the bases of these heads have a rectilinear meander design like an "S" which appears to represent the neck joint. The limbs of many of the figures, but especially the angels, are shown with bone-like interior structures. Noses are depicted as rings or other geometric shapes. Interlocking, salient canines are common in the mouths of the mythical figures, especially the earlier ones, and in numerous cases they are depicted as an "N" with the tips of the canines not projecting beyond the row of teeth. When the hands are shown grasping some object, it is common to see the thumb or thumbnail projecting beyond the line of the knuckles. Staffs and other bands may terminate in a "fan" with oval base and three or four projecting fillets. Finally, the iconographic constellation is replete with trophy heads. They are found dangling from hands, bound to elbows, or at the base of staffs, although staffs may also terminate in headless bodies or complete human figures with bound arms.

Tiahuanacoid iconography is found in a variety of media. The most impressive is monumental stone sculpture which is limited to Tiwanaku and south *altiplano* sites. The icons occur on anthropomorphic sculptures in the round, but they are never the principal themes for the sculptures. Rather, they are incised with fine lines on the torsos and heads of the figures as though they represent decorations on the woven apparel of the principal person.

Tiahuanacoid icons also occur on sculpted façades of Tiwanaku's buildings, such as the Gate of the Sun. In these examples a combination of fine line incision and low-relief *champlave* were employed to provide a two-dimensional effect very reminiscent of a woven wall hanging.

Polychrome-painted and, in some regions, press-molded decorations on ceramics are the second most visible media of Tiahuanacoid icons. These are found north of the *altiplano*. A Middle Horizon 1B cache of oversize, human effigy pots from Conchopata, Ayacucho shows that the Tiahuanacoid figures are represented on the garments of the persons (Cook 1979). Consequently, representations of Tiahuanacoid icons in sculpture and ceramic decoration may both be secondary media derived from fancy, woven apparel.

Textiles with Tiahuanacoid motifs are found in burials from the arid coast of Peru and Chile, and less frequently in the highlands where they have been preserved in dry caves (Conklin 1970, Sawyer 1963, Wassén 1972). The most frequent finds are poncho-like shirts of dyed wool produced with a tapestry technique. Obviously, they belong to an ancient highland technical tradition and are the antecedents of Inca shirts. Head bands and square hats with peaked corners are also common, and occasionally large sheets with tapestry or painted designs are found, such as the example discovered at Pachacamac by Uhle (1903: fig. 1a–e).

Tiahuanacoid figures are found on carved wood and carved bone where dry conditions insure good preservation. In the southern, Tiwanaku sphere, the most common wood artifacts are shallow trays employed in ritual snuffing of hallucinogenic powders believed to have been manufactured from seeds of the *Anadenanthera*. Bone artifacts include snuffing tubes. Curiously, these snuff trays are virtually unknown north of the *altiplano* and wooden artifacts with Tiahuanacoid designs are generally kero-shaped goblets. However, it could be that both the trays and cups were employed in taking hallucinogens, stimulants, and cures, so they may be functional equivalents of one another. The recipients of wood have not been studied in detail, but they may be very important for the history of Tiahuanacoid art. Perishable but portable artifacts of wood or woven wool seem to be vehicles far more appropriate for diffusing religious motifs than massive statues or fragile pots.

Tiahuanacoid motifs are also known from carved gourds, and luxury items of metal, shell, and semi-precious stones. Mural paintings of the figures are known from the North Coast of Peru.

There can be little doubt that Tiahuanacoid iconography belongs to a mythical tradition with its roots in late Chavín culture. The front-face deity has its origin in the staff god as depicted on the Raimondi Stone while the Tiahuanacoid attendant angels recapitulate the anthropomorphic hawk and eagle of the columns of the Black and White Portal, as well as other more human figures with and without wings from Chavín de Huántar. The arrangement of the deity, viewed front-face and flanked by a profile attendant figure on its right and left, is also found in Chavín art (Rowe 1962b: figs. 16, 9, 10, and 27).

The intermediary style between Chavín and Tiahuanacoid iconography is that of Pucara. A rather divergent front-face deity is known from ceramic designs (Rowe and Brandel 1970: figs. 14 and 17), but a small Pucara stone sculpture of the front-face deity has staffs, headdress, and other Tiahuanacoid-like attributes (Rowe 1976: lams. 15–19). Profile attendant angels are also present, carrying staffs as they do in Tiahuanacoid art, although the known examples lack wings (Rowe and Brandel 1970: figs. 4–9). Finally, trophy heads are common, and there are feline, bird, and staff-like icons as well (Rowe and Brandel 1970: figs. 20, 23, 30–5, 37, 62, and 63).

Radiocarbon dates from the type site of Pucara suggest that it was abandoned by AD 200, leaving a hiatus of two or three centuries before the diagnostic icons are likely to have appeared at Tiwanaku around AD 500. This temporal separation is also consistent with the stylistic difference between Pucara and the Tiahuanacoid icons from Tiwanaku. Only one small sculpture fragment from Tiwanaku (Créqui-Montfort 1906: fig. 11) has elements, and especially the trophy head appendages, which are very similar to those of Pucara. All other specimens seem well differentiated stylistically from Pucara antecedents, although shared features such as "N" shaped canines, belted garments, and a peculiar zig-zag design may identify a group of icons from Tiwanaku which are the earliest examples from the site. These figures include abbreviated versions of the front-face deity and angels shown in horizontal, floating positions (Posnansky 1945: vol. II, fig. 140a).

Examination of the earliest Tiahuanacoid iconography from Ayacucho, that of the elaborately decorated ceramic offering found at Conchopata by Julio Tello (Cook 1979, Menzel 1964, 1977), reveals that the Middle Horizon 1A figures of Ayacucho share more with the Tiwanaku icons on sculptures believed to be early than they do with the apparently later figures on sculptures such as the Gate of the Sun. However, the early specimens from the two areas are not so similar to one another that one set could be easily derived from the other. The most likely interpretation is that an early Tiahuanacoid iconography was derived from Pucara and gave rise almost simultaneously to the Tiahuanacoid figures of Tiwanaku and of Ayacucho.

One possible candidate for an early Tiahuanacoid art that could be ancestral to both of the better-known styles comes from a find on the eastern slopes of the Andes, adjacent to the *altiplano* (Wassén 1972). At Niño Korin the well-preserved burial of a medicine man or herbalist curer was found in a dry cave with all his ritual paraphernalia, including specimens of the plants employed. Radiocarbon dates are confusing, but two of the four suggest a date between AD 350 and 400. Among the artifacts are a wooden snuff-tablet decorated with an attendant angel that has a Pucara-like trophy head on its chest, and a basket with polychrome abbreviated front-face deity design (Wassén 1972: fig. 5, color pl. 1).

The Niño Korin site lies within the homeland of the Callahuaya Indians, famed herbalist curers who travel throughout the Andes selling their remedies. They are so important in the Ayacucho area that they are among the foreigners imitated by costumed performers in contemporary village rituals (B. J. Isbell 1978: 141). The find of the prehistoric curer's burial suggests that ancestors of the Callahuayas were making journeys throughout the Central Andes by the 4th century AD and that their ritual paraphernalia was decorated with an early form of Tiahuanacoid iconography derived from Pucara. Belief in mythical beings associated with the curing rituals could have been spread by traveling Callahuaya shamans, and if the curers distinguished themselves with clothing marked with the same beings as their ritual items, then their textiles and curing paraphernalia would have provided the artistic antecedents for Tiwanaku and Huari versions of Tiahuanacoid art. In fact, the first copies of the mythical icons might have been made to distinguish costumed performers of local origin who imitated the traveling curers in village rituals much like those of today.

The introduction of Tiahuanacoid iconography to Conchopata by traveling curers may not account for all the interactions between Ayacucho and the southern *altiplano* in Middle Horizon 1A. At Huari, near the center of the architectural core, a semi-subterranean temple has been found (Isbell and Spickard [n.d.]). It is associated with ceramics of Epoch 1A (Knobloch 1981) and has a C14 date of AD 580 ± 60 for its construction period. Unlike Tiwanaku's semi-subterranean temple, the Huari example is square, measuring 24.11 m to a side, and it is constructed of rectangular and polygonal blocks perfectly fitted to one another. Vertical ashlers characteristic of Tiwanaku are absent. It could be that the Huari temple belongs to a local tradition, or was introduced from elsewhere, although the general form and excellence of the stone work strongly imply an origin at Tiwanaku. However, traveling curers would not introduce monumental temples, so Huari's relations with Tiwanaku were probably independent of and more direct than Conchopata's.

What is clear is that the construction of a semi-subterranean temple at Huari did not initiate a Tiwanaku-like ceremonially focused theocracy into the Ayacucho area. The temple at Huari functioned for only a century or so, and secondary or tertiary ceremonial complexes of the same form are unknown. Subsequently, in Middle Horizon 1B, the semi-subterranean temple was covered and a new architectural compound was constructed over it. This compound, which may have housed administrators, possesses a form characteristic of Huari provincial administrative architecture that was widely spread throughout the Peruvian highlands in Epoch 1B (Brewster-Wray 1982, Schreiber 1978). Simultaneously, in Epoch 1B, the Ayacucho Valley began to experience a shift in settlement locations and sizes until a pattern characteristic of a hierarchical, centralized state emerged.

It appears that contact between Tiwanaku and Huari, and the construction of a semi-subterranean temple at Huari, introduced centralized, hierarchical political organization into Ayacucho rather than the old Tiwanaku religion. This novel organizational structure was combined with the secular administration of vertical archipelagos to establish what may be the first centralized secular state, and perhaps even empire, to emerge in the Andes. Tiahuanacoid iconography probably was adopted at Huari when Conchopata was annexed into the state hierarchy. The icons, which might have represented some sort of universal creator concept, were probably incorporated into the legitimization of the universal state being established by Huari.

During Epoch 1B of the Middle Horizon, Huari reorganized the peoples of the Central Andes, and it is likely that its new political power and economic practices began to convert the capital into a city. These successes can, in large part, be attributed to a brilliant administrative invention by Huari politicians, an invention that was to set a unique course for Andean civilization.

Huari administrators transformed a system of vertical archipelago economics based on reciprocal exchange among comparable units into revenue collection by the state. The essence of the new system involved the collection of labor rather than goods, and the disguise of compulsory labor for the state with all the trappings of traditional, reciprocal exchange of labor.

Labor tax is well described for the 16th-century Inca state. Maurice Godelier has called this system the "Inca mode of production."

> By compelling the peasants to come in their holiday clothes to work on the lands of the State and the Sun, by providing them with food and drink, the Incas were employing the former mode of production based on reciprocal obligations between members of local communities, where both the form and the obligation were known and understood by all; in this way they shaped new relations of production, founded on oppression and domination since the

producers had now lost part control of their labour and its product.
Godelier 1977: 188

Archaeological correlates of the "Inca mode of production" are not difficult
to identify. The house of the chief of 1,000 families of Chupachu Indians was
identified by its impressive size, number of rooms, large kitchen, copies of
Cuzco Inca ceramics, and the great number of colander sherds (Thompson
1967). These latter are especially important for they were required for the production of *chica*, maize beer, that was the appropriate drink to offer in recipro-
cation for work. Although the study of the chief's house was only partial, it is
likely that its size reflected the chief's greater storage requirements and need
for women to process food. The large kitchen was required for simultaneous
preparation of food and drink for many members of the community. Finally,
the chief must have had sufficient cooking vessels and an unusually large
number of serving vessels in which *chica* and food were distributed to persons
who had contributed labor.

At the level of the state, similar facilities were required, but in enormous
magnitude. Morris (1972a, 1974, 1978, Morris and Thompson 1970) has
shown that the Inca administrative capital of Huanuco Pampa had vast
storage facilities, huge community kitchens, residences for women involved in
preparation of food and drink, immense quantities of ceramics for service and
cooking, and barrack-like residences for citizen taxpayers who were rotated
through the capital.

Keatinge (1974) argues that an Inca-like system of labor tribute maintained
Chan Chan and the Late Intermediate Period Chimu State. In support of this
position, he notes the existence of a number of planned architectural compounds in the immediate hinterland of Chan Chan which possessed three-
sided rooms that have been interpreted as offices for administrators. Some of
these compounds contained large kitchens where food could have been prepared for entire work gangs. However, the most explicit support for his
interpretation comes from the Quebrada del Oso site, isolated in the desert
adjacent to the Chicama–Moche inter-valley canal where an outlet irrigated
extensive agricultural fields. Here, almost all the abundant surface sherds are
from bowls appropriate for serving food and drink. Clearly, the Quebrada del
Oso installation was a state facility designed to meet the state's "reciprocal"
obligations to its citizen workers by generously treating them to feasts and
drinking bouts.

Jargampata is located about 20 km from Huari, in the neighboring San
Miguel Valley, next to several hundred hectares of easily irrigated land (Isbell
1977). It includes various residential structures which appear to have been
built in a series of unplanned, room-by-room additions. A single planned compound was built in two construction periods probably beginning early in
Middle Horizon 2. It consists of a square enclosure with elongated hall-like

rooms along two sides, a double room in one end of the enclosure, a large patio, and other features common in Huari constructions. There is no evidence of domestic occupation in the compound, although a dense concentration of charcoal and bone located between the double room and the enclosure wall may have been a community kitchen. The compound seems to have been a state administrative facility in charge of agricultural production on irrigated lands. Excavations in and around the administrative compound revealed five ceramic phases. The first predated the construction of the compound, while the last postdated the collapse of Huari. The frequency of open-bowl vessel forms in the two phases was 45.8% and 39% respectively. Three intervening phases represent occupational trash deposited while the enclosure functioned as a Huari administrative compound. The frequency of open-bowl forms from these sequential deposits is 54.9%, 55.3%, and 61.9%. The corresponding frequency change was in necked jar forms, which constituted 45.8% and 49.4% of the vessel shapes in the early and late phases, but only 33.3%, 30.9%, and 26.9% of the ceramic forms in the three phases during which the installation functioned as a state-administrative unit. Excavations in residential areas revealed ceramic frequencies similar to those of the early and late phases – about 40% to 45% open bowls, 40% to 45% necked jars, and 10% to 20% rarer forms such as spoons, bottles, flasks, incurving vessels, miniature vessels, colanders, etc. This frequency distribution appears to represent normal domestic refuse. Vessel shape frequencies with 10% to 20% rare forms, but 55% to 60% open bowls, and about 25% to 30% necked jars, belong to a distinct activity set. It is clear that the activity implied involved serving a large number of persons from a smaller number of cooking pots than would be found in the case of family kitchens. The most probable explanation is feasting and drinking bouts held by state administration, and if the recipients were local people responsible for working the adjacent irrigated lands, the "Inca mode of production" is demonstrated at Jargampata during Epoch 2 of the Middle Horizon.

Huari's administrative system may have provided an antecedent to much more of the Inca state than even the "Inca mode of production." It is likely that the Inca network of provincial administrative capitals, linked by highways, with *tambo* way stations in between was developed by Huari. Investigation of Huari provincial administrative facilities is still extremely incomplete, but the data do provide a sketchy outline surprisingly similar to Inca administrative structure (Isbell and Schreiber 1978, Lumbreras 1974a, Schreiber 1978).

Three Huari governmental compounds have been identified and described. They include Jincamocco (Schreiber 1978), Viracochapampa (McCown 1945), and Pikillaqta (Sanders 1973). Spickard (1982) has shown that they share a number of architectural features with the Moraduchayuq compound at Huari, which was constructed in Middle Horizon 1B. Among the shared features are well-planned and carefully bonded foundations of entire modular units; a floorplan which emphasizes repetition of modular units in parallel rows; modular units that have patios with elongated rooms arranged serially around the courtyard; two or more stories in the elongated rooms with the upper floor supported by a single row of projecting stones, or corbels, on the interior of both walls; raised platforms of bench-like constructions against each of the elongated rooms around the patio that were probably covered by broad eaves projecting from the roofs of the rooms; walls of angular stone set in clay mortar and generally finished with a thick clay plaster and thin white facing of lime or gypsum; carefully prepared floors with layers of tamped earth and gravel fills, often with a white plaster surface; a system of drains placed under the floors; and rectangular doors and niches whose sizes varied with their functions. These similarities, plus the presence of Huari-style pottery, leave no doubt that the planned enclosures belong to a Huari provincial organization.

Jincamocco is the smallest of the three Huari provincial centers and covers about four hectares. Because of its small size, it is the most intensively excavated and Schreiber (1978) shows that it can be compared with an Inca *tambo*. Furthermore, she demonstrates that a Huari highway must have passed through Jincamocco on its way to the coast, even though actual remains of the road have not been excavated.

Viracochapampa lies 700 airline km north of Huari in the valley of Huamachuco. At the natural highland entrance to the Cajamarca Valley, and to the coastal Moche Valley, Viracochapampa possessed a strategic location appropriate for a provincial capital. Its perimeter wall enclosed an area in excess of 30 hectares, but well-preserved architecture is visible only in the central third of the enclosure where there is no evidence of continuous cultivation of the land. The modest stratigraphic cuts excavated in the ruins by McCown (1945) provide no direct evidence concerning prehistoric activities at the site.

Pikillaqta is located in Cuzco's Lucre Basin, 250 airline km southeast of Huari. It is larger than Viracochapampa, covering at least 50 hectares, and lies on the natural pass south toward the *altiplano* as well as west toward the Apurimac River and Huari. Excavations at Pikillaqta have been scant but Barreda (personal communication) has encountered Huari-style ceramics of Middle Horizon 1B. Sanders (1973) has studied and mapped the visible architecture, identifying extensive storage facilities which compare in volume with those of Huanuco Pampa, as well as barrack-like quarters for temporary residents. He concluded that the facility functioned as a garrison, even though the outer walls lack parapets, ascending steps, and other features characteristic of fortifications. More likely, Pikillaqta was like Huanuco Pampa. Its storehouses were filled with food and supplies to be distributed in return for labor tributed to the state. Some of its barracks were occupied by female specialists who prepared maize beer and feast foods in huge kitchens. Other facilities were destined for elite male administrators but most of the living space was occupied by successive work gangs engaged in paying tribute through labor. Investigations at Pikillaqta by McEwan (1979, 1980, 1981) will certainly provide new information about the activities that were carried out on the site. However, the magnitude of this Huari administrative facility, and its functions inferred from architectural forms, are both consistent with the "Inca mode of production" as Huari's chief revenue-raising device.

Viracochapampa and Pikillaqta appear to represent second-order capitals in a Huari state or empire. They can be referred to as provincial administrative centers. Jincamocco may be an example of a third-order administrative installation or *tambo*.

The distribution of Huari provincial centers never has been determined fully, so the sphere of Huari political control has been defined more on the basis of art-style distribution than direct evidence of administrative facilities. Viracochapampa and Pikillaqta may have been Huari's most distant capitals, which might explain their size. However, at the Otuzco site, 100 km farther north in Cajamarca, Huari pottery is found on the surface, and walls of a rectangular enclosure with elongated rooms on two of its sides may represent a Huari compound. About 70 km farther north, Shady and Rosas (1977) report Huari influence in the ceramics at Chota, and site survey has been far too limited to discount the possibility of administrative installations in the area. In the south, Rowe (1956) reports Huari-style pottery in the Sicuani area, about 75 km beyond Pikillaqta. However, this appears to be the frontier of the Huari style, and, near Puno, Tiwanaku pottery is found.

Between these extremes there is very little information. However, to the north of Huari, several diagnostic architectural compounds have been reported. Only 50 km away, near the town of Huanta, is Inkaraqay, or Azangaro as it is also called (Isbell and Schreiber 1978, Anders 1981). In Huancayo are Wari Willka and Calpish, while slightly north of Cerro de Pasco, near Yanahuanca, John Hyslop (personal communication) observed what may be a Huari enclosure next to the Inca highway. Following the Inca highway through Huanuco, MacNeish, Patterson, and Browman (1975: 60) report Wisajirca, which may be an important Huari regional capital near La Union. Farther north in the Callejón de Huaylas, Vescelius and Amat (personal communication) located Honco Pampa near the old Vicos Hacienda. Situated only 180 km south of Huamachuco, Honco Pampa may have been the last regional capital before reaching Viracochapampa.

Descriptions of the Huari administrative centers show that they contrast sharply with the ceremonial towns and temples of the Tiwanaku III theocracy. These latter lacked residential facilities for leaders and bureaucrats as well as for other specialists involved in food preparation. No barrack-like quarters are found, nor are there storehouses or community kitchens.

The North Coast during the Early Intermediate Period appears to have been organized along the same lines as the Tiwanaku theocracy, although Moseley (1978b: 523–4) has argued that the local system of revenue collection was like that of the Incas, and perhaps antecedent to the Inca institution. He points out that a first-order capital with huge pyramids was located in the Moche Valley, while all the valleys to the north and south possessed at least one similar but smaller pyramid complex which should represent dependent, second-order capitals. The largest pyramid at the first-order capital, Huaca del Sol, was built of columnar units, each containing adobe bricks bearing a unique kind of mark. These have been interpreted as makers' marks identifying the social group responsible for the bricks, and demonstrating that its members had paid their labor tribute, which probably included all the activities necessary to complete one modular unit of the building (Hastings and Moseley 1975). However, there is no evidence that any of these capitals had extensive storage facilities, community kitchens, specialists to prepare food and drink, or other correlates of the "Inca mode of production." Authority and power appear to have been backed by asymmetric religious obligations rather than through transformation of traditional bonds of reciprocity.

It is very unlikely that the "Inca mode of production," as described by Godelier (1977), characterized either the Tiwanaku III theocracy or the North Coast Moche polity. Rather, this system of administration and revenue collection was invented by Huari rulers about AD 600 in Middle Horizon 1. It was spread through much of the Central Andes as a result of Huari's policies of provincial reorganization, probably reaching the North Coast by that means. Subsequently, this same form of labor tribute was instigated by the Chimu and Inca states, giving Andean civilization much of its unique flavor.

Huari presence on the coast of Peru is more difficult to interpret than in the highlands. However, in keeping with the Inca analogy, provincial administrative centers are virtually absent. The Incas succeeded in controlling the coast without constructing their own costly facilities, so it must be assumed that traditional coastal patterns of revenue collection contrasted with the "Inca mode of production," and that some form of indirect administration was employed.

Menzel (1964, 1968, 1977) feels that the Robles Moqo and Atarco ceramic styles of the South Coast are so similar to the ceramic styles of Huari that they demonstrate the incorporation of the South Coast into the Huari state. It would appear that Huari began its colonizing of the Nasca Valley late in the Early Intermediate Period, and in Middle Horizon 1B took over the entire area north to Chincha and Cañete. Perhaps in Epoch 2, dominion was extended farther south, reaching the Siguas Valley (Santos Ramirez 1977). However, Feldman and Moseley (personal communication) have surveyed the hilltop settlement of El Baul in the Moquegua Valley near the Chilean border. Their discovery of Ocros- and Chakipampa-style pottery demonstrates Huari presence far to the south in Epoch 1B of the Middle Horizon. This puzzling discovery may reveal that in Epoch 1B, Huari was practicing conquest and direct rule in the highlands, conquest and indirect rule on the coast, and at the same time establishing colonial archipelagos in more distant places.

On the Central Coast, the Nieveria ceramic style of Middle Horizon 1B also indicates Huari incorporation. However, Menzel (1964, 1968, 1977) feels that, during Epoch 2, a new and independent power center appeared at Pachacamac. The basis of her argument is the appearance and marked popularity of an icon depicting a flying critter that Menzel named the "Pachacamac Griffin." Since the griffin icon was not a religious theme at Huari, Menzel felt that it revealed religious schism and the political independence of Pachacamac. However, recent excavations in the Moraduchayuq compound of Huari have revealed representations of the "Pachacamac Griffin" as well as other icons and ceramic decorations best known at Pachacamac. Consequently, the iconographic separation, religious schism, and political independence of Pachacamac must be seriously doubted. Could it be that the Moraduchayuq compound at Huari was the residence of a social group especially associated with Pachacamac and the Central Coast?

North of Pachacamac, near the mouth of the Supe Valley, is the Chimu Capac site that was visited by Max Uhle. This is perhaps the only coastal Huari settlement that may include highland style Huari administrative architecture. However, maps and detailed architectural descriptions are unavailable so its form and function remain something of a mystery.

Rafael Larco Hoyle (1948) was the first specialist in the archaeology of the North Coast to state that the area had been conquered by Huari. His studies were based on ceramic styles, but subsequent examination of shifts in settlement patterns as well as religious themes in mural painting have tended to confirm his conclusions. On the other hand, several recent scholars have emphasized continuity in North Coast ceramics, religious themes, and settlement patterns, casting doubt on the inference that Huari conquered and administered that region. More research will be required to settle this question. However, the demonstration that the "Inca mode of production" had its origin in Huari institutions, and only subsequently became an important component of North Coast, Chimu administration, shows that Huari was responsible for significant reorganization on the North Coast, whether conquest and incorporation were involved or not.

In conclusion, Huari must be granted a position of great significance in the evolution of Andean civilization. The origin of urbanism in the Andes is not yet determined, but Huari grew into a large and important city after its rise to power in the Middle Horizon. The first state has not been identified either but Huari became the seat of a hierarchical and highly centralized state government. The evolutionary process was complex and probably involved marked population growth as well as the administration of diverse economic resources located far from the capital. However, the stimulus that seems to have brought about profound changes was the introduction of, and subsequent experimentation with, an organizational structure developed at Tiwanaku. Simultaneously, a convenient set of religious beliefs with corresponding iconic symbols was also introduced into Ayacucho, and elaborated into an appropriate vehicle for an expansionist ideology.

Whether Huari was the origin of Andean urbanism and state administration or not, it was the creator of a unique technique of revenue collection and a vast administrative structure. Referred to as the "Inca mode of production" (Godelier 1977), labor was demanded of the citizens. Food and drink were given in return by the state in an imitation of reciprocal bonds among kinsmen and community members. This special system of administration gave a unique flavor to Andean civilization that lasted until its demise from European pressures of acculturation. In order to manage its financial affairs, the Huari government constructed elaborate administrative facilities that included storehouses, specialists who prepared feast foods and drink, barrack-like quarters, community kitchens, vast quantities of serving vessels, and connecting highways throughout the highlands. Huari's control of the coast is less well understood, but the appearance of the "Inca mode of production," complete with appropriate facilities in the hinterland of Chan Chan, shows that this late coastal state was based on a Huari model.

7

The Late Intermediate Period

JEFFREY R. PARSONS
&
CHARLES M. HASTINGS

SCOPE AND OBJECTIVES

This chapter makes no attempt to review all archaeological and ethnohistoric research that relates to the Late Intermediate Period. A good deal of important work is not mentioned at all in our discussion. In part this relates to limitations of space. Just as important, however, has been our decision to focus on those areas for which information is sufficiently abundant and complete so as to provide a reasonable basis for making inferences about societal organization. To this end we have selected four principal regions for discussion: 1) the Chimú domain on the North Coast; 2) the Upper Mantaro–Tarma drainage in the Central Sierra; 3) the Chillón-Rimac-Lurín valleys on the Central Coast and adjacent sierra; 4) the Upper Urubamba drainage and northern Titicaca Basin in the Southern Sierra.

We have tried to select areas which correspond to the full range of geographic diversity within the Central Andes. This is because we believe that the natural environment plays an important role in the behavior of preindustrial cultural systems, which (because of high transportation and communication costs) are closely constrained by the potentials and limitations for subsistence production of comparatively small regions. Thus, one tactic for describing and explaining cultural variability over space is to consider the natural variability within the area of concern.

For the Central Andes, this means that we should take into account examples of development in (a) the low-lying oasis valleys on the desert coastal plain, (b) the rugged intermontane valleys and high puna grasslands of the sierra, and (c) the heavily vegetated slopes and valleys in the montaña and ceja de montaña, along the humid eastern margins of the sierra. In ecological terms, the Andean sierra has come to be associated with the concept of "verticality" (Murra 1972) – a strategy of economic self-sufficiency, implemented at the household, community, or regional levels, which involves the simultaneous and direct exploitation of several different, vertically defined zones. This strategy is particularly feasible in the sierra, where local vertical relief often exceeds 2,500 m over very short horizontal distances. A diversified agricultural base, coupled with camelid herding in the high puna grasslands, means that a great variety of productive activities are viable (even though, as Winterhalder and Thomas (1978) point out, they may not always be highly productive) virtually anywhere that vegetation grows – up to the lower edge of the sterile "frost desert" at about 4,700 m elevation (Troll 1970: 33). As Rostworowski (1977b) has noted, this "vertical" sierra ecology contrasts quite markedly with the much more "horizontal" configuration of the coastal valleys. In the latter context, most agriculture is restricted to comparatively narrow bands of irrigated land on the valley floors, and the only significant complementary food production (for large, sedentary societies) is fishing along the marine littoral.

Despite our concern with the implications of environmental diversity on cultural development, we view socio-cultural stresses and constraints as the dominant determinants of cultural behavior. It follows that in order to understand cultural behavior in the Late Intermediate Period, we must investigate societal organization, utilizing ethnohistoric sources where available, but depending primarily on archaeological approaches to society. We think that some of the most productive of such approaches are those which have recognized and emphasized the regional dimension, especially in light of the degree of environmental diversity encountered at the regional level. Consequently, we have been most attracted to those data sets which offer the greatest possibilities for reconstructing spatial and chronological variability in Late Intermediate settlement systems.

Our interests stem ultimately from an overall research strategy which seeks to describe and explain prehistoric cultural evolution, both in specific regions and cross-culturally. Unfortunately, not since Steward's (1949) seminal effort more than 30 years ago have Andean archaeological data figured significantly in attempts to generalize broadly about cultural evolutionary processes. This latter objective is clearly well beyond the scope of this chapter. However, our major purposes will be achieved if we at least can suggest some of the directions in which archaeological research on the Late Intermediate Period might best move in the near future so as to become more relevant for general studies of Archaic State society.

THE NORTH COAST

Introduction

Nowhere in the Central Andes has the precolumbian past been more intensively investigated than on the Peruvian North Coast. Several generations of archaeologists have compiled an impressive literature on the prehistoric record of this lowland desert coastal plain. Here we will be primarily concerned with the character of the 15th-century Chimú state, the development of

Fig. 7.1 Sites relevant to the text.

this state after about AD 1000, and the impact of antecedent Middle Horizon organization on the evolutionary trajectory of the Chimú socio-cultural system. Our main emphasis will be on the comparatively well-studied Chimú core area between Virú and Lambayeque, although we will also consider the significance of more fragmentary evidence from the three or four valleys south of Virú and from the Pariñas-Chira area to the north.

Chan Chan: the Chimú capital

The nucleated core of Chan Chan covers an area of about 6 km^2 (Keatinge and Day 1973: 278, Moseley and Mackey 1974: 1, Moseley 1975b: 220). Its population variously has been placed at between 25–30,000, on the basis of a provisional room count (Moseley 1975b: 223), and a minimum of 68–69,000, on the basis of a generalized appraisal of the abundance of domestic architecture (Day 1974: 187, West 1970: 84).

Very significant progress has been made in inferring some aspects of the use of space within Chan Chan. The Chan Chan–Moche Valley Project (e.g., Keatinge and Day 1973, Day 1974, Moseley 1975b, Moseley and Day 1982) has demonstrated a hierarchy of architectural units within Chan Chan which may reasonably be associated with a three-tier social hierarchy. Several investigators (Conrad 1981, Andrews 1974, Keatinge and Day 1973) have argued convincingly that the nine great compounds were built sequentially by successive Chimú rulers, and that they combined the functions of royal entombment, elite residence, centralized storage, and closely administered redistribution. In particular, the role of distinctive U-shaped buildings in controlling access to storerooms throughout Chan Chan seems undeniable and highly significant. These structures, together with their offertory caches of exotic artifacts and sacrificed humans and camelids, appear to manifest a distinctly state-level component of Chimú polity which can be traced widely in space, and whose distribution can be used to approximate the regional extent of Chimú imperial control.

Finds of spindle whorls and metal-working tools in archaeological contexts (e.g., Moseley and Mackey 1973: 328) are highly suggestive that many craft specialists lived and worked in the non-elite sectors of Chan Chan (Topic 1982: 161–5). For many years several concentrations of scoria within the center were taken as evidence for large-scale metal-smelting. However, chemical analyses (Lechtman and Moseley 1975) have shown conclusively that this scoria was not produced by metal-smelting, or by any other purposive productive activity. It is likely, as Moseley and Mackey (1973: 329) suggest, that manufacturing at Chan Chan was not of the large-scale variety which the scoria deposits had once seemed to imply.

A still unresolved dimension of Chan Chan's development is its areal extent and configuration at various stages during the several centuries of its existence. For most purposes, Chan Chan can still be discussed only synchronically. The time of Chan Chan's initial foundation is still not firmly established (e.g., Moseley 1978a: 8, Menzel 1977: 23, Donnan and Mackey 1978: 219). Our inclination is to regard as very suspect any claims for significant occupation at Chan Chan much before about AD 1000.

Chan Chan's end point is somewhat easier to deal with. The site is known to have been occupied only partially, or perhaps even largely abandoned, by the time of initial Spanish contact in 1532 (Moseley and Mackey 1973: 320, Moseley 1975b: 39). Both documentary and archaeological evidence clearly indicate that the center played a distinctly secondary role after the Inca Conquest in about 1470 (Andrews 1974: 262, Conrad 1977).

The Chimú heartland: the Moche Valley

It seems probable that there was only a limited Late Intermediate population residing outside Chan Chan in the Moche Valley. Although the regional settlement data are still incompletely presented, our understanding is that there are only some six or seven significant Late Intermediate rural sites in the Moche Valley (Keatinge and Day 1973, Keatinge 1974, 1975, Donnan and Mackey 1978). Three of these sites were walled compounds whose architectural features (including U-shaped buldings) clearly denote close linkages to the Chan Chan elite. These three sites are found rather widely and evenly distributed, always in close association with irrigation canals and fields of the same period. These characteristics, together with the apparent absence of permanent household residence and suggestions of communal kitchens, provide the basis for Keatinge's (1974) argument that the three sites represent rural administrative centers which facilitated the operation of state-controlled hydraulic works by means of periodic concentrations of laborers in sparsely settled areas. (For a radically different view, however, see Farrington 1978.)

The other four Moche Valley rural sites are agricultural communities, the largest of which (Cerro de la Virgen) is estimated to have contained some 1,000 persons (Keatinge 1975: 217). These settlements are distributed rather evenly throughout the valley, probably in order to facilitate direct access to all agricultural lands. In contrast to the three rural administrative centers, these agricultural settlements provided full-time residence for households, and are architecturally very similar to non-elite sectors of Chan Chan itself.

Frankly, we are puzzled about why there seem to be so few Late Intermediate rural settlements and such a small Moche Valley rural population. *If we can assume that all significant sites have been located and reported*, then we must be dealing with a highly structured regional system, tightly controlled by the central authority at Chan Chan. The fact that S. Pozorski's (1979: 179) analysis of plant remains from Cerro de la Virgen suggests a strong preoccupation with cotton production might imply some degree of agricultural

specialization in rural communities. This in turn implies a centralized redistributional network linking different kinds of rural agricultural specialists
with Chan Chan. The carefully controlled storehouse complexes in the capital
take on great significance in this regard.

It is interesting that S. Pozorski (1979: 179–80) has found little evidence for
the consumption of camelids in the middens of Moche Valley rural sites. This
seems to contrast strongly with the comparatively camelid-rich diet of non-
elite Chan Chan residents. This contrast may reflect the less effective partici-
pation of rural people in the redistributional networks focused on the Chan
Chan elite. It may also mean that camelid production in the Chimú domain
was managed and controlled directly and exclusively by the Chan Chan elite
– not surprisingly, in view of the difficulty in securing adequate pasturage in
a desert zone where the primary grazing lands were along canals and in the
fallow fields of intensively irrigated areas directly managed by the state.

Furthermore, we must be dealing with a Moche Valley regional system
which is quite small in terms of overall population size. If Chan Chan contained about 30,000 persons, then there may have been fewer than 35,000 in
the entire Moche Valley during the Late Intermediate Period. The Moche
Valley settlement system was thus extraordinarily top-heavy. There must have
been many food producers residing within Chan Chan. Almost certainly the
sunken fields that cluster so tightly around the capital (Parsons and Psuty
1975) were cultivated by urban people. The briefly mentioned (e.g., Keatinge
1975: 217) tiny Late Intermediate sites scattered throughout the Moche
Valley may represent temporary encampments of urban residents during
periods of intensive agricultural activity.

The Chimú domain: south (Virú to Huarmey) and north (Chicama to Lambayeque)

Although the details are still very sketchy, there is some additional suggestion
that the Late Intermediate population decline observed in Virú (Willey 1953:
297, 395) may be more generally characteristic of the southern North Coast
as a whole. For one thing, David Wilson's (1980, personal communication)
recently completed survey in the nearby Santa Valley indicates a comparable
decline. Similarly, both Proulx (1973a: 6, 1973b: 66) in Nepeña, and
Thompson (1964b: 97) in Casma, comment on the probable decline of Late
Intermediate sites and population after an impressive Middle Horizon peak.

In the large valleys of the northern half of the Chimú domain (Chicama to
Lambayeque), available evidence suggests population stability, or even expansion, relative to the Middle Horizon. Large Late Intermediate sites are numerous, especially in Jequetepeque and Lambayeque (e.g., Schaedel 1951,
Ubbelohde-Doering 1967, Trimborn 1973, 1979, Keatinge 1977a, 1977b,
1978, 1982, Keatinge and Conrad 1983). In particular, Keatinge's (1982)

briefly reported Jequetepeque survey suggests a build-up of Late Intermediate occupation there on a scale seemingly without parallel to the south of Moche. However, it also appears that some (most?) of this build-up was in areas newly colonized through massive irrigation projects constructed and centrally administered by the Chimú state (Eling 1978: 413, Keatinge 1977b: 5, 1982: 220). As in the Moche Valley itself, we may be dealing with a situation in the large northern valleys in which Late Intermediate settlement is closely tied to a centrally managed hydraulic network.

It appears that provincial administrative centers with direct links to Chan Chan existed in all valleys within the Chimú domain. This has been best demonstrated at Farfán in the Jequetepeque Valley and Chuquitoy Viejo in Chicama, where recent work (Keatinge 1977a, 1977b, 1982, Moseley 1978b: 533, Keatinge and Conrad 1983, Conrad 1977) has demonstrated close architectural parallels with Chan Chan that are best understood as manifestations of direct control by the capital center. The strategic location of both sites also is suggestive of their role as nodes in the Chimú administrative hierarchy.

U-shaped structures and small walled compounds resembling those at Chan Chan, Farfán, and Chuquitoy Viejo also have been reported at much more modest sites in Virú (the V-124 site – Collier 1955: 97–8), Nepeña (Collier 1955: 98, Proulx 1973a: 6, 1973b: 68), and possibly in Casma (Collier 1955: 98). It is likely that, like Farfán and Chuquitoy Viejo, these sites are manifestations of Chimú provincial administration at the height of Chan Chan's influence. Their small size relative to Farfán and Chuquitoy Viejo probably reflects the comparatively marginal role of the southern North Coast valleys in the Chimú domain. There certainly is no indication, anywhere south of Moche, of the impressive build-up of irrigation canals and large sites which characterizes the Late Intermediate occupation in the Jequetepeque and Lambayeque drainage.

Aside from Farfán and Chuquitoy Viejo, large Late Intermediate settlements are known at Pacatnamú (*c.* 100 hectares) and Gallito Ciego (*c.* 25 hectares) in Jequetepeque (Keatinge 1978: 30, 1982: 213), and at Purgatorio (Tucume), Chotuna, Apurlec, and possibly Pampa Grande in the Lambayeque drainage (Trimborn 1973, 1979, Day 1975: 8). In marked contrast to Farfán, Chuquitoy Viejo, V-124, etc., most of these sites (excepting only Gallito Ciego) appear to have had long occupations dating back continuously to Middle Horizon and even Early Intermediate times. Furthermore, they generally lack the distinctive architectural features (such as U-shaped buildings and storerooms) so closely associated with centralized administration at Chan Chan (although such architectural forms apparently are anticipated at Pampa Grande in Middle Horizon times (Day 1975: 9–10). Instead, numerous large pyramidal platforms (which are not abundant at Chan Chan) are often the outstanding architectural features.

Although they remain very poorly understood, there seems little doubt that such long-occupied sites as Pacatnamú, Apurlec, Chotuna, and Tucume were functionally quite distinct from Chan Chan, on the one hand, and newly founded imperial provincial administrative centers (such as Farfán, Chuquitoy Viejo, etc.), on the other. Keatinge (1977a) has argued convincingly that Pacatnamú played a distinctly ceremonial role in the Chimú regional hierarchy. It is possible that places like Pacatnamú, Apurle, Chotuna, and Tucume represent older, established capitals of small regional states which were incorporated into the Chimú domain at some point in the Late Intermediate Period. For whatever reasons, the Chimú authorities seemingly did not choose to base their provincial administration at these older capitals, but preferred to build new centers, presumably at localities more strategic to their own concerns (which probably included management of greatly expanded hydraulic networks).

Rowe (1948a: 32, 34) long ago argued, largely on the basis of ethnohistoric sources, that Chimú domination extended north to south along the Peruvian coast from Tumbez to the Chillón River. Archaeologically there is little good indication of significant Chimú impact south of Supe or north of Lambayeque. The massive fortress-like site of Paramonga, at the mouth of the Fortaleza Valley, is sometimes cited as the southernmost outpost of Chimú authority (e.g., Bushnell 1956: 116). However, we know of no good evidence for Chimú presence at that site. Late Chimú pottery is, however, reported in the nearby Supe Valley (Strong, Willey, and Corbett 1943: 196), and also at the Infantas site in the lower Chillón (Stumer 1954b: 117–18). Chimú pottery also occurs, in a ceremonial context, at the Pachacamac center in the lower Lurín (Keatinge 1978: 38–9). The significance of this Chimú material on the Peruvian central coast, where it occurs unaccompanied by any other evidence for Chimú presence (such as architectural features that are found from the Casma Valley northward), remains questionable. We suspect that it reflects the ritual or economic realm more than the political domain.

In the far north, Lothrop's (1948: 65) work in the Chira Valley suggests a decidedly limited Chimú impact. It is likely that the great Sechura desert wasteland to the north of Lambayeque constituted an effective barrier to the easy expansion of hydraulically based Chimú civilization. Ecuadorian spondylus shell obviously moved in substantial quantities into offertory caches at major Chimú centers. However, the absence of important Chimú centers on the far northern coast of Peru suggests that such movement was waterborne, as it was at the time of initial Spanish contact (Lothrop 1932).

Ethnohistoric sources (Rowe 1948a) and archaeological data (Thompson 1973a: 368, 1976: 100, Topic and Topic 1978: 618) suggest rather clearly that there was little significant Chimú control of the adjacent sierra to the east. On the other hand, preliminary observations of a major build-up of Late Intermediate occupation along strategic routes in the upper Moche drainage

(Topic and Topic 1978) are suggestive of some Chimú impact, of a less direct sort, in the Northern Sierra. There can be little doubt that Chan Chan, and probably other major Late Intermediate coastal centers, obtained large quantities of raw materials from the highlands (e.g., some of the metal ores and wool yarn needed for craft production). Nevertheless, the absence of Chimu administrative centers in the highlands, and the paucity of Chimú-related pottery in upland areas, suggest that highland products were controlled and acquired in a much different way than were coastal materials by the Chimú state.

Hydraulic agriculture and Chimú geopolitics

In the Moche Valley, canal building on a comparatively large scale dates back into the early phases of the Early Intermediate Period (Moseley 1978a: 29, Farrington and Park 1978: 256). During the early Late Intermediate, additional canals were constructed in the lower Moche Valley, with particular emphasis upon previously uncultivated plains to the north and east of Chan Chan. A disastrous flood during the early 12th century (Nials *et al.* 1979a: 5) apparently destroyed a large section of the network. Nevertheless, repairs were carried out and expansion continued. By the mid 13th century, a number of canals within the Moche Valley had reached their maximal length, and the massive (84 km) Chicama–Moche inter-valley canal had been built. During this same period there are good indications that intra- and inter-valley canals of comparable magnitude were being constructed in the Jequetepeque and Lambayeque drainages (Eling 1978, Keatinge 1982).

The construction, maintenance, and regulation of water-flow through large-scale canal networks in a desert environment have a series of important implications for Chimú economic and political organization. We noted earlier the settlement pattern data which indicated centralized administration of canal and field operations in the Moche and Jequetepeque valleys. Also notable is a pattern of continuous opening up of new agricultural fields in previously uncultivated areas. This can be related to certain environmental factors – e.g., the encroachment of dunes in the southern Moche Valley and, possibly, subtle tectonic tilting and uplift which reversed or reduced old canal gradients to the point that effective water-flow could not be maintained (Ortloff, Moseley, and Feldman 1982: 575–6). We also strongly suspect that the emphasis on irrigating new lands may be related to the reduction of fertility through salt accumulation in old fields, much as was the case in the arid plains of southern Mesopotamia (Jacobsen and Adams 1958).

For whatever reasons such new terrain was developed, the practice obviously required great labor inputs for building canals of ever-increasing length. It is unlikely that any group or institution apart from the state itself would have been able to recruit and manipulate the human labor necessary for such massive construction projects. Such canal-building also would have necessitated great engineering competence to achieve the proper gradients and cross-sectional forms. The fact that such competence generally was achieved (Ortloff, Moseley and Feldman 1982, Farrington and Park 1978, Farrington 1979) makes a good argument for the existence of a "specialized branch of government devoted to collecting, analyzing, and abstracting hydraulic observations ... [and] technical liaison activities coupled into Chimu administrative functions" (Ortloff, Moseley, and Feldman 1982: 593).

It is now known that the Chicama–Moche inter-valley canal was of minor, even inconsequential, value as a source of water for Chan Chan. Despite the tremendous investment in labor, engineering skills, and administrative overhead, very little water actually ever flowed through the massive system. The inter-valley canal now appears largely to have been abandoned early in the 13th century (Ortloff, Moseley, and Feldman 1982: 593, but see Farrington 1978: 124–6). This failure is attributed to technical difficulties in maintaining water flow – either 1) subtle tectonic tilting in the critical drainage divide region (Ortloff, Moseley, and Feldman 1982: 589), or 2) irresolvable problems with canal erosion (Farrington and Park 1978: 266–7, Farrington 1979: 13). It is tempting to associate Chimú imperial expansion during the later Late Intermediate with the growing difficulties of providing adequate water to Chan Chan and its immediate sustaining area.

Finally, it is noteworthy that effective Chimú control apparently never extended eastward into the adjacent sierra (see above). This might be taken as additional support for interpreting the Chimú state as a polity preoccupied with the operation of large-scale canal irrigation in the coastal valley plains.

The Moche–Chimú transition

Certainly one of the most complex problems in North Coast prehistory concerns the Moche–Chimú transition. Despite the fact that both socio-cultural systems appear to have centered in the Moche Valley, it has always proved difficult to link them developmentally. A widely accepted view holds that Moche development was drastically altered in the Middle Horizon by "Huari-Tiahuanacoid" intrusions emanating from the central Peruvian coast, and perhaps ultimately from the center of Huari in the south-central highlands (Willey 1971: 164). A series of changes in ceramic technology, pottery decoration, burial patterns, architectural forms, settlement types, and ritual art have pointed to significant influences from the south (Willey 1953: 389, 394, 397, Collier 1955: 135–7, Donnan 1972). This influence sometimes has been interpreted as military invasion (Strong 1948: 101, Willey 1948: 13, Willey 1953: 354, Collier 1955: 136).

On the other hand, Chimú antecedents also can be perceived in somewhat different terms. Settlement-pattern continuities observed between the Early

Intermediate Period and Middle Horizon of Virú (Collier 1955: 137) are suggestive of strong cultural continuity as well. Moseley (1973) has argued forcefully that urban communities existed in the Moche Valley prior to the Middle Horizon, and thus represent an independent development not induced by Huari or other external influence. Throughout the southern North Coast the occurrence of actual Huari, or even "Coast Tiahuanaco," pottery is extremely limited (Collier 1955: 112, Collier 1962: 415, Donnan and Mackey 1978: 213), and the little which does occur seems to be of exclusively funerary provenience. North of the Moche–Chicama valleys, Huari-Tiahuanacoid influence in ceramics and architecture alike generally is understood to be rare. Huari influence is manifest in mural art of the final phases of the Moche culture, e.g., Huaca Facho in Lambayeque (Donnan 1972) and Huaca de la Luna in the Moche Valley (Mackey and Hastings 1982). In the case of the Luna murals, this influence is traced to Middle Horizon textile designs thought to have diffused into the valley via non-militant means. Indeed, much Huari-Tiahuanacoid "influence" on the North Coast may have been produced by peaceful interchange of material goods and/or ideological concepts (e.g., Shady and Ruiz 1979). Taken together, these various considerations make it clear that Chimú antecedents are quite complex, and our understanding of them remains very incomplete.

During the Middle Horizon (Moche V phase), the two largest known North Coast centers were at Galindo, in the Moche Valley, and at Pampa Grande, in Lambayeque (Moseley 1973, Day 1975). Both were on the order of 4 km^2 in area, and neither shows any significant Huari-Tiahuanacoid influence in ceramics or architecture. A detailed description of Galindo has yet to be published, but extensive work at Pampa Grande (Day 1975, Shimada 1978, Anders 1977) shows many architectural features (walled enclosures, U-shaped structures, storeroom complexes) which anticipate distinct Chan Chan features. As Day suggests, these architectural parallels imply some organizational similarities between Moche V and early Chimú.

The abandonment of Galindo in Middle Horizon times may reflect some degree of stress in the Moche Valley during that time. As Shimada (1978: 572–3) suggests, some of this stress may have derived from pressures exerted by an expanding Huari-affiliated polity to the south. This may have reinforced problems deriving from salinization of irrigated land, etc. The reported rarity or absence of Moche V pottery from the entire southern North Coast (Donnan 1973: 126, Donnan and Mackey 1978: 210–11) also suggests a contraction of the Mochica polity in Middle Horizon times.

It is probably something more than mere coincidence that the Chimú capital developed in an area which seems to have been a Middle Horizon frontier zone on the Peruvian North Coast. This frontier separated a southern region where Huari-Tiahuanacoid "influence" definitely was present (though still poorly understood), from a northern region where such influence was much less notable. This observation may provide a useful perspective on Chimú origins. Although much less is understood about the origins of Inca Cuzco, this highland center also developed (probably roughly contemporaneously with Chan Chan) at another Middle Horizon frontier zone, between the spheres of Huari and Tiahuanaco in the southern highlands (see, e.g., Lumbreras 1978: 108–9). The origins of Cuzco and Chan Chan early in the second millennium AD may well share some common developmental processes.

THE UPPER MANTARO–TARMA DRAINAGE

Introduction

In shifting our focus from the North Coast to the Central Sierra, we must deal with a vastly different ecological configuration, a much richer ethnohistoric record, and a much less well-known archaeological record. Prior to the 1960s, archaeological research on the Late Intermediate Period was quite limited. Since then investigation has focused primarily on two regions: 1) the upper reaches of the Huallaga and Marañon drainages; and 2) the Upper Mantaro and Tarma drainages. Because of space limitations, we will discuss here only the latter area.

The Huanca, Tarama, and Chinchaycocha – ethnohistoric perspectives

We will examine here the highland area extending between Huancayo in the south to Lake Junín in the north and the adjoining upper montaña as far east as the Chanchamayo Valley. This area encompasses portions of the former Huanca, Tarama, and Chinchaycocha provinces of the Inca empire (see Rowe 1946: map 3), plus the eastern margins of imperial domination. The Huanca "ethnic" group, probably the largest and most powerful in the region, occupied the broad expanse of the Mantaro Valley between Huancayo and Jauja as well as several fertile side valleys and the adjoining uplands. Chinchaycocha Province centered on the high plateau of Lake Junín and lay mostly within the puna zone. The Tarama (also "Taruma") ethnic group spread across the rugged ridge-and-valley terrain below the eastern rim of the Junín puna. Beyond the territorial limits of these groups, as well as those of their Inca masters, Campa and/or Amuesha peoples occupied the Chanchamayo valley and its tributaries in the montaña.

The ethnohistoric record is generally poor for the Chinchaycocha, Tarama, Campa, and Amuesha, but for the Huanca there is an abundance of documentary information relevant to the Late Intermediate Period (e.g., Matos Mendieta 1959b, Lumbreras 1960, 1974a, Espinosa 1971, Hastings 1978, Levine 1979). From these documentary studies it is known that the Huanca were a major pre-Inca ethnic group which offered serious resistance to Inca penetration in the 1460s and later joined forces with the Spanish to overcome Inca domination. As a province of Tawantinsuyu, the Huanca heartland was organized into three administrative units, each of which cross-cut the region's major ecological subdivisions from puna to valley to upper montaña. Furthermore, there is good evidence that Inca administrators significantly restructured economic production throughout the Huanca region to meet Cuzco's imperial needs (see, e.g., Levine 1979: 62–4).

The documentary sources have been useful in only a general way, however, in discerning Huanca political and economic organization prior to the Inca conquest. The three-part administrative subdivision during the Late Horizon appears to have been imposed by Cuzco for its own purposes with little if any basis in pre-Inca organizational structure. The size of stable pre-Inca Huanca polities has not been ascertained with any confidence from ethnohistoric materials, although there is some suggestion (Levine 1979: 44) that the very largest such unit was about half the size of one of the Late Horizon tripartite divisions. The Huanca appear ethnohistorically to have been a politically fragmented people, fraught with internal hostilities stemming from competition over borders and resources. Alliances between Huanca subgroups were predominantly shifting and ephemeral, based on immediate political and economic expediency. The fragmented political character of the Late Intermediate Huanca is further emphasized by their failure to present a unified front to Inca incursion.

The Huanca and Tarama–Chinchaycocha – archaeological perspectives

Archaeological contrasts between the Huanca and combined Tarama–Chinchaycocha regions are striking (Fig. 7.2). In the Tarama–Chinchaycocha region, Late Intermediate sites are characterized by 1) distinctive red-on-buff pottery; 2) small size (only a handful of sites exceed 2 or 3 hectares); 3) a highly defensible location, usually on narrow ridgecrests (Figs. 7.3–7.6); 4) a predominance of circular buildings, which in many sites are intermingled with rectangular, multi-story structures probably used as storehouses (Fig. 7.7); 5) an absence of obvious public architecture; 6) few spatially discrete storage complexes, apart from the above-mentioned rectangular buildings dispersed throughout many sites; and 7) a wide distribution of sites across a number of sub-valleys but concentrated mainly on high ridges with access to puna grazing land above and terraced farmland on the sides of the valleys. The largest settlements (5–10 hectares) were mainly on this puna–valley juncture and, to a lesser extent, on the eastern rim of the sierra overlooking the upper montaña.

In the Huanca area, by contrast, we find 1) a completely different ceramic assemblage; 2) a pronounced site-size hierarchy, with many sites on the order of 5–10 hectares in area, several between 15 and 40 hectares, and one of more than 100 hectares; 3) a marked dichotomy between small, low-lying sites and large, walled hilltop sites (Figs. 7.8–7.10); 4) a near absence of rectangular buildings; 5) a suggestion of modest public architecture in the form of small complexes of sizeable rectangular and circular buildings around small, central plazas in a few of the larger sites; 6) the presence of formal storage complexes (*qollqa*) of uncertain antiquity, found along both margins of the main Mantaro Valley; and 7) a pronounced site clustering in one major sub-valley,

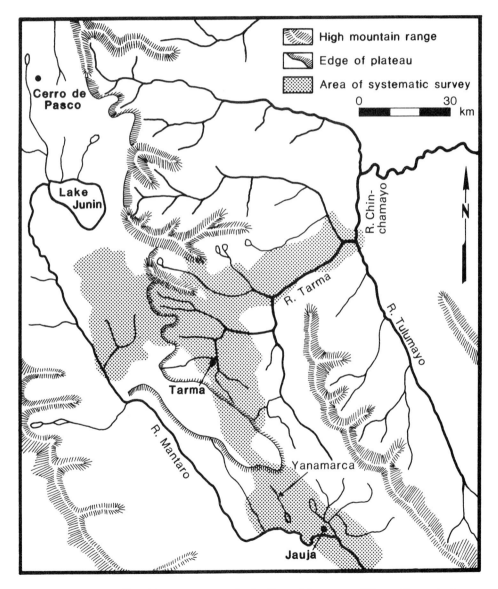

Fig. 7.2 University of Michigan survey area in the Upper Mantaro and Upper Tarma drainages of the Central Highlands.

the Yanamarca, which features unusually productive soils and close proximity
to the largest expanse of puna grasslands in the environs of Jauja. In both the
Huanca and Tarama–Chinchaycocha regions population density was greatest
near the puna–valley juncture.

Many Late Intermediate sites in the Huanca and Tarama–Chinchaycocha
areas are remarkably well preserved and exhibit the same absence of site planning that everywhere characterizes Late Intermediate settlement in the sierra.
In both areas settlement is generally compact and nucleated, with tight clustering of residential architecture. Many of the better-preserved sites show a
rather casual configuration of structures along irregular, narrow alleyways. In
some of the few published site maps (e.g., Lavallée 1973, Parsons and Matos
Mendieta 1978, Earle, D'Altroy, and Le Blanc 1978c, Orellana 1973, Bonnier
and Rozenberg 1978a, 1978b) there is an obvious tendency for small groups
of 2–6 buildings to cluster around a small open patio, often associated with
small storage facilities and tombs. These building clusters probably represent
household units.

Although most sites are characterized by a comparatively nucleated residential pattern, occupational density varies considerably from site to site and
possibly also between ethnic groups. A density of 47 buildings per hectare is

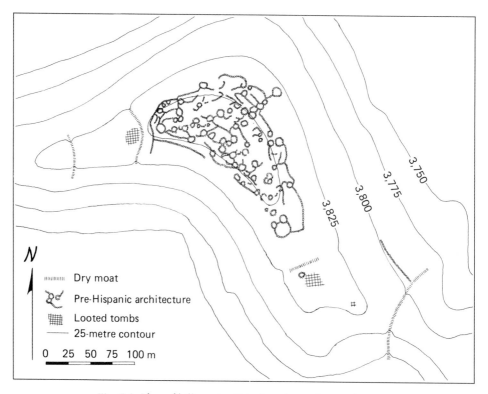

Fig. 7.3 Plan of hilltop site (Rinripata), northeast of Tarma.

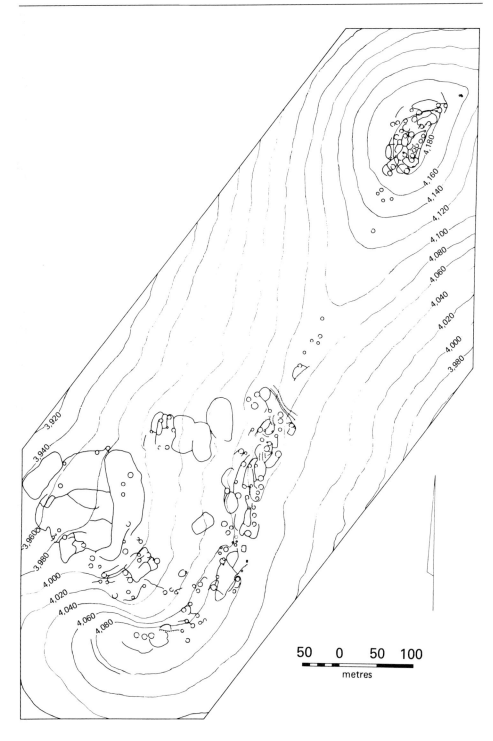

Fig. 7.4 Plan of hilltop site (Paraupunta), northeast of Tarma.

Fig. 7.5 Walled ridgetop site near Tarma.

Fig. 7.6 Section of massive outer wall at a small hilltop site near Tarma.

Fig. 7.7 Multi-story rectangular architecture at hilltop site near Tarma.

Fig. 7.8 Vertical air photograph of a walled hilltop site near Jauja, Upper Mantaro drainage. Total length about 400 m.

relatively high for the Tarama area (Parsons and Hastings 1977: 38), and the average building density of Chinchaycocha sites may have been slightly lower than that of the Tarama. By contrast, densities of 128 and 208 buildings per hectare have been measured in parts of two large Huanca sites of the Yanamarca Valley (Earle *et al.* 1979: 20). In the Asto region of the neighboring Anqara ethnic group to the southeast, Lavallée (1973: 114) recorded an average of about 135 buildings per hectare at five sites. This wide range of densities undoubtedly is linked to a variety of factors, such as local topography, duration of site occupation, household economics, redistributive organization, and, quite possibly, differences in the measurement methods employed by archaeologists. We may note, however, that the highest densities in the region under consideration appear to be those of the largest Huanca sites, and it is doubtful that such densities exist anywhere in the Tarama–Chinchaycocha area.

Even in these large Huanca centers there are no known architectural features indicative of the high degree of intra-community organization implicit in the walled compounds of major Chimú sites and some Middle Horizon sites. However, in both the Huanca and Tarama–Chinchaycocha regions there are at least suggestions of dual organization at the village or supra-village levels. Many sites are comprised of two spatially distinct subdivisions, some of which are separated by a major stone wall bisecting the

Fig. 7.9 Section of large hilltop site near Jauja, Upper Mantaro drainage.

settlement. Distinctive site pairings can be recognized in a number of cases, in which two separate settlements of comparable size and complexity occur close together along a single ridgecrest, or atop a pair of closely spaced hills.

The technology, but not necessarily the underlying economic principles, of Late Intermediate storage appears to differ significantly between the Huanca and Tarama–Chinchaycocha regions. There is a tremendous build-up of formal storage facilities in the vicinity of the Inca administrative center at Jaujatambo (at the edge of modern Jauja) which are clearly associated with Inca imperial administration (Parsons and Hastings 1977, Earle *et al.* 1979). However, there are also smaller groups of very similar buildings downvalley from Jaujatambo which are not so obviously associated with the Inca state. Some are isolated complexes well removed from residential settlement and contain virtually no surface pottery, whereas others are found within or just adjacent to Huanca residential sites where standard Late Intermediate pottery predominates in surface collections. Our own provisional interpretation (see also Earle *et al.* 1979, Earle *et al.* 1980) is that all formal, detached storage facilities in the greater Jauja area are Late Horizon in date and therefore linked to administrative policies of the Inca state. This differs significantly from the conclusions of some earlier workers (e.g., Browman 1970: 233, MacNeish, Patterson, and Browman 1975: 66, Matos Mendieta 1966: 96–8) who

Fig. 7.10 Example of a well-preserved circular house at a large hilltop site near Jauja, Upper Mantaro drainage.

assigned many of these features to the Late Intermediate Period. If we are correct, then even the Huanca, the largest and most centralized of local Late Intermediate polities, do not appear to have been involved in any large-scale redistributional strategies which such storage facilities would imply.

There is also very little evidence of collective, centrally controlled storage in Tarama settlements. A few possible exceptions warrant mention. In two sites in the main Tarma Valley there is a complex of about a dozen small, continuous, rectangular rooms stacked in two levels against a massive wall, but their use as storage facilities remains hypothetical (Figs. 7.6, 7.11). To the northeast of Tarma, a row of circular, stone-paved buildings with window-like entrances may have been a small but central storeroom complex in a large site on the way to the montaña. Most perplexing of all are two sizeable sites in the high puna west of Tarma which contain several dozen two-story rectangular structures and no circular buildings. Otherwise, Tarama storage appears to have been managed below the level of the community or village, perhaps at the household or extended family level. We suspect the distinctive two-story rectangular structures dispersed throughout most Tarama settlements were built for such local-unit storage. These structures do not exist in the northeast section of Tarama territory, but their function may have been duplicated by small circular buildings and building alcoves similarly dispersed throughout the sites.

In the Middle Mantaro, Lavallée (1973: 103) uncovered subterranean storage pits in Anqara villages, and comparable facilities, invisible at the ground surface, could exist at Huanca or Tarama sites. These pits, as well as the dispersed non-residential structures discussed for the Tarama, fit well with a model of household or extended family storage, and nowhere in the Huanca–Tarama–Chinchaycocha region do we see convincing evidence for a well-established pattern of centrally controlled, community-wide storage during the Late Intermediate Period.

The most obvious contrast between the Late Intermediate occupations of the Huanca and Tarama–Chinchaycocha regions is in scale and density. Both regions show a strong, direct correlation between the local productive potential of agriculture and herding and the size and density of occupation. The small and dispersed character of Tarama–Chinchaycocha settlement is almost certainly related to topographic limitations on productivity: narrow ridges with limited pasturage, steep mountainsides difficult to farm, and very little valley-bottom farmland. Conversely, the much greater overall population size and higher concentration of population in the Huanca region, particularly the Yanamarca Valley, are undoubtedly linked to the massed agricultural potential of extensive, highly fertile bottomlands and hillsides.

The combined ethnohistoric and archaeological evidence for the Huanca and Tarama–Chinchaycocha areas points to significant differences in the Late Intermediate societal structure of these ethnic groups. The Huancas stand out

Fig. 7.11 Outer wall of Tarama–Chinchaycocha site with rectangular rooms stacked against opposite side.

as the larger, more powerful group and appear, based on settlement-pattern data, more hierarchical and centralized. The large hilltop centers of the Yanamarca Valley have a distinctly urban character and are unparalleled in scale anywhere in the region. Furthermore, recent investigations of a canal system linking together several of the largest sites (Hastorf, personal communication) suggest a certain degree of high-level cooperation among these centers. On the other hand, the operation of centralized storage and redistributive systems has yet to be demonstrated for the Huancas, and the documentary sources are insistent on the fragmented character of political organization prior to the Inca conquest.

Cultural and organizational distinctions are considerably more blurred between the Tarama and Chinchaycocha groups. We have discussed them as a single entity partly because the ethnohistoric sources often referred to them as such. Both groups shared common ceramic and architectural traditions and from an archaeological standpoint appear inseparable, the principal difference being the predominantly agricultural orientation of the Tarama versus the pastoral orientation of the Chinchaycocha (Figs. 7.12, 7.13). Even this one contrast is not entirely straightforward; since an archaeological boundary is not visible between groups, we cannot be sure that the Tarama did not range onto the puna, or that the Chinchaycocha did not occupy parts of the Tarma

Fig. 7.12 Section of large hilltop site on the Junín puna. Note the circular houses in the foreground and the ancient *corrales* below.

or other valleys below the puna (Hastings 1978). Archaeological recognition of ethnohistoric ethnicity looms large as a problem in working out Late Intermediate socio-economic organization (Thompson 1970).

Archaeological determination of ethnic identity is a somewhat less troublesome but nonetheless complex task between the Tarama–Chinchaycocha and the Huanca, and also, as we will discuss below, between both these groups and their montaña neighbors. Contrasts in ceramics and architecture enable us in most cases to distinguish Tarama–Chinchaycocha sites from Huanca sites, but imbalances in the frontier between these groups may provide some insight into the nature of ethnic territoriality and relationships across ethnic boundaries during the Late Intermediate Period. The unbalanced character of this particular frontier is expressed in 1) a wide distribution of Huanca pottery in trace amounts across much of the Tarama territory; and 2) considerable mixing of the two ceramic traditions in sites just into the Tarama side of the frontier. This mixing of traditions extends along the frontier zone all the way into the montaña. In recent excavations in the northeast rim of the Tarma highlands, Hastings has encountered dwellings with predominantly Huanca pottery inside a Tarama settlement, bringing to mind *mitmaq* models of settlement known ethnohistorically for the Late Horizon. Documentary sources allude to exchange between these groups and give no hint of political domination by one or the other. However, the rather lopsided archaeological manifestations

Fig. 7.13 Example of ancient camelid corral in the Junín puna.

of the interaction between them suggest that the more populous, hierarchically structured Huanca may have played the more active, if not dominant, role in ordering their relationship with the Tarama–Chinchaycocha.

Huanca and Tarama–Chinchaycocha settlement in the upper montaña

The upper montaña region presented a number of economic opportunities to occupants of the adjoining Huanca and Tarama-Chinchaycocha sierra. Despite its formidable terrain, inhospitable climate, and seemingly impenetrable vegetation, the upper montaña embodies a wealth of natural resources and offers distinct advantages to the Andean farmer. A greater variety of crops can be grown than in the highlands and usually in a significantly shorter period of time. Of special importance is the relatively early scheduling of agricultural cycles on the warmer, wetter slopes of this region. For example, potatoes harvested in the upper montaña several months earlier than those at higher elevations may alleviate year-end shortages developing in households of the sierra.

Archaeological and ethnohistoric evidence indicates that Late Intermediate peoples of the Huanca and Tarama–Chinchaycocha highlands took advantage of these opportunities. Sixteenth-century sources describe the flow of lowland products into the main Mantaro Valley from a series of specialized agricultural settlements in the upper montaña (see, e.g., Espinoza 1973, Hastings 1978, 1980, Levine 1979). For the most part, each of these outposts was associated with one and only one of the three administrative Huanca subdivisions, but we know nothing of how they may have related to the pre-Inca political structure. Levine (1979: 43) argues that the attainment of direct control over montaña resources, and the implementation of this control through verticality strategies, may have been important factors in the evolution of a degree of centralized leadership among the Late Intermediate Huanca.

Four of the Huanca outposts were spaced at intervals along the Tulumayo Valley, an upper continuation of the Chanchamayo. A recent archaeological survey by one of us (Hastings) in the upper montaña revealed small, Late Intermediate Huanca sites in the vicinities of three of the locations named by the documents (Comas, Uchubamba, and Monobamba), and it is apparent that Huanca occupation of the forested Tulumayo drainage was more widespread and dispersed than implied by the ethnohistoric sources. No highland groups other than the Huancas have as yet been identified at these sites.

Sixteenth-century tribute records published by Rostworowski (1975) disclose that Chinchaycocha payments to the Spaniards in the 1540s included sizeable quantities of coca and maize. The fact that neither crop can be grown in the Chinchaycocha heartland indicates that this group was in some way tied into a vertically structured economy cross-cutting ecological zones. Maize could have been procured from the Tarama valley bottoms, but coca had to be obtained from the upper montaña. The ethnohistoric literature is of very limited use in identifying Chinchaycocha and Tarama sources of coca. One probable source was the Chinchaycocha linkage to an elaborate exchange network among Huánuco ethnic groups to the north, and another could have been coca fields in the general environs of the lowest Huanca outpost (Vitoc) in the Tulumayo (Hastings 1978). Apart from these possibly multi-ethnic sources, the main flow of lowland products into the Tarama–Chinchaycocha sierra would most likely be from the immediately adjacent section of upper montaña, an area for which we are dependent mainly upon archaeological survey.

Hastings's survey in this area demonstrates a more-or-less continuous distribution of Tarama–Chinchaycocha sites from the Junín puna down the eastward draining valleys into the upper montaña. Late Intermediate sites were found in mainly two levels of elevation within the transitional zone from sierra to montaña. The relatively few sites of the upper level are located on exposed ridgecrests above 4,000 m, in an area of mixed pastoral and high-elevation agricultural potential. One of these sites (Paraupunta) contains about 150 buildings, a few of which are the centrally positioned, paved structures discussed above as possible storage facilities, and ranks among the largest settlements in the entire Tarama–Chinchaycocha region. These ridgetop sites are linked via several ancient trails to smaller, low-level sites on the sides of deep, forested canyons between 2,000–3,000 m (Figs. 7.14, 7.15), where a considerable variety of valley crops are grown and harvested well in advance of their high-sierra counterparts. Today, both levels are symbiotically bound within the economic structure of a single *comunidad*, and it is tempting to project a similar relationship back to the Late Intermediate Period. This would be in keeping with the politically fragmented character hypothesized for the Tarama–Chinchaycocha ethnic group(s), whereby products of the eastern slopes were controlled by a locally resident subgroup rather than by 1) the ethnic group as a whole, or 2) a central hierarchy representing the group as a whole.

The same frontier-zone intermingling of Huanca and Tarama–Chinchaycocha cultures we discussed for the sierra also applies to the upper montaña region. Of three major canyons leading into the Chanchamayo montaña, the southernmost (Tulumayo) appears to have been predominantly Huanca, the northernmost (Ulcumayo) exclusively Tarama–Chinchaycocha, and the middle (Tarma) a mixture of both.

The outermost settlements of these highland groups are situated just a few kilometers from village sites once occupied by natives of the montaña (Fig. 7.16), almost certainly those peoples known since early hispanic times as the Campa and/or Amuesha (Lathrap 1970, Smith, personal communication). Archaeologically speaking, the lowland group appears quite distinct from its highland neighbors: occupation is concentrated mainly on alluvial terraces of

Fig. 7.14 Tarama–Chinchaycocha site just below the timberline in the Tarma Canyon.

Fig. 7.15 Fortified Tarama–Chinchaycocha site on a prominent spur in the Tarma Canyon.

broad valleys, stone architecture is absent or poorly executed, and the local pottery tradition is entirely different. Exchange between groups is indicated by trace amounts of highland pottery in lowland sites and vice-versa. There may perhaps have been some overlap, but for the most part the Campa/Amuesha occupied a discrete territory below and apart from sierra settlements. Nowhere do the Campa/Amuesha sites occur above the limit of manioc cultivation (about 1,800 m), but sierra occupation reached below this line.

Vast tracts of Tarama–Chinchaycocha and Huanca territories have yet to be surveyed before ethnic boundaries can be determined more fully, but approximate territorial limits are now known between these groups and along their montaña frontier. The contiguous territory of each group traverses an extraordinary environmental gradation from puna to valley to montaña, a vertical range of almost 3,000 m. The upper montaña region of the Tarama–Chinchaycocha was relatively compact and accessible to the sierra heartland, whereas Huanca possessions in the montaña were considerably more distant and widespread.

Preliminary findings suggest contrasting cultural adaptations to these geographical differences, which in turn relate to basic contrasts in the groups as a whole. The upper- and lower-level sites discussed in the eastern extremity of the Tarama–Chinchaycocha region cluster as one of several discrete subgroups within the greater ethnic territory. Late Intermediate settlement size within this subgroup is distinctly hierarchical, with Paraupunta as the dominant site surrounded by a few small high-elevation and many far-flung low-

Fig. 7.16 Tarama–Chinchaycocha fortifications around a site on the eastern frontier.

elevation sites. A plausible model for the ethnic group as a whole, which on a holistic level appears completely non-centralized, would see sierra-based subgroups deriving eastern products via intra-ethnic exchange mechanisms from largely self-sufficient, perhaps semi-autonomous subgroups based in the upper montaña.

Such a model appears less plausible for the Huanca lowlands, although archaeological research there has barely begun. Rather, the broad distribution of sites similar in size over a tremendous area would be more in keeping with a more direct relationship between sierra and montaña settlements, one which perhaps could have been instrumental in – or produced by – the emergence of hierarchical structure in Huanca settlement.

The Middle Horizon–Late Intermediate transition

One of the major contributions of recent work in the Jauja area is a refinement of Late Intermediate ceramic chronology (Earle *et al.* 1980, C. LeBlanc, personal communication). This has permitted an unparalleled diachronic perception of the development of Huanca local organization over the 400-plus years preceding Inca conquest in the 1460s. This chronological refinement reveals a marked dichotomy between 1) an early phase of the Late Intermediate characterized by small, low-lying settlements and comparatively low overall population, and 2) a late phase characterized by large, walled sites situated on hilltops, and a substantial population increase. Most low-lying sites appear to have been abandoned in the late phase, although several were again reoccupied during the subsequent Late Horizon. The shift to high, defensible sites was slightly anticipated in the early phase of the Late Intermediate by the foundation of a few new hilltop settlements.

As Earle *et al.* (1980) point out, the early Late Intermediate in the Jauja area represents considerable continuity with the antecedent Middle Horizon in terms of overall settlement configuration. The real break in settlement patterning does not occur until the drastic transformations of the late Late Intermediate. These changes presumably reflect the development of a markedly higher degree of local political centralization characteristic of the ethnohistorically known Huanca. Clearly this development involved intensified hostilities.

We would expect the impact of Middle Horizon Huari on the Upper Mantaro–Tarma drainage to have been a critical factor shaping the course of Late Intermediate development throughout this region. Situated less than 200 km to the southeast of Jauja, the Middle Horizon capital must have had a significant interest in the broad floor of the main Mantaro Valley between Huancayo and Jauja. The presence of two major Huari-related temples in the Wari Willka area near Huancayo is ample evidence of this interest (Matos Mendieta 1968a, MacNeish, Patterson, and Browman 1975: 60). Browman

(1974a: 191) has argued that Huari influence in the main Mantaro Valley produced a basic transformation from a primary reliance upon herding during Early Intermediate times to a fully agricultural mode of life and substantial population growth in the Middle Horizon. While we cannot agree with the specifics of Browman's argument, we would agree in more general terms that some sort of Huari impact was quite important during the later 1st millenium AD. The importance of the permanent spring at the Wari Willka temple as the legendary Huanca origin point is certainly suggestive of the importance of Huari influence in the Upper Mantaro during the Middle Horizon (Matos Mendieta 1968b).

Apart from the Wari Willka temple, there is very meagre archaeological evidence of Huari influence from anywhere in the Upper Mantaro–Tarma drainage. So much is this the case, that it has proved very difficult for two recent projects even to identify Middle Horizon occupation with any confidence (Parsons and Hastings 1977, Earle *et al.* 1980). Clearly, one of the key problems for future archaeological research in the Upper Mantaro should be an improved definition of Huari influence. Earls and Silverblatt (1978), for example, have suggested that movements and relocations of peoples through the implementation of Huari imperial policies may have helped produce the regional "ethnic" configuration upon which subsequent developments were founded.

THE CENTRAL COAST AND ADJACENT SIERRA

Introduction

Here we will focus primarily on three adjacent valleys of the Pacific slope – the Chillón, the Rimac, and (to a lesser degree) the Lurín. Archaeological and ethnohistoric sources are in general agreement about the rather modest scale of Late Intermediate socio-political development in this region. Nowhere is there any indication of the overarching organization which characterized the North Coast Chimú. In her documentary analysis, for example, Rostworowski (1977a: 22) concludes that shortly before the Inca conquest there were two separate "kingdoms" in the three-valley area: 1) the Colli, who effectively controlled the lower and middle reaches of the Chillón, and 2) the Ychma, centered at Pachacamac in the lower Lurín, who controlled the lower and middle portions of the Rimac and Lurín valleys. These kingdoms themselves comprised rather loosely integrated entities of small "ethnic" groups dependent upon a major "lord" whose own base of operations was in the irrigated coastal plain.

Although there is much less information for other areas, it appears that comparable polities, focused on one or two adjacent coastal valleys, everywhere characterized the coastal sector to the south of the Chimú domain

– the Chancay, Chincha, and Ica being the best known of these coastal valley states (Lumbreras 1974a: 191, Rostworowski 1977a: 105–251, Menzel 1959, 1966, 1976, Menzel and Rowe 1966). The distribution of distinctive ceramic complexes appears to conform to the ethnohistorically defined pattern (see, e.g., Dillehay 1976: 429, Stumer 1954a: 142, Strong, Willey, and Corbett 1943: 89–90).

Documentary studies (e.g., Rostworowski 1977b: 26, 27, 78, etc.) indicate that major Central Coast polities of the later Late Intermediate were engaged in a variety of relationships with less centralized, but increasingly expansive, groups in the higher parts of the same valleys – e.g., the Canta in the Upper Chillón, and the Yauyos in the higher portions of the Rimac, Lurín, Chilca, Mala, and Cañete valleys. These upvalley/downvalley relationships involved open hostility and warfare, punctuated by periods of comparative peace. It appears that militaristic confrontations were becoming increasingly prevalent, as archaeological finds of hilltop fortifications in the middle and lower Chillón Valley attest (Dillehay 1976: 420–3). Furthermore, these confrontations involved not only upvalley/downvalley antagonists, but also increasingly aggressive sierra groups who warred against each other (Rostworowski 1977b: 78, 81–2, 87). Rostworowski's analysis indicates that a major factor in the intense inter-group conflict that characterized the whole area was competition over access to the restricted prime coca-producing lands at intermediate elevations (300–1,000 m altitude) on the Pacific slope.

The Chillón Valley case study

Dillehay's (1976, 1977, 1979) recent archaeological investigations in the Chillón Valley provide a nice complement to ethnohistoric studies of the same area. His work purposefully cross-cuts the full environmental diversity of the valley, from the coastline and broad irrigated plain of the lower valley, through the narrow *quebradas* of the middle valley, into the high puna at altitudes in excess of 4,000 m at the upper end of the drainage system. He found a high degree of correspondence between the documented locations of some 15 specific pre-Hispanic "ethnic" groups and sections of the Chillón Valley where archaeological sites still are identified with the same ethnic names by modern inhabitants. Late Intermediate ceramic variability did not correspond to these ethnic units, but distinct regional differences were perceived on a more general level: Late Intermediate sites in the lower and middle valley were rather closely linked by the presence of specific ceramic types, while there was no such linkage between lower and upper valley sites. The archaeological record thus reinforces ethnohistoric interpretations that the lower and middle valleys were politically separate from the upper valley in late pre-Inca times. Similarly, the presence in the lower valley of the largest and architecturally most complex sites (e.g., Caraballo, Collique) also supports the documented dominance of lower-valley groups.

Another important dimension of Dillehay's study is his finding that middle-valley sites also have some ceramic links to upper-valley settlements during the Late Intermediate. These ceramic linkages appear to conform to an ethno-historically documented pattern of alliances between middle- and upper-valley ethnic groups in late pre-Hispanic times (Dillehay 1976: 417). These alliances seem to have been founded on attempts by middle-valley groups to ensure their security and survival by facilitating the highlanders' access to coca. Thus, the middle-valley groups, while politically subordinate to lower-valley centers, possessed sufficient autonomy to be able to buffer their rather precarious position through advantageous alignments with adjacent sierra groups which were beyond the control of the dominant lower-valley powers.

Although the specifics of these Late Intermediate middle-upper valley align-ments remain obscure, additional insight is provided by Dillehay's detailed analysis of Huancayo Alto, a unique site strategically situated in the middle Chillón, about 60 km inland from the coast. This center, whose overall area is about 14 hectares (Dillehay 1979: 25), has a long occupational sequence that extends over more than 1,500 years from the Early Intermediate Period through the Late Horizon. The importance of the site during Late Intermediate times is reflected by the abundance of distinctive ceramic types and by four 14th-century radiocarbon dates (Valastro, Davis, and Varela 1978: 269). This unusually long occupation undoubtedly reflects the site's enduring import-ance as a node which facilitated the access of many groups to a diversified set of resources *in the absence of any overall political unification* (prior to Inca conquest in the later 15th century).

The key features of Huancayo Alto – a series of terraces (which may have functioned for drying coca), formal public storage facilities, and suggestions of multi-ethnic occupation – are suggestive of a rather complex organization through which goods such as coca and camelid products were stored, pro-cessed, and redistributed throughout the valley from this strategic locus. This organization remains incompletely understood, but it may have been based partly on periodic residence at Huancayo Alto by people from several different parts of the Chillón Valley. Dillehay's (1979: 30) argument (based primarily on ethnohistoric evidence) that Huancayo Alto was not a locus of major politi-cal power during Late Intermediate times is particularly interesting. We are not convinced that Dillehay is correct. Huancayo Alto seems to be the largest settlement in the middle Chillón, and, on this basis at least, would appear to be an important focus of political power.

The Middle Horizon–Late Intermediate transition

The Central Coast was clearly a florescent region during the Middle Horizon. Major Middle Horizon centers are known at Cajamarquilla and Pachacamac. Menzel (1968: 94, 1977: 67) has argued forcefully that Pachacamac chal-lenged, or replaced, Huari dominance on the Central and North Coasts during the second half of the Middle Horizon. Pachacamac (in the lower Lurín) also continued to be an important ritual and political center in Late Intermediate times – we already have seen that it probably constituted a major link with the Chimú (Keatinge 1978: 38–9). It is possible that a comparable Middle Horizon–Late Intermediate continuity may also exist at Cajamarquilla (in the lower Rimac). We also have noted that Huancayo Alto, in the middle Chillón, was another important Middle Horizon site which continued to function during the Late Intermediate. Stumer (1954b: 173, 177–8) also has located several sites in the lower Chillón where both Middle Horizon and Late Intermediate occupation occur. Clearly there is some degree of socio-political continuity between the later Middle Horizon and the earlier Late Intermediate. There is at least a hint that Central Coast ceramic traditions were more broadly shared during the earlier part of the Late Intermediate than later in the period (Strong, Willey, and Corbett 1943: 89–90, Patterson and Lanning 1964: 116). This lends additional support to the notion of Middle Horizon–Late Intermediate continuity, and may signify that, just as in the better-studied Upper Mantaro (see above), the socio-cultural changes that occurred on the Central Coast between the earlier and later phases of the Late Intermediate were more pronounced than those that accompanied the Middle Horizon–Late Intermediate transition.

At first glance, the Middle Horizon–Late Intermediate transition on the Central Coast would appear to offer a great contrast to what we seem to have on the North Coast, where influences from Huari were less direct. However, there are some suggestions of significant parallels between the two regions. For one thing, in both regions the clearest Huari-related ceramics occur in limited contexts, most of which are ritual and funerary (see, e.g., Stumer 1954a: 143, Shady and Ruiz 1979, Strong, Willey, and Corbett 1943: 89). Secondly, there may be similarities in settlement-system role between Pacatnamú and Pachacamac (Keatinge 1978), both of which are major Late Intermediate ritual centers with long time depth. Thirdly, there may be developmental analogs between Cajamarquilla and Galindo, two major Middle Horizon centers, possibly of predominantly secular orientation, whose importance did not continue into Late Intermediate times, but whose presence strongly affected the transition from one era to the next.

THE SOUTHERN SIERRA

Introduction

This is another region for which a rich ethnohistoric literature can be integrated with the archaeological record in order to achieve deeper understanding of the Late Intermediate Period. During the past decade there have been important new investigations in two regions – the Cuzco area in the

Upper Urubamba drainage, and the Titicaca Basin (especially on the Peruvian side of the international border). Our discussion will focus on these areas, and will attempt to address two inter-related problems: 1) the consequence of the collapse of the two major Middle Horizon capitals at Huari and Tiahuanaco, and 2) the formation of the early (pre-imperial) Inca state at Cuzco.

The Upper Urubamba drainage

The presence of the Inca imperial capital at Cuzco understandably has shifted archaeological interest in this region toward the physical remains of the Late Horizon. Although Rowe (1944) long ago defined the Late Intermediate Killke ceramic complex at Cuzco, it was not until the late 1960s that systematic archaeological research on the Late Intermediate was renewed in the Cuzco environs (Dwyer 1971, Rivera 1971). Between 1969 and 1973, Kendall (1974, 1976) carried out surveys and excavations in the lower Urubamba Valley some 80 km northwest of Cuzco, near the sierra–montaña juncture. At the same time there have been new interpretations of documentary sources which bear upon the Late Intermediate period (Rostworowski 1970, 1978a, Lumbreras 1978, Zuidema 1979).

The documentary sources indicate that Cuzco emerged as an important power center as a result of intensive and protracted warfare with a variety of neighboring polities – the most important of which were the Chanka, in the Ayacucho region to the west, and the Colla, in the western Titicaca basin to the southeast (see, e.g., Lumbreras 1978: 103). There are indications, too, that hostilities and competition also proceeded within the Cuzco heartland as specific groups sought predominance at the local level (Rostworowski 1970: 92). Lumbreras (1978: 103, 104, 109) has stressed that these conflicts in Late Intermediate times must be understood in the context of their Middle Horizon antecedents. That is, hostilities would have focused on the Cuzco region precisely because this area was 1) a strategic frontier province of the Middle Horizon Huari domain, and 2) a region which also had close links (manifested by ceramic similarities – Ibarra Grasso 1965: 161) with the Titicaca Basin. Lumbreras reasons that with the collapse of centralized authority in later Middle Horizon times, the local Cuzco elite would have found it both necessary and advantageous to assert themselves against the remnants of both the old Middle Horizon powers.

Dwyer's (1971) surveys and excavations in the Cuzco basin have defined some general features of Late Intermediate occupation there. One important contribution of his work is the demonstration that the Late Intermediate Killke ceramic complex is directly ancestral to the subsequent Inca, and has its roots in the local material of the antecedent Early Intermediate Period and Middle Horizon (Dwyer 1971: 135, 136, 148). Kendall (1976: 98) shows that a similar relationship exists between Late Intermediate architecture of the general Cuzco region and imperial Inca architecture. These findings strongly indicate predominantly local roots for Inca state development. Dwyer (1971: 40–1) also finds that the Killke pottery style includes a fair degree of variability from one valley to another within the general Cuzco area. Whether this variability related to socio-political, chronological, or functional factors cannot yet be ascertained.

Within the immediate Cuzco Valley, Dwyer (1971: 24–40, 145–6) reports that most Late Intermediate sites (which include settlements measuring between about 12 and 60 hectares) are not found in defensible settings, but tend to occur rather closely spaced atop low ridges or on intermediate slopes at no great distance above the valley floor. Outside the immediate Cuzco Valley, however, in adjacent localities, all Late Intermediate sites so far discovered occur in defensive hilltop settings. This contrast is quite marked. If the sites located are indeed a representative sample (Dwyer's survey, like Dillehay's in Chillón, was not systematic enough to guarantee this), then the conclusion can only be that there was something special about the Cuzco Valley at this period. The nature of this special quality remains obscure.

Working some 80 km from Cuzco, lower in the Urubamba drainage, Kendall (1976) found an area of substantial Late Intermediate occupation, with very limited evidence for any earlier settlement. Ceramics are generally similar to the Killke material of the Cuzco Valley, although there are some significant differences between the two areas in terms of domestic architecture and settlement patterns. Kendall has been able to phase her ceramic material, and she finds that most of the sites of the early Late Intermediate are situated on hilltops. Later in the period there was some downward shift to locations closer to the valley floor (*Ibid*. p. 99). Many of these lower sites continued to be occupied in Late Horizon times. At this point one might wonder whether the low-lying Late Intermediate sites that Dwyer reports in the Cuzco Valley belong primarily to this same late phase. It is also interesting to note that Kendall's lower Urubamba study area seems to show precisely the reverse of what happened in the Huanca area of the Upper Mantaro, where the late Late Intermediate saw a pronounced upward settlement shift (see above). The principal cause for this rather marked contrast may have been the development of a more centralized Late Intermediate polity in the Cuzco area. Such a polity may have been more effective than were the contemporary Huanca in keeping the peace over sizeable regions, and thereby reduced the need for defensible settlement.

There is as yet no good information on site size in the lower Urubamba study area. In general terms, however, these settlements seem to approximate those we have already described for the Late Intermediate in some parts of the Central Sierra: communities of modest size, comprised of nucleated clusters of predominantly round domestic buildings, often containing precincts of small rectangular buildings which seem to be storage facilities.

The Titicaca Basin

There is extensive 16th-century documentation for this region (e.g., Diez de San Miguel 1964 [1567]). The most complete ethnohistoric studies bear upon two large "kingdoms": the Lupaca (Lupaqa) on the southwest, and the Colla (Qolla) on the north and northwest of Lake Titicaca (Rowe 1946: map 3, Murra 1968, Lumbreras 1974d). The existence of a half-dozen other socio-political groups is also known for the broad regions east and south of Lake Titicaca. In the early 16th century these polities were hierarchically organized, with authority that extended over large contiguous areas of several thousand km^2 of rolling puna and adjacent lower valleys of the high Titicaca Basin. These Late Horizon kingdoms also controlled access to montaña and coastal resources through detached "colonies" of dependents which resided permanently in the latter areas, several days' journey from the Titicaca core area (Murra 1968, 1972, 1979, Trimborn *et al.* 1975, Isbell 1968). Even in Late Horizon times, however, there was considerable hostility between the principal Titicaca kingdoms, and inter-group warfare probably played an even more significant role prior to the Inca conquest.

After the 1460s, all these Titicaca kingdoms were administrative provinces of the Inca empire. Ethnohistoric sources and the archaeological record make it clear that Inca conquest and control brought about significant change. For example, recent archaeological investigations of the Qolla capital at Hatunqolla, near modern Puno, show that this site is exclusively Late Horizon, with strong Inca influence in ceramics and architecture (Julien 1979). Similarly, the six principal Lupaqa centers show comparable Inca influence: Inca pottery is generally predominant, and all but one lie on the main Inca road (Hyslop 1976: 167–8). For our present concern with the Late Intermediate period, we must consider the degree to which the historically documented Late Horizon situation reflects the pre-Inca era. We have seen already that the Huanca of the Upper Mantaro were considerably more cohesive, both politically and economically, in Late Horizon times than they had been during the antecedent Late Intermediate. Clearly, the ethnohistoric sources must be used with care in reconstructing pre-Inca patterns.

The archaeological record indicates that the documented 16th-century divisions have some real significance, in at least a general way, for the Late Intermediate Period. Bennett (1950: 97), for example, indicates that the Qolla, Lupaqa, Pacasa, and Omasuya groupings can be associated generally with distinctive pre-Inca mortuary pottery. M. Tschopik (1946: 52) has shown that variability in tomb architecture (*chullpas*) of probable Late Intermediate date can likewise be linked with these regional groupings. Archaeologists also have noted the abundance of small Late Intermediate sites in the small coastal valleys of far-southern Peru and northernmost Chile (Trimborn *et al.* 1975,

Nuñez 1968). These sites provisionally have been interpreted as settlements of colonists from the sierra, linked politically and economically with their home-lands in the Titicaca Basin. Although the specifics of these coastal-sierra relationships must still be demonstrated archaeologically (see, e.g., Murra 1979), the presence of Tiahuanaco-related Middle Horizon ceramics in the same general area (see, e.g., Schaedel 1957, Stumer 1954c) is suggestive of considerable time depth to these linkages.

The upper montaña north of the Titicaca Basin is archaeologically virtually unknown, but ethnohistoric sources refer to small Lupaqa settlements main-tained in the region for the production of coca (Diez de San Miguel 1964). Isbell (1968) briefly explored parts of the upper Inambari watershed and encountered sites as large as "several hundred" buildings surrounded by extensive agricultural terracing. On the basis of architectural style, they are dated tentatively to Inca and immediately pre-Inca periods.

It has long been known that the collapse of Tiahuanaco in late Middle Horizon times was followed, or perhaps accompanied, by a shift to defensible, hilltop sites throughout the Titicaca Basin. Bennett (1933, 1950) and Ryden (1947, 1957) long ago reported walled hilltop settlements of this era in Bolivia, some of which contained over 1,000 houses (Bennett 1950: 94). More recent work in Peru has produced a similar picture (Lumbreras and Amat 1968: 89, 90). Because settlements of terminal Middle Horizon (Tiahuanaco V) and Late Intermediate date are so much more numerous than earlier sites (Ponce Sanginés 1972: 58, Bennett 1950: 96), it would appear likely that over-all population was increasing as well – although it must be recalled that at least a part of this increase in site numbers probably is linked to the decay of massive Middle Horizon centers, such as Tiahuanaco itself. These general features of Late Intermediate occupation lend a certain credence to documentary reports of intensive hostility as a characteristic of pre-Inca times.

Hyslop's (1976, 1977a, 1977b) survey in the Lupaqa area offers an import-ant new perspective on Late Intermediate development in the northern Titicaca Basin. This survey was not systematic enough to ensure that a rep-resentative sample of site locations was obtained. Nevertheless, some well-defined patterns emerge from which useful tentative conclusions can be drawn.

1) There seems to have been a significant population expansion during the Late Intermediate relative to the antecedent Middle Horizon: 13 Middle Horizon sites were located in the study area, as opposed to 25 Late Inter-mediate settlements (Hyslop 1976: 80, 109). Several of the Late Intermediate sites are quite large, and one, with an estimated habitation area of 150 hectares (*Ibid.* p. 116), is substantially larger than the largest known Huanca site near Jauja.

2) After the Middle Horizon there was a pronounced shift in settlement

location away from low-lying land near the lakeshore to hilltop localities well removed from the lake (Hyslop 1976: 92, 109). All major Late Intermediate sites in the study area are walled hilltop communities at elevations over 4,000 m. Their location in agriculturally marginal terrain, and the indications of camelid pens at most sites, are suggestive of the expansion and intensification of herding.

3) The Late Intermediate saw the appearance of another new site type: elite cemeteries containing large burial towers (*chullpas*). These tomb complexes appear to have replaced temples and shrines as primary ceremonial foci after the end of the Middle Horizon (Hyslop 1976: 136–7, 222). The sociological implications of this change are not clear, but this, more than any other single factor, lends some credence to suggestions from historical linguistic studies that Aymara speakers may have replaced Puqina speakers in parts of the Titicaca Basin early in the second millenium AD (*Ibid.*).

4) There appears to be a well-defined Late Intermediate site-size hierarchy (Hyslop 1976: 116). One site covers 150 hectares, four sites are 30 hectares or somewhat larger, several are somewhat larger than 10 hectares, and several are less than 10 hectares. This hierarchy suggests that some degree of organizational complexity and political centralization existed prior to Inca encroachment in the 1460s. There are no clear indications of such organization in Hyslop's study area prior to the Late Intermediate. A degree of Late Intermediate architectural and ceramic variability within the study area also may be indicative of socio-political subdivisions within this hierarchy (*Ibid.* pp. 221–2).

5) The shift from Late Intermediate to Late Horizon was marked by settlement-pattern changes as profound as those which accompanied the Middle Horizon/Late Intermediate transition. The principal settlements which can be ceramically and architecturally linked to the Inca conquerors all occur in low-lying localities along the Inca road, near the lakeshore (Hyslop 1976: 200). Although the old hilltop settlements further inland may have continued to be at least partially occupied during the Late Horizon, only the *chullpa* cemeteries show any obvious Inca ceramic or architectural influence (*Ibid.* pp. 201, 223). The six historically documented Lupaqa centers can all be identified on the ground – all were obviously intended to facilitate Inca provincial administration, and there is little or no relationship between them and the pre-Inca settlement system (*Ibid.* pp. 166–8). The principal socio-political link between the Late Intermediate and the Late Horizon is the continued use by the Lupaqa elite of their old cemeteries, where they now built increasingly elaborate tombs incorporating Inca architectural styles. As Hyslop (*Ibid.* p. 201) suggests, this latter feature probably reflects the increasing wealth and prestige of indigenous elites who were incorporated into the Inca provincial administrative hierarchy.

CONCLUSIONS

Throughout this review we have been hampered by two principal defects in the Late Intermediate data base: the general absence of a refined chronology suitable for our purpose, and an inadequate ability to perceive the regional structure of society. It is painfully apparent that future archaeological research should focus very heavily on these two key problems. All too often we have been forced to talk in static terms about a period nearly 500 years long which must ultimately provide critical information regarding the dynamics of decay in major inter-regional cultural systems of the Middle Horizon and the dynamics of development for Late Horizon pan-Andean organization. All too often we potentially have been misled by non-representative samples of archaeological remains provided by the existing published literature. On the other hand, we hope we also have emphasized the more positive side of the picture, for it is clear that many important insights emerge from what already has been accomplished.

The primary focus of this chapter has been the spatial and temporal variability in economic and socio-political organization. There is one outstanding dichotomy that has long been apparent: the contrast between the regional Chimú state and the much more fragmented polities characteristic of other areas. We have suggested a close relationship between Chimú political organization and large-scale hydraulic agriculture. On the other hand, there are large valleys on the central and southern coasts where irrigation and agriculture would appear to be just as intimately related, but where it appears that political organization was much less centralized and expansive.

There seems to be an undeniable correlation between socio-political development and the local resource base in Late Intermediate times. Everywhere we have found cultural systems whose size and complexity varied directly with the degree to which they were underwritten by massed agricultural/herding resources. The Chimú, the Huanca, and the Killke-phase Cuzco polity all stand out in this respect. On the other hand, we could ask why large Late Intermediate cultural systems failed to develop in such places as the lower Chillón–Rimac valleys, or in the Titicaca Basin, where comparable resource bases exist.

Recent investigations have emphasized the importance of the movement of diverse resources between populations living in ecologically distinct regions in close spatial proximity. It seems apparent that during Late Intermediate times this movement probably took place in the absence of over-arching systems of political control which integrated these same areas during the subsequent Late Horizon. Late Horizon models of inter-zonal political and economic integration must be modified appropriately for the Late Intermediate context.

Late Intermediate polity and economy will never be comprehensible until the antecedent Middle Horizon is better known. Everywhere we have found it difficult to discuss the transition between these periods. In part this relates to inadequate chronological controls over early phases of the Late Intermediate Period. However, it also has a lot to do with inadequate views of Middle Horizon organization which have been based much too heavily on decorated funerary pottery – a very restricted data base.

III

PAN-ANDEAN EMPIRE AND THE USES OF DOCUMENTARY EVIDENCE

8

Progress and prospect in the archaeology of the Inca

CRAIG MORRIS

Travelers of the nineteenth century, such as Squier (1877), were very interested in the remains of Inca settlements and recorded many of them. But during the early years of scientific archaeology in the Andes, Inca materials were given only passing consideration. The focus was on translations from the early Spanish sources and commentaries on them (Means 1920, 1928). Andean archaeology was busy discovering the extent of the pre-Inca past, and there seemed almost to be a feeling that archaeology could add little to the apparently full record to be found in Cieza, Garcilaso, and other standard chronicles.

Bingham's (1930) historic work at Machu Picchu and Bandelier's (1910) in the Lake Titicaca region would seem to be exceptions to this. Both made some surprisingly modern attempts at determining the uses of Inca buildings, but their methodologies were not yet up to their interests, and their expeditions were intellectually more akin to those of the nineteenth-century travelers than to archaeology as it was then beginning to be practiced. The work of Valcárcel at Machu Picchu and in Cuzco (Valcárcel 1934) and of Uhle (1923) at Tumebamba, Chincha (Uhle 1924), and other locations somewhat more seriously began to integrate the Inca material into an overall outline of Andean material culture history. Ambrosetti (1907–8) and Nordenskiöld (1924a) documented important Inca remains in Argentina and Bolivia respectively. Rowe added his definition of the *Killke* series and his classic descriptions of Inca architecture and ceramics in *An introduction to the archaeology of Cuzco* (Rowe 1944). It was this work that really brought serious and sustained archaeological consideration specifically to the Inca. In the year following that work, chronological questions were addressed using the historic sources (Rowe 1945), and that was followed by his critical consideration of the evidence contained in the written record for reconstructing *Inca culture at the time of the Spanish Conquest* (Rowe 1946). Scientific interest in the Inca finally had begun to match their hold on the popular imagination.

In 1959 Menzel's paper, "The Inca occupation of the South Coast of Peru," set the stage for a series of developments that would allow Inca archaeology to assume a new role in the 1960s and 1970s. Menzel's work demonstrated, on

Fig. 8.1 Sites relevant to the text.

the one hand, that written sources and archaeology can be effectively used together and, on the other, that archaeology in and of itself can add significantly to our understanding of the Inca. She perceived that stylistic variables are not just markers of time, but indicators of historical events. Stylistic chronology when sensitively interpreted in its overall archaeological context is not an empty framework, but a "mirror of history" which reflects the character of societies and their institutions. Even on substantive questions the last word on the Inca had not been written in the sixteenth century. Menzel closed her article with a challenge: "Instead of lamenting the absence of written records in the Andean area, we have only to look closely at the abundant evidence which has survived from the past in the form of archaeological associations. The answers to many of our questions can be found in the ground" (Menzel 1959: 141).

During the 1960s and 1970s archaeological research on the Inca began, finally, to take its full place alongside the study of the completely prehistoric period. Inca projects were still quantitatively few, but their goals were now more ambitious. Virtually all of that research has taken advantage of the historical data, either as a general source of models or as explicit points of reference on specific sites and regions. Its range has spanned the full spectrum of contemporary archaeology.

For purposes of discussion, the recent and continuing accomplishments are divided into four categories of research. The first and second categories deal with the more traditional archaeological concerns with the distribution of artifacts in time and space. The third is the use of archaeology to reconstruct activity patterns which then contribute to an understanding of lifeways and of economic and political institutions. The fourth is a still rather experimental approach, closely tied to structural studies in ethnohistory and ethnology, which looks at various aspects of planning and design as reflections of broad principles of structure and organization.

It is obvious at the outset that these discussions cannot be complete. They are intended only to indicate the general directions of research, and many contributions necessarily are omitted. It is also evident that the categories crosscut each other to a certain extent and are inter-related. Concrete examples of work carried out have usually contributed to more than one of the "categories." Though most archaeologists tend to put special emphasis on one or the other of these kinds of research, this is not an attempt to classify archaeologists. The point rather is to stress the legitimacy and importance of several goals and approaches to the common end of understanding Andean civilization in the last century before the arrival of the Spanish.

THE MEASUREMENT OF TIME

The basic archaeological chronology for the Inca was published almost forty years ago by John Rowe (1944). Using a thorough analysis of the written record, Rowe was able to argue that Cabello de Balboa's dates for the last three Inca rulers are at least approximately correct (Rowe 1945). It is apparent from the sources that the real Inca expansion began only during the reign of Pachacuti, which Cabello de Balboa dates from 1438 to 1471 (Rowe 1945: 277). The pottery styles associated with the expanding empire in provincial areas are those related to the Cuzco Series defined by Rowe (1944: 47–9). There is stratigraphic evidence that the Killke Series, also found in the Cuzco area, immediately precedes the Cuzco Series. Rowe believes this pottery to associate with the pre-expansion period of the Inca, thought to have begun around AD 1200. The temporal divisions are thus simple and the timespan quite short, especially the period of empire:

> Late Inca (Cuzco Series): *c*. 1428–*c*. 1532
> Early Inca (Killke Series): ?1200–*c*. 1438

In comparison with archaeology as a whole this already represents a fine-grained and rather reliable chronology. However, in centrally directed complex societies such as the Inca the pace of significant change can be so rapid that even smaller temporal units are necessary. We cannot properly study the expansion of an enormous empire unless we can work out chronological controls that allow us to see its shape and nature at different points in its development.

The first promising step in the direction of subdividing the Late Inca Period into phases has been taken by Katherine Julien in her research at Hatungolla near Lake Titicaca (Julien 1978). She has established a three-phase chronology for Hatungolla based on stratigraphy and a detailed analysis of the shape and design attributes of the pottery. The three phases together are estimated to cover a time span of 70 to 90 years, corresponding roughly to the period of the Inca occupation of the site (Julien 1978: 214–15). Julien does not attempt to assign absolute dates to her three phases, but the possibility of achieving a chronology with time units of only about 30 years is indeed impressive.

For a chronology to have maximum utility it must be extendable to other areas of the Inca realm. To my knowledge equivalent stratigraphy has not so far been excavated elsewhere. The style sequence worked out by Julien involves a complex inter-relationship between the Cuzco Inca ceramic tradition and local Lake Titicaca styles. Thus it cannot be applied as it is to other regions, for different local styles interacted in many different ways with the Cuzco tradition. Nevertheless, there are tantalizing hints which may reflect changes in the Cuzco tradition itself, and therefore be of broad utility in empire-wide chronology. For example, there is a possibility of a chronological difference between the well-known Mode A and Mode B polychrome decoration. "The evidence seems to be fairly good for the chronological precedence of Mode A design at Hatungolla. Since both Mode A and Mode B are rendered in good Cuzco Inca style, the local patterns may be following a sequence of events in Cuzco closely, and Mode A may have an earlier stylistic beginning than Mode B. At the same time a neck fragment in Phase I suggests Mode B composition, though it does not imitate choice of pigments or drawing techniques" (Julien 1978: 208). It is obvious from the caveat that Julien does not yet consider the case established, but it is these kinds of determination, based on the kind of detailed analysis she employs, that one hopes will provide a new degree of chronological control for Inca archaeology in the future.

GEOGRAPHIC VARIATIONS IN ARTIFACTS

The traditional chronicles tended to encourage a monolithic Cuzco-centered view of the Inca state that, whether despotic or benevolent, was governed by a set of relatively uniform principles. Perhaps the most important advances of Inca studies in recent years have been the emergence of new "provincial" perspectives on Tawantinsuyu. Both ethnohistory and archaeology have made important contributions to our present conception of an enormously varied and complex domain where principles of rule altered with changing imperial objectives and with the regional differences the Inca encountered as their territory expanded. Although the Cuzco rulers certainly had some general principles that guided their governance, the state was formed out of diverse peoples and remained a patchwork of different polities and ethnicities at the time of the European invasion.

The publication and analysis of a series of administrative records dealing with local groups in the early post-Spanish period has been a major factor in the new emphasis on the groups of which the empire was composed. One of these documents, the *visita* of the Huánuco region, was partially published beginning in the 1920s (Ortiz de Zúñiga [1562] 1920–5, 1955–61), but its importance was not fully appreciated until the 1960s (Murra 1962, 1966, Ortiz de Zúñiga [1562] 1967, 1972). *Visitas* of the Lupaca kingdom (Diez de San Miguel [1567] 1964) and a series of slightly later *visitas* of the Collaguas (Pease 1977a) have provided important new data for the regions near Lake Titicaca and Arequipa. The work of Maria Rostworowski (1977b, 1978b) using various coastal sources has documented many contrasts between highlands and coast. Jorge Hidalgo has drawn together some of the information on the ethnic groups the Inca encountered in what is now Chile (Hidalgo 1972). These are only some major examples from what is now a very rich literature on Andean ethnographic diversity in the 16th century (see Pease 1978: ch. 1).

Archaeological advances in understanding the variation within Tawantinsuyu have so far been piecemeal, the results of isolated efforts in various parts of the Andes. We have known at least since the work of Bennett (1944) that the variation in the ceramics of the period is enormous and that the domination of Cuzco is very difficult to detect in some areas where it is documented in the written sources.

Fig. 8.2 Map of Tawantinsuyu: general area covered by the Inca Empire at the time of the Spanish Conquest. Principal roads, sites, and capitals of modern republics are indicated.

The area is so vast that any complete study of styles and materials through its entirety is not feasible (Fig. 8.2). John Hyslop's (1984) recent research on the Inca road system is the first attempt at a systematic sampling of the empire as a whole, and aside from new information on the roads it gives us a comparative perspective on several areas under Inca domination.

One of the first examples of specifically non-Cuzco research which pointed out internal differences was that of Menzel (1959), alluded to above. Both the substantive and methodological guidelines for the study of regional differences during the Inca period were laid down in her classic paper. She used the major components of the archaeological record, i.e., architecture, ceramics, and site locations, to draw inferences about political boundaries and the nature of the relationship between those units and their conquerors in Cuzco. Other "provincial" studies have followed, with research on the more peripheral areas of the empire in Argentina, Bolivia, Chile, and Ecuador especially active.

It is obviously not possible here to summarize or integrate this great wealth of information on the regional variation in Tawantinsuyu. Instead, I would like to address a few comments to the specifically archaeological matters of the patterns of variation, particularly stylistic variation, in artifacts from region to region. The work to date shows considerable potential for the comparative study of artifact variation over broad areas. At least three kinds of question may be answered by such studies: (1) Ethnic and political units may be identified, their boundaries mapped, and the movement of populations suggested; (2) The interactions between local styles and the imperial style of Cuzco can serve as a rough guide for suggesting the nature of the varying relationships between Cuzco and the "provinces"; (3) The actual movement of goods may give important information on forms of economic and political organization.

The identification of ethnic and political units

Archaeologists generally have assumed that geographic patterning in the distribution of artifact styles indicates cultural boundaries that in turn correlate somehow with social or political units. There is no reason to believe, however, that the relationship between stylistic distributions and socio-cultural units is in any sense precise. Much work is needed on style distributions in circumstances where socio-political boundaries are known from non-archaeological evidence. In the Andean case it is necessary to conduct surveys where ethnic and political divisions for the Inca, or immediately post-Inca, period are described in the written sources.

One of the places where this has been done, at least in a preliminary fashion, is the Huánuco region (Thompson 1967, 1968) (Fig. 8.3). The correspondence there between the archaeological results and the independent written evidence

Fig. 8.3 Map of Huánuco Pampa: overall site plan. Note *usnu* in center and *qoíqas* (storehouses) to the southwest.

is encouraging, but less than perfect. While the material styles of the several groups inspected by Iñigo Ortiz can be recognized, certain towns seem to belong archaeologically to groups different from those to which they are assigned in the *visita*. In this case, the written information may reflect an alignment that was relatively new at the time the inspection was made, but the discontinuity does emphasize the care that must be used in accepting either the written or archaeological evidence alone in identifying groups and drawing boundaries.

Yet another complication in the archaeological study of local divisions in Inca times is the existence of several classes of groups or divisions. For example, divisions such as *pachaca* and *waranga* were localized in space, at least to some extent. But such divisions are mentioned in different contexts and are probably of a different character from those which are given individual names and apparently have an "ethnic" identity. The socio-cultural nature of such basically political and accounting divisions is often unclear in the written sources, and their archaeological exploration is certain to be a complicated undertaking since we have no guide at this point as to what their material or stylistic references might be. However, by working in areas where the existence of the various kinds of units and divisions is clearly signaled in the written record, we should be able to coordinate the ethnohistoric and archaeological data to locate boundaries and at the same time gain a better understanding of the content of the various classes of units and the ways in which they inter-relate.

Relationships between local styles and the Cuzco style

The questions of the inter-relationships between Cuzco and the local building blocks of its empire are obviously not independent of the questions of the nature and boundaries of the local units. Data collected for one purpose also serve the other. A case in point, yet again, is Menzel's research on the Peruvian South Coast. Some of her conclusions on the differing degrees of Inca influence and control implied by the pottery, and substantiated by other evidence, are worth summarizing, for they provide models with which to approach other areas.

The regions of Ica and Chincha were both regions of well-developed centralized authority when the Inca arrived on the South Coast. In both cases, the Inca apparently took advantage of the existing centralization for the establishment of their own rule. The results, however, as seen in the ceramics, are far from identical. In Ica the local ceramic tradition is altered by the appearance of a new Ica Inca style which incorporates some recognizable Inca elements, but was a basically new style – distinct from both Cuzco ceramics and the previous local styles. In Chincha grave lots the local ceramic tradition declines markedly, both in quality and in frequency of occurrence. Imported and

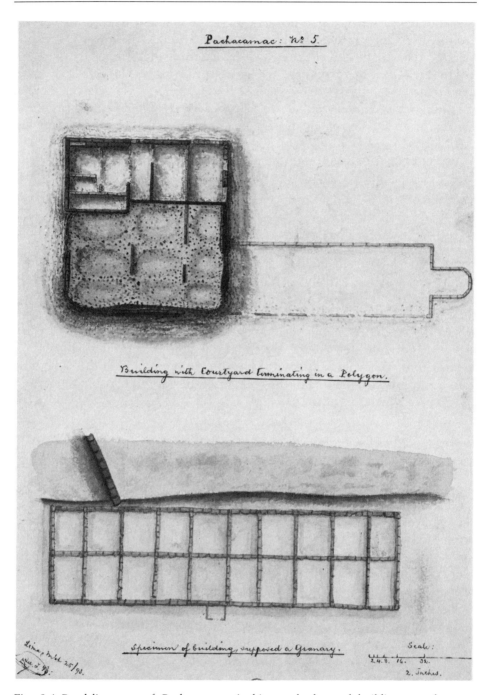

Fig. 8.4 Bandelier map of Pachacamac. Architectural plans of building complexes at Pachacamac, dated March 25, 1893, entitled "Building with courtyard terminating in a polygon"; "Specimen of building, supposed a granary."

imitation Inca ceramics are important along with a new Chincha Inca style which combines local elements with Inca designs and elements from other regions. The various Inca-related styles seem to be generally accepted, and are associated with lower levels of the society as well as with the elite. While a set of Inca ceramic styles is associated with the elites of both Chincha and Ica, the Inca elements permeate the ceramics of the society at large to a much greater extent in Chincha. The difference in the effect of the Inca conquest on the two regions is made all the more striking by their stylistic histories after the European invasion. In Ica there was a marked florescence of motifs characteristic of the immediately pre-Inca period as the ceramic decorations associated with Inca rule were "swept away." In Chincha there was no such reaction to the fall of Tawantinsuyu (Menzel 1959: 226–31). In the South Coast areas of Acari and Nazca, styles associated with Inca rule are found mainly in administrative centers built by the state along its roads. The local styles are not greatly affected and there is no reaction following the fall of the Inca. This third South Coast pattern with relatively rare occurrences of specifically Inca pottery except in administrative centers built by the state Menzel believes to indicate a lack of centralized authority at the time of the Inca arrival. The pattern in which Inca-related pottery is limited largely to contexts of political authority with little modification of local styles is very similar to the situation in the Chupaychu region of Huánuco (Thompson 1967, Morris 1978). The Chupaychu were one of several small groups in an area with no suggestion of a strong centralized authority. And certainly the region was not characterized by a tradition of fine ceramics.

The data from Tawantinsuyu as a whole are still too spotty to allow us to assess the meaning of stylistic variability in terms of the different patterns of rule that presumably in part produced it. But with increasing amounts of information on the Late Horizon from the outlying regions (see, e.g., Raffino 1978, González 1980, Silva Galdames 1977–8, Stehberg 1976, Niemeyern 1969–70, Llagostera 1976, de Mesa and Gisbert 1973, Meyers 1976, Plaza Schuller 1976, Alcina Franch 1978, Rivera Dorado 1978), some means of systematizing the ways we look at Inca–local relationships are beginning to be attempted. González (1980), for example, has suggested a series of categories for Inca period ceramics related to the extent to which each category reflects a relationship to the Cuzco style associated with the state. He also has proposed a classification of sites which should be helpful in the various regions.

In 1972 I suggested that large Inca administrative centers might be associated mainly with attempts to control politically fragmented regions. In a somewhat similar vein, Miguel Rivera Dorado (1978) has hypothesized an inverse relationship between the "level of development and integration" of an area and the expectation of finding abundant Cuzco forms and designs in locally made vessels. It is reasonable that Cuzco-created administrative mechanisms would be more necessary in areas where existing organizational forms were not adequate for Inca purposes. Likewise, Inca vessel attributes may have had more prestige in areas not already centralized. However, the Chincha area is a prominent exception to this, and we must realize that many variables affected the nature of Inca rule and its durable material remains.

While we await the results of more systematic studies involving a variety of regions it may be useful to suggest that two variables in the regional situation seem to stand out at this time in influencing settlement pattern, site characteristics, and ceramic attributes. These are the degree of existing political centralization just mentioned and the extent to which Inca rule was resisted. These of course are apart from ecological variables that set up patterns of resource distribution and, in turn, affected Inca plans and actions. An example of a previously centralized region which accepted the hegemony of Cuzco peacefully may be Chincha – where a substantial Inca component was grafted onto an important local center and Cuzco ceramic elements were pervasive in local wares associated with people of various social levels. In these cases we would not expect a rapid abandonment of Inca elements when the empire was overthrown. In the case of zones with relatively well-developed mechanisms of central control which resisted Inca domination we might expect rather minimal Inca architectural remains associated with principal centers, and perhaps even the partial abandonment of such centers as local control was disarticulated. The ceramic pattern might be rather like Menzel's description for

Fig. 8.5 Cuzco–Inca vessel forms. Adapted from Rowe 1944.

Ica referred to above. The previous local style is replaced with a new local style which incorporates some Cuzco elements, but remains highly individualistic. We might further expect such a style to be abandoned with the fall of Tawantinsuyu, as was the case in Ica.

In regions where a suitable political mechanism was not in place the Inca probably attempted to create one. Administrative centers were built from the ground up and the ceramics associated with them made under state supervision incorporating large numbers of Cuzco attributes. Such ceramics were probably limited largely to the state centers and the direct lines of political authority. The influence of this "state style" on the local styles would have varied in terms of many factors – among them the extent to which local groups embraced or rejected Inca rule and, probably, the distance from Inca state centers. The example which comes to mind here is the Huánuco region; the variation on this pattern may have been the case in many peripheral regions of the empire where pre-existing polities were rather small. The state installations themselves would have varied enormously with shifting objectives as well as differing possibilities based on economic, strategic, and environmental circumstances. There are indications, for example, that the large centers with high frequencies of easily recognizable Inca ceramics common in the Peruvian Central Highlands may be quite rare in the southern tier of the empire.

As a result of work in several regions of Tawantinsuyu we can now appreciate some of the very great variability in the regions ruled and in the obviously flexible approach to rule. As research continues we hope to be able to recognize some patterns and principles in that regional variation. With better communication between the numerous scholars of various nationalities working on the topic, progress should be rapid.

The movement of goods

Systematic studies of sources and movements of products have not yet been undertaken on any significant scale for the Inca period. The promise of such studies for resolving several problems related to the nature of Tawantinsuyu, however, is considerable. Most obviously, following the flow of goods from their sources of production to their ultimate use and disposal offers an opportunity to examine exchange systems. If the tendency we noted in Huánuco for the flow of certain goods to follow lines of political authority can be confirmed more broadly, these studies could provide valuable political data as well. For example, the extent to which exchange involved reciprocities and redistribution can be examined as I have explored elsewhere (Morris 1978), provided that the contexts in which goods are produced and used are also carefully studied.

In planning future work on the distribution of Late Horizon artifacts we must be acutely aware of the complexities of interpreting patterns of distribution. The past tendency to refer to an object found far from its locale of production as simply a "trade piece" is, fortunately, fast disappearing from archaeology. But it remains difficult to control contextual information sufficiently well to understand the long-distance movements of artifacts. We must also be aware that all of the goods in an economy do not circulate in exactly the same way and evaluate the specific variables likely to affect the movement of given products. Although certain principles of socio-political organization and exchange affect all goods, the heavy ceramics that constitute most of our evidence probably will not have patterns like those of more portable and ritually valuable textiles. Subsistence food products are likely to have yet another "circuit" or "circuits" of exchange.

We are fortunate in Inca studies that at least part of the critical context for interpreting distribution patterns can come from written sources. The *visitas* and other administrative records mentioned previously are especially valuable in defining the socio-political units within and between which items move. In the future we can anticipate an increase in sophisticated technical studies of artifact distribution in relation to the sources of the raw materials from which they are made. Carefully combined with the contexts of manufacture, distribution, and consumption as reconstructed from the archaeological and

Fig. 8.6 Inca ceramic vessels. Collected in 1896 on the Island of Titicaca, Bolivia, these are Bolivian variations of Inca-Cuzco design. Nos. B/1890, ht 40.5 cm; B/1908, ht 31.0 cm. Courtesy American Museum of Natural History.

written records, these should provide important new insights into the organization of Inca society and economy.

FUNCTIONAL STUDIES: THE RECONSTRUCTION OF LIFEWAYS AND INSTITUTIONS

While studies of geographic variation in architecture, ceramics, and other artifacts are essential to assessing the nature of the Late Horizon, they cannot stand alone. Eventually we need to know in some detail the patterns of human activities and organization in a wide range of Tawantinsuyu's varied regions. Some of this, of course, is available from the written sources, but these need to be supplemented. Archaeology can provide this kind of information through activity-pattern reconstruction in sites with good primary context and through systematic settlement-pattern studies of the kind first done by Willey (1953) and more recently carried out by Parsons and his colleagues in the Tarma region (Parsons and Matos Mendieta 1978). Since settlement-pattern surveys do not normally focus on Inca matters specifically, I will not deal with them here, except to comment that the regional approach they embody is essential and that it is unfortunate that more studies of this nature have not been done for the Andean area.

It is somewhat paradoxical that the explicit aim of activity reconstruction has been more characteristic of the study of early societies than of late ones.

Fig. 8.7 Inca ceramic vessels. Tripod bowl, pedestal bowls, and collared jar; Cuzco-Inca form. Nos. B/8866, ht 19.1 cm; B/2501, ht 12.0 cm; B/2507, ht 9.8 cm; B/8935, ht 13.2 cm. Courtesy American Museum of Natural History.

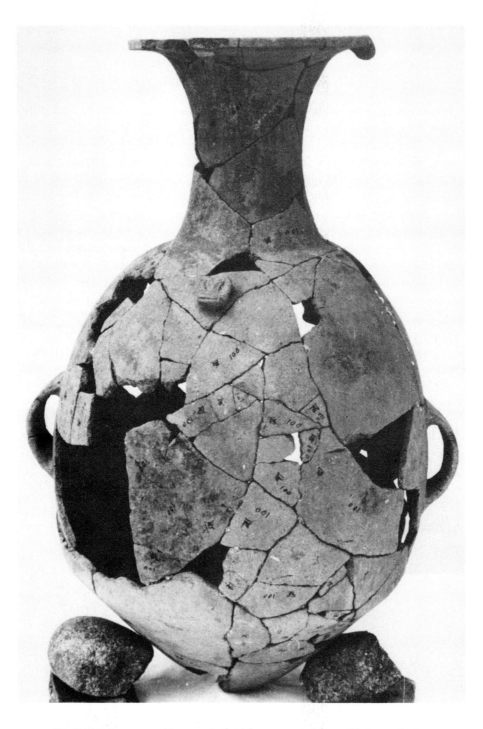

Fig. 8.8 Reconstructed Inca aryballoid from excavations at Huánuco Pampa.

This circumstance is as true for Andean archaeology as for the discipline as a whole. Part of the reason for this is the complexity of activity reconstruction for complex societies. Reconstruction of relatively specific non-subsistence activities is needed for most problems, and these in turn require situations of excellent archaeological context. The artifacts must be found in association patterns that reflect their use and the socio-cultural circumstances prevailing in the society which uses them. What the archaeologist usually finds, of course, is patterns of artifact disposal or abandonment rather than functional articulation with activities.

There are two further conditions that complicate activity-pattern studies in complex societies. The first has to do with the richness of the record. As societies evolve materially and technologically the range of activities with material references increases. At the same time that this opens up new avenues for the study of spheres such as religion and social organization, it creates an archaeological record which is in a sense cluttered with evidence of complicated overlapping activities and therefore difficult and costly to unravel.

The second special condition is that the pace of change in complex societies is rapid. Artifacts tend to flow through the system rapidly and to have their positions rearranged frequently. This is not conducive to the ideal conditions of context just mentioned. In addition, since all more elaborate archaeological goals depend on first establishing contemporaneity, as the pace of change

Fig. 8.9 Inca tunic, Island of Titicaca, Bolivia; Colonial Period. Found inside a carved stone chest near the site of Muro-Kato. The presence of silver tinsel silk yarns in the figures in the lower border indicates Spanish influence. Tapestry weave. No. B/1500, length 97.8 cm, width 80.0 cm. Courtesy American Museum of Natural History.

quickens certain changes may take place more rapidly than we can measure them. Some problems, thus, must await the development of more precise chronological controls, as discussed earlier.

Reconstructions of activities can proceed successfully so long as sites with exceptional context are found or methods worked out whereby worthwhile results can be obtained from less than ideal preservation of horizontal context. For example, general information on subsistence and technological activities can usually be recovered adequately from a small sample even if only a disposal context is available, so long as chronology can be controlled.

Fortunately many sites with exceptional context are available for Inca archaeology. In many parts of Tawantinsuyu new installations were built by the state on virgin ground. After enduring less than a century, the empire collapsed in most areas within a very few years of the European invasion, resulting in the rapid abandonment of many sites. Some disorder of course resulted in the aftermath of the European decapitation of the state, but some of the more isolated sites appear to have artifact distribution patterns which reflect the last days of the Inca period remarkably well. The sites have complex

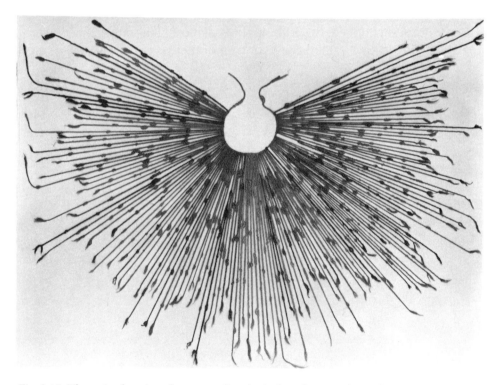

Fig. 8.10 The *quipu* functioned as a recording device based upon a decimal system. The recording units are the knots, which are coded by size, location, relative sequence, and color. Modern variations are still used in Highland Peru today, although in a simplified form. No. B/8705, side-to-side width *c*. 120 cm. Courtesy American Museum of Natural History.

internal structuring of both architecture and artifact distribution; the structuring was left basically intact as the sites were abandoned in the 15th century and not essentially modified by minimal European occupation and use. I have worked in two such sites in the Peruvian Central Highlands which demonstrate, I feel, the feasibility of even rather ambitious goals of activity reconstruction. Some of the results of that work are published in preliminary form and need not be summarized here (Morris and Thompson 1970, Morris 1966, 1967, 1971, 1974, 1975, 1980). Among the other research which has aimed either explicitly or implicitly at Late Horizon activity patterns and the socio-cultural institutions that shaped them, that of Timothy Earle and his colleagues in the Upper Mantaro Valley has been especially notable (Earle *et al.* 1980). The comparative survey of Inca architecture by Gasparini and Margolies (1980) has been aimed in part at function and activity reconstruction. John Hyslop's entire Inca road survey referred to above should make a major contribution to the understanding of the function of various sites and architectural complexes. His survey and mapping in the site of Incawasi in the Cañete Valley will contribute data pertinent to activity identification in a critical Inca coastal site.

There is a need to expand the functional approach, developing more archaeological projects that look explicitly at social, economic, and political issues. In particular it would be useful to have the results of large-scale intra-site studies based on excavations to compare with those now emerging from the Peruvian Central Highlands. It is necessary to keep in mind, however, that certain classes of Late Horizon site are better candidates for activity-pattern studies than others, and these may not be evenly distributed throughout Tawantinsuyu. It is primarily state installations in the provinces which have those attributes of rapid building and abandonment bracketing a short occupation. Many of these, of course, have been adversely affected by relatively recent occupation or cultivation, but others have survived thanks to their isolation. Certain activities in a state society can be studied only in its capital. Inca Cuzco, of course, is gone except for a few fragments. Several other sites in the region are well preserved, however, and these can be profitably studied. Ann Kendall's (1974) research at Cusichaca, which includes functional considerations among its objectives, should give us some indication of the productivity of such research in that area. Luis Watanabe's investigations in areas not previously "cleaned" at Machu Picchu should add some badly needed activity data on that still enigmatic site. The publication by Alcina Franch (1976) and his colleagues of the full documentation of the architecture and ceramics of Chinchero provides critical functional information on that site.

While championing the contribution that functional studies can make to numerous issues regarding the Inca period, one must hasten to recommend caution. The broad applicability of the approach for complex societies has not yet been demonstrated. It is obviously difficult, costly, and not appropriate to

Fig. 8.11 Silver alpaca figure from the Island of Titicaca. The corrugated exterior effect is achieved with hammered sheet silver soldered into place. Details are accentuated with repoussé and chasing. No. B/1619, ht 23.8 cm. Courtesy American Museum of Natural History.

Fig. 8.12 Hollow silver figurine in diagnostic Inca style. These figurines are often found as offerings and are sometimes clothed in miniature textile garments. From the Island of Coati, Lake Titicaca, Bolivia. No. B/9608, ht 15.7 cm. Courtesy American Museum of Natural History.

all sites and regions. Yet it clearly does work for certain topics and cases; storage is perhaps its greatest success to date. The final conclusion in all of these considerations is that for many important questions the archaeological study of activities is the only source of answers.

STRUCTURAL APPROACHES: IDEOLOGY AND PRINCIPLES OF ORGANIZATION

We come finally to the most tentative and difficult to assess recent advances in the study of the material remains of the Inca. These involve a wedding of the structuralist-oriented studies of the written sources and modern ethnographic evidence to the results of archaeological field work. Here we not only have to face the questions a traditionally positivist discipline such as archaeology must ask of structuralist studies, we also must contend with the lack of an adequate and accepted methodology for a structural approach to archaeological data. Without pursuing the broader epistemological problems, it seems evident that such approaches are as promising as they are dangerous and difficult. They at least represent a way in which limited information can be organized to build models to help understand the material record. If some independent information on similar themes can come from ethnohistoric and ethnographic

Fig. 8.13 Cuzco stone masonry with mortarless joints.

sources the process of cross-checking referred to previously can help keep us out of the arid territory of so many purely archaeological attempts to "model" the social and cultural dimensions of dead societies without any ties to known groups.

The beginnings of these approaches go back to R. Tom Zuidema's classic, and difficult to decipher, study of the organization of holy places (wakas) in the vicinity of Cuzco (Zuidema 1964). This work has been followed by a rich body of research, much of it by Zuidema and his students, examining a wide range of themes from a primarily structuralist perspective. We are interested here only in those studies which have specifically examined aspects of the material record to see how they correspond to the organizational principles derived from written sources and ethnographic field work. Zuidema's original study of the ceque system of Inca Cuzco did not concern itself with the working out on the ground of the principles by which the Inca holy places were organized. Later he did attempt to locate some of these sites, largely in terms of assessing their relationship to astronomical phenomena and the calendar, work carried out in part in collaboration with Anthony Aveni (Zuidema 1982). Janet Sherbondy (1980) has made extensive studies of the irrigation systems in the vicinity of Cuzco, tracing the water courses in relation to information on the groups which controlled them. Her analysis has looked at the water system in terms of the ritual calendar and the principles which organized it in space and by socio-political hierarchies. I myself have made a tentative effort (Morris 1980) to look at the site plan of Huánuco Pampa in terms of some of the spatial and hierarchical principles suggested by the ceque system and ethnographic work, such as that of Isbell (1978). The exact nature of the correspondences between the site plan and principles of organization derived from ethnohistoric and ethnographic sources cannot be ascertained with the information presently available. However, I have no doubt that dualism, tripartition, and quadrapartition were guiding principles in the division and organization of space at Huánuco Pampa, as they were to the organization of the ceque system. Furthermore, the hierarchical positions of the spaces created seem to show a general similarity to patterns of the ceques – though there are also some unexplained differences.

Several other attempts to look at spatial organization in the Late Horizon are now under way. The evidence so far collected is not sufficient to allow us to begin to draw specific generalizations regarding site planning. Indeed, in this too it is the diversity within Tawantinsuyu that is most notable. I feel confident, however, that such studies, as fraught with difficulties as they are, are essential. It is probable that the Andean concern with lines which connect, and also separate or divide, spaces and people is ultimately linked to such well-known features of Inca governance as the road system and the occupation and organization of a vast territory. While a strict and uniform set of principles probably was not followed, it is likely that some of the variation within and between regions is patterned, and when more data are available and analyzed we will find reason in them. I think we can see accumulating clues suggesting a distinctly non-European system of organization, and even of growth. Studies of spatial organization and related issues are likely to contribute fundamentally to our discovery of the nature of that system.

Most of our knowledge of the Inca still comes from the written sources. For a general summary of Inca culture one is still best directed to Rowe's (1946) classic review of the ethnohistoric material; for economic and political analysis one should turn to Murra's (1975, 1980) ethnohistoric work. The contributions of archaeology at this point constitute mainly verification, amplification, and modification of some of that material. Even the realms of subsistence and technology, where archaeology traditionally scores well, have received only passing consideration. We know that the Inca controlled the largest territory of any New World state; apparently this was achieved through some balance of military force, large-scale population relocation, and a kind of reciprocity in which state generosity on feast occasions and in support of people working on state projects mobilized vast amounts of human labor to finance the governmental enterprise.

In the preceding pages I have tried to suggest some of the ways in which archaeology's primary strategies have contributed to the existing sketch. In all cases, prospect clearly exceeds progress. The importance of gaining a thorough understanding of the Late Horizon extends beyond the fascination with that brief one-century interlude in the history of Andean civilization. The Inca period represents our best chance for understanding purely native Andean institutions. The evidence from ethnography, important for details on communities and overall principles of organization, cannot provide evidence on the upper levels of socio-political organization destroyed by European subjugation. The written evidence is the source of critical clues and hypotheses, but it is limited by the interests and perceptions of people not trained to observe an unfamiliar culture. The material record is the most uncontaminated, but it is fragmentary and expensive to study. The only viable approach is an eclectic one which combines the efforts of various specialists in anthropology and history. Archaeology must assume a more active role, combining the various approaches discussed here. By putting these complementary tactics together Inca scholars can construct the critical benchmark, providing a source of models and hypotheses that are useful for looking both backward and forward through the history of Andean culture.

9

From event to process: the recovery of Late Andean organizational structure by means of Spanish colonial written records

PATRICIA J. NETHERLY

HISTORY, ANTHROPOLOGY, AND ARCHAEOLOGY IN THE ANDES

In general it may be fairly stated that Andean archaeologists have not made effective use of the documents and accounts from the early Spanish colonial occupation of the Andean region in their reconstruction of late pre-Hispanic society and culture. Worse, there has developed among some archaeologists a tendency to utilize one or another scrap of documentary information as an "ethnohistorical datum" without proper citation or much regard for provenience. This state of affairs is difficult to explain, particularly since there have been several comprehensive surveys of documentary sources referring to the pre-Hispanic cultures of the Andes and these have been available for some years. A limited list would include Rowe (1946, 1948a), Murra (1956, 1970, 1980), and Wachtel (1977). A careful reading of these works would provide an initial entry into the large literature upon which Andean ethnohistory is based. This is particularly unfortunate because very often new insights for the interpretation of information contained in written accounts come from archaeological research.

By the same token, attempts to foster the combined use of archaeological and written information in a reciprocal fashion have been received with respect, but seldom imitated. In general these studies have been of two kinds. The first begins with a specific documentary account and proceeds to complement the written information with archaeological field study. The archaeological and ethnographic field studies carried out in Huánuco by John Murra and his associates between 1963 and 1966 were deliberately guided by information provided in a detailed administrative inspection tour of the region in 1567 (Murra 1962, Ortiz de Zúñiga 1967, 1972). On a more concrete level the field study of the Inca bridges of the region was the field study of a particular kind of structure of primordial importance to the pre-Hispanic transportation and communication networks, which may be considered typical of a class of artifacts – but not necessarily of all Inca or pre-Inca bridges. The organization of the construction and maintenance of such bridges was

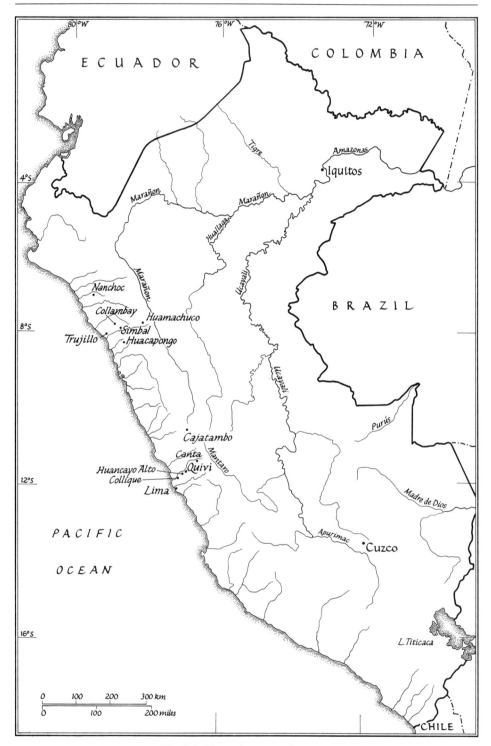

Fig. 9.1 Sites relevant to the text.

described in detail in testimony presented in colonial litigation (Thompson and Murra 1966, Mellafe 1965, 1967). In this case the organizational details, which are unrecoverable archaeologically, were present in the written record together with clues for the location of the bridges which could then be identified on the ground.

The second type of study has used information derived from documents as a means of generating new hypotheses that may be tested archaeologically and in the process provide a wealth of unanticipated information. This procedure characterizes Morris's work at Huánuco Pampa (1972b, 1974, 1976a, 1976b, 1978, 1979, 1980, 1981, Morris and Thompson 1970, Murra and Morris 1976). In his archaeological study of the Middle and Upper Chillón Valley and adjacent highland areas, Dillehay also took extensive colonial documentation on coast–highland relations as his point of departure (Dillehay 1976, 1977, 1979). A synchronic description of late pre-Hispanic Chimú and Chimú-Inca society on the North Coast also has provided many new questions for archaeological research (Netherly 1977a, 1977b, 1978, 1984). In the latter case there was no single coherent account and a synthetic description of late pre-Hispanic society had to be based on fragmentary and scattered sources.

The stumbling blocks to greater integration of the use of documentary sources into archaeological research of the appropriate periods – the 15th and 16th centuries AD and perhaps the 14th as well – lie in a failure to grasp the underlying similarities in historical, archaeological, and ethnological inquiry as well as the technical differences which distinguish them. Expanding upon an analysis offered long ago by Evans-Pritchard (1962: 23–5) it can be noted that all three disciplines operate on different analytical levels which are similar in degree of abstraction. The primary level is one of basic data-gathering: archaeological field data, description of discrete events as recorded in written sources, direct ethnographic field observations of human behavior. In each case there is a greater universe of information than the investigator can possibly record and a selection must be made. Whether acknowledged or unacknowledged, this selection is based upon a classification of the primary data resulting from a ranking based on the postulates of the particular discipline. At the same time all three disciplines enjoin a self-conscious objectivity upon their practitioners.

In order to invest the primary data with "meaning" or relevance, it is necessary to proceed to a further level of abstraction. At this level the historian will deal with a processional series of events in, for example, the history of the development of a particular institution, in the course of which an attempt will be made to establish logical relations of causation. E. H. Carr puts it very neatly:

> History therefore is a process of selection in terms of historical significance. To borrow Talcott Parsons' phrase once more, history is

"a selective system" not only of cognitive, but of causal, orientations to reality. Just as from the infinite ocean of facts the historian selects those which are significant for his purpose, so from the multiplicity of sequences of cause and effect he extracts those, and only those, which are historically significant; and the standard of historical significance is his ability to fit them into his pattern of rational explanation and interpretation. Other sequences of cause and effect have to be rejected as accidental, not because the relation between cause and effect is different, but because the sequence itself is irrelevant. The historian can do nothing with it; it is not amenable to rational interpretation, and has no meaning either for the past or the present. Carr 1962: 99

The anthropologist, on the other hand, has proceeded from ethnographic to ethnological analysis and seeks to uncover the relations between events and the nature of institutions – which are made up of regularly recurring concatenations of relations. At this analytical stage the archaeologist is constructing regional chronologies and cultural histories.

There is a higher level of analysis in all these disciplines, however. For historians it is comparative history – a level on which the analysis is clearly in processual terms. The ethnologist also compares institutions and processes and seeks underlying universal regularities. Archaeology has focused much in recent years upon processual analysis. The point to remember is that the primary and secondary modes of analysis must occur before proceeding to a processual analysis, or instead of science we will find ourselves in the realm of fantasy.

At this point we can turn to a consideration of the role of ethnohistory with a better notion of the boundaries within which it can operate. Ethnohistory may be defined as the study of non-Western peoples by means of historiographic techniques using an anthropological analytical framework. Anthropological archaeologists and ethnologists share such an anthropological perspective. It is the historiographic techniques which appear formidable; they do, indeed, introduce a series of requirements which have not always been met.

First of all, those attempting ethnohistorical studies must control the language of record, which may well be different from their own and from that of the indigenous peoples they study. Secondly, the student of ethnohistory must control the historiographic techniques which permit the evaluation of the authenticity, veracity, and trustworthiness of written sources and the information they contain (Bloch 1949). Archaeologists who have already adjusted to the acquisition of mastery over statistics and the use of computers as essential analytical tools – both of which require considerable effort – will grant the reasonableness of this requirement.

It is also necessary to know something of the culture of those who write down the original observations about a given society. As readers of such written records, we can observe the object of our study only indirectly through the eyes of another individual, frequently from a culture and time quite different from our own (Netherly 1970). Fig. 9.2 summarizes the nature of the observations frequently necessary in this sort of study and shows how the recording observer acts as a filter between the student and the object of his study.

Ethnohistory or historical anthropology can be seen to be a particular combination of methodologies corresponding to the exigencies of the analytical situation, rather than a separate discipline. The development of social structures in the past or the history of a non-literate culture are extremely difficult for the ethnohistorian to recover through documents written after contact with a literate culture, although some help may come from archaeology, linguistics, and oral history. Often the only study there may be of a precontact society is a synchronic analysis of the social structure at the moment of contact or in the period immediately before contact. A diachronic or processual analysis for the contact period becomes possible when a non-literate society

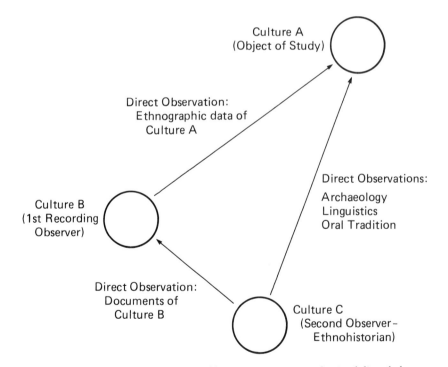

Fig. 9.2 Direction of perception is indicated by arrows. Data are obtained directly by means of archaeology, linguistics, or oral tradition. Ethnographic information about Culture A is perceived directly by the First Observer, the recorder, but indirectly through the written record by the ethnohistorian or Second Observer.

has been in contact with a literate one over a period of time and a number of observations have been recorded, or where it is possible to extend the record backward in time archaeologically. In all cases where the recording observer wrote earlier than this century, a special effort is required of the ethnohistorian to come to terms with the cultural assumptions of the original observer, as well as the standard external and internal historiographic critiques of the document and its contents.

In summary it should be understood that ethnohistory is not a discipline but a series of investigative techniques. As the Peruvian scholar Franklin Pease G. Y. has noted, there exists no corpus of "ethnohistorical documentation" (1977b: 178), nor are unprovenienced "ethnohistorical data" a magical quick fix of somehow greater efficacy or weight, because they are written, than information obtained by other means. Like ceramic analysis, ethnohistorical research requires long hours of application and painstaking work. As Flannery (1977) has noted, "old-fashioned" scholarship is part of the intellectual heritage of our larger discipline.

For the study of the pre-Hispanic past in the Andes we are fortunate in that there is an extraordinarily rich archaeological record and a multitude of documents of all kinds from the early decades of Spanish domination when remnants, at least, of the complex Andean society were still functioning. The case study presented below is a good example of the movement between disciplines and levels of analysis which characterizes the attempt to understand many of the processes present in the Andes in the immediately pre-Hispanic past.

COCA AND INCA STRATEGIES OF CONTROL
ON THE WESTERN FLANKS OF THE ANDES

We are becoming increasingly aware of the importance of coca (*Erythroxylum coca*) in the religious and cosmological beliefs of Andean peoples. Its political significance during Inca times, at least, is also well established. Likewise, recent archaeological surveys by Dillehay in the Chillón Valley and Hyslop in southern Peru attest to the construction of large flights of terraces on the western slopes of the Peruvian Andes destined in particular for the cultivation of coca and maize. Such terracing can be found from Arica in the south to the valleys of the north.

Today legal, commercial coca cultivation on the western slopes of the Andes is found only in the Department of La Libertad on the North Coast. It is particularly prevalent in the area around Simbal located on a tributary of the Moche River (see Fig. 9.3).

The close juxtaposition of differing ecozones characteristic of tropical mountains is present in the Andes. Following the geographer Carl Troll, a three-dimensional arrangement of climatic type, plant formations and landscapes can be discerned in this region consisting of (1) vertical change from sea level to the region of permanent snow, (2) a change from north to south according to latitude, and (3) a change from east to west generally from more to less precipitation (Troll 1970: 34, fig. 15).

The geographic zone favored above all others for coca production in pre-Hispanic times lies on the western side of the Andean cordilleras. It lies above the *chala* – the cool, moist, coastal zone covered by clouds through the influence of the cold Peru Current (Pulgar Vidal 1972: 50–4, Koepcke 1954). This maritime-influenced coastal zone extends inland 30 to 50 km to an altitude just under 1,000 m above sea level at 12° S. Lat. on the Central Peruvian coast (Koepcke 1954). The region lying above this zone to an altitude of about 2,400 m is frequently considered one unit (see Pulgar Vidal 1972: 56). Insolation is greater in this region and the natural vegetation of the zone on the Central Coast is characterized by associations of columnar cactus at 1,000 m followed by communities of *Caroca* (*mito*) and *Jatropha* (*huarango*) thorn

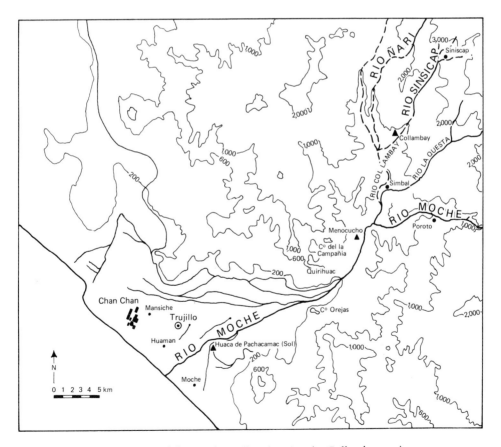

Fig. 9.3 Map of the Moche Valley showing the Collambay region.

scrub. These are succeeded at 2,100 m by a scrub steppe. Both zones above 1,400 m may be associated with seasonal grasses (Koepcke 1954: 18).

My own observations of the vegetation zones on the western slopes of the Andes between 7° and 9° S. Lat. lead me to suggest that at the latitude of the Jequetepeque Valley and to the north there is greater humidity, and these vegetational zones are lowered some 400–600 m. Thus columnar cactus occurs at 300 m and below; the thorn scrub is present in some areas at 900 m. On the other hand, in the Sinsicap drainage (9° S. Lat.), a tributary to the Moche River which extends from 300 to 3,000 m, the plant succession above 1,000 m did not differ so markedly from that reported for the Rimac Valley on the Central Coast by Koepcke (1954).

The internal complexity of the ecozones on the western slopes between 800 and 2,400 m in the south or 300–3,000 m in the north has not been fully studied. In the following discussion we will adhere to the 16th-century term for the ecozone called the *chaupiyunga*, "between hot and cold" (Vazquez de Espinoza [1630] 1948: no. 1225), which designated a region characterized by a warm, sunny climate with little variation, lying above the coast or *chala* and below the lower sierra *quishua* zone. This description clearly refers to the ecozone lying along the western flanks of the cordillera between 800–1,200 m at 12° S. Lat. and between 300–1,800 m at 9° S. Lat. This area was used for the production of coca, *ají* (*Capsicum* sp.), fruits, and maize.

The cultivation of coca in this zone goes back 4,000 years on the Central Coast, but an initial date for its production in this region has not been established (Patterson 1971b). In all probability the first dates for cultivation will prove to be even earlier in the north. Plowman (1979, 1984) has described the botanical characteristics of cultivated coca and those traits that distinguish the Trujillo variety of coca (*Erythroxylum novogranatense* var. *truxillense*; see Fig. 9.4) – drought tolerance and superior taste – from the variety grown on the eastern slopes of the Andes. Thus we find the preferred form of coca, a cultigen of enormous cultural significance for Andean peoples, and an ecozone especially propitious for its cultivation, the *chaupiyunga*, occurring as a band along the western slopes of the Andes between the coastal climatic province and the temperate areas of the highlands. An origin myth for coca, collected in Cajatambo above the Chancay and Huaura valleys, appears to refer to coca grown on the western slopes of the cordillera in both valleys. In it coca is described as having been the exclusive prerogative of the Sun, a reflection of the great religious importance of this crop (Duviols 1973).

What is most significant about the data on coca production in this region during the period immediately before the Spanish Conquest is the light they shed on the socio-economic organization of the use of this resource zone by the societies of the coast and highlands in the Late Intermediate Period and the reorganization of coca exploitation in this region under the highland-based Inca state.

Until very recently nothing was known about the relative significance of the *chaupiyunga* as a coca-producing zone for the highland societies of the western cordillera. For the inhabitants of the coast, where fruit, *ají*, and even coca can be grown within the maritime climatic province, the *chaupiyunga* region represents a supplemental zone of greater productivity, particularly of coca and *ají*. For the inhabitants of the adjacent highlands, however, the *chaupiyunga* represents in many cases the only zone in which these cultigens could be grown. Highland pressure upon the *chaupiyunga* region was probably always intense.

The basic model for the competition between highland and lowland groups for the coca-producing *chaupiyunga* ecozone derives in the first instance from 16th-century litigation over the coca lands of Quivi (Fig. 9.5) in the middle Chillón Valley (Rostworowski 1967–8, Murra 1972). These lands are located at about 1,100 m above sea level at the junction of the Arahuay River with the Chillón. The fields were watered by irrigation canals which drew water from the Arahuay. The area produced coca, fruit such as *pacae* and *lúcuma*, *ají*, maize, and cotton. The detailed information presented in the colonial documentation has been complemented and corroborated by archaeological research, a most unusual situation in the Andes (Dillehay 1976, 1977, 1979).

Fig. 9.4 Coca bushes (*Erythroxylum novogranatense* var. *truxillense*) growing in the shade of pacae trees (*Inga feuillei*) at Collambay in 1976. Photo by T. Plowman. Collambay lies within the *chaupiyunga* zone of the Moche Valley.

The testimony presented in the litigation indicates that during the Late
Intermediate Period, Quivi was subject to the *kuraka* or lord of Collique,
located on the coast in the Lower Chillón Valley. In the pre-Inca period, by
means of increased military pressure on the part of the highland groups of
Canta, a portion of the Quivi coca lands was ceded to this highland group.
Witnesses from adjacent ethnic groups in the valley testified that the Canta
people enjoyed a certain right to this ecozone because it was watered by the
Quivi River (the Arahuay), which had its source in their territory
(Rostworowski 1967–8: 55–6). A second highland group, the Chacalla, sub-
ject to the Yauyos of Huarochirí, occupied the highland salient between the
Chillón and Rimac rivers. In addition to the access they already enjoyed to

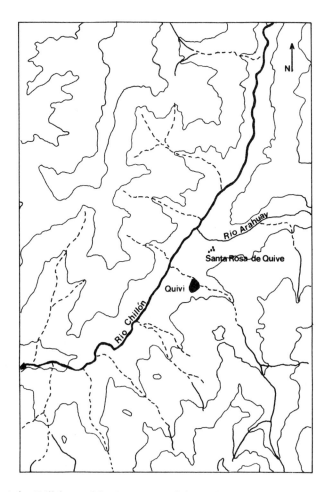

Fig. 9.5 Map (after Dillehay) of the Quivi area of the Middle Chillón Valley. The pre-Hispanic
settlement of Quivi is indicated. The coca lands lay between the settlement and the Arahuay
River on land that sloped toward the Chillón. Water to irrigate these terraced fields was brought
by canals whose intakes were located on the Arahuay.

chaupiyunga lands in the Mama (Sta. Eulalia) Valley in the Rimac drainage, the Chacalla were also able to gain access to coca-producing lands at Quivi some two generations before the Inca conquest (Rostworowski 1967–8: 14, 21, 41, Murra 1972: 447). Thus, well before the advent of the Inca, the coastal polity of Collique had abandoned its monopoly of the Quivi coca lands in order to retain partial access to this region of high coca productivity.

The nature of the Inca administration and control of the coca-producing zone of Quivi appears clearly in the testimony of the litigation. Briefly summarized, a portion of the Quivi lands held by the people of Quivi subject to Collique, together with a portion of the Canta Islands at Quivi, was seized by an Inca official in the name of the conquering Inca, Topa Inca Yupanqui, and his Coya or principal wife. These lands were cultivated by *mitmaq* from the Chacalla, part of the highland Yauyos ethnic group. The *mitmaq* were transferred populations which retained their socio-political and ethnic ties with their home base. A marker was set up in the name of the Inca at the western boundary of the Canta lands to demarcate the political division between coastal and highland peoples (Rostworowski 1967–8: 56–7). The *mitmaq* from Chacalla numbered between 150 and 200 households and were drawn from both moieties of Chacalla (Rostworowski 1967–8: 21, 32). They were charged with the cultivation of coca for the Inca and also with other responsibilities of service to the Inca state: serving as *chasqui* or runners, and as bearers (Rostworowski 1967–8: 20, 57).

At the time Huayna Capac became the principal Inca ruler, a new parcel of coca lands at Quivi was confiscated for the use of the new Inca. These lands were taken from the Quivi lands held by the people of Canta and a new political boundary marker was set up between the highlands: Canta territory, and the coast: the *mitmaq*, Quivi, and *yungas*, at the western edge of Quivi pueblo (the archaeological site known as Quibi Viejo) (see Fig. 9.5).

From the point of view of the Inca state organization, the use of *mitmaq* from a loyal subject group like the Yauyos ensured the production of coca for the Inca state in the name of the Inca and his principal wife or Coya and provided trustworthy runners and bearers for state service. The *mitmaq* also acted as a military garrison, keeping both the coastal population of Quivi and Collique and the restive Canta highlanders under observation.

Coca production itself was under the care of the *kuraka principal* or paramount lord of the Atun Yauyos group of Huarochirí. Of the total production from the Inca coca fields, some 150–60 sacks (*costales*), 4 or 5 were given to the lords of Chacalla for distribution to the lords of their ethnic group. The other crops grown – maize, *ají*, yuca, potatoes, and fruit – were used to maintain the *mitmaq*, but in what proportion is not clear. The Inca goveror of the administrative center at Jauja sent to Quivi for coca and *ají* to replenish his supplies on at least one occasion (Rostworowski 1967–8: 33). Fruit cultivation, particularly of *guayaba* or *pacae* (*P. inga*), was associated

Fig. 9.6 A silver figurine of a member of the Inca aristocracy. This man has the long, stretched ear lobes caused by the large cylindrical earspools worn by men of the Inca elite. The Spanish called such men *orejones*, or "big ears." The figurine has a large quid of coca in his left cheek. Such figurines were richly dressed and had feather headdresses. Dumbarton Oaks Collection, Washington, D.C.

with the production of coca (see Fig. 9.4). The dried fruit seems to have been an important item in the Inca redistribution network and has been recovered along with coca leaf in the archaeological excavation of the storehouses of the Inca administrative center at Huancayo Alto, just to the west of Quivi in the Chillón Valley (Dillehay 1976, 1979).

In contrast to these lands under indirect, but close, state control, other *chaupiyunga* lands of the *waranqa* of Huancayo in the Chillón Valley provided the Inca state with tribute which included 45 large baskets of coca, 36 large baskets of *ají*, 45 small reed caskets (*pectacas*) of "*suara de coca*" (*mate*), as well as dried birds, dried fruit, and dried crayfish – all products of this ecozone. The *waranqa* of Huancayo also cultivated a small garden of coca which was harvested and taken fresh as an offering for the cult of the Sun (Martínez Rengifo 1963: 65). The lord of the *waranqa* of Huancayo received 25 baskets of coca each *mit'a* or harvest (Martínez Rengifo 1963: 64) in addition to *ají*, maize, beans, sweet potatoes, yuca, and cotton planted and harvested for him by his subjects. It would seem that the people of Huancayo, like those of Canta, retained direct control over their coca production, incurring the obligation of producing a part of their harvest for the Inca state. The 45 baskets of coca given to the Inca state by the 900 households of Huancayo is notably less than the production of 150–60 sacks of coca by the 150–200 *mitmaq* from Chacalla. We do not know whether the baskets or "*cestos*" mentioned in the Martínez Rengifo *visita* to Huancayo in 1571 were equivalent to the sacks or "*costales*" of the Quivi litigation of 1559. It is possible that the Inca used a common unit of measure for the two neighboring groups and that it is the translation which is at variance. On the other hand it may be that the method of packing the coca was different in the two groups. The highland Chacalla would have access to wool to make sacking; the lowland Huancayo would have access to the raw materials to make baskets. Either container would provide the ventilation needed for the coca. If we assume that the measures are equivalent, then the Inca state received about one-third the quantity of coca from the 900 households of Huancayo as from the Inca coca fields at Quivi. It is also possible that the 5 sacks of coca given by the Chacalla *mitmaq* to their own lord is in line with the 20 baskets given to the *waranquakuraka* (literally "lord of a thousand households") of Huancayo by his subjects, although clearly the quantity is much smaller. Structurally, this assured the Inca state of the loyalty of the regional rulers. At the same time, the greater productive efficiency achieved by placing *mitmaq* on lands assigned to the Inca in a zone of high productivity is also obvious.

The foregoing detailed description of the location and administration of Inca coca fields in the Middle Chillón Valley is justified because it serves as a model for Inca control of coca production in other areas, where Inca coca fields are known to have existed, but detailed information on production and administration is lacking.

Inca coca fields are reported from Collambay in the Sinsicap Valley (Fig. 9.7), a tributary of the Moche River, in land titles to the former Hacienda Collambay dating from the mid 16th century (ANP Aguas 3.3.18.68). The Inca coca lands formed the nucleus of the 16th-century hacienda. Today the area between Simbal and Collambay leads the rest of the Department of La Libertad in coca production. It outstrips the analogous area in the Moche Valley around Poroto, where coca is cultivated on a much-reduced scale.

The 16th-century land titles were granted to the *encomendero* of Huamachuco, don Juan de Sandoval, in 1562 and confirmed in 1565 and 1567. All required testimony by local and provincial indigenous lords as to the past ownership of the land. In each case it is clear that the lands in question had been three enclosed fields, named Yapon, Arensa, and Guancha, located at about 800 m above sea level on alluvial terraces on the west bank of the Sinsicap River in a location topographically analogous to that of the coca lands at Quivi (see Fig. 9.5). The total extension of the Inca lands was 12 *fanegadas* or 36 hectares (90 acres).

The land was watered by canals drawn from the Sinsicap River. It is evident from the colonial documentation that this river has limited water and if the Collambay lands were to be exploited, the cultivators in the upper Sinsicap

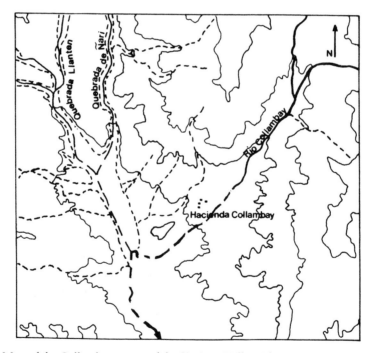

Fig. 9.7 Map of the Collambay sector of the Sinsicap Valley. The Sinsicap River is here called the Río Collambay. As at Quivi, the sloping alluvial terrace on the west bank formed by the river and the seasonal streams in the lower Quebrada de Ñari was the location of the Inca coca fields at Collambay. Coca is still grown there today (see fig. 9.4).

Valley must have been enjoined from drawing off all the flow for their own fields. The Inca state enjoyed the authority to do this. During the thirty years between the defeat of the Inca by the Spanish and 1562, however, the Collambay lands were not cultivated, perhaps out of fear or respect for the Inca, but more probably because local ethnic groups preferred to use the water upstream for their own lands.

In the immediately pre-Hispanic period the small ethnic groups in the Sinsicap Valley appear to have been subject to the *kuraka* of Mochal in the Moche Valley and he in turn to the *kuraka* of Huamachuco. This is another instance of the redrawing of the political boundaries between coast and highlands at the expense of the coastal states by the Inca state. This policy assured the Incas' highland allies, in this case the Huamachuco, of access to abundant *chaupiyunga* lands, and at the same time restricted the remnant Chimu rulers to the area between the confluence of the Sinsicap and the Moche (i.e., Quirihuac) and the sea.

This is in sharp contrast to the distribution of ceramics in the Middle Moche and Sinsicap valleys throughout the ceramic sequence. Reconnaissance shows coastal ceramics are abundant in this region and highland sherds appear much less frequently and as exotics. Recent archaeological survey by Theresa and John Topic in the Middle Moche Valley and the lower Sinsicap Valley around Simbal indicates that this region has been a zone of contact between coastal and highland peoples with coast influence particularly marked in the Middle Valley during Moche and Chimú times and hilltop fortifications a characteristic of the settlement pattern (Topic and Topic 1982). The presence of fortifications is surely also indicative of the intensity of highland pressure. Keatinge (1974) had earlier reported a Chimu elite residential/administrative structure at Quirihuac (see Fig. 9.3). What is remarkable as the result of this archaeological work is the absence of a regional Inca installation in the Middle Moche Valley (Topic and Topic 1982) similar to the one in the Huacapongo branch of the Virú Valley (Willey 1953), Huancayo Alto in the Chillón (Dillehay 1976), or the center in the Nanchoc branch of the Zaña Valley (Netherly 1976, 1977a, 1977b, Dillehay and Netherly 1983).

The three fields at Collambay were taken by the Inca ruler (probably Huayna Capac) through an Inca official. Yapon and Guancha were assigned to the Inca, while Arensa was assigned to the *mother* of the Inca. They produced coca and *ají* (ANP Aguas 3.3.18.68).

The fact that these fields were walled with *tapia* is noteworthy. *Tapia* walls around fields are not common outside Chan Chan. One informant testified that the walls around Yapon were built by men from Túcume, who returned to their home when they were finished (ANP Aguas 3.3.18.68: f. 108). The reason alleged for walling the fields was to prevent the foxes from entering and urinating on the coca, perhaps a desecration. The Agustinian Fathers in their relation about Huamachuco in the 1540s describe a cult of several animals

Fig. 9.8 A Moche portrait jar from Chepén with a broken spout depicts a one-eyed man with a coca quid in his left cheek. In Moche iconography such individuals seem often to have fulfilled ritual functions, perhaps as shamans (E. P. Benson, personal communication). Coca and coca chewing are frequent themes in Moche iconography usually in religious contexts, indicating the importance of coca to this North Coast civilization which flourished almost a millennium before the conquest of Chimor. Courtesy American Museum of Natural History.

Fig. 9.9 A Chimú–Inca face jar in a provincial and syncretic style. The Inca removed some of the finest of Chimú pottery-makers to the Highlands, but they also required local potters to work according to Inca stylistic canons, sometimes with odd results. The peculiarities may also have been the fruit of a passive resistance. The man represented on the jar has a large coca quid in his right cheek. Unlike the Inca silver figurine (Fig. 9.6), the ears are plain, probably indicating that this individual represents a local personage. Courtesy American Museum of Natural History.

such as skunks (*zorrino*) and other pests to prevent their harming the crops (Agustinos [1550] 1918: 38).

Without discounting the Andean belief, it is also possible to suggest several political considerations which may have motivated the Inca. Walling the fields was a means of displaying the Inca presence in a hostile, coastal zone. This seems to be the best explanation for bringing workmen from so far away as Túcume to build the wall. There were surely groups close by who could have built walls more economically. However, Túcume is known as a regional polity which was loyal to the Chimú and hostile to the Inca (Cabello Valboa [1586] 1951: 468), and this may have been an exemplary punishment for them as well. The walls also controlled access to the fields and protected them against thieves (cf. Calancha 1638: Lib III Cáp. 2, Lizárraga [1603–8] 1968: Cáp. CXIII: 98).

It is also interesting that these fields were abandoned at the Spanish conquest and were not brought into cultivation again until the *encomendero* began to use them thirty years later. The only exceptions are two occasions when the *kuraka* of Huamachuco in the Highlands and the *kuraka* of Mochal in the Middle Moche Valley ordered maize and *ají* planted in them (ANP Aguas 3.3.18.68). The shrinking populations of the post-Hispanic period must have had other fields in which they grew what coca they needed.

It was very common in the first years after the Spanish conquest for local peoples to recover lands seized from them by the Inca. This was the case of Quivi, for example. The question then arises as to why the Inca fields at Collambay were not cultivated for nearly thirty years after the defeat of the Inca. The most logical answer in Andean terms is that none of the nearby highland groups had prior claim to them. I would suggest that the Collambay fields may have been taken from either Chimú state lands or from those of one of the Chimú lords, whose claim to them could not have been made in colonial times because of the Spanish perpetuation of the Inca political boundaries and the dismembering of the Chimú state (Netherly 1976, 1977b). Furthermore, the witnesses from Huamachuco who testified at the establishment of title for Juan de Sandoval were all highlanders and would not be likely to mention a coastal claim.

The policy of containment followed by the Inca state with regard to the defeated Chimor kingdom has been described elsewhere (Netherly 1976, 1977b). It was consistently carried out in other northern valleys, such as Virú, as well (Netherly 1976, 1977b). The redrawing of the political boundary at 300 m not only gave the highlanders greater access to *chaupiyunga* lands, but also placed the Inca coca fields in friendly territory.

In the Sinsicap Valley, as in the Chillón, the mechanism used by the Inca to obtain multiple access to coca production was to assign coastal coca lands as personal lands of the Inca ruler and his close kin. In Collambay lands were assigned to the mother of the Inca; in Quivi they were given to his Coya or principal wife. This procedure was used in addition to requiring contributions in kind from groups with coca lands, as in the case of *waranqa* of Huancayo in the Chillón Valley. Additionally, in a fashion comparable to the policy followed in the Chillón Valley, where a significant portion of the coca-producing zone was put under the control of the adjacent highland province, the Sinsicap Valley with the Middle Moche Valley became part of the highland province of Huamachuco in Inca times.

The similarity of the patterns reported from Quivi and Collambay suggests a highly consistent Inca policy toward a particular ecozone, which was aligned longitudinally along the western slopes of the Andean cordillera, the coca-producing *chaupiyunga*, because of the ritual and political significance of the coca crop. This uniformity in policy can be contrasted with the variable Inca treatment of the defeated valley states of the North, Central, and South Coast regions (Netherly 1976, 1977b).

In many ways the combined ethnohistorical and archaeological information about the Middle Chillón Valley and Quivi are unique in the Andes. They are particularly valuable because they illuminate the interaction between different ethnic groups across an ecological frontier and the redefinition of political boundaries by state-level polities with reference to a particular ecozone. The combined evidence for Quivi serves as a model which permits interpretation of the scantier written evidence from Collambay in the Moche drainage. Although archaeological survey has been carried out in this area, it was directed toward other questions (Topic and Topic 1982). Further archaeological research, particularly between Mochal and Con Con in the Middle Moche Valley, should add new insights. In contrast, the Inca presence in the Huacapongo branch of the Virú Valley reported by Willey (1953), and the comparable Inca administrative center in the Nanchoc branch of the Zaña Valley, on a principal route to the highlands of Cajamarca (Netherly 1976, 1977b, Dillehay and Netherly 1983), lack written references. However, our understanding of their significance is greatly enhanced by the documentary information available for Quivi and Collambay. This evidence permits the framing of hypotheses as to possible function which can then be tested through archaeological research.

IV
CONTRIBUTIONS FROM THE SELVA

10

A view from the tropical forest

J. SCOTT RAYMOND

In studies of the evolution of Andean civilization, often more attention has been paid to long-distance diffusion of ideas and traits from Mexico and across the Pacific than to possible contributions from cultures in the nearby tropical forest regions of Peru and Bolivia. The view which prevailed until recently among Andeanist archaeologists and anthropologists held that the rugged terrain of the eastern Andes, the high rainfall and the dense foliage of the cloud forest generally limited cultural development in the Upper Amazon to a simple farmer-fisher/hunter-gatherer stage and discouraged settlement, conquest, or intensive exploitation of the area by the Andean kingdoms and states. This view seemingly was confirmed by the historic accounts of the native cultures of the region and by frustrated attempts of Europeans to establish permanent settlements and develop commerce in the tropical forest.

Another contributing factor has been the general bias among historians of culture in believing that the ecology of an arid area is more conducive to the evolution of agrarian societies and hence to the development of high civilization than is the ecology of a tropical forest. In Peru there seemed no reason to doubt this assumption. Unlike Mesoamerica where it was necessary to explain the apparent anomaly of lowland Maya civilization (see Meggers 1954), the achievements of the Andean civilizations, culminating in the Inca Empire, stood in marked contrast to the achievements of the neighboring tropical forest peoples of the montaña.[1] Moreover, the bounty of archaeological remains preserved in the Peruvian desert attested the early development of plant domestication, monumental architecture, weaving, status differentiation, and many of the other characteristics associated with civilization.

That a chapter on the tropical forest is included in this volume is a sign that archaeologists now are paying more serious attention to the prehistoric cultural events of the montaña and their possible impact on the evolution of civilization in Peru. There is a growing recognition that, particularly with respect to the development of agriculture, the tropical forest cultures made important contributions to the beginnings of Peruvian civilization and that there was an ongoing commerce and contact among the peoples of the coast, highlands, and tropical forest.

Fig. 10.1 Sites relevant to the text.

There is a huge disparity in the quantity and quality of archaeological information available from the coast and highlands of Peru and the tropical forest. Despite a growing interest in tropical forest archaeology, that disparity is likely to continue to increase. The wet, warm environment of the forest is not kind to cultural remains; with the high rate of decay, organic substances do not survive long. And, since houses and the majority of artifacts are made out of wood, cane, bone, reeds, and other plant and animal remains, the only cultural residues which preserve to attest the prior existence of a settlement, under most circumstances, are ceramics and the rare objects made of stone and metal. The large rivers of the Upper Amazon, which provide an attractive environment for man to exploit, are also guilty of destroying evidence of occupation. Riverside settlements which escape erosion eventually may be buried in tons of sediment from the annual floods. Furthermore, the archaeological sites which survive are usually camouflaged by a blanket of vegetation.

It is an absurd understatement to say that there are gaps in the archaeological record of the Peruvian tropical forest. Gaping holes would be a more appropriate description, and it is unlikely that many of these holes will be filled. However, if we are to progress in our understanding of the prehistoric cultures of the tropical forest and their relationship to the Peruvian civilizations, we cannot become preoccupied with the lack of data; rather, we must recognize that the data are biased and that we must avoid being overly empirical in using the evidence. In this chapter, instead of giving a comprehensive review of the archaeolaogical evidence from eastern Peru and attempting a current synthesis of the culture history, I shall use archaeological, ethnohistorical, ethnological, and ecological information to consider the modes by which cultural interchange between the tropical forest and the highland and coastal regions of Peru might have occurred. I begin with a brief review of environmental factors and follow with a description of three different settlement systems which I use to define patterns of lowland–highland contact. Finally, I attempt to look at highland–lowland contact from a diachronic perspective by considering how the archaeological data fit with these proposed patterns.

ENVIRONMENTAL FACTORS

At the frontier between Peru and Ecuador the Andes are narrower and lower in altitude than they are at any other point in the long chain which reaches from northern South America to Tierra del Fuego. This narrow range, sometimes called the Chamaya Highlands, divides the northern extension of the Peruvian desert from the westernmost extension of the Amazonian rainforest and, through several low mountain passes, affords relatively easy travel between the two regions. From the Chamaya Highlands the tropical rainforest spreads eastward and southward along the flanks of the Andes and up the several valleys which subdivide the Peruvian Andes into a series of northwest–southeast-trending ranges (Fig. 10.2). On the west side, the Peruvian desert grades northward into the rainforest and tropical savannahs of western Ecuador. Thus the arid heartland of Peruvian civilization is bordered by tropical rainforest to the north and east. A transect in northern Ecuador would show a symmetric vegetational profile with the Andes ascending from tropical rainforest on the west and east. However, from southern Ecuador to northern Chile and Argentina an asymmetric pattern prevails; the coastal desert of the Pacific side contrasts markedly with the rainforest on the east (Troll 1968: 46).

The green blanket of vegetation seen when traveling by air over the eastern Andes gives the montaña a uniform appearance. This apparent homogeneity is illusory for it masks a diversity of landforms, plant communities, and microenvironments, all of which have important implications for man's settlement of the area. Local climate and vegetation is affected mainly by altitude, latitude, and exposure to the easterly trade winds. The cloud forest of the ceja, an evergreen broad-leafed forest with dense foliage, occurs along the steep eastern slopes of the Andes where they meet the moisture-laden winds from the Amazon (Fig. 10.3). The tree-line, at an altitude of 3,500–4,000 m, is

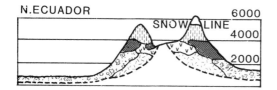

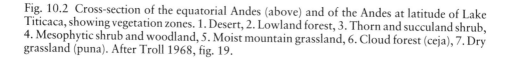

Fig. 10.2 Cross-section of the equatorial Andes (above) and of the Andes at latitude of Lake Titicaca, showing vegetation zones. 1. Desert, 2. Lowland forest, 3. Thorn and succuland shrub, 4. Mesophytic shrub and woodland, 5. Moist mountain grassland, 6. Cloud forest (ceja), 7. Dry grassland (puna). After Troll 1968, fig. 19.

determined mainly by the occurrence of frost. Above the cloud forest and below the snow-line, is a zone of constantly moist mountain grassland: *pajonal*. Generally the ceja vegetation grows to a higher altitude in the valleys than it does on the ridges between valleys because of the decreased danger of frost and the higher humidity in the valleys. Montane forest with a series of arboreal canopies reaching a height of 60–70 m gradually replaces the dense tangle of cloud forest below 2,000–1,500 m (Fig. 10.4).

Local topography is a strong factor affecting climatic and vegetation patterns. High mountains may block the moisture-laden airs, creating rain-shadows. Under such circumstances the windward side of the ridge may be covered with lush tropical vegetation while the leeward side supports a thorn forest. The deep valleys, which act as wind tunnels for the moist air from the Amazon, create topoclimatic conditions which result in marked contrasts in precipitation/vegetation patterns over very short distances (Troll 1968).

It is generally true that soils in the moist tropics are infertile. The hot and wet conditions lead to rapid weathering and depletion of soil minerals. Characteristically, such soils are acidic, high in aluminum and iron-oxides, and have a very shallow organic layer. Soil types in the montaña have not yet been thoroughly studied; however, it seems a fair guess that there is a great deal more variation in soil types than is commonly expected in the moist tropics

Fig. 10.3 View of ceja and sierra from the montaña, Apurimac Valley.

because of the mountainous terrain and the variability in parent rock material, geomorphology, and climate. Limestone outcrops, which occur in some of the valley systems, may ameliorate the acidity of some soils (e.g., the soils of the Alto-Pachitea; Allen 1968, Allen and Tizon 1973). The soils of the flood plains, which are renewed annually by the deposition of sediment, contrast markedly with the older soils between the rivers. The extent of the flood plain, then, which varies significantly between the various valleys, is an important factor in considering agricultural potential. Tropical-forest farmers have partly overcome the poor soils of the moist tropics by practicing shifting agriculture; however, in considering the effectiveness of this practice in the Peruvian montaña, slope and other factors affecting soil erosion must be taken into account.

Game and fishing are the two principal sources of protein in the montaña, although palm fruits may be an important secondary source. These resources are not distributed evenly over the landscape. Generally, the concentration of animal biomass is far greater along the riparian zones than between the rivers; however, because of the variability of the upper montaña topography, this is

Fig. 10.4 Cloud forest of the *ceja de la montaña*.

not as fixed a rule as it is in the lower montaña and the Amazon Basin. In some areas the forest gives way to grasslands; the largest example of this is in the Gran Pajonal at the headwaters of the Pachitea River.

In considering the economic importance of the montaña to highland peoples, it is not enough merely to study environmental variables in the montaña; one must also take account of relevant variables in the adjacent highland areas. Here we must take note of general differences between the northern and southern parts of the Central Andes. Rainfall in the Andes is affected, generally, by the same meteorological factors which affect rainfall in the Amazon Basin. Thus the valleys, mountains, and high grasslands become successively drier from north to south. In the north the valley bottom lands are generally broader, the slopes are better watered – permitting dry cropping of some drought-sensitive plant foods such as maize – and the cloud cover during the rainy seasons reduces the diurnal range of temperatures. In the valleys of the Marañon, Huallaga, Apurimac, and Urubamba, the vegetation of the montaña penetrates deeply into the mountains. Among these valleys, the Marañon is unique in that its short western tributary valleys reach up into the Cordillera Blanca to meet the headwaters of rivers which descend to the Pacific coast.

In the south the montaña is juxtaposed mainly to the cold, high, and dry environment of the Peru–Bolivian *altiplano*. The valleys are higher and narrower, and the headwaters of the Madre de Dios do not penetrate as deeply into the Andean core. The high altitude and clear skies cause a greater range in diurnal temperatures: night frosts and high daytime temperatures are common. These ecological differences, which noticeably contributed to the variance in the native economies of northern and southern Peru,[2] may have shaped the cultural forms of interaction between highlanders and lowlanders distinctly in the two regions, a topic which will be taken up later in this chapter.

SETTLEMENT SYSTEMS AND THE ECOLOGY OF THE MONTAÑA

Three prevailing patterns describe the cultural systems of settlement in the montaña. These derive mainly from differences in the economic systems. The dominant system of the lower montaña is that which Lathrap (1968a, 1970) refers to as Tropical Forest Culture. This pattern is best exemplified today by the Panoan-speaking Shipibo and Conibo who occupy the riparian zone along the main stream of the Ucayali River.

The second pattern is highly varied and less clearly defined, which can be attributed to the fact that it is found in the more varied environments of the interfluves, the smaller tributary valleys and in the hilly terrain of the upper montaña. Generally, it is true that this pattern is characterized by smaller settlements, which are less permanent and less likely to be integrated into centralized social, political, and economic systems. The modern Arawak-speaking Campa, Machiguenga, Piro, and the Panoan-speaking Amahuaca, Remo, and Cashibo exemplify this pattern (Fig. 10.5).

The third pattern is found in the narrow valleys and along the slopes of the upper montaña and the ceja. The ethnic groups found in this pattern are of highland origin, and it is basically an extension of the highland agrarian system. Unlike the two other systems, this one is not self-sufficient but is tied closely to social, political, and economic networks in the highlands.

The emergence and spread of the tropical riverine systems

Lathrap (1968, 1970) has argued cogently that the tropical forests of South America are not particularly propitious for the settlement of people dependent mainly on hunting and gathering. In the heart of the forest, neither game nor edible plant foods are found in concentrations. It is unlikely, then, that the Amazon Basin was inhabited by man to any significant extent until fishing technologies and the rudiments of horticulture were begun. If that is correct,

Fig. 10.5 Small Campa settlement on the Ene River.

then the montaña was probably not occupied for the first several thousand years after man first entered the South American continent. During the late Pleistocene/early post-Pleistocene, the belt of grassland bordering the upper edge of the cloud forest may have extended further down the flanks of the Andes. If it was rich in game it was probably part of the route followed by the early hunting cultures as they spread southward to Patagonia. But, there would have been little incentive for man to colonize the forested lands of the montaña, although there is ongoing debate concerning the extent to which the tropical forests contracted during drier episodes of the late Pleistocene (Meggers 1979).

As mentioned earlier, most of the evidence for prehistoric settlement in the montaña consists of ceramic-bearing sites. Lathrap's discoveries at Yarinacocha (Lathrap 1958, 1962, 1970) define a cultural sequence extending back to at least the beginning of the second millennium BC. The antiquity of the sequence at Yarinacocha is matched at the Casa de La Tia site in the upper Pachitea Valley. There Allen discovered the Cobichaniqui ceramic phase associated with radiocarbon dates – *c*. 1600 BC – rivaling dates for the earliest ceramic complexes from the highlands or coast.[3]

The context of the sites at Yarinacocha (Lathrap 1968b) and on the upper Pachitea suggests that these sites are remnants of early settlements of Tropical Forest Culture, i.e., that there was a definite orientation to the resources of the river and riparian zone. By studying the ancient meander scars of the rivers and the patterns of sedimentation, Lathrap has argued persuasively that the Yarinacocha settlements were situated along an active channel of the Ucayali at the time they were occupied.

Extrapolating from the archaeological evidence to the evidence for the dispersion of linguistic families, Lathrap (1970) infers that the early sites on the Ucayali and Pachitea rivers are remains of an ancient colonization of the tributaries of the Upper Amazon by Proto-Arawak-speaking peoples. Some archaeologists are reluctant to accept the correlation of linguistic and archaeological entities; nevertheless, it is interesting that Lathrap's model is in essential accord with Steward and Metraux (1948: 535), who concluded that the Arawak were part of an early migration into the montaña from the Amazon.

The logic of Lathrap's argument becomes more apparent when it is put in the context of the riparian settlement system. An expanding economic system based on exploiting the resources of the riparian zone would not acquire territory in a radiating pattern across the Amazon Basin but would be channeled by the highly desired and very productive flood plains of the major rivers. In the Upper Amazon colonization would continue into the eastern Andes to the limits of effective flood-plain farming, fishing, and efficient canoe travel. The demographic impact on the highlands will be considered later in the chapter.

There is no direct evidence that this pattern of settlement was based on agriculture; however, it is difficult to understand how a series of large settlements along the Amazonian rivers could have been sustained without food production. As Sauer (1952) and Lathrap (1968a, 1970) have pointed out, the lush vegetation of a tropical forest does not contain concentrated stands of single species. Food plants are scattered among thousands of other plant species. Sedentism, which would have been favored by a fishing-based economy, could arise on the Amazonian rivers only if the local flora were manipulated so that food plants were concentrated within daily walking distance of the village. Thus (see Lathrap 1977b), it may have been the evolution of the tropical fishing economies which led to the fundamental change in man's relationship to the land, from gathering wild plant products to deliberate attempts to increase the percentage of local edible flora. This pattern may have had its onset in the Central Amazon as early as the 7th or 8th millennium BC (Lathrap 1970). There is no direct evidence from the Central Amazon to support that contention; however, ceramic-bearing settlements dating to the end of the 4th millennium BC (uncorrected radiocarbon years) are known from the mouth of the Amazon (Meggers and Evans 1978), the tropical lowlands of northern Columbia (Reichel-Dolmatoff 1965), and the tropics of western Ecuador (Damp 1979), a distribution which is consistent with a model of expansion out of the Central Amazon. Plant remains are scarce in such sites: however, at Real Alto in Ecuador evidence of maize, jack beans (*Canavalia* sp.), and achira (*Canna edulis*) has been discovered (Pearsall 1979, Damp 1979). This evidence, together with the pattern of settlement which favors the flood plains (Zavallos *et al.* 1977, Damp 1979, Raymond, Marcos, and Lathrap 1980), suggests an early emergence of the tropical riverine settlement system in the area surrounding the Central Andes.

Settlement of the interfluves and the valleys and hills of the upper montaña

Population density in the montaña is significantly lower in the areas away from the large flood plains. Denevan (1976) estimates that in late pre-Hispanic times these areas had population densities of *c.* 0.8/km², while a density of 14.6/km² may have been achieved along the main river systems. However, it is wrong to think that this low density was distributed evenly over the diverse terrain of the interfluves, valleys, and hills of the upper montaña. The lower population densities are attributable mainly to the lesser availability of food resources. Protein may have been the critical nutrient limiting population growth, although that is a subject of ongoing study and debate (see for example Denevan 1972, Gross 1975, and Beckerman 1979). Since, as described earlier in this chapter, agricultural potential, game concentrations, and fishing resources vary significantly in the montaña, it is to be expected that there were corresponding variations in the size and density of human populations.

Along the major river systems, there was probably a clinal diminution in overall population density as there was a gradual reduction in the size of the flood plains going from the lower montaña into the narrower valleys of the Andean foothills. This may have been true, for example, along the Ucayali–Tambo–Ene–Apurimac system, where archaeological evidence suggests that prehistoric cultures of a common tradition may have been linked in a loose political and economic system (Raymond, DeBoer, and Roe 1975). However, there may have been abrupt changes in the size and density of the settlements at the junctures of the major rivers corresponding to abrupt changes in the flood plain caused by the increased volume of water. Perhaps the most significant change would have been the point in the river system where ox-bow lakes – natural fish reservoirs – begin to occur.

Individual characteristics of the river systems must be taken into account in assessing food resources. The occurrence of rapids limits the penetration of certain Amazonian fish species into the rivers of the upper montaña and may affect fish density. Gradient, generally, affects the size of the flood plain and thus limits the good agricultural land, as does the shape of the valley. The valleys of the small tributary streams are generally poor in food resources, and in these and on neighboring hills population density would have been very low. But, even in those areas, there is considerable variation in the availability of food.

The origin of settlement in the upper montaña may have been through the forced displacement of people from the flood plains (Lathrap 1968a). As long as there was fresh flood plain to settle, competition for the resources could be resolved by community or tribal fissioning and migration, but eventually, unless population growth was stabilized, some groups would be forced into the smaller valley systems and into the interfluvial zones. On the Central Ucayali, where the archaeological record is best known, competition for the flood plain seems to have been in full swing by the start of the second millennium BC.

Settlement along the eastern Andean slopes

While anthropologists have traditionally regarded the ceja as a cultural-ecological boundary separating the highland and lowland cultures, recent archaeological, ethnohistorical, and ethnographical research has shown that in both ancient and modern times highlanders have exploited land and controlled territory well beyond the cloud–forest frontier. Extensive terrace systems were built along the sides of the steep sloping valleys to expand highland agricultural systems (Isbell 1968, 1974, Lathrap 1970, Bowman 1916: 77). Settlements, ranging in size and complexity from small isolated stone buildings to fortifications and temples with monumental stone architecture, have been found in the ceja (Thompson 1973b, Bonavia 1964, 1968, 1970, 1975, Bonavia and Ravines 1967, Lathrap 1970) and in the valleys below (Raymond

1972, 1976, Kendall 1976). Inca control of the forested Vilcabamba was probably equivalent to imperial control over the other provinces, and as Lyon (1981) has pointed out, its control was probably crucial for the conquest and defense of the neighboring highland regions. The Lupaca kingdom of the Titicaca region held distant agricultural lands in the montaña (Murra 1968), as did the ancient peoples of Huanuco (Murra 1972). This practice, which persists to modern times, is an extension of the Andean economic system which aims at community self-sufficiency and control of a maximum number of resource zones.

Factors affecting the extent and nature of highland colonization of the montaña varied. A principal determinant was the demand for tropical forest products. Coca, highly valued among Andean peoples, was probably always the main commodity imported. However, in the dry, cold punas of southern Peru and Bolivia, which are best suited to llama herding and the cultivation of frost-resistant tubers, the agricultural lands of the montaña may have been important for maize production as well. Among the many other products brought to the highlands from the montaña were: cotton, chili peppers, fruits, exotic herbs and drugs, feathers, birds, monkeys, tapir feet (Murra 1968, 1972, Miller 1836, Raymond 1979). The greater labor expenditure required to clear and cultivate the very steep slopes and heavy vegetation of the ceja would have encouraged colonization deeper into the montaña; however, that had to be weighed against greater traveling distance from the highland settlements and the increased vulnerability to marauding lowland Indians. Soil fertility, rainfall patterns, and altitudinal factors affecting plant growth would also have determined the areas selected for settlement. Coca plants apparently are tolerant of very poor soils (personal observation), but maize and peanuts are not. However, coca is subject to certain fungus diseases, the incidence of which increases at lower altitudes (Brush 1974: 294–5, Gade 1967).

The geographical relationship of the montaña to the highland resource zones is the primary determinant of the local patterns of settlement, tenancy, economic specialization, and networks of interchange (Brush 1974: 280). If the resource zones are near one another, i.e., within one or two days' walk, then all the resources may be exploited from a single highland village, and settlements in the montaña may be either non-existent or small and scattered. Resources which are widely spaced and require several days' walk lead to a pattern of settlement which Murra (1972) has called the Archipelago type. The principal villages are in the highlands but satellite communities are established in the montaña. The permanency and size of the settlements in the montaña are a function of the distance, relative economic importance of the resources, and the extent to which it is necessary to protect the lands occupied from neighboring ethnic groups – of both highland and lowland origin.

If the resource zones are large and continuous but strung out over a long valley system, then an extended, multi-ethnic settlement pattern may develop with products moved via a trade and market system (Brush 1974: 294–5, Gade 1967). Under such circumstances permanent settlements of highlanders would be established in the montaña.

Highland–lowland interface

From the foregoing, it is apparent that the interface between highland and lowland societies was probably affected strongly by variations in the natural ecology of the montaña. The main factors affecting the pattern and density of settlement among the tropical forest societies were: 1) the size and gradient of the rivers; 2) the length and breadth of the flood plains; 3) the density and accessibility of the aquatic, terrestrial, and arboreal biomasses; and 4) the fertility of the soils. Those factors affecting the highland societies were mainly: 1) the gradients of the valley slopes; 2) the distances between the ceja and centers of highland settlement; and 3) the rainfall, temperature, topographic and cultural conditions in the adjacent highland valleys which would affect the need for products of the montaña. Since there is generally an inverse relationship between altitude and the availability of the resources which contribute to settlement density and stability for the tropical forest systems, the highland and lowland land-use patterns should usually have been complementary – i.e., there should have been little cause for competition over resources. Exceptions to this might have occurred: 1) where only a short distance separates the ceja from the flood plain environment, e.g., the central Marañon, central Huallaga, and the lower Apurimac valleys; 2) when expanding lowland societies attempted to colonize a warm, moist highland valley (because of climatic variables cited above this is more likely to have occurred in the northern than the southern highlands); and 3) when, for economic reasons, expanding highland states sent colonists deep into the montaña.

Cultural interchange between highlanders and lowlanders may have occurred through the mutual influence of groups occupying neighboring regions and through formal commercial networks. Broad areas of the montaña were inter-connected by trade until relatively recently. Salt, dart poisons, pottery, and stone were exchanged between riverine and non-riverine societies in the montaña (DeBoer, 1981b), and the major rivers were commercial highways which connected the montaña with the rest of Amazonia. The intensity of trade with the highlands would have been affected by cultural-ecological factors. *Pongos* (rapids) would have interrupted the integration of riverine trade between the lower and upper montaña. The Marañon, Huallaga and Urubamba rivers, with respectively the *pongos* of Manseriche, Aguirre, and Manique, contrast with the Apurimac River, which is easily navigated by canoes up to about 700 m. The river gradient above the *pongos* determined whether transport continued by canoe or on foot. Riverine trade most likely would have been confined to the dry season when the rivers are more placid.

In the parts of the upper montaña which are distant from the major flood plains and which were occupied by multi-ethnic, scattered populations, exchange of goods occurred either on a small scale between individuals or in the context of periodic markets, such as the annual one held by the Piro at El Encuentro in the Urubamba Valley for the purpose of trading with highlanders (Lyon, 1981). The intensity and integration of the highland–lowland commercial ties also would have been a function of the extent of the trade networks in the highlands and between the highlands and the coast. The advent of broad regional exchange networks in the highlands with llama caravans should have brought an increase in trade with the montaña.

A DIACHRONIC PERSPECTIVE ON MONTAÑA–HIGHLAND INTERACTION

The settlement systems which are described above were functioning at the time of the Hispanic Conquest and provided the context for interaction between the peoples of Amazonia and the Central Andes in the late prehistoric period. We cannot fully document the emergence of these systems archaeologically, nor, considering the poor conditions for preservation of cultural remains in the tropical forest, are we ever likely to have very complete evidence. However, archaeological research in Peru over the past few decades indicates that cultural inter-relationships between the coast, highlands, and montaña go back several thousand years.

One of the strongest arguments favoring early contact with the montaña stems from the research which has been carried out in connection with the beginnings of agriculture in Peru. Few, if any, of the plants which occur as cultigens in the Peruvian coastal sites, beginning as early as the 3rd millennium BC, are native to the coastal region, and many can be shown to be derived from plant communities found in the moist tropics east of the Andes (Pickergsill 1969). Since they are full-blown domesticates from the time of their first occurrence, they imply the prior existence of agricultural economies in a nearby moist tropical environment: i.e., western Ecuador and/or the Peruvian montaña.

Botanical remains preserved in sites of the arid Peruvian coast, then, provide insight for the reconstruction of cultural events which occurred in the tropical forest. Two fundamental questions which they raise are: 1) What was the cultural context in which these plants were domesticated? 2) What were the cultural mechanisms which account for their transmission across the Andes to the coast?

A probable answer to the first question already has been addressed earlier in the chapter, in the section discussing the emergence of the tropical riverine settlement systems. Evidence cited there suggests that the major flood plains of the moist tropics in South America were settled by societies practicing farming/fishing economies at least 1,000 years before agriculture first appeared in coastal Peru. While it is still a point of controversy, archaeological evidence from western Ecuador suggests that this subsistence pattern was established in the Guayas Basin and in the tropical river valleys of coastal Ecuador by the middle of the 4th millennium BC. A radiocarbon date from ridged fields in the lower Guayas drainage (James Parsons, personal communication) indicates that possibly there were efforts to intensify agricultural production of the flood plain as early as the middle of the 3rd millennium BC.

Broad regional interaction is attested by similarities in ceramics between sites in western and eastern Ecuador and the Peruvian montaña at this same time (Lathrap 1970, 1974, Braun 1971, Porras 1975). The low mountain passes of the Peru–Ecuador frontier would have made such contact relatively easy. Moreover, the fact that the agricultural plant complexes from the coastal sites derive from plant species found in different parts of Amazonia and the montaña indicates that agriculture was already a widespread phenomenon east of the Andes.

Answering the second question involves still further speculation. The transmission of cultigens from the tropical forest to the coast cannot be passed off simply as diffusion. Rather, the cultural mechanisms by which such transmissions took place must be considered. A trade network could explain the transfer of cultigens from one region to another if groups in both regions were already practicing agriculture – the new cultigens would simply be incorporated into the existing inventory of cultivated plants. On the other hand, if conveyance of farming technology is involved as well, which seems to be the case here, then more complex patterns of social and economic interaction must be invoked.

An expansion of the tropical riverine systems during the 5th, 4th, and 3rd millennia BC would have carried this subsistence pattern up the eastern Andean valleys into the upper montaña to the terminus of the flood plain. This process of colonization may have continued up into the mountain basins in northern Peru where the valleys are lower and broader and the rainfall permits dry cropping on the slopes as well as flood-plain farming. The presence of village sites in the upper Huallaga Valley by the end of the 3rd millennium BC may have been the result of such processes (Izumi 1971, Izumi, Cuculiza, and Kano 1972). Indeed, the Kotosh Wairajirca ceramics share stylistic characteristics with the Tutishcainyo complex in the Ucayali Basin (Lathrap 1970, Lathrap and Roys 1963) and with the Valdivia complex in Ecuador (Meggers, Evans, and Estrada 1965: 174–5).

Earlier, I hinted at the unique characteristics of the Marañon Valley with respect to its proximity to the low mountain passes of the Chamaya highlands and its adjacency to the Cordillera Blanca in northwestern Peru. Colonization of the Marañon could have brought the tropical forest societies into close and regular contact with occupants of the highland valleys in the Cordillera

Blanca. If the evidence from Guitarrero cave in the Callejón de Huaylas is indicative of a common subsistence pattern in the North Highlands, then limited agriculture may have prevailed in that region from as early as 8500 BC (Smith 1980b). A chili pepper (probably *Capsicum chinense*) dated between the 9th and 6th millennia BC (Smith 1980a) is the earliest evidence of an Amazonian cultigen. This and other tropical lowland cultigens could have been assimilated gradually by the highland cultures as a result of prolonged social and economic interaction.

The mechanisms of socio-economic contact between the highlands and coast are taken up in other chapters, so I will not discuss them here. However, it seems to me that if the North Highlands was the route by which agriculture was brought to the coastal valleys, then either transhumance, which has recently fallen into disfavor as an explanation (Moseley 1972), or limited migration from highlands to coast must be invoked.

A second route to the coast which would have been accessible from the Marañon Valley is through the low mountains which back the desert in the far North Coast of Peru. There in the Amotape mountains on the west side of the Andes, Richardson (1973) has found possible evidence of agricultural economies dating to the preceramic period.

There is no evidence of trans-Andean contact – montaña to coast – in southern Peru and Bolivia at this time. However, this could be partly a function of lack of research. At the beginning of the Initial Period, *Arachis hypogaea*, the peanut, and *Capsicum baccatum*, a species of chili pepper, occur in coastal Peruvian sites, and both are believed to have come from plants native to eastern Bolivia.

Throughout the Initial Period there are signs in northern Peru of continued regular contact with the montaña and, perhaps, with tropical western Ecuador as well. From the evidence it is hard to say whether most of this can be ascribed to extended trade networks or whether more integrated social and economic patterns were involved. Some of the similarities may even be ascribed to parallel developments from a common cultural heritage.

Cultigens from the moist tropics continue to be added to the inventory of cultivated plants from the coastal sites. Of these, sweet potatoes, *Ipomoea batatas*, and manioc, *Manihot esculenta*, are probably the most important food plants.[4] Manioc does not occur until the end of the Initial Period, and if Lathrap's (1973) identification of it on the Obelisk Tello at Chavín de Huántar is correct, its appearance, or increased popularity, on the coast may have been connected with the spread of the Chavín cult.

Connections with the montaña are also apparent in the art, the iconography, the ceramic technology, and in features of the ceremonial centers. The engraved gourd from Huaca Prieta (Bird 1963a) is strikingly similar in its decoration to ceramic imitation carved gourds of the Valdivia complex (Lathrap, Collier, and Chandra 1975). Its feline design is an early example of religious iconography shared by art styles found over a broad part of northern Peru and Ecuador.

While the development of ceramic technology is earlier in the tropical forest than on the Peruvian coast and in the highlands (at least 1,000 years earlier in Ecuador), the simple range of neckless ollas, the predominant vessel form in the Peruvian Initial Period sites, cannot be shown to derive from any of the tropical forest ceramic complexes. At Kotosh (Izumi 1971, Izumi, Cuculiza, and Kano 1972) the neckless olla tradition seems to have been assimilated by a tradition originating in the montaña. However, as ceramics begin to take on a ceremonial function in Peru, parallels with the montaña ceramics occur. Double-spout-and-bridge vessels and round-bottomed bowls of the South Coast, with resist and zoned polychrome post-fire painting, are similar to ceramics of the Kotosh Wairajirca and the Tutishcainyo complexes. Perhaps this indicates that the trade connections between the South Coast and the high-lands of Huancavelica, attested by obsidian trace-element analysis as early as Preceramic times (Burger and Asaro 1977: 44), was extended eastward to the montaña early in the Initial Period (Browman 1974b). Also, the stirrup-spout bottles and the polished flaring-sided bowls, which become part of the set of Chavín prestige wares (Patterson 1971c), may have antecedents in tropical lowland complexes (Lathrap 1971a).

While there are regional differences in the ceramic complexes of the montaña at this time, there are also signs of continued regional interaction. Evidence of trade and mutual influence is found in the ceramics of Cerro Narrío in southern Ecuador, Bagua at the bend of the Marañon, Kotosh in the upper Huallaga and Tutishcainyo in the Ucayali Valley. At Bagua (Shady and Rosas 1980) and Kotosh (Izumi 1971) camelid remains are evidence of close contact with the highlands. As Shady and Rosas (1980) point out, Pacopampa is strategically located to control trade between the montaña, highlands, and coast. And, the discovery of a Bagua-style vessel in the Jequetepeque Valley suggests that more than just the exchange of economic goods may have been involved.

Chavín is the subject of an earlier chapter of this volume, so I shall not dwell on it here. However, in this context it is important to point out that the tropical forest aspect of its iconography, which Tello (1943) and Lathrap (1971a, 1971b, 1973, 1974) have so clearly identified, can be plausibly related to long-standing social, economic, artistic, and ceremonial inter-connections between southern Ecuador, the northern Peruvian montaña, the northern Peruvian highlands, and the Peruvian coast.

The apparent strength of this close cultural relationship with the montaña cultures wanes during the Early Horizon. This may have been the result of emerging regionalism in the highlands and the establishment of political boundaries. From that point onward the inter-regional contact seems to have taken on a more commercial flavor, although tropical forest products may have continued to find their way to the coast via llama caravans (Browman 1974b).

Colonization of the steep terrain of the upper montaña apparently began during the Early Intermediate Period. This phenomenon is attested by a number of sites found in the ceja zone from the Marañon Valley to south-eastern Bolivia. Lathrap (1970) and Isbell (1974) in separate essays have proposed that this process was the result of a demographic expansion of Quechua-speaking peoples who, through the development of terraced agriculture, were able to dominate successfully what had hitherto been unexploited territory. Lathrap suggested that the colonization began in Bolivia and spread northward, but Isbell, relying on more recent linguistic and archaeological evidence, argued that a north–south spread makes more sense. In an earlier, more conservative hypothesis, Bonavia and Ravines (1967) explained the phenomenon as a general territorial aggrandizement on the part of Andean polities.

Few sites have yet been investigated and reported adequately, and criteria for dating many of the sites are wanting. Nevertheless, recognizing these and many other shortcomings in the data, it is possible to make some cautious generalizations about the evidence.

The sites generally are situated on or above steeply sloped hillsides which sometimes incorporate systems of stonefaced terraces (Isbell 1968). Ceramics are rare at some sites (Bonavia 1964), but generally they are littered with coarse ceramic ware. Lathrap (1970) referred to this simply as the "coarse ware tradition", but Isbell (1974) prefers to call it a series – the CB series – which cautiously recognizes a cultural–historical tradition with broad temporal and geographical boundaries. The diagnostic characteristics of the CB series are flaring-necked ollas and sub-hemispherical bowls with red-brown surfaces and coarse temper.

According to Isbell, the beginnings of the CB series can be traced to ceramic complexes dating to the end of the Early Horizon in the central and northern highlands of Peru. During the Early Intermediate Period, it spread as far south as northern Bolivia. Isbell makes a plausible historical connection to people who speak Quechua and includes the Inca ceramics as a late and fancy variant of the CB series. Since the linguistic diversity of Quechua is greater in the north highlands and since Quechua B is restricted mainly to that area, southward dispersion of Quechua, paralleling that of the CB series, seems plausible. If the Quechua had developed terraced farming, as both Lathrap and Isbell argue, this coupled with maize farming would have provided them with the means to cultivate the steep slopes of the ceja which could have effected a rapid spread along the eastern flanks of the Andes. Terracing has proved an effective means of cultivating maize in the steep cold valleys of southern Peru. However, Isbell suggests that it is more likely that it was developed in the north, where maize could first have been dry-farmed on the gentle, well-watered slopes of the valleys which are found from southern Ecuador to northern Peru. An expansion of cultivation to the steeper slopes of the valleys could have led to the development of terracing as a response to the need to prevent soil erosion, a factor of critical importance in adapting the agricultural system to the ceja environment.

Isbell's model has a compelling logic, and I have not been able to do justice to the nuances and implications of his argument in this short summary. However, it rests mainly on a linguistic–ecological scheme which some may find unconvincing. Perhaps current research by Hastings (personal communication) in the Tarma Valley will shed more light on the subject of the role of the montaña in the evolution of terraced farming.

A formal economic network with the montaña may have emerged earlier in the Titicaca region than it did in the valleys of the north. Whereas in central and northern Peru a single community may have easy access to puna valley, and montaña resources, such a situation is far less common in the south. The peoples of the high, dry punas of Titicaca, which are eminently suited to llama-herding, the cultivation of frost-resistant tubers and the production of freeze-dried foods – chuño – must rely on the warm valleys of the montaña or the coast for several important products: e.g., maize, cotton, coca. On the other hand, transport of these goods was made easier by the ready availability of large numbers of llamas. A caravan with rations of chuño and charqui (dried meat) was capable of traveling for several days into the eastern jungles.

Archaeological evidence for the emergence of this system is scant. The early occurrence of eastern Bolivian crops in coastal Peru, cited above, may indicate the beginnings of regular long-distance commerce between the montaña and the coast in that region; however, I have already suggested other probable mechanisms by which the dispersal of those cultigens might have taken place. Nordenskiöld (1917, 1924b: 227–8) suggests that similarities between ceramic styles from sites in the Llanos de Mojos and Tiahuanaco-style ceramics at Misque are indicative of prehistoric contact between lowland tropical forest tribes and the Andean states; however, the similarities are not sufficiently close to argue the case with conviction. Ryden (1957) has discovered evidence of Tiahuanaco-era settlements in the eastern valleys immediately to the east of Lake Titicaca. The ceramics from these sites seem stylistically to be a mixture of features of the CB series and the Tiahuanacoid tradition.

There are numerous unsubstantiated reports of "Inca" ruins in the eastern forest of Bolivia. These are worth investigating; however, they cannot yet be regarded as evidence of highland settlement. The only published report of these is a brief one by Denevan (1966: 23) which describes a site on the upper Beni River with rock walls standing 2 to 3 m high, rock-lined canals and ceramics reputed to be of highland origin. The site is locally referred to as an Inca fort, but of course it could well pre-date the Late Horizon by many centuries. Metalled roads which descend from the mountains to the eastern lowlands and which were obviously used and maintained by the Incas may well have followed long-standing prehistoric trails; however, evidence of the antiquity of these will probably always elude us (Stothert-Stockman 1967).

Evidence of transfer of goods from the montaña to the highlands comes from a Classic Tiahuanaco grave reported by Wassén (1972). From the associated items he identifies the grave as that of a prehistoric traveling medicine man, known from historic accounts of the cultures of the Titicaca area as *callahuayas*. One of the items associated was a package of *Ilex guayusa*, a caffeine-rich herb. That and the hallucinogenic snuffs, which are implied by a kit of tubes and tablets included in the burial, must have been brought to the highlands from the eastern Andean slopes.

A synergistic model seems best to explain the evolution of the highland–lowland economic networks in southern Peru and Bolivia. The success of the Archipelago settlement systems, characteristic of the area in late prehistoric and early historic times, would have rested in large part on the ability of highland polities to protect their distant colonies from hostile tropical forest groups occupying the montaña and to provide a commercial outlet for the products. Conversely, increasing control of the importation and redistribution of the montaña products would have strengthened political and religious centralization in the highlands.

In the montaña east of Huari, there is, as yet, no evidence of highland settlement during the Early Intermediate Period, although the cultural remains of Caballoyuq and other sites studied by Bonavia (1964) in the ceja have yet to be dated with certainty. By the Middle Horizon, however, sites which are probably Huari colonies were established in the lower Apurimac Valley below the ceja, where the gentle slopes of the valley bottom could be utilized (Raymond 1976, Raymond, DeBoer, and Roe 1975). Although there is no evidence of fortification, the larger size of two of these sites suggests that they were frontier settlements, built to define a territorial boundary and to trade with tropical forest peoples. Downstream from these sites lies the site of the Granja de Sivia (Raymond 1972, Raymond, DeBoer, and Roe 1975), which may have been occupied contemporaneously by Panoan-speaking peoples. The 20-plus km separating the Huari outposts from the Granja de Sivia would have been an effective buffer zone between the polities.[5] Contact with the people at the Granja de Sivia would have linked the Huari empire to a vast trade network along the Apurimac–Ene–Tambo–Ucayali river systems and ultimately to the Amazon itself. During historic times the Panoans were aggressive traders over a vast part of the Peruvian montaña (DeBoer 1981b). Copper artifacts from the Granja de Sivia and Cumancaya on the Ucayali and from surface finds elsewhere in the montaña attest to this trade; however, it probably included a number of perishable products as well.

Trade of this sort between highlanders and lowlanders, which persists to modern times (Camino 1977, Lyon 1981), probably waxed and waned during the prehistoric periods, as did the extent and intensity of colonization of the montaña by highlanders. If the Apurimac Valley is representative of other eastern valleys, then these processes were intensified during periods of imperial expansion in the highlands when large tracts may have been incorporated as provinces into the imperial structure. But, the desire for products of the montaña, particularly coca, is a long-standing, basic part of Andean culture, and so the commercial ties survived the fall of the empires. Trade in exotic luxury goods such as tapir's feet, feathers, and pets probably diminished, but the local ethnic groups continued to defend their coca-growing lands, the produce from which they either used themselves or exchanged with other highland peoples for highland products or usufruct of mountain resources which they did not possess.

CONCLUSION

In his short note "On basic highland culture" published in *A Reappraisal of Peruvian Archaeology*, Rowe (1948b) states that the eastern boundary of highland culture is difficult to define and that the montaña Indians may have shared basic Andean traits with the highland peoples. This statement stands in marked contrast to one made by Bennett in the same volume (Bennett 1948: 4), in which he says that the "Peruvian co-tradition . . . certainly does not exist in the jungle." Research over the past thirty years underscores the truth of Rowe's remark. The history of cultural evolution in the Peruvian Andes and on the Peruvian coast cannot be studied without regard for cultural events which took place in the forested eastern provinces of the country. During the formative stages, the Tropical Forest Cultures had a significant impact on the evolution of the Peruvian agrarian system and may have contributed directly to the basic social and religious fabric of Andean civilization. While in the later periods cultural interchange continued, the montaña became more important as a source of exotic goods which were brought to the highlands and coast via trade networks and as an area which the highland peoples colonized to produce goods vital to their economies. During both the Inca and Huari empires, parts of the montaña may have been treated as provinces, and probably from the onset of the Christian era, the kingdoms of southern Peru and Bolivia maintained colonies in distant parts of the montaña. While the modern-day Andean Indian shows open antipathy toward the *chunchos*, which is what he calls the Indians of the montaña, he owes much of his cultural heritage to his "savage" neighbors of the jungle.

Notes

1 A variety of terms has been used to designate the forested terrain of the Upper Amazon. The quadrant of their empire which the Incas called Antisuyu comprised

a large part of the area, and that term is occasionally found in modern usage (see Savoy 1970). Yungas, another Quechua word, is used generally to refer to the eastern lowlands of Bolivia and sometimes to parts of the Peruvian Upper Amazon; however, its meaning can be ambiguous since it also sometimes designates the arid western lowlands in Peru. Geographers (e.g., Tosi 1960) have defined highly specific terminology to convey subtle micro-environmental differences in the region. Added to this confusion in nomenclature are the local folk taxonomies, which vary regionally. *Selva* (jungle), sometimes subdivided into *selva alta* and *selva baja*, is gaining currency in anthropological literature. However, I prefer to use *montaña*, a term which has a long history of use among Peruvianists (cf. Steward 1948, Steward and Faron 1959, Lathrap 1970). By *montaña* I mean the forested eastern Andean slopes of Ecuador, Peru, and Bolivia including the lowland area immediately adjacent to it. Upper montaña and lower montaña distinguish the broken, hilly terrain of the mountains from the low flat land. *Ceja de la montaña* (eyebrow of the montaña), or simply *ceja*, designates the cloud forest which constitutes the uppermost edge of the tropical rainforest.

2 Troll (1958, 1968) argues convincingly that llama herding and the invention of the freeze-dried potato (*chuño*) were prerequisites to the evolution of sedentism in the dry punas of southern Peru and Bolivia.

3 Sites of comparable age have not been found elsewhere in the Peruvian montaña; however, that is probably a function of the lack of research. Cultural-ecological factors may have restricted this expansion along some of the river valleys, but there is no reason to believe that the Ucayali and Pachitea were uniquely suited for settlement. Shady and Rosas (1980, Lathrap and Weber 1972) have discovered a ceramic sequence extending back to the Initial Period in the Marañon Valley, and further research in that valley is promising. Discoveries of ceramic sites in the Pastaza Valley (Porras 1975) dating to the end of the 3rd millennium BC bespeak the presence of such settlements in the Upper Amazon of Ecuador at this time.

4 Even on the Peruvian coast, where conditions for preservation are probably better than any region besides the frozen Arctic, one must be very cautious in using empirical evidence of organic remains (Cohen 1975, Begler and Keatinge 1979) and wary of jumping to the conclusion that the first occurrence of a plant in an archaeological sequence marks its earliest presence in the area or indicates its general economic importance. Root crops, because they are usually consumed *in toto* and because their moist, fleshy tubers are subject to rapid decay, do not preserve well in archaeological sites. Thus, we must regard the evidence of manioc as suggestive of its first cultivation on the coast, bearing in mind that it may well have been present several centuries earlier.

5 In a recent study of the late prehistoric archaeology and early historic documents of the Ucayali, DeBoer (1981a) suggests that competition for the flood plain is evinced in a distinctive settlement pattern in which the largest and militarily most powerful settlements border a contested and virtually unoccupied buffer zone. The evidence from the Apurimac suggests that a similar pattern may have obtained on the highland–lowland interface under circumstances where the riverine pattern was contiguous to territory densely settled by highlanders.

V
SYNTHESIS

11

A summary view of Peruvian prehistory

RICHARD W. KEATINGE

This chapter is a summary and, to a degree, a synthesis of the major points made in the preceding chapters. It also offers a few observations on the directions of future research in Peru, together with some general comments on issues of increasing concern to archaeologists working in the region. The organization of the chapter follows that of the major subdivisions of the book, and few bibliographical references will be cited since they are available in other chapters.

OVERVIEW

As is clear from the preceding chapters in this book, the archaeological remains of prehistoric societies found in Peru are as varied as the geography and myriad of ecological zones found throughout the region. Without question, Peru constitutes one of the great archaeological areas of the world. And yet, progress in obtaining a better understanding of the region's prehistory has been almost glacial in its movement.

Partly, this slow pace of increasing knowledge is due to the tremendous wealth of the archaeological remains themselves, abetted in some geographical zones by incredible preservation. The desert coast is a case in point, where the dryness of the climate has created an "American Egypt," an archaeologist's paradise. Whole valleys are yet to be scientifically surveyed and studied. Even major sites, some known since the time of the Spanish Conquest, have yet to be thoroughly investigated.

On the other hand, the slow accretion of information on Peru's prehistory is also due partly to the understandable inability of the Peruvian nation to finance a large-scale and ongoing program of archaeological research. As a Third World country, Peru's governmental priorities necessarily have been oriented towards food, housing, and medical care for the populace, not to mention the general goal of the industrialization of the country. There simply never has been sufficient funding available from the government to mount the kind of continuous program of professional training, excavation, and research which is even minimally necessary given the wealth of remains.

In addition, while there has been notable foreign interest in undertaking expeditions to Peru, especially from the United States, western Europe, and Japan, these have not occurred in sufficiently large numbers over many years to offset the lack of support for an intensive and organized indigenous effort. Partly because of this, Peru's national patrimony has suffered irretrievable damage in some areas due to intensive looting and the impact of industrialization.

Fueled by the demand from the antiquities markets of the western industrialized societies, the looting of Peru's archaeological sites has become something of a national pastime, particularly in rural areas of the country. Sites have been gutted by gangs of looters, known as *huaqueros*, and fragile information on the context and provenience of archaeological remains has been lost forever. Again, archaeological sites are so numerous, and many are so far from population centers, that policing them is simply impractical. The end result is that much of the portable artifactual remains of Peruvian prehistory has ended up in the possession of antiquities dealers, collectors, and museums. Only recently has there been a concerted effort in the United Nations to obtain world agreement on attacking the problem of the looting of the Third World's cultural heritage – for the Peruvian case represents but one of the more blatant examples of this problem.

With the foregoing comments as background, it seems fair to emphasize to the reader that while we certainly know more about the prehistory of Peru than we did forty years ago – when the previously mentioned Institute of Andean Research conference on Peruvian archaeology was convened in New York City – we nevertheless are barely more than scratching the surface in some areas, and only sharpening our trowels in others.

Early inhabitants and settlement

As seems amply demonstrated in the contributions by Rick and Chauchat, whether one is dealing with the highlands or the coast, issues of chronology, earliest evidence, and adaptation are only beginning to be attacked for the Peruvian preceramic. The question of the existence of a "pre-projectile point" stage of technological development has served to muddy the waters of early Peruvian prehistory, just as it has in other parts of the New World. The push by some investigators to show that the site they have excavated is not only the earliest occupied in the region but also that its artifactual content proves the existence of a pre-projectile point stage of development has so far served only to confuse the literature on Peru, as it has elsewhere.

For years, as Chauchat points out, the work of Lanning and Patterson on the Central Coast served to obscure and inaccurately define the age and sequencing of the coastal Peruvian preceramic. Work at the sites of Chivateros and Oquendo, perhaps more than any other, formed the basis of a lithic sequence which was, at best, inaccurately dated and poorly conceived. Accepted uncritically and in the absence of additional work in the same area, claims of great antiquity for human habitation of the region and the appearance of an orderly progression of sequential evidence became entrenched in the literature.

Based on what now appears to be an inaccurate assessment of the lithic evidence from the Central Coast region of Ancon, Preceramic Periods I–IV as defined by Lanning simply do not represent viable criteria to use in attempting to develop a chronology for the coastal preceramic.

Similarly, for the highlands, Rick questions the utility of preceramic periods based on changes in stone tools, with changes in one area equated as synchronomous with changes in another. As Rick argues, such changes would imply sweeping economic transformations as well as rapid dispersion and reception of style in stone tools. None of this has been adequately demonstrated for the Central Andes.

As with Chivateros and Oquendo materials for the coast, the Pacaicasa materials from Pikimachay Cave excavated by MacNeish represent a parallel example for the highlands of inconclusive data pushed to the point of extremes. Clearly, on the basis of currently available evidence from Pikimachay, claims for a late Pleistocene human occupation of the highlands in association with extinct megafauna and a pre-projectile stage of technological development are unsupportable.

As is evident in the contributions by Rick and Chauchat, a true understanding of the early preceramic stages of development is still very much in its infancy. Ecological diversity, so evident as one transects the country from west to east, must have played a fundamental and distinguishing role in human adaptation during these early time periods, just as it did in later ones.

While we still know very little about the early preceramic of Peru, the work of Rick and Chauchat is suggestive of the kind of useful results which can be obtained when an emphasis is placed on issues related to variable patterns of adaptation, mobility, seasonality, and sedentism. While we do not know precisely when the earliest human occupation of the Central Andes took place, we do know that certainly by 9000–8000 BC human occupation adapted to a hunting and gathering way of life was widespread. By this time, lithic technologies are well defined and the stage set for the build-up of sedentary populations which gradually came to characterize the Late Preceramic and Initial periods.

The transition from a hunting and gathering way of life to one based on sedentary villages represents a critical archaeological focus for the Peruvian region, just as it does in other parts of the world where a similar process took place. Rosa Fung Pineda's contribution amply documents the range of variation in types of site and their locations which roughly characterize the time when this gradual transformation took place.

While in other parts of the world where the transition from a hunting and gathering way of life to one based on sedentary villages was founded on the development of a stable food supply made possible through the domestication of plants and animals, in Peru the case may have been more variable.

For the highlands, domestication of plants and animals seems to have formed the basis of sedentary life. However, for the coast – at least certain parts of it – Moseley has argued that the vast marine resources of the Pacific Ocean provided the basis for an early and sustained sedentary population. While not discounting the importance of agriculture and the domestication of animals, Moseley argues that, at least initially, the caloric inputs from these developments simply paled before the advantages represented by the exploitation of the nearby marine resources. Certainly if Chauchat is correct in his interpretation of the use of the highly sophisticated Paijan projectile points in fishing, the littoral orientation of coastal populations was well established at an early date.

The settlements of the Late Preceramic at such coastal sites as Rio Seco and Aspero indicate the level of increasing complexity achieved by preceramic societies, associated with what must have been a more complex social life. Unquestionably, these Late Preceramic developments are part of an area-wide trend which saw an increase in population and associated emphasis on the construction of monumental pyramids, the latter presumably indicating the growing importance of religion and a society directed by a temple hierarchy.

The focus on the construction of temple pyramid mounds beginning in the Late Preceramic is a prelude to even greater mound proliferation during the Initial Period. The hallmark of this period is the introduction of ceramics, which are present in fully developed form. On the basis of present emphasis, the earliest ceramic technology may have developed somewhere in the northern Andean area, perhaps in Ecuador, and diffused southward to the Peruvian area, possibly via a tropical forest route.

Sechín Alto in the Casma Valley, sharing a U-shaped plan characteristic of many temple complexes of this period, represents perhaps the largest pre-columbian monument ever constructed on the South American continent. What has become increasingly obvious in the last forty years is that the levels of cultural evolution achieved by the Late Preceramic and Initial Period societies in Peru were far greater and extensive than previously imagined. Sites thought to have been significantly later or assignable to the later Early Horizon on the basis of their assumed association with the Chavín phenomena are now known to date to the Late Preceramic or Initial periods. Thus, sites such as Sechín Alto, Las Aldas, Aspero, and Garagay are all indicative of a level of social complexity previously thought to have developed much later.

While incomplete evidence from the highlands and coast indicates the maintenance of regional idiosyncrasies, shared architectural attributes of stepped pyramidal construction, U-shaped plan, and sunken pits suggest the existence of certain elements of a shared belief system. Whatever the nature of the interaction which spawned these elements, they nevertheless indicate that the crucial basis for the complexity of Peruvian society was established through the cultural processes at work during the Late Preceramic and Initial periods.

The florescence of complex society

The archaeological data from the Early Horizon, traditionally defined by the appearance of the Chavín art style across the Peruvian region, constitute the material remains of processes already in full swing by the end of the Initial Period. As Burger points out, far too much emphasis has been placed on the theory that Chavín represented a pan-Andean religious movement that served somehow to unify a large portion of the region.

I would strongly agree with the notion that the order of discovery of archaeological sites dating to the Late Initial Period and Early Horizon greatly colored interpretations of the nature and spread of what appears best defined as the Chavín religious cult. Clearly, had a better understanding of site chronologies for the Central and northern coasts been available at the time of Tello's work at Chavín de Huántar in the Central Highlands, it seems unlikely that this great highland site would have dominated interpretations of the Early Horizon in the way it has for much of this century.

Though not denying the importance of Chavín as a religious force, Burger's argument that care must be taken in identifying cultural manifestations as directly related to the Chavín cult rather than of local origin is well taken. These latter Chavínoid artifacts, upon closer examination, are shown by Burger to "portray the symbols of non-Chavín religious cults which flourished prior to or contemporary with the cult promoted by the Chavín de Huántar temple."

Suffice it to say that while the Chavín cult may well be responsible for the consolidation of a pan-Peruvian religious foundation, this foundation itself was based upon earlier, regional precursors. Acceptance of artistic attributes of the Chavín cult was in many cases highly selective. This is not especially surprising given the well-entrenched local or regional religions already established in the Initial Period and early part of the Early Horizon. Interpretations of the importance of the Chavín cult as well as the site of Chavín de Huántar as the source of the cult's spread have been complicated by what appears to have been the portrayal of numerous traditional, local deities with selective artistic attributes having Chavín affinities.

As I have argued elsewhere (Keatinge 1981: 178), the variation in regional manifestations of Chavín so amply demonstrated in Burger's analysis provides an example of the interpretive problem inherent in the iconographic analysis of prehistoric religions (Lyon 1979: 97). In this case such variation may in part be attributed to religious syncretism, together with the fact that acceptance of the Chavín religious ideology was selective (and short lived), varying by degrees from area to area.

Furthermore, the evidence suggests that the Chavín religion may have been reinterpreted and combined with local belief systems, perhaps to enhance its level of acceptance by different regional audiences. At the least, the religious theology spread by Chavín must have been manipulated autonomously by the individual temple centers (Willey 1948: 10). Such distinct religious manifestations need not automatically suggest a proselytizing missionary religion, which would reasonably be expected to produce a much more unified iconographic system. Rather, the current evidence can also be interpreted as indicating a truly vast array of different temples or shrines that variously emphasized local or regional pantheons, or embellished local gods with differing degrees of Chavín-influenced attributes, and were tied, perhaps, in a loose fashion to a pan-Andean belief system.

As Burger suggests, if Moseley is correct about the impact of El Niño related floods and consequent devastation of coastal societies, then this environmental destabilization may have provided at least a partial impetus for the spread and acceptance of Chavín as a kind of crisis cult. It might also explain the temporary nature of the cult's existence, which Burger argues did not exceed much more than two centuries in most areas.

Following the unifying theme of research represented by Chavín and its variations, the archaeological record for the Early Intermediate Period appears anything but cohesive. In fact, deciphering the overall record for this period might be appropriately likened to trying to understand an elaborate tapestry by viewing it through a cover into which have been cut a series of small, randomly distributed holes. Which is to say, for much of the central Andean region the Early Intermediate Period still constitutes a fragmented period in our understanding of the area's prehistory.

Perhaps more than by anything else, this period of time is known by the extraordinary funerary ceramics associated with the Moche culture of the North Coast and the Nasca culture of the South Coast. The societies which produced these ceramics are representative of the kind of regional polities which apparently typified the period. Their derivation following the demise of Chavín is unclear, though the central and perhaps unifying role of the religious system characteristic of earlier periods clearly remained intact.

Unfortunately, as Conklin and Moseley indicate, the fragmentary record for the period makes the comparative use of pattern analysis extremely tentative. Attempting to discern diagnostic patterns of culture requires a fuller archaeological data base than is currently available. Nevertheless, some suggestive and even useful patterns can be extracted from the record.

The socio-political patterns which can be discerned for the Early Intermediate Period conform to the classic definition of a period – regional differentiation and even isolation with little evidence of pan-Andean integration. On the coast, multi-valley or regional polities such as Moche or Lima contrast with the fragmented "fiefdoms" of the Santa Valley. In the highlands, small, independent cultural groups appear to have been the norm. Yet we know that Early Intermediate Period societies continued to be characterized as labor-intensive and driven by a religious zeal which was expressed by an emphasis on architectural monumentality and elaborate funerary paraphernalia, just as in earlier times.

Even though in the last forty years much has become clearer regarding the cultural evolutionary processes at work during the Early Intermediate Period, it is still fair to say that this period of time as well as the Middle Horizon which follows it requires much more work. We know far more about, for instance, Moche iconography and mortuary practices than we do about the demise of Chavín and the rise of Huari and Tiwanaku.

Isbell's comment that "scarcity of information promotes speculation" is perhaps no place more relevant than in reference to the prehistoric record for the Middle Horizon. I will not review the nuances of this statement, which are well covered in Isbell's contribution. Huari, undeniably a critical site in elucidating the true nature of the Middle Horizon, has suffered from a variety of destructive factors which have made interpretation especially difficult. This has allowed only for continued speculation on the site's impact on the evolution of Andean civilization.

Tiwanaku, on the other hand, has suffered less from destructive factors and is simply under-studied for a site of its magnitude and importance. Similar statements could be made about other large sites in Bolivia and the southern sierra. This, too, has allowed for more speculation to entrench itself in the literature, much of it based on limited studies of ceramic distribution.

As Isbell notes, there is little doubt that Huari and Tiwanaku share common attributes and that "some kind" of interaction took place between these two great centers. And it seems equally clear that "some kind" of interaction took place between these two great centers and different parts of the Central Andes. The major issue, particularly as it pertains to Huari (since Tiwanaku's sphere of influence seems to have been confined largely to the *altiplano* region of the Southern Highlands), concerns the precise nature of this interaction.

While the presence of Huari politico-economic control seems best documented for the Southern Highlands and South Coast regions, beyond these areas the extent of Huari control or influence is still an issue of dispute. Recent work by Topic and Topic at Viracochapampa in the Northern Highlands, long posited as a Huari provincial center, would seem to call into question the impact of Huari on the Northern Highlands. Though Viracochapampa is still viewed as intrusive to the region, it incorporates architectural attributes such as multi-story building techniques which are indigenous to the northern region and which were in use there prior to the Middle Horizon.

Furthermore, Viracochapampa apparently was abandoned before completion and Huari's impact on the area, though not discounted, is interpreted as less than major. Rather, it is the indigenous Middle Horizon site of Marcahuamachuco which may have exercised the more important influence, impacting the central sierra to the south as Huari influence spread northward.

Though on the basis of currently available evidence the issue of Huari dominance as well as its politico-economic influence must be left open, I remain highly skeptical of arguments which posit actual Huari presence or military dominance beyond the Central Highlands–Central Coast region. Even there, I question the nature of Huari interaction, which may well have been different from what it was in the Southern Highlands–South Coast area. I am not convinced, for instance, that the data can support claims of a Huari invasion of the North Coast, nor do I believe that the lack of a major Moche V (i.e. Middle Horizon) site in the Moche Valley indicates that the Moche "capital" was transposed to Pampa Grande in the Lambayeque Valley due to "pressure" from an expanding Huari empire.

On the other hand, I do believe that the change of North Coast burial patterns from the extended position characteristic of Moche I–V (dating from the Early Intermediate Period to the Middle Horizon) to the flexed burials characteristic of the Chimú (dating to the Late Intermediate Period) indicates that something of considerable importance impacted the entire North Coast during the Middle Horizon. Coupled with the appearance of Huari-influenced iconography on ceramics, textiles, and murals, one cannot deny that, at least in the sphere of religion, the impact of Huari may well have been profound.

If the change in North Coast religious practices was due somehow to interaction with Huari, then Huari influence on the economic organization of North Coast Late Intermediate Period society may have been equally profound, even without actual conquest and occupation. Surely the North Coast was not isolated from these influences. On the other hand, while not denying the possibility of important Huari influence, I nevertheless tend to view later North Coast development as largely the product of a long indigenous process in the region. While outside influences no doubt played a role, they were incorporated into an already well-defined North Coast cultural system.

With the Late Intermediate Period the attention of archaeologists is focused on the florescence of regional Andean societies prior to their incorporation into the Inca Empire of the Late Horizon. This period, then, constitutes the last phase of cultural development reflective of native regional patterns before the impact of militaristic and administrative policies promulgated by the largest precolumbian empire ever created in the New World.

As Parsons and Hastings emphasize, one of the difficulties in attempting to understand the polities and economies of the Late Intermediate Period is the fact that the antecedent Middle Horizon still remains relatively unknown. The transition between the two periods, as indicated by such things as the changes in burial patterns on the North Coast, represents a critical period in our understanding of Andean cultural evolution.

Moreover, in studying the Late Intermediate Period we lack detailed chronologies for many regions. In a period that spans some 500 years, detailed chronologies, particularly ceramic chronologies, are necessary in order to control the crucial factor of time. Without this control, we are relegated to generalities and speculation. The process of developing such chronologies is long, hard, tedious and, some would not hesitate to say, boring. But this kind of work forms the basis for a more accurate sequencing of sites as well as providing a stronger basis for insights into processes and events.

Dominating the archaeological literature for the Late Intermediate Period is the information on the Chimú state of the North Coast. Due to both its size and the intensity of study over the last twenty years, we probably know more about the Chimú than any other Late Intermediate period polity. The Moche Valley, heartland of the Chimú and the location of their capital city, Chan Chan, has been the focus of almost continuous archaeological investigations since 1969. The results of this research, well summarized by Parsons and Hastings, provide a picture of the politico-economic organization of a pre-Inca state which was urban, militaristic, and characterized by an agricultural system based on large-scale irrigation networks.

Though there is still a great deal to be learned about the Chimú, sufficient data now exist to utilize this North Coast society in the comparative study of ancient civilizations. Even though we lack the eyewitness accounts and ethnohistoric data available for the Inca, archaeological research has resulted in enough insight into the general maintenance and functioning of the Chimú state to clearly establish it as one of the best exampales of a prehistoric complex society in the New World.

For much of the rest of the Late Intermediate Period, the record still remains rather spotty. Nowhere else is their evidence for the development of the kind of massive centralized authority represented on the North Coast. In the Upper Mantaro–Tarmo drainage of the Central Highlands, for example, the areas occupied by the Huanca and Tarama–Chinchaycocha provide a contrast in areal organization. On the basis of settlement pattern data, the large hilltop centers of the Huanca and the small, dispersed hamlets of the Tarama–Chinchaycocha are almost certainly representative of distinct adaptations to topographic limitations on productivity. The Huanca region provides a far greater agricultural potential and thus supported a much larger population, while the Tarama–Chinchaycocha region is more marginal in terms of productive potential. Yet even in the Huanca region, where huge walls and internal subdivisions at various sites have caused Parsons and Hastings to refer to the "urban character" of these centers, there is no evidence for redistribution or centralization of production such as would be implied by the existence of storage facilities.

But, perhaps most importantly, both the archaeological and ethnohistorical evidence indicate that the peoples of the Huanca and Tarama–Chinchaycocha highlands took advantage of the Upper Montana region to the east. In so doing, they were able to exploit the more productive agricultural climate on the warmer, wetter eastern slopes of the Andes, while at the same time gaining access to a wealth of natural resources. This effective colonization of the Upper Montaña region by highland peoples represents a typical pattern of vertical resource exploitation which Murra has presented as part of his archipelago model for resource access and organization of production in Andean societies.

On the Central Coast, the solidification of Pachacamac as a major pilgrimage center in the Lurín Valley is of major importance. Rostworowski has presented ethnohistoric evidence that belief in the deity of Pachacamac was spread over considerable distances, possibly even to the tropical forest, through associated temples established in various regions. Evidence from the site of Pacatnamú on the North Coast also tends to substantiate both the widespread influence of Pachacamac and a connection between different religious centers. Unquestionably, given what we now know about the importance of Pachacamac, additional research at the site might shed new light on both the prehistoric religious system and the long-distance connections which are referred to in the ethnohistoric sources.

As was the case earlier, during the Late Intermediate Period trade and contact between the distinct environmental zones of the Central Andean region played an important role in the development of an increasingly interconnected society. Though still separated by social, political, and ethnic boundaries, evidence from the Late Intermediate Period suggests that Andean societies did maintain some sort of shared religious heritage based on a foundation layed down in earlier time periods. Pachacamac may well be a key to a better understanding of that heritage.

Pan-Andean empire and the uses of documentary evidence

The chapters by Morris and Netherly provide an example of the interplay between archaeological evidence and ethnohistoric records. Though utilized with great caution in abstracting much beyond the Late Horizon, ethnohistoric records occasionally bring a note of clarity to our understanding of Peruvian prehistory that is simply not achievable in any other way. Details of social organization, politico-economics, conquest, and religion known for the Inca due to the existence of documentary evidence would simply be irretrievable if we were forced to rely on archaeological research alone. Sadly, this also points up how much we must be missing for earlier societies for which there are no written sources whatsoever.

In his review of research on the Inca, Morris makes an important point that there were apparently distinct differences between Inca society as described in the chronicles of the Cuzco region and the organization which was established in the far-flung provinces of the empire. While the classic view of Inca society found in the traditional chronicles, still best presented in John Rowe's seminal work of the 1940s, can be accepted as a fairly accurate portrayal of the situation which existed at the center of the Inca Empire, this classic view must be tempered considerably in reference to the provinces incorporated into the expanding Inca state.

It must also be kept in mind that the Inca Empire was a very late phenomenon in Andean prehistory and existed for less than a century prior to the arrival of the Spanish. Much of the territory annexed by the Inca had been part of the empire for only a very short period of time. In some cases, the Spanish Conquest cut short consolidation of these annexations with the result that, without the chronicles, reliance on the archaeological evidence would not be sufficient to demonstrate Inca dominance of a distant province.

As Morris indicates, research in non-Cuzco, provincial settings has shed new light on the impact of Inca expansion on conquered territories. Clearly, Inca administration of annexed regions was flexible and not necessarily predictable on the basis of patterns encountered in other provinces of the empire. Indications of Inca domination cover a range of archaeological evidence. For example, there are the definite material remains of state administrative centers such as Huánuco Pampa in the Central Highlands, built on virgin soil as an intrusive settlement to provide centralized control over the region. This contrasts sharply with the almost total lack of archaeological evidence for Inca presence at Chan Chan (or in the entire Moche Valley, for that matter), the capital of the North Coast Chimú Empire known from ethnohistoric sources to have been conquered by the Incas.

Morris and Netherly demonstrate that, where it exists, the written record of observations can provide important clues leading to a better understanding of unique Andean institutions. However, even where documentation does exist, we must remember that the observations were made through the sieve of a sixteenth-century Spanish world view by people untrained to record the meeting of two cultures which, without doubt, could hardly have been more different.

The significance of contributions such as Netherly's is to demonstrate the importance of interplay between the archaeological record and the written record when the latter is available. Carefully used, as in the work of Murra and his colleagues in the Huánuco region, interpretations of prehistoric data grounded in sound documentary evidence can produce a thread leading to a clearer perception of Andean beliefs and institutions. I am convinced that twentieth-century archaeologists are ill equipped, not unlike the sixteenth-century Spanish, to comprehend the true meaniang of the Andean past without clues provided by the ethnohistoric accounts. Even so, I would argue, the prehistoric peoples of the Peruvian region developed politico-economic and belief systems so different from our own, that much of the detail of these systems is lost forever, even for areas where documentary evidence does exist.

Contributions from the Selva

Scott Raymond's chapter on tropical forest culture serves to emphasize the greatly increased importance given to cultural developments on the eastern slopes of the Andes by archaeologists concerned with Peruvian prehistory. In retrospect, it seems strange that not until relatively recently has major attention focused on the contributions of montaña societies to the evolution of ancient civilization in Peru. Clearly, peoples occupying the Andean highlands did not reach the eastern slopes of the mountains and simply peer over the edge. Nor did the occupants of the lowlands reach the highlands and simply stare across the puna in amazement. Unquestionably, there was interaction between these two groups, very likely dating from the earliest occupation of the regions.

As Raymond cogently points out, even given the tremendous gaps in the evidence due to poor preservation and lack of research in the lowlands, there is nevertheless sufficient data to support a strong argument for continuous commerce and contact between the peoples of the highlands, tropical forest, and the coast. Evidence of early and ceramic-bearing cultures in the montaña rivals that dated for the highlands and the coast. The coastal appearance of fully domesticated plants, which evidently underwent the necessary genetic transformations in the lowland region, strongly suggests that the origins of both agricultural and ceramic technology in the civilizations of the coast and highlands may be traced to their introduction from the tropical forest region.

The importance of coca to interaction between the montaña and Andean communities in other geographical localities cannot be underestimated. For thousands of years and, as we are becoming all too aware, up to the present, coca has been the major export of the tropical forest region. The economic and ritual importance of coca in prehistoric societies likely played a role in the development of the Archipelago pattern of settlement, proposed by Murra as a uniquely Andean model involving colonization for the purpose of controlling resource zones. Control of the ceja region of the montaña by highland peoples would have meant access to some of the best lands for the production of coca.

The long-distance trade and interaction between the tropical forest and other regions facilitated not only the transfer of tangible items, but also the transfer of ideas. At least some of the iconographic motifs and decorations occurring in different artistic media at highland and coastal sites dating to the Early Horizon, if not earlier, almost surely owe their existence to intense contact with the tropical forest. As such, the evolution of the belief systems associated with the Initial Period and Early Horizon, a time when the nucleus of what was to become a generalized but nevertheless shared pan-Andean religion likely developed, may be intimately intertwined with longstanding and complex connections involving trade and access to resources on the eastern side of the Andes.

Concluding remarks

As mentioned at the beginning of this chapter, the study of Peruvian prehistory has made significant strides in the last forty years. In the last twenty years, all of the authors included in this book have made important contributions to that effort. Thus, the view of active field archaeologists who are constantly confronted with the theoretical and methodological realities of interpreting the Peruvian data is strongly represented in this volume. In that sense, the chapters assembled here represent the current assessments of a group of individuals similar to the one present at the 1947 conference.

While the study of cultural and ceramic chronology is still very much a focus of research in many parts of Peru, just as it was in 1947, sufficient data have been collected for some time periods for archaeologists to begin asking larger, more processual and evolutionary questions. No longer is the Virú Valley sequence the template for cultural development, or the montaña given short shrift in terms of its contributions to the development of complex society in Peru. Ceramic sequences are better known throughout the region and interdisciplinary projects are more the rule than the exception.

Nevertheless, there are still many questions to be asked and many regions to be explored. Crucial sites like Huari and Tiwanaku remain to be thoroughly researched, and whole valleys in virtually every region remain to be surveyed systematically. Issues such as the Moche–Chimú transition on the North Coast or the nature of Nasca settlement on the South Coast still remain to be resolved. Furthermore, if Moseley is correct about the impact of tectonic uplift and landscape-scouring floods on the coast, a reasonably complete picture of site location and change through time may be totally lost to us for much of the Peruvian coastal region. Acceptance of Moseley's argument means that a radically different aproach must be taken in studies attempting to reconstruct prehistoric settlement patterns in areas affected by the posited changes in environment and terrain.

In conclusion, while there is still much to be learned about Peruvian prehistory, the picture of cultural evolution for the region is definitely becoming clearer. The evidence available is in sufficiently intelligible form that the Peruvian case can now firmly claim its place in comparative studies with other world areas where complex societies and pristine states arose. Future research on a wide variety of problems will continue to clarify the patterns of development and change which accompanied the evolution of prehistoric civilization in Peru, truly one of the richest archaeological areas on earth.

ACKNOWLEDGEMENTS

CHAPTER 1. John Rick thanks B. Bocek for editorial assistance, and T. Lynch, R. S. MacNeish, and H. E. Wright, Jr, for help with figures and unpublished data.

CHAPTER 2. Archaeological investigations in the Cupisnique desert were sponsored by the Centre National de la Recherche Scientifique and the French Ministry of Foreign Relations. Radiocarbon measurements were made under the direction of Mme Georgette Delibrias at Gif-sur-Yvette. Dr Jean-Paul Lacombe, Laboratory of Physical Anthropology, Bordeaux University, studied the human skeletons. Prof. Elizabeth Wing, Florida State Museum, studied the faunal remains from the middens. Claude Chauchat is also indebted to Prof. Robert Hoffstetter, National Museum of Natural History in Paris, for his determination of pleistocene vertebrate remains in the field, and to Frédéric Engel for permission to study his collections in Lima. Paul Ossa and Santiago Uceda generously shared their unpublished reports and data and gratitude is also due to Pierre Yves Demars, of the CNRS, who undertook an important part of the field work in Cupisnique.

CHAPTER 3. Rosa Fung Pineda would like to express her appreciation to L. G. Lumbreras and A. Bueno Mendoza, for sharing unpublished reports and data.

CHAPTER 4. Richard L. Burger would like to express his appreciation to Lucy Salazar, Jeffrey Quilter, Thomas Patterson, and Elizabeth Boone. Work on this chapter was carried out as a Fellow in Pre-Columbian Studies at the Dumbarton Oaks Research Library and Collection in 1980–1. José Pinilla, Shelia and Thomas Pozorski, and Robert Bird shared their unpublished reports and data, for which the author is very grateful.

CHAPTER 5. William J. Conklin and Michael E. Moseley would like to thank Anthony Aveni, Alan Sawyer, David Browman, the late Junius Bird, Alan Kolata, and Gary Vescelius for sharing unpublished reports and data.

CHAPTER 6. William H. Isbell offers special thanks to all who have participated in the Huari Urban Prehistory Project. Richard MacNeish generously allowed study of unpublished manuscripts and site survey information from the Ayacucho Archaeological-Botanical Project. Messrs Amat and Barreda, and John Hyslop,

Michael Moseley, and Gary Vescelius shared unpublished reports and data with the author. Lynda Spickard read and commented on a preliminary version of the chapter, assisting significantly in its revisions. However, the author alone bears responsibility for the interpretations presented.

CHAPTER 7.   Jeffrey R. Parsons and Charles M. Hastings are greatly indebted to Sergio Chavez for his assistance with bibliographic materials. We also much appreciate the generosity of several people who have shared their unpublished reports and data with us: Elizabeth Bonnier, Geoffrey Conrad, Kent Day, Timothy Earle, Ian Farrington, Christine Hastorf, Richard Keatinge, Daniele Lavallée, Catherine LeBlanc, Terry Levine, Michael Moseley, Catherine Rozenberg, Richard C. Smith, and David Wilson. Very special thanks go to Ramiro Matos Mendieta, who has so greatly facilitated recent field work in the Upper Mantaro–Tarma drainage.

CHAPTER 9.   Portions of this chapter were read at the 1976 Meeting of the American Anthropological Association in a paper entitled "Inca Coca Lands on the North Coast of Peru." The research on which it is based was carried out in Peru from 1971–4 with the support of a Foreign Area Fellowship Program Fellowship for field research (1971–3) and NSF Dissertation Improvement Grant No. SOC-74-19928 (1974). This support is gratefully acknowledged.

   Patricia Netherly would also like to thank Michael E. Moseley, Director of the Harvard Moche–Chan Chan project, and Carol Mackey, the Co-Director, for many courtesies extended while she was in Trujillo; and Geoffrey Conrad and Cristóbal Campana who visited the Collambay–Simbal region with her on two different occasions.

CHAPTER 10.   Scott Raymond particularly thanks Warren DeBoer, who read earlier drafts of the chapter and gave frank and helpful criticism of his ideas. Thanks go also to Donald Lathrap, whose ideas continue to inspire me, and William Isbell, who has been a stimulating intellectual sparring partner over the years. Personal communication helpful in the preparation of the chapter is acknowledged from James Parsons. There are countless other friends, colleagues, and students who deserve credit for many of the ideas expressed in the text of my chapter; but the list is too long to include them all.

CHAPTER 11.   Richard W. Keatinge would like to thank Michael E. Moseley for the guidance and support upon which the inspiration for this volume is based.

BIBLIOGRAPHY

Agustinos (Religiosos) 1918 [1550]. Relación de la religión y ritos del Perú . . . In H. Urteaga, ed., *Informaciones acerca de la religión y goberino de los incas*. Lima: Imp. & Lib. Sanmartí

Alcina French, J. 1976. *Arqueología de Chinchero*, 2 vols.: I, *La Arquitetura*; II, *Cerámica y Otros Materiales*. Madrid: Ministerio de Asuntos. Exteriores, Direccion General de Relaciones Culturales, Junta para la Protección de Monumentos y Bienes Culturales en el Exterior

   1978. Ingapirca: arquitectura y áreas de asentamiento. *Revista Española de Antropología Americana* [Trabajos y Conferencias], pp. 127–46. Madrid: Facultad de Geografia e Historia, Universidad Complutense de Madrid

Allen, W. L. 1968. A ceramic sequence from the Alto Pachitea, Peru: some implications for the development of tropical forest culture in South America. Unpublished PhD dissertation, Univ. Illinois, Urbana

Allen, W. L. and J. H. Tizon 1973. Land use patterns among the Campa of the Alto Pachitea, Peru. In *Variation in Anthropology*, ed. D. W. Lathrap and J. Douglas, pp. 137–53. Urbana: Illinois Archaeological Survey

Alva, W. and C. Elera 1980. Summary of work at the formative site of Morro de Eten. *NorPARG Newsletter* 3: 2

Ambrosetti, J. B. 1907–8. Exploraciones arquelógicas en la ciudad prehistorica de "La Paya" (Valle Clahaquí, Provincia de Salta). *Revista de la Universidad de Buenos Aires* 8 (Sección Antropología 3), 2 vols., Facultad de Filosofía y Letras, Buenos Aires: M. Biedma é hijo

Anders, M. B. 1977. Sistema de depositos en Pampa Grande, Lambayeque. *Revista del Museo Nacional* 43: 243–79

   1981. Wari experiments in statecraft. Unpublished paper, presented at the 4th Andean Archaeology Colloquium, Austin, Texas

Andrews, A. P. 1974. The U-shaped structures at Chan Chan, Peru. *Journal of Field Archaeology* 1: 241–64

[ANP] Archivo de la Nación, Perú, Sección Histórica, Aguas 3.3.18.63

Bandelier, A. F. 1910. *The Islands of Titicaca and Koati*. New York: Hispanic Society of America

Bawden, G. L. 1977. Galindo and the nature of the Middle Horizon in northern coastal Peru. Unpublished PhD dissertation, Harvard Univ.

   1982. Galindo: a study in cultural transition during the Middle Horizon. In *Chan*

Chan, Andean Desert City, ed. M. E. Moseley and K. C. Day, pp. 285–320. Albuquerque: Univ. New Mexico Press

Beckerman, S. 1979. The abundance of protein in Amazonia: a reply to Gross. *American Anthropologist* 81 (3): 533–60

Begler, E. and R. Keatinge 1979. Theoretical goals and methodological realities: problems in the reconstruction of prehistoric subsistence economies. *World Archaeology* 11 (2): 208–26

Benavides, M. 1965. Estudio de la cerámica decorada de Qonchopata. Unpublished BA thesis, Univ. Nacional de San Cristobal de Huamanga, Ayacucho, Peru

　1979. Notas sobre excavaciones en Cheqo Wasi, Wari. *Investigaciones* 2 (2): 26. Ayacucho, Peru: Universidad Nacional de San Cristobal de Huamanga

Bennett, W. C. 1933. Archaeological hikes in the Andes. *Natural History* 33 (2): 163–74

　1934. Excavations at Tihuanaco. *Anthropological Papers of the American Museum of Natural history* 34 (3)

　1936. Excavations in Bolivia. *Anthropological Papers of the American Museum of Natural History* 35: 331–505

　1943. The position of Chavín in Andean sequences. *Proceedings of the American Philosophical Society, Philadelphia, 1942* 86: 323–7

　1944. Excavations in the Callejón de Huaylas and at Chavín de Huántar. *Anthropological Papers of the American Museum of Natural History* 39 (1)

　1946. The archaeology of the Central Andes. In *Handbook of South American Indians*, II, ed. J. Steward, pp. 61–148. Washington, DC: Smithsonian Institution, Bureau of American Ethnology Bulletin 143

　1948. The Peruvian Co-Tradition. In *A Reappraisal of Peruvian Archaeology*, ed. W. C. Bennett, pp. 1–7. Menasha: Memoirs of the Society for American Archaeology no. 4

　1950. Cultural unity and disunity in the Titicaca Basin. *American Antiquity* 16 (2): 89–89

　1953. Excavations of Wari, Ayacucho, Peru. *Yale University Publications in Anthropology* no. 49

Bennett, W. C. and J. Bird 1949. *Andean Culture History*. American Museum of Natural History, Handbook Series no. 15. New York; 2nd rev. edn, 1960

Berger, R., G. J. Ferguson, and W. F. Libby 1965. UCLA radiocarbon dates IV. *Radiocarbon* 7: 347. *American Journal of Science*

Beynon, D. E. and M. I. Siegel 1981. Ancient human remains from Central Peru. *American Antiquity* 46: 167–78

Bingham, H. 1930. *Machu Picchu, A Citadel of the Incas*. Washington, DC: Memoirs of the National Geographic Society

Bird, J. B. 1948. Preceramic cultures in Chicama and Virú. In *A Reappraisal of Peruvian Archaeology*, ed. W. C. Bennett, pp. 21–8. Menasha: Memoirs of the Society for American Archaeology no. 4

　1963a. Pre-ceramic art from Huaca Prieta, Chicama Valley. *Ñawpa Pacha* 1: 29–34

　1963b. Technology and art in Peruvian textiles. In *Technique and Personality*, Lecture Series Number Three. New York: Museum of Primitive Art

Blanton, R. E. 1972. Prehispanic settlement patterns in the Ixtapalpa peninsula region, Mexico. *Occasional Papers in Anthropology* no. 6. Dept of Anthropology, Pennsylvania State Univ.

Bloch, M. 1949. *Apologie pour l'histoire ou métier d'historien.* Paris: Armand Colin

Bonavia, D. 1964. Investigaciones en la ceja de selva de Ayacucho: informe de la primera expedición científica Huamanga. *Arqueológicas: Publicaciones del Instituto de Investigaciones Antropológicas.* Lima: Museo Nacional de Antropología y Arqueología

1965. Arqueología de Lurín. Seis sitios de ocupación en la parte inferior del valle. *Tesis Antropologicas,* no. 4, ed. Instituto de Estudios Etnológicos del Museo Nacional de la Cultura Peruana y Departamento de Antropología de la Universidad Nacional Mayor de San Marcos. Lima: Museo Nacional de la Cultura

1968. *Las Ruinas del Abiseo.* Lima: Universidad Peruana de Ciencias y Tecnologia

1970. Investigaciones Arqueológicas en el Mantaro Medio. *Revista del Museo Nacional* 35: 211–94

1975. Ecological factors affecting the urban transformation in the last centuries of the pre-Columbian era. In *Advances in Andean Archaeology,* ed. D. L. Browman, pp. 393–410. The Hague: Mouton

1979. Consideraciones sobre el complejo Chivateros. In *Arqueologia Peruana: Investigaciones Arqueológicas en el Perú, 1976,* ed. R. Matos Mendieta, pp. 65–74. Lima

1982a. El complejo Chivateros: una aproximación tecnológica. *Revista del Museo Nacional* 46: 19–37

1982b. *Los Gavilanes.* Corporación Financiera de Desarrollo S.A. Cofide and Instituto Arqueológico Aleman

Bonavia, D. and A. Grobman 1978. El origen del maíz andino. *Estudios Americanistas* 1: 82–91. Homenaje a Herman Trimborn. Bonn: Instituti Anthropos de San Agustín

1979. Sistema de depósitos y almacenamiento durante el período precerámico en la costa del Perú. *Journal de la Société des Américanistes* NS 65: 21–45

Bonavia, D. and R. Ravines 1967. Las fronteras ecológicas de la civilización Andina. *Amaru* 2: 61–9

Bonnier, E. and C. Rozenberg 1978a. L'habitat en village a l'époque préhispanique dans le bassin Shaka-Palcamayo, Dept de Junín, Pérou. *Bull. Inst. Français d'Etudes Andines* 7 (1–2): 49–71

1978b. Note complementaire sur l'habitat en village, a l'époque préhispanique, dans le bassin Shaka-Palcamayo, Dept de Junín, Pérou. *Bull. Inst. Français d'Etudes Andines* 7 (3–4): 59–60

Bordes, F. 1961. Typologie du Paléolithique ancien et moyen. Bordeaux: Imprimerie Delmas. New edn, 1979, in *Les Cahiers du Quaternaire,* I. Paris: Editions du CNRS

1970. Reflexions sur l'outil au Paléolithique. *Bulletin de la Société Préhistorique Française* CRSM 7: 199–202

Bowman, I. 1916. *The Andes of Southern Peru: Geographical Reconnaissance along the Seventy-Third Meridian.* New York: American Geographical Society

Braun, R. 1971. Cerro Narrío reanalyzed: the formative as seen from the southern

Ecuadorian highlands. Unpublished paper, presented at Primer Simposio de Correlaciones Antropológicas Andino-Mesoamericano, Salinas, Ecuador

Brewster-Wray, C. 1982. Huari architecture: form and function. Unpublished paper, presented at the 10th Annual meeting of the Midwest Conference on Andean and Amazonian Archaeology and Ethnohistory, Ann Arbor

Browman, D. L. 1970. Early Peruvian peasants: the culture history of a Central Highlands valley. Unpublished PhD dissertation, Harvard Univ.

   1974a. Pastoral nomadism in the Andes. *Current Anthropology* 15 (2): 188–96

   1974b. Trade patterns in the Central Highlands of Peru in the first millennium BC. *World Archaeology* 6: 322–9

   1977. External relationships of the Early Horizon ceramic style from the Jauja-Huancayo-Basin, Junín. *El Dorado* 11: 1–23

   1980. Tiwanaku expansion and altiplano economic patterns. *Estudios Arqueológicis* 5: 107–20

   1981. New light on Andean Tiwanaku. *American Scientist* 69 (4): 408–19

Brush, D. B. 1974. El lugar del hombre en el ecosistema Andino. *Revista del Museo Nacional* 40: 277–99

Bueno Mendoza, A. and T. Grieder 1979. Arquitectura precerámica de la Sierra Norte. *Espacio* 1 (5): 48–55

   1980. La Galgada nueva clave para la arqueología andina. *Espacio* 9: 49–55

   1981. Arte y cultura precerámica. *Espacio* 10 (3): 50–7

Burger, R. L. 1979. Resultados preliminares de excavaciones en los distritos de Chavín de Huantar y San Marcos, Perú. In *Arqueología Peruana: Investigaciones Arqueológicas en el Perú, 1976*, ed. R. Matos Mendieta, pp. 133–55. Lima: Centro de Proyección Cristiana

   1980. Trace-element analysis of obsidian artifacts from Pachamachay, Junín. In *Prehistoric Hunters of the High Andes*, ed. J. W. Rick, pp. 257–61. New York: Academic Press

   1981. The radiocarbon evidence for the temporal priority of Chavín de Huantar. *American Antiquity* 46

   1983. Pojoc and Waman Wain: two Early Horizon villages in the Chavín heartland. *Ñawpa Pacha* 20: 3–40

   1984a. *The Prehistoric Occupation of Chavín de Huantar, Peru*. University of California Publications in Anthropology

   1984b. Archaeological areas and prehistoric frontiers: the case of formative Peru and Ecuador. In *Social and Economic Organization in the Prehispanic Andes*, ed. D. Browman, R. L. Burger, and M. A. Rivera, pp. 37–71. Oxford: BAR International Series 194 (Proceedings, 44th International Congress of Americanists, Manchester, 1982)

Burger, R. L. and F. Asaro 1977. *Trace Element Analysis of Obsidian Artifacts from the Andes: New Perspectives on Prehispanic Economic Interaction in Peru and Bolivia*. Berkeley: Energy and Environment Division, Lawrence Berkeley Laboratory, Univ. California

   1978. Obsidian distribution and provenience in the Central Highlands and Coast of Peru during the preceramic period. *Contributions of the University of California Archaeological Research Facility* 36: 51–83

1979. Análisis de Rasgos Significativos en la Obsidiana de los Andes Centrales. *Revista del Museo Nacional* 43 (1977): 281–325

Burger, R. L. and L. Salazar-Burger 1980. Ritual and religion at Huaricoto. *Archaeology* 33 (6): 26–32

Burger, R. L., F. Asaro, and H. Michel 1984. The source of the obsidian artifacts at Chavín de Huántar. In *The Prehistoric Occupation of Chavín de Huantar, Peru*, by R. L. Burger, Appendix E, pp. 263–70. Berkeley: Univ. California Press

Bushnell, G. H. S. 19546. *Peru.* London: Thames and Hudson; US edn, 1957, New York: Praeger

Cabello Valboa, M. 1951 [1586]. *Miscelánea antártica.* Lima: Instituto de Etnología, Universidad Nacional Mayor de San Marcos

Calancha, A. de la 1638. *Crónica moralizadora del orden de San Agustín en el Perú . . .* Barcelona: Pedro Lacavalleria

Camino, A. 1977. Trueque, correrías e intercambios entre los Quechuas andinos y los Piro y Machiguenga de la montaña Peruana. *Amazonia Peruana-Ecología* 1 (2): 123–40

Cárdenas Martin, M. 1977. *Informe preliminar del trabajo de campo en el valle Santa* (Departamento de Libertad Ancash). Manuscript Seminario de Arqueología, Instituto Riva-Agüero, Pontificia Universidad Católica del Perú, Lima

1979. Obtención de una cronología del uso de los recursos marinos en el antiguo Perú. *Arqueología PUC* (19–20): 3–26. Publication no. 104, Instituto Riva-Agüero, Pontificia Universidad Católica del Perú, Lima

Cardich, A. 1958. Los yacimientos de Lauricocha. Nuevas interpretaciones de la prehistoria Peruana. *Studia Praehistórica* 1

1959. Ranracancha: un sitio prehistórico en el Departamento de Pasco, Perú. *Acta Praehistórica* 3/4: 35–48

1964. Lauricocha: fundamentos para una prehistoria de los Andes Centrales. *Studia Praehistorica* 3

1976. Vegetales y recolecta en Lauricocha: Algunas inferencias sobre asentamiento y subsistencia preagrícola en los Andes Centrales. *Relaciones de la Sociedad Argentina de Antropología* 10: 27–41

Carmack, R. M. 1972. Ethnohistory: a review of its development, definitions, methods, and aims. In *Annual Review of Anthropology*, I, ed. B. J. Siegel, A. R. Beals and S. A. Tyler, Palo Alto, California

Carr, E. H. 1962. *What Is History?* London: Macmillan

Carrión Cachot, R. 1948. La cultura Chavín; dos nuevas colonias: Kuntur Wasi y Ancón. *Revista del Museo Nacional* 2 (1): 123–72

Casafranca, J. 1960. Los nuevos sitios arqueológicos chavinodes en el Departamento de Ayacucho. In *Antiguo Peru: Espacio y Tiempo*, ed. R. Matos Mendieta, pp. 325–34. Lima: Librería-Editorial Juan Mejía Baca

Castro de La Mata and D. Bonavia 1980. Lumbosacral malformations and Spina Bifida in a Peruvian preceramic child. *Current Anthropology* 21: 515–16

Chauchat, C. 1972. Ensayo de tipología lítica del precerámico Peruano. *Revista del Museo Nacional* 38: 125–32

1976. The Paiján complex, Pampa de Cupisnique, Peru. *Ñawpa-Pacha* 13 (1975): 85–96, pls. XXIX–XXXVI

1977. Problemática y metodología de los sitios líticos de superficie: El Paijanense de Cupisnique. *Revista del Museo Nacional* 43: 13–26

1978. Recherches préhistoriques sur la Côte nord du Pérou. *Bulletin de la Société Préhistorique Française* 75 (8): 253–6

1979. Additional observations on the Paiján complex. *Ñawpa Pacha* 16 (1978): 51–64, pl. X

1982. Le Paijanien du désert de Cupisnique: recherches sur l'occupation préhistorique de la Côte nord du Pérou au début de l'Holocène. [I, 719pp.; II, 11 pls.] Unpublished dissertation, Univ. Bordeaux 1

Chauchat, C. and J. M. Dricot 1979. Un nouveau type humain fossile en Amérique du Sud: l'Homme de Paiján (Pérou). *Comptes-rendus de l'Académie des Sciences* 289: 387–9

Chauchat, C. and J. P. Lacombe 1984. El hombre de Paijan: el más antiguo Peruano? *Gaceta arqueológica andina* 11: 4–6, 12

Chauchat, C. and J. Zevallos Quiñones 1980. Una punta en cola de pescado procedente de la costa norte del Perú. *Ñawpa Pacha* 17 (1979): 143–6, pl. XXVIII

Chávez, K. L. M. 1977. Marcavalle: the ceramics from an Early Horizon site in the Valley of Cuzco, Peru, and implications for South Highland socioeconomic interaction. Unpublished PhD dissertation, Univ. Pennsylvania

Cieza de León, P. 1947. Pt 1 of *La Crónica del Perú*. Madrid: Biblioteca de Autores Españoles 26

1967. *El Señorío de los Incas*, Pt 2 of *La Crónica del Perú*. Lima: Instituto de Estudios Peruanos

Clapperton, C. M. 1972. The Pleistocene moraine stages of west-central Peru. *Journal of Glaciology* 11 (62): 255–62

Cobo, B. 1892–5. *Historia del Nuevo Mundo*. Seville: Sociedad Bibliofilos Andaluces

Coe, M. D. 1972. Olmec jaguars and Olmec kings. In *The Cult of the Feline Conference*, ed. E. Benson, pp. 1–12. Washington, DC: Dumbarton Oaks Research Library and Collection

Cohen, M. 1975. Some problems in the quantitative analysis of vegetable refuse illustrated by a Late Horizon site on the Peruvian coast. *Ñawpa Pacha* 10–12: 49–60

1979. Archaeological plant remains from the Central Coast of Peru. *Ñawpa Pacha* 16: 23–50

Cohn, B. S. 1968. Ethnohistory. In *Encyclopedia of the Social Sciences*. New York: Macmillan and The Free Press

Collier, D. 1955. Cultural chronology and change as reflected in the ceramics of the Viru Valley, Peru. Chicago: Field Museum of Natural History, *Fieldiana: Anthropology* 43

1962. Archaeological investigations in the Casma Valley, Peru. *Akten des 34 Internationalen Amerikanistenkongress*, Vienna, 1958, pp. 411–17. Vienna: Verlag Ferdinand Berger

Colson, E. 1977. A continuing dialogue: prophets and local shrines among the Tonga of Zambia. In *Regional Cults*, ed. R. P. Werbner, pp. 119–39. New York: Academic Press

Conklin, W. J. 1970. Peruvian textile fragment from the beginning of the Middle Horizon. *Textile Museum Journal* 3 (1): 15–24

1971. Chavin textiles and the origins of Peruvian weaving. *Textile Museum Journal* 3 (2): 13–19

1974a. An introduction to South American archaeological textiles with emphasis on materials and techniques of Peruvian tapestry. In *Archaeological Textiles*, ed. P. L. Fiske, pp. 17–30. Washington, DC: The Textile Museum

1975a. Pampa Gramalote textiles. In *ibid.*, pp. 77–92.

1978. The revolutionary weaving inventions of the Early Horizon. *Ñawpa Pacha* 16: 1–12

1979. An introduction to South American archaeological textiles. *Archaeological Textiles*, Irene Emery Roundtable on Museum Textiles. Washington, DC: The Textile Museum

1985. Pucara and Tiahuanaco tapestry: the beginning of an altiplano weaving tradition. *Ñawpa Pacha* 21

1985a. The architecture of Huaca Los Reyes. In *Early Ceremonial Architecture of the Andes*. Washington, DC: Dumbarton Oaks

1985b. Pucara and Tiahuanaco tapestry: time and style in a sierra weaving tradition. *Ñawpa Pacha* 21: 1–44

Conrad, G. W. 1977. Chiquitoy Viejo: an Inca administrative center in the Chicama Valley, Peru. *Journal of Field Archaeology* 14: 1–18

1981. Cultural materialism, split inheritance, and the expansion of ancient Peruvian empires. *American Antiquity* 46: 3–26

Cook, A. G. 1979. The iconography of empire: symbolic communication in seventh-century Peru. Unpublished MA thesis, State Univ. of New York, Binghamton

Cordy-Collins, A. 1976. An iconographic study of Chavin textiles from the South Coast of Peru: the discovery of a Pre-Columbian catechism. Unpublished PhD dissertation, Univ. of California, Los Angeles

1977. Chavín art: its shamanic/hallucinogenic origins. In *Pre-Columbian Art History*, ed. A. Cordy-Collins and J. Stern, pp. 353–62. Palo Alto, CA: Peek Publications

1979a. Cotton and the Staff God: analysis of an ancient Chavín textile. In *Junius B. Bird Pre-Columbian Textile Conference*, ed. A. Pollard Rowe, E. P. Benson and A.-L. Schaffer, pp. 51–60. Washington, DC: The Textile Museum and Dumbarton Oaks, Trustees for Harvard University

1979b. The dual divinity concept in Chavín art. *El Dorado* 3 (2): 1–31

1980. An artistic record of the Chavín hallucinatory experience. *The Masterkey* 54: 84–93

Créqui-Montfort, Count G. de 1906. Fouilles de la mission scientifique française à Tiahuanaco. *Verhandlungen des XIV Internationalen Amerikanisten Kongresses*, Stuttgart, pt 2, pp. 531–51

Cruikshank Dodd, E. 1969. The image of the word. *Berytus Archaeological Studies* 18: 35–79

Damp, J. E. 1979. Better homes and gardens: the life and death of the early Valdivia community. Unpublished PhD dissertation, Univ. Calgary, Alberta

Davis, E. L. 1963. The desert culture of the western Great Basin: a lifeway of seasonal transhumance. *American Antiquity* 29: 202–12

Day, K. C. 1974. Walk-in wells and water management at Chan Chan, Peru. In *The Rise and Fall of Civilizations*, ed. J. Sabloff and C. Lamberg-Karlovsky, pp. 182–90. Menlo Park, CA: Cummings Publications Co.

    1975. *Midseason Report, ROM Lambayeque Project*. Toronto: Office of the Chief Archaeologist, Royal Ontario Museum

DeBoer, W. 1981a. Buffer zones in the cultural ecology of Aboriginal Amazonia: an ethnohistorical approach. *American Antiquity* 46 (2): 364–77

    1981b. The machete and the cross: Conibo trade in the late seventeenth century. In *Networks of the Past. Proceedings of the 12th Annual Conference of the University of Calgary Archaeology Association* (1979), ed. P. Francis, F. Kense and P. G. Duke, pp. 30–47

Deetz, J. and E. Dethlefsen 1965. The Doppler Effect and archaeology: a consideration of the spatial aspects of seriation. *Southwest Journal of Anthropology* 21: 196–206

Denevan, W. M. 1966. The Aboriginal cultural geography of the Llanos de Mojos in northeastern Bolivia. *Ibero-Americana* no. 48, Univ. California Press, Berkeley

    1972. Campa subsistence in the Gran Pajonal, eastern Peru. *Actas y Memorias del XXXIX Congreso Internacional de Americanistas* (Lima) 4: 161–70

    1976 (ed.). *The Native Population of the Americas in 1492*. Madison: Univ. Wisconsin Press

Diez de San Miguel, G. 1964. *Visita hecha a la provincia de Chucuito por Garci Diez de San Miguel en el Año 1567. Documentos Regionales para la Etnología y Etnohistoria Andina*, I, 1–299. Lima: Casa de la Cultura Peruana

Dillehay, T. D. 1976. Competition and cooperation in a pre-Hispanic multi-ethnic system in the Central Andes. Unpublished PhD dissertation, Texas, Austin

    1977. Tawantinsuyu, integration of the Chillón Valley, Peru: a case of Inca geopolitical mastery. *Journal of Field Archaeology* 4 (4): 397–405

    1979. Pre-Hispanic resource sharing in the Central Andes. *Science* 204: 24–31

Dillehay, T. D. and P. J. Netherly 1983. Exploring the Upper Zaña Valley of Peru; a unique tropical forest setting offers new insights into the Andean past. *Archeology* 37 (4): 23–30

Dillon, W. P. and R. N. Oldale 1978. Late quaternary sea level curve; reinterpretation based on glacio-tectonic influence. *Geology* 6: 56–60

Dollfus, O. 1981. El reto del espacio andino. *Perú Problema* 20. Lima: Instituto de Estudios Peruanos

Donnan, C. B. 1964. An early house from Chilca, Perú. *American Antiquity* 30: 137–44

    1972. Moche-Huari murals from northern Peru. *Archaeology* 25 (2): 85–95

    1973. Moche occupation of the Santa Valley, Peru. *Univ. California Publications in Anthropology* 8

Donnan, C. B. and C. J. Mackey 1978. *Ancient Burial Patterns of the Moche Valley, Peru*. Austin: Univ. Texas Press

Dricot, J. M. 1979. Descubrimientos de dos esqueletos humanos asociados a la cultura Paijanense. In *Arqueología Peruana*, ed. R. Matos Mendieta, pp. 9–15. Lima: Seminario "investigaciones arqueológicas en el Perú 1976" (April 1976), Universidad Nacional Mayor de San Marcos

Duviols, P. 1967. Un inedit de Cristóbal de Albornoz: la instrucción para descubrir todas las guacas del Pirú y sus camayos y haziendas. *Journal de la Société des Américanistes* 56 (1): 7–39

  1973. Un mythe de l'origine de la coca (Cajatambo). Institut Français d'Études Andines, *Bulletin* 2 (13)

Dwyer, E. B. 1971. The early Inca occupation of the Valley of Cuzco, Peru. Unpublished PhD dissertation, Univ. California, Berkeley

Earle, T. K. 1972. Lurin Valley, Peru: Early Intermediate Period settlement development. *American Antiquity* 37 (4): 467–77

Earle, T. K., T. N. D'Altroy, and C. J. LeBlanc 1978a. Arqueología regional de los períodos prehispánicos tardíos en el Mantaro. In *El Hombre y la Cultura Andina*, ed. R. Matos Mendieta, II, pp. 641–72. Lima: Univ. Nacional Mayor de San Marcos, III, Congreso Peruano

  1978b. Regional archaeology of the Late Hispanic periods in the Upper Mantaro. Unpublished report, Dept Anthropology, UCLA

  1978c. Preliminary report of the 1978 field season of the Upper Mantaro research project. Unpublished report, Dept Anthropology, UCLA

Earle, T. K., T. N. D'Altroy, C. J. LeBlanc, C. A. Hastorf, and T. Y. Levine. 1980. Changing settlement patterns in the Upper Mantaro Valley, Peru. *Journal of New World Archaeology* 4 (1), Institute of Archaeology, UCLA

Earle, T. K., C. Hastorf, C. LeBlanc, and T. D'Altroy 1979. Preliminary report of the 1979 field season of the Upper Mantaro research project. Unpublished report, Dept of Anthropology, UCLA

Earls, J. and I. Silverblatt 1978. Ayllus y etnías de la region Pampas-Qaracha – el impacto del imperio Incaico. In *El Hombre y la Cultura Andina*, ed. R. Matos Mendieta, II, pp. 157–77. Lima: Univ. Nacional Mayor de San Marcos, III Congreso Peruano

Eickelman, D. 1977. Ideological change and regional cults, Maraboutism and ties of "closeness" in western Morocco. In *Regional Cults*, ed. R. P. Werbner, pp. 3–28. New York: Academic Press

Eling, H. H. 1978. Interpretaciones preliminares del sistema de riego antiguo de Talambo en el Valle de Jequetepeque, Peru. In *El Hombre y la Cultura Andina*, ed. R. Matos Mendieta, II, pp. 401–19. Lima: Univ. Nacional Mayor de San Marcos, III Congreso Peruano

Engel, F. 1956. Curayacu, a Chavinoid site. *Archaeology* 9: 98–105

  1957a. Early sites on the Peruvian coast. *Southwestern Journal of Anthropology* 13: 54–68

  1957b. Sites et établissements sans céramique de la Côte péruvienne. *Journal de la Société des Américanistes* NS 46: 67–155

  1958. Algunos datos con referencia a los sitios precerámicos de la costa peruana. *Arqueológicas* 3

  1962. *Elementos de Prehistoria Peruana*. Lima: Stylos

1963. A preceramic settlement on the Central Coast of Perú: Asia, Unit 1. *Transactions of the American Philosophical Society* (Philadelphia), NS 53, pt 3

1964. El precerámico sin algodón en la costa del Perú. *Actas y Memorias del XXXV Congreso Internacional de Americanistas* (México, 1962) 3: 141–52

1965. *Historia Elemental del Perú Antiguo*. Lima: Libreria-Editorial Juan Mejía Baca

1966a. *Paracas. Cien Siglos de Cultura Peruana*. Lima: Libreria-Editorial Juan Mejía Baca

1966b. *Geografía humana prehistórica y agricultura precolombina de la Quebrada de Chilca*. Lima: Universidad Agraria

1966c. Le complexe précéramique d'el Paraiso (Pérou). *Journal de la Société des Américanistes* NS 55 (1): 43–96

1969. On early man in the Americas. *Current Anthropology* 10: 225

1970a. Exploration of the Chilca Canyon, Perú. *Current Anthropology* 11: 55–8

1970b. *Las lomas de Iguanil y el complejo de Aldas*. Lima: Universidad Agraria

1970c. La grotte du megatherium a Chilca et les ecologies du haut-Holocene Peruvien. In *Echanges et Communications*, ed. J. Pouillon and P. Miranda. The Hague: Mouton

1971. D'Antival à Huarangal. *L'Homme* 11 (2): 39–57

1973. New facts about pre-columbian life in the Andean lomas. *Current Anthropology* 14: 271–80

1976. *An Ancient World Preserved: Relics and Records of Prehistory in the Andes*. New York: Crown Publishers

Espejo Nuñez, J. 1951. Exploraciones arqueológicas en las cabeceras del Pukcha (Perú). *Cuadernos Americanos* 61 (2): 139–52

1955. Gotush nuevos descubrimientos en Chavín. *Baessler-Archiv* NS 3: 123–36

Espinosa, W. 1971. Los Huancas, aliados de la conquista. *Anales Científicos de la Universidad del Centro del Perú* 1: 9–198

1973. *La Destrucción del Imperio de los Incas*. Lima: Retablo de Papel Ediciones

Estete, M. de 1968. Noticia del Perú (ca. 1535). In *Biblioteca Peruana*, Primera Serie, I. Lima: Editores Técnicos Asociados SA

Evans-Pritchard, E. E. 1962. *Essays in Social Anthropology*. London: Macmillan

Farrington, I. 1978. Irrigación prehispánica y establecimientos en la costa norte del Perú. In *Tecnología Andina*, ed. R. Ravines, pp. 117–28. Lima: Instituto de Estudios Peruanos

1979. *Open Channel Hydraulics and Hydrology: Towards an Understanding of Prehistoric Irrigation Systems in Peru*. Vancouver: 43rd International Congress of Americanists

Farrington, I. and C. C. Park 1978. Hydraulic engineering and irrigation culture in the Moche Valley, Peru: *c*. AD 1250–1532. *Journal of Field Archaeology* 5: 255–68

Feldman, R. A. 1977a. Preceramic corporate architecture from Aspero. Paper presented at The Andean Preceramic Symposium, 76th Annual Meeting of the American Anthropological Association, Houston, Dec. 2, 1977

1977b. Life in ancient Perú. *Field Museum of Natural History Bulletin* 48: 12–17

1980. Aspero, Perú: architecture, subsistence economy, and other artifacts of a pre-ceramic maritime chiefdom. Unpublished PhD dissertation, Harvard Univ.

Fergusson, G. and T. Rafter 1959. New Zealand 14C age measurements. *New Zealand Journal of Geology and Geophysics* 2 (1): 208–41

Flannery, K. V. 1965. The ecology of early food production in Mesopotamia. *Science* 147: 1247–56

1968. The Olmec and the Valley of Oaxaca: a model for inter-regional interaction in formative times. In *Dumbarton Oaks Conference on the Olmec*, ed. E. Benson, pp. 79–110. Washington: Dumbarton Oaks Research Library and Collection

1977. Review of *Mesoamerican Archaeology: New Approaches*, ed. N. Hammond. *American Antiquity* 42: 659–61

Flores Espinoza, I. 1960. Wischqana, sitio temprano en Ayacucho. In *Antiguo Perú: Espacio y Tiempo*, ed. R. Matos Mendieta, pp. 335–44. Lima: Librería-Editorial Juan Mejía Baca

Fung Pineda, R. 1969. Los anzuelos de concha de Las Aldas: un análisis comparativo. *Boletín del Seminario de Arqueología* 4: 29–43

1972a. Las Aldas: su ubicación dentro del proceso histórico del Perú Antiguo. *Dédalo* 5 (9–10). Sao Paulo: Museo de Arte y Arqueología

1972b. El temprano surgimiento en el Perú de los sistemas socio-políticos complejos: planteamiento de una hipótesis de desarrollo original. *Apuntes Arqueológicos* 2: 10–32

1972c. Nuevos datos para el período de cerámica inicial en el Valle de Casma. *Arqueología y Sociedad* 7–8: 1–12

Fung Pineda, R., C. Cenzano, and A. Zavaleta 1972. El taller lítico de Chivateros, valle del Chillón. *Revista del Museo Nacional* 38: 61–72

Fung Pineda, R. and C. Williams León 1979. Exploraciones y excavaciones en el valle de Sechín, Casma. *Revista del Museo Nacional* 43 (1977): 111–55

Gade, D. 1967. Plant use and folk agriculture in the Vilconota Valley of Peru: a cultural–historical geography of plant resources. Unpublished PhD dissertation, Univ. Wisconsin, Madison

Garbett, K. 1977. Disparate regional cults and a unitary field in Zimbabwe. In *Regional Cults*, ed. R. P. Werbner, pp. 55–92. New York: Academic Press

Gasparini, G. and L. Margolies 1980. *Inca Architecture*. Trans. P. J. Lyon. Bloomington: Indiana Univ. Press

Gayton, A. E. 1967. Textiles from Hacha, Perú. *Ñawpa Pacha* 5: 1–14

Godelier, M. 1977. *Perspectives in Marxist Anthropology*. Cambridge Univ. Press

González, A. Rex 1980. Patrones de asentamientos Incaicos en una provincia marginal del imperio, implicaciones socio-culturales. Unpublished manuscript, Wenner-Gren Symposium (Vienna): *Settlement Patterns: Retrospect and Prospect*

Gonzalez, E., T. Van Der Hammen, and R. F. Flint 1965. Late quaternary glacial and vegetational sequence in the Valle de Lagunillas, Sierra Nevada del Cucuy, Colombia. *Leidse Geologische Mededelingen* 32: 157–82

Grabar, A. 1968. *Christian Iconography: A Study of its Origins*. Bollingen Series, vol. 35. Princeton Univ. Press

Grieder, T. 1975. A dated sequence of building and pottery at Las Haldas. *Ñawpa Pacha* 13: 99–112

Grieder, T. and A. Bueno Mendoza 1981. La Galgada: Peru before pottery. *Archaeology* 34 (2): 44–51

Grobman, A. and D. Bonavia 1978. Pre-ceramic maize on the north-central coast of Perú. *Nature* 276: 386–7

Grobman, A. *et al.* 1977. Study of pre-ceramic maize from Huarmey, north central coast of Perú. Harvard University, *Botanical Museum Leaflets* 25 (8): 221–42

Gross, D. R. 1975. Protein capture and cultural development in the Amazon Basin. *American Anthropologist* 77 (3): 526–9

Grossman, J. 1972a. Early ceramic cultures of Andahuaylas, Apurimac, Perú. Unpublished PhD dissertation, Univ. California, Berkeley

   1972b. An ancient gold worker's tool kit; the earliest metal technology in Perú. *Archaeology* 25: 270–5

   1976. Demographic changes and economic transformations in the south-central highlands of pre-Huari Peru. Paper presented at the Northeastern Anthropological Meetings (Middletown, Conn.); *Ñawpa Pacha* 21 (1983): 45–126

Hansen, B. C. S., H. E. Wright, Jr, and J. P. Bradbury 1984. Pollen studies in the Junín area, central Peruvian Andes. *Geological Society of America Bulletin* 95: 1454–65

Hastenrath, S. 1967. Observations on the snowline in the Peruvian Andes. *Journal of Glaciology* 6: 541–50

Hastings, C. 1978. Huánuco, Tarma, and Jauja: a study of interzonal economic organization in Central Peru. Unpublished paper, on file at Univ. Michigan Museum of Anthropology, Ann Arbor

   1980. Sierra–Selva contact in the eastern Andes of Peru: the Tulumayo Valley. Unpublished report, on file at Univ. Michigan Museum of Anthropology, Ann Arbor

Hastings, C. M. and M. E. Moseley 1975. The adobes of Huaca del Sol and Huaca de la Luna. *American Antiquity* 40 (2): 196–203

Hester, J. J. 1973. Late Pleistocene environments and early man in South America. In *Peoples and Cultures of Native South America*, ed. D. R. Gross, pp. 4–18. New York: Doubleday

Heusser, C. J. 1966. Late-Pleistocene pollen diagram from the province of Llanquihue, southern Chile. *Proceedings of the American Philosophical Society* 110: 269–306

Hidalgo, L. J. 1972. *Culturas Protohistóricas del Norte de Chile: El Testimonio de los Crónistas*. Santiago: Editorial Universitaria

Hill, B. 1975. A new chronology of the Valdivia ceramic complex from the coastal zone of Guayas Province, Ecuador. *Ñawpa Pacha* 10–12: 1–32

Hodder, I. 1977. The distribution of material culture items in the Baringo District, W. Kenya. *Man* 12: 239–69

   1982. *Symbols in Action: Ethnoarchaeological Studies of Material Culture*. New York: Cambridge Univ. Press

Hyslop, J. 1976. An archaeological investigation of the Lupaca Kingdom and its origins. Unpublished PhD dissertation, Columbia Univ.

1977a. Hilltop cities in Peru. *Archaeology* 30 (4): 218–26

1977b. Chulpas of the Lupaca zone of the Peruvian High Plateau. *Journal of Field Archaeology* 4: 149–70

1984. *The Inka Road System*. New York: Academic Press

Ibarra Grasso, D. E. 1965. Prehistoria de Bolivia. La Paz: Editorial, "Los Amigos del Libro"

Instituto Nacional de Planificación 1969. *Atlas Histórico Geographico y de Paisajes Peruanos*. Lima: Instituto Nacional de Planificacion

Isbell, B. J. 1978. *To Defend Ourselves: Ecology and Ritual in an Andean Village*. Latin American Monographs, no. 47, Institute of Latin American Studies, Univ. Texas, Austin

Isbell, W. H. 1968. New discoveries in the montaña, southeastern Peru. *Archaeology* 21 (2): 108–14

1974. Ecología de la expansión de los Quechua-Hablantes. *Revista del Museo Nacional de Antropología y Arqueología* 40: 139–55

1977. The rural foundation for urbanism. *Illinois Studies in Anthropology*, no. 10, Univ. Illinois Press

Isbell, W. H. and K. Schreiber 1978. Was Huari a state? *American Antiquity* 48 (3): 372–89

Isbell, W. H. and L. E. Spickard [n.d.]. From ceremonialism to bureaucracy: an interpretation of a Huari compound. Unpublished manuscript, Dept Anthropology, State Univ. New York, Binghamton

Ishida, E. *et al.* 1960. *Andes; The Report of the University of Tokyo Scientific Expedition to the Andes in 1958*. Tokyo: Bijitsu Shuppan Sha

Izumi, S. 1971. The development of the formative culture in the ceja de montaña: a viewpoint based on the materials from the Kotosh site. In *Dumbarton Oaks Conference on Chavín*, 1968, ed. E. P. Benson, pp. 49–72. Washington, DC: Dumbarton Oaks Research Library

Izumi, S. and T. Sono 1963. *Andes 2: Excavations at Kotosh, Perú, 1960*. Tokyo: Kadokawa Publishing Co.

Izumi, S. and K. Terada 1966. *Andes 3: Excavations at Pechiche and Garabanzal, Tumbes Valley, Perú, 1960*. Tokyo: Kadokawa Publishing Co.

1972. *Andes 4: Excavations at Kotosh, Peru, 1963 and 1966*. Univ. Tokyo Press

Izumi, S., P. J. Cuculiza, and C. Kano 1972. Excavations at Shillacoto, Huánuco, Perú. *Bulletin* no. 3, Univ. Tokyo Museum

Jacobsen, T. and R. Adams 1958. Salt and silt in ancient Mesopotamia. *Iraq* 22: 186–96

Jones, G. D. and R. Kautz 1981. Issues in the study of New World state formation. In *The Transition to Statehood in the New World*, ed. G. D. Jones and R. R. Kautz, pp. 3–34. New York: Cambridge Univ. Press

Julien, C. J. 1978. Inca administration in the Titicaca Basin as reflected at the provincial capital of Hatungolla. Unpublished PhD dissertation, Univ. California, Berkeley

1979. Investigaciones recientes en la capital de los Qolla, Hatungolla, Puno. In *Arqueología Peruana*, ed. R. Matos Mendieta, pp. 199–213. Lima: Universidad Nacional Mayor de San Marcos

Julien, M., D. Lavallée, and M. Dietz 1981. Les sépultures préhistoriques de Telarmachay. *Boletín del Instituto Francés de Estudios Andinos* 10 (1–2): 85–100

Kano, C. 1972a. Excavaciones en Shillacoto, Huánuco. *Revista del Museo Nacional* 36 (1975): 52–62 (*Actas y Memorias del XXXIX Congreso Internacional de Americanistas*, Lima, 1970, vol. 3)

1972b. Pre-Chavín cultures in the Central Highlands of Peru: new evidence from Shillacoto, Huánuco. In *Cult of the Feline Conference*, ed. E. P. Benson, pp. 139–52. Washington: Dumbarton Oaks Research Library and Collection

1979. The origins of the Chavín culture. *Dumbarton Oaks: Studies in Pre-Columbian Art and Archaeology*, no. 22

Kaplan, L. 1980. Variation in the cultivated beans. In *Guitarrero Cave: Early Man in the Andes*, ed. T. F. Lynch, pp. 145–8. New York: Academic Press

Kauffman Doig, F. 1964. Los estudios de Chavín (1553–1919). *Fenix* 14: 147–249

1970. *Arqueología Peruana*. Vision Integral. Lima: Promocion Editorial Inca, SA

1971. *Arqueología Peruana*. Vision Integral 5th edn. Lima: Ediciones PEISA

1978. *Manual de Arqueología Peruana*, 6th edn. Lima: Ediciones PEISA

Kaulicke, P. 1975. *Pandanche. Un Caso del Formativo en los Andes de Cajamarca*. Lima: Seminario de Historia Rural Andina, Universidad Nacional Mayor de San Marcos

1976. *El Formativo de Pacopampa*. Lima: Seminario de Historia Rural Andina, Universidad Nacional Mayor de San Marcos

Kautz, R. R. 1980. Pollen analysis and paleoethnobotany. In *Guitarrero Cave: Early Man in the Andes*, ed. T. F. Lynch, pp. 45–59. New York: Academic Press

Keatinge, R. 1974. Chimu rural administrative centers in the Moche Valley, Peru. *World Archaeology* 6 (1): 66–82

1975. Urban settlement systems and rural sustaining communities: an example from Chan Chan's hinterland. *Journal of Field Archaeology* 2: 215–27

1977a. Religious forms and secular functions: the expansion of state bureaucracies as reflected in prehistoric architecture on the Peruvian North Coast. *Annals of the New York Academy of Sciences* 293: 229–45

1977b. Reconocimiento de sitios arqueológicos efectuados por el proyecto de irrigación Jequetepeque–Zaña. Unpublished paper

1978. The Pacatnamu textiles. *Archaeology* 31 (2): 30–41

1980. Archaeology and development: the Tembladera sites of the Peruvian North Coast. *Journal of Field Archaeology* 7: 467–75

1981. The nature and role of religious diffusion in the early stages of state formation: an example from Peruvian prehistory. In *The Transition to Statehood in the New World*, ed. G. D. Jones and R. R. Kautz, pp. 172–87. New York: Cambridge Univ. Press

1982. Economic development and cultural resource management in the Third World: an example from Peru. *Journal of Anthropological Research* 38: 211–22

Keatinge, R. and G. W. Conrad 1983. Imperialist expansion in Peruvian prehistory: Chimu administration of a conquered territory. *Journal of Field Archaeology* 10: 255–83

Keatinge, R. and K. C. Day 1973. Socio-economic organization of the Moche Valley,

Peru, during the Chimu occupation of Chan Chan. *Journal of Anthropological Research* 29 (4): 275–95

Kelley, D. H. and D. Bonavia 1963. New evidence for pre-ceramic maize on the coast of Peru. *Ñawpa Pacha* 1: 39–42

Kendall, A. 1974. Architecture and planning at the Inca sites in the Cusichaca area. *Baessler-Archiv* NS 22: 73–137

  1976. Preliminary report on ceramic data and the pre-Inca architectural remains of the (Lower) Urubamba Valley, Cuzco. Baessler-Archiv 24: 41–159

Kitzinger, E. 1977. *Byzantine Art in the Making*. Cambridge, Mass.: Harvard Univ. Press

Knobloch, P. 1981. The Huari transition: exchange and integration of stylistic information. Unpublished paper, presented at the 21st Annual Meeting of the Institute of Andean Studies, Berkeley

Koepcke, M. 1954. Corte ecológico transversal en los Andes del Perú central con especial consideración de las aves, Universidad Nacional Mayor de San Marcos, Museo de Historia Natural "Javier Prado," *Memorias* no. 3, Lima

Kosok, P. 1965. *Life, Land and Water in Ancient Peru*. New York: Long Island Univ. Press

Kroeber, A. 1925. The Uhle pottery collections from Supe. *Univ. California Publications in American Archaeology and Ethnology* vol. 21

  1944. Peruvian archaeology in 1942. *Viking Fund Publications in Anthropology* vol. 4. New York: Wenner-Gren Foundation

  1947. Esthetic and recreational activities: art. In *Handbook of South American Indians*, V, ed. J. Steward, pp. 411–92. Washington, DC: Smithsonian Institution, Bureau of American Ethnology Bulletin 143

  1953. Paracas Cavernas and Chavín. *Univ. California Publications in American Archaeology and Ethnology* 40 (1953): 313–32

Kubler, G. 1970. Period, style and meaning in ancient American art. *New Literary History* 1 (2): 127–44

  1975. *The Art and Architecture of Ancient America: The Mexican, Maya, and Andean Peoples*. Harmondsworth, Middlesex: Penguin Books

La Barre, W. 1971. Materials for a history of studies of crisis cults: a bibliographic essay. *Current Anthropology* 12 (1): 3–44

Lanning, E. P. 1958. Cerámica antigua de la costa peruana: nuevos descubrimientos. Unpublished paper, presented at the Mesa Redonda de Ciencias Antropológicas (January 7–13, 1958). Instituto de Etnología y Arqueología, Universidad Nacional Mayor de San Marcos, Lima. 2nd, corr. edn, 1960, Institute of Andean Studies, Berkeley

  1962. Review: Andes. The report of the University of Tokyo Scientific Expedition to the Andes in 1958 by Eiichiro Ishida *et al. American Antiquity* 27: 594–5

  1963a. A pre-agricultural occupation on the Central Coast of Peru. *American Antiquity* 28: 360–71

  1963b. A ceramic sequence for the Piura and Chira coast, North Peru. *Univ. California Publications in American Archaeology and Ethnology* 46 (2)

  1965. Early man in Peru. *Scientific American* pp. 68–76

  1967a. *Peru before the Incas*. Englewood Cliffs, NJ: Prentice-Hall

1967b. *Preceramic archaeology of the Ancón–Chillón region, Central Coast of Perú.* Report to the National Science Foundation on research carried out under Grant GS-869, 1965–6

1970. Pleistocene man in South America. *World Archaeology* 2: 90–111

1974. Western South America. In *Prehispanic America*, ed. S. Gorenstein, pp. 65–86. New York: St Martin's Press

Lanning, E. P. and E. Hammel 1961. Early lithic industries of western South America. *American Antiquity* 27 (2): 139–54

Lanning, E. P. and T. C. Patterson 1967. Early man in South America. *Scientific American* pp. 44–50

Lapiner, A. 1976. *Pre-Columbian Art of South America.* New York: Harry N. Abrams

Larco Hoyle, R. 1938. *Los Mochicas*, I. Lima: Casa Editorial, "La Crónica"

1941. *Los Cupisniques.* Lima: Casa Editorial, "La Crónica" y "Variedades" SA

1945. *Los Cupisniques.* Buenos Aires: Sociedad Geográfica Americana

1946. A culture sequence for the North Coast of Peru. In *Handbook of South American Indians*, II, ed. J. Steward, pp. 149–75. Washington, DC: Smithsonian Institution, Bureau of American Ethnology Bulletin 143

1948. *Cronología Arqueológica del Norte del Perú.* Buenos Aires: Sociedad Geográfica Americana

1966. *Peru.* Trans. J. Hogarth. New York: World Publishing

Lathrap, D. W. 1958. The cultural sequence at Yarinacocha, eastern Peru. *American Antiquity* 23 (4): 379–88

1962. Yarinacocha: stratigraphic excavations in the Peruvian montaña. Unpublished PhD dissertation, Harvard Univ.

1968a. The hunting economies of the tropical forest zone of South America: an attempt at historical perspective. In *Man the Hunter*, ed. R. B. Lee and I. Devore, pp. 23–9. Chicago: Aldine

1968b. Aboriginal occupations and changes in river channel on the central Ucayali, Peru. *American Antiquity* 33 (1): 62–79

1970. *The Upper Amazon.* Ancient Peoples and Places Series, vol. 70. New York and Washington, DC: Praeger; London: Thames and Hudson

1971a. The tropical forest and the cultural context of Chavin. In *Dumbarton Oaks Conference on Chavin* (1968), ed. E. P. Benson, pp. 73–100. Washington, DC: Dumbarton Oaks Research Library

1971b. Complex iconographic features shared by Olmec and Chavin and some speculations on their possible significance. *Actas del Primer Simposio de Correlaciones Antropológicas Andino – Mesoamericano*, July 1971, Salinas, Ecuador

1973. Gifts of the cayman: some thoughts on the subsistence basis of Chavín. In *Variation in Anthropology: Essays in Honor of John C. McGregor*, ed. D. W. Lathrap and J. Douglas, pp. 91–105. Urbana: Illinois Archaeological Survey

1974. The moist tropics, the arid lands and the appearance of great art styles in the New World. In *Art and Environment in Native America*, ed. M. E. King and I. R. Taylor, Jr, pp. 115–58. The Museum, Texas Tech University, Special Publication no. 7. Lubbock: Texas Tech Press

1977a. Farming communities and the demands of archaeology. *Science* 195: 1319–21

1977b. Our father the cayman, our mother the gourd: Spinden revisited, or a unitary model for the emergence of agriculture in the New World. In *Origins of Agriculture*, ed. C. A. Reed, pp. 713–52. The Hague: Mouton

Lathrap, D. W. and L. Roys 1963. The archaeology of the Cave of the Owls in the upper montaña of Peru. *American Antiquity* 29 (1): 27–38

Lathrap, D. W. and R. Weber 1972. Lowland South America. *Current Research, American Antiquity* 37 (2): 273–4

Lathrap, D. W., D. Collier, and H. Chandra 1975. *Ancient Ecuador: Culture, Clay and Creativity 3000–300 BC*. Chicago: Field Museum of Natural History

Lathrap, D. W., J. G. Marcos, and J. Zeidler 1977. Real Alto: an ancient ceremonial center. *Archaeology* 30: 2–13

Lavalle, J. de and W. Lang 1979. Arte y tesoros del Perú, pt 3: *Pintura* [Paintings]. Introductions by L. Lumbreras and J. W. Reid. Lima: Banco de Crédito del Perú

Lavallée, D. 1973. Estructura y organización del habitat en los Andes centrales durante el período intermedio tardío. *Revista del Museo Nacional* 39: 91–116

Lavallée, D. and M. Julien 1975. El habitat prehistórico en la zona de San Pedro de Cajas, Junín. *Revista del Museo Nacional* 41: 81–127

Lavallée, D., M. Julien, and J. Wheeler 1982. Telarmachay: niveles precerámicos de occupación. *Revista del Museo Nacional* 46: 55–127

Lechtman, H. 1980. The Central Andes: metallurgy without iron. In *The Coming of the Age of Iron*, ed. T. Wertime and J. Muhly, pp. 267–334. New Haven: Yale Univ. Press

Lechtman, H. and M. E. Moseley 1975. The scoria at Chan Chan: non-metallurgical deposits. *Ñawpa Pacha* 10–12: 135–70

Levine, T. Y. 1979. Prehistoric political and economic change in highland Peru: an ethnohistorical study of the Mantaro Valley. Unpublished MA thesis, Dept Anthropology, UCLA

Lizárraga, F. R. de 1968 [1603–8] *Descripción de las Indias*. Madrid: Atlas

Llagostera, A. 1976. Hipótesis sobre la expansión Incaica en la vertiente occidental de los Andes Meridionales. In *Homenaje al Dr Gustavo Le Paige*, ed. Hans Niemeyer, pp. 203–18. Santiago: Imprenta Universidad Católica de Chile (orig. Anales de la Universidad del Norte no. 10, Antofagasta, Chile

Lothrop, S. K. 1932. Aboriginal navigation off the west coast of South America. *Journal of the Royal Anthropological Institute* 62: 229–56

1941. Gold ornaments of Chavín style from Chongoyape, Peru. *American Antiquity* 6 (3): 250–62

1948. Pariñas-Chira archaeology: a preliminary report. *American Antiquity* 13 (4): 53–65

Ludeña, H. 1970. San Humberto, un sitio formativo en el Valle de Chillón (Informe Preliminar). *Arqueología y Sociedad* 2: 36–45

Lumbreras, L. G. 1960. Algunos problemas de arqueología Peruana. In *Antiguo Perú*, ed. R. Matos Mendieta, pp. 129–48. Lima: Juan Mejía Baca

1969. *De los Pueblos, Las Culturas y Las Artes del Antiguo Perú*. Lima: Francisco Moncloa Editores, SA

1971. Towards a re-evaluation of Chavín. *Dumbarton Oaks Conference on Chavín* (1968), ed. E. P. Benson, pp. 1–28. Washington, DC: Dumbarton Oaks Research Library

1973. Los estudios sobre Chavín. *Revista del Museo Nacional* 38: 73–92

1974a. *The Peoples and Cultures of Ancient Perú.* Trans. B. J. Meggers. Washington, DC: Smithsonian Institution Press

1974b. Sobre los origenes del estado y las clases sociales [1968]. In *La Arqueología Como Ciencia Social*, ed. L. Lumbreras, pp. 211–40. Lima: Ediciones Histar

1974c. Las fundaciones de Huamanga: hacia una prehistoria de Ayacucho. Lima: Editorial "Nueva Educación" for "El Club Huamanga"

1974d. Los reinos post-Tiwanaku en el área altiplánica. *Revista del Museo Nacional* 40: 55–85

1974e. Informe de labores del proyecto Chavín. *Arqueológicas* 15: 37–55

1977. Excavaciones en el Templo Antiguo de Chavín (sector R); Informe de la Sexta Campaña. *Ñawpa Pacha* 15: 1–38

1978. Acerca de la aparición del estado Inka. In *El Hombre y la Cultura Andina*, ed. R. Matos Mendieta, pp. 101–9. Lima: Universidad Nacional Mayor de San Marcos

1979. Críticas y perspectivas de la arqueología Andina. *Documento de Trabajo* no. 1. Lima: Proyecto Regional de Patrimonio Cultural Andino UNESCO/PNUD

Lumbreras, L. G. and H. Amat 1968. Secuencia arqueológica del altiplano occidental del Titicaca. *Actas y Memorias del 37 Congreso Internacional de Americanistas* 2: 75–106

Lynch, T. F. 1967. The nature of the Andean preceramic. *Occasional Papers of the Idaho State University Museum* no. 21

1970. Excavations at Quishqui Puncu in the Callejón de Huaylas, Peru. *Occasional Papers of the Idaho State University Museum* no. 26

1971. Preceramic transhumance in the Callejón de Huaylas, Peru. *American Antiquity* 36: 139–48

1974. The antiquity of man in South America. *Quaternary Research* 4: 356–77

1980. *Guitarrero Cave: early man in the Andes.* New York: Academic Press

1982. Current research: Andean South America. *American Antiquity* 47: 209–14

Lyon, P. 1979. Female supernaturals in ancient Peru. *Ñawpa Pacha* 16: 95–140

1981. An imaginary frontier; prehistoric highland–lowland interchange in the southern Peruvian Andes. In *Networks of the Past. Proceedings of the 12th Annual Conference of the University of Calgary Archaeology Association* (1979), ed. P. Francis, F. Kense, and P. G. Duke, pp. 4–18

McCown, T. D. 1945. Pre-Incaic Huamachuco: survey and excavation in the region of Huamachuco and Cajabamba. *Univ. California Publications in American Archaeology and Ethnology* 39 (4): 223–400

McEwan, G. F. 1979. Principles of Wari settlement planning. Unpublished MA thesis, Dept Anthropology, Univ. Texas, Austin

1980. New data on the Pikillacta site, Cuzco, Peru. Unpublished paper, Dept Anthropology, Univ. Texas, Austin

1981. Archaeological survey of the Lucre Basin, Cuzco, Peru: an investigation of the impact of the Wari imperial expansion on the culture history of the South

Highlands. Unpublished paper, Dept of Anthropology, Univ. Texas, Austin

Mackey, C. and C. Hastings 1982. Moche murals from the Pyramid of the Moon. In *Precolumbian Art History*, ed. A. Cordy-Collins, pp. 293–312. Palo Alto, CA: Peek Publishers

MacNeish, R. S. 1969. *First Annual Report of the Ayacucho Archaeological–Botanical Project*. Andover, MA: R. S. Peabody Foundation for Archaeology

  1977. The beginning of agriculture in central Peru. In *Origins of Agriculture*, ed. A. Reed, pp. 753–80. Hague–Paris: Mouton

  1979. The early man remains from Pikimachay Cave, Ayacucho Basin, Highland Peru. In *Pre-Llano Cultures of the Americas: Paradoxes and Possibilities*, ed. R. L. Humphrey and D. Stanford, pp. 1–48. Washington, DC: Anthropological Society of Washington

  1980. *Review of Prehistoric hunters in the High Andes by J. W. Rick. American Scientist* 68: 705

  1981. Synthesis and conclusions. In *Prehistory of the Ayacucho Basin, Peru*, ii, ed. R. S. MacNeish *et al.*, pp. 199–257. Ann Arbor: Univ. Michigan Press

MacNeish, R. S., A. Nelken-Terner, and A. Garcia Cook 1970. *Second Annual Report of the Ayacucho Archaeological–Botanical Project*. Andover, MA: R. S. Peabody Foundation for Archaeology

MacNeish, R. S., T. C. Patterson, and D. L. Browman 1975. The central Peruvian prehistoric interaction sphere. Andover, MA: Papers of the R. S. Peabody Foundation for Archaeology, vol. 7

MacNeish, R. S., R. K. Vierra, A. Nelken-Terner, and C. J. Phagan 1980. *Prehistory of the Ayacucho Basin, Peru*, III: *Nonceramic Artifacts*. Ann Arbor: Univ. Michigan Press

MacNeish, R. S., A. G. Cook, L. G. Lumbreras, R. K. Vierra, and A. Nelken-Terner 1981. *Prehistory of the Ayacucho Basin, Peru*, II: *Excavations and Chronology*. Ann Arbor: Univ. Michigan Press

Marcos, J. G. 1978. The ceremonial precinct at Real Alto: organization of time and space in Valdivia society. Unpublished PhD dissertation, Univ. Illinois

Markham, C. 1910. A comparison of the ancient carvings of Tiahuanacu and Chavin. *Verhandlungen des XVI Internationalen Americanisten Kondresses* (Wien and Liepzig, 1908), pp. 389–99

Martinez Rengifo, J. 1963. La visita de Guancayo, Maca y Guaravni 1571. In Waldemar Espinoza, "La Guaranga y la reducción de Huancayo," *Revista del Museo Nacional* 32: 58–69

Mason, J. A. 1957. *The Ancient Civilizations of Peru*. Harmondsworth, Middlesex: Penguin Books

Matos Mendieta, R. 1959a. Exploraciones arqueológicas en Huancavelica. Unpublished BA thesis, Universidad Nacional Mayor de San Marcos, Lima

  1959b. Los Wanka, datos históricos y arqueológicos. *Actas del 2 Congreso Nacional de Historia del Perú* (Lima) 1: 187–210

  1966. La economía durante el período de reinos y confederaciones en Mantaro, Perú. *Actas del 36 Congreso Internacional de Americanistas* (Sevilla) 1: 95–9

  1968a. A formative period painted pottery complex of Ancón. *American Antiquity* 32: 226–32

1968b. Wari-Wilka, Santuario Wanka en el Mantaro. *Cantuta* 2: 116–28

1972. Alfareros y agricultores. In *Pueblos y Culturas de la Sierra Central del Perú*, ed. D. Bonavia and R. Ravines, pp. 35–43. Lima: Cerro de Pasco Corp.

1973. Ataura: un centro Chavín en el Valle del Mantaro. *Revista del Museo Nacional* 38 (1972): 93–108

1975. Prehistória y ecología humana en la punas de Junín. *Revista del Museo Nacional* 41: 37–80

1980. La agricultura prehispánica en las punas de Junín. *Allpanchis Phuturinqa* 14: 91–108

Matsuzawa, T. 1974. Excavations at Las Haldas on the coast of central Perú. *Series of Cultural Anthropology* no. 2. *The Proceedings of the Department of Humanities* 59: 3–44. Tokyo: Univ. Tokyo Press

1978. The formative site of Las Haldas, Perú: architecture chronology. Trans. I. Shimada. *American Antiquity* 43: 652–73

Mazess, R. B. and D. W. Zimmerman 1966. Pottery dating from thermoluminescence. *Science* 152: 347–8

Means, P. A. 1920. Aspectos estético-cronológicos de las civilizaciones Andinas. *Académia Nacional de Historia, Boletin* 1: 195–226

1928. Biblioteca Andina, pt 1. *Transactions of the Connecticut Academy of Arts and Sciences* 29: 271–525

Meggers, B. J. 1954. Environmental limitation on the development of culture. *American Anthropologist* NS 56: 801–24

1979. Climatic oscillation as a factor in the prehistory of Amazonia. *American Antiquity* 44 (2): 252–66

Meggers, B. J. and C. Evans 1978. Lowland South America and the Antilles. In *Ancient Native Americans*, ed. J. D. Jennings, pp. 543–92. San Francisco: W. H. Freeman

Meggers, B. J., C. Evans, and E. Estrada 1965. Early formative period of coastal Ecuador: the Valdivia and Machalilla phases. Washington, DC: *Smithsonian Contributions to Anthropology* vol. 1

Mejía Xesspe, T. 1968. Pintura Chavinoide en los lindes del arte rupestre. *Revista "San Marcos"* 9: 15–32

1972. Algunos restos arqueológicos del período Paracas en el Valle de Palpa, Ica. *Arqueología y Sociedad* 7–8: 78–86

1978. Importancia prehistórica de la "Huaca Florida" en el Valle de Lima. *III Congreso Peruano El Hombre y la Cultura Andina (Lima 1977), Actas y Trabajos* 2: 493–520, ed. R. Matos Mendieta

Mellafe, R. 1965. La significación histórica de los puentes en el virreinato peruano del siglo XVI. *Historia y Cultura* 3: 134–40.

1967. Consideraciones históricas sobre la visita. In Iñigo Ortiz de Zúñiga, *Visita de la provincia de León de Huánuco [1562]*, I, *Visita de las cuatro waranqa de los Chupachu*. Huánuco, Peru, Universidad Nacional Hermilio Valdizán

Menzel, D. 1959. The Inca occupation of the south coast of Peru. *Southwestern Journal of Anthropology* 15: 125–42

1964. Style and time in the Middle Horizon. *Ñawpa Pacha* 2: 1–105

1966. The pottery of Chincha. *Ñawpa Pacha* 4: 77–144

1968. New data on the Huari empire in the Middle Horizon, Epoch 2A. *Ñawpa Pacha* 6: 47–114

1976. *Pottery Style and Society in Ancient Peru: Art as a Mirror of History in the Inca Valley, 1350–1570.* Berkeley: Univ. California Press

1977. *The Archaeology of Ancient Peru and the Work of Max Uhle.* Berkeley: R. H. Lowie Museum of Anthropology, Univ. California

Menzel, D. and J. Rowe 1966. The role of Chincha in late pre-Spanish Peru. *Ñawpa Pacha* 4: 63–76

Menzel, D., J. Rowe, and L. E. Dawson 1964. *The Paracas Pottery of Ica: A Study in Style and Time.* Berkeley: Univ. California Press

Mercer, J. H. 1972. Chilean glacial chronology 20,000 to 11,000 Carbon-14 years ago: some global comparisons. *Science* 176: 1118–20

Mesa, J. de and T. Gisbert 1973. *Los Incas en Bolivia. Historia y Cultura*, I, pp. 15–50. La Paz: Universidad de San Andres

Meyers, A. 1976. Die Inka in Ekuador. *Bonner Americanistische Studien* no. 6, ed. U. Oberem

Middendorf, E. 1895. *Peru. Beobachtungen und Studien uber das Land und seine Bewohner während eines 25 jahrigen Aufen-halts*, III, *Das Hochland von Peru.* Berlin: Robert Oppenheim

Miller, G. W. 1836. Notice of a journey to the northward and also to the eastward of Cusco and among the Chunchos Indians in July 1835. *Journal of the Royal Geographical Society of London* 6: 174–86

Mohr Chavez, K. 1981. The archaeology of Marcavalle, an Early Horizon site in the Valley of Cuzco, Peru. *Baessler-Archiv* 29

Moore, S. F. 1969. Descent and legal position. In *Law in Culture*, ed. L. Nader, pp. 374–400. Chicago: Aldine

Morales, D. 1977. Excavaciones en Las Salinas de San Blas. *Seminario Arqueológico* 1: 27–48. Lima: Seminario de Historia Rural Andina, Universidad Nacional Mayor de San Marcos

1980. *El Dios Felino en Pacopampa.* Lima: Seminario de Historia Rural Andina, Universidad Nacional Mayor de San Marcos

Morris, C. 1966. El Tampu Real de Tunsucancha. In *Cuadernos de Investigación, Antropología 1* (Universidad Nacional Hermilio Valdizan, Huánuco), pp. 95–107

1967. Storage in Tawantinsuyu. Unpublished PhD dissertation, Univ. Chicago

1971. The identification of function in provincial Inca architecture and ceramics. *Actas y Memorias del XXXIX Congreso Internacional de Americanistas* (Lima) 3: 135–44. Also published in *Revista del Museo Nacional* 37.

1972a. El Almacenaje de dos Aldeas de los Chupaychu. In *Visita de la Provincia de León de Huánuco [1562], Iñigo Ortiz de Zúñiga, Visitador*, ed. J. Murra, II, pp. 383–404. Huánuco, Peru: Universidad Nacional Hermilio Valdizán

1972b. State settlements in Tawantinsuyu: a strategy of compulsory urbanism. In *Contemporary Archaeology: A Guide to Theory and Contributions*, ed. M. P. Leone. Carbondale: Southern Illinois Univ. Press

1974. Reconstructing patterns of non-agricultural production in the Inca economy: archaeology and ethnohistory in institutional analysis. In *The Reconstruction of*

Complex Societies, ed. C. Moore, pp. 49–68. Cambridge, MA: American Schools of Oriental Research

1975. Sampling in the excavation of urban sites: the case at Huánuco Pampa. In *Sampling in Archaeology*, ed. J. Mueller, pp. 192–208. Tucson: Univ. Arizona Press

1976a. Master design of the Inca. *Natural History* 85 (10)

1976b. The archaeological study of Andean exchange systems. In *Social Archaeology: Beyond Subsistence and Dating*, ed. C. Redman et al. New York: Academic Press

1976c. The Spanish occupation of an Inca administrative city. In *Actes*, vol. 9-B, International Congress of Americanists. Paris

1979. Maize beer in the economics, politics, and religion of the Inca empire. In *Fermented Food Beverages in Nutrition*, ed. C. F. Gastineau *et al.* New York: Academic Press

1980. Huánuco Pampa: nuevas evidencias sobre urbanismo inca. *Revista del Museo Nacional* 42

1981. Tecnología y organización inca del almacenamiento de víveres en la sierra. In *Runakana Kawasayninkupaq Rurasqankunaqa: Tecnología del Mundo Andino*, ed. H. Lechtman and A. M. Soldi. Mexico DF: Universidad Nacional Autónoma de México

[1980]. Architecture and the structure of space at Huánuco Pampa. [To be published] in *Inka Architecture and Planning* [tentative title], ed. G. Gasparini and L. Margolies. Caracas: Ediciones Venezolanas de Antropología

Morris, C. and D. Thompson 1970. Huánuco Viejo: an Inca administrative center. *American Antiquity* 35 (3): 344–62

Moseley, M. E. 1972. Subsistence and demography: an example of interaction from prehistoric Peru. *Southwestern Journal of Anthropology* 28: 25–49

1973. The development of urbanism in the Moche Valley, Peru: challenging the invasion–urbanism axiom. Unpublished paper, presented at the Annual Meeting, American Anthropological Association (San Francisco)

1975a. *The Maritime Foundations of Andean Civilization*. Menlo Park, CA: Cummings

1975b. Chan Chan: Andean alternative of the preindustrial city. *Science* 187: 219–25

1976a. Master design of the Inca. *Natural History* 85 (10)

1976b. The Spanish occupation of an Inca administrative city. *Actes*, XLII International Congress of Americanists (Paris), vol. 9-B

1978. The archaeological study of Andean exchange systems. In *Social Archaeology: Beyond Subsistence and Dating*, ed. C. Redman, M. J. Berman, E. V. Curtin, W. T. Langhorne Jr, N. M. Versaggi, and J. C. Wanser, pp. 135–327. New York: Academic Press

1978a. An empirical approach to prehistoric agrarian collapse: the case of the Moche Valley, Peru. In *Social and Technological Management in Dry Lands, Past and Present, Indigenous and Imposed*, ed. N. Gonzalez, pp. 8–44. New York: American Association for the Advancement of Science, Selected Symposia, X

1978b. The evolution of Andean civilization. In *Ancient Native Americans*, ed. J. D. Jennings, pp. 491–541. San Francisco: W. H. Freeman

1978c. Pre-agricultural coastal civilizations in Peru. *Carolina Biology Reader 90*. Burlington, NC: Carolina Biological Supply Co.

1982. Human exploitation and organization on the North Andean Coast. In *Chan Chan: Andean Desert City*, ed. M. Moseley and K. Day, pp. 1–24. Albuquerque: Univ. New Mexico Press

1983. Patterns of settlement and preservation in the Viru and Moche valleys. In *Prehistoric Settlement Patterns*, ed. E. Z. Vogt and R. Leventhal, pp. 423–42. Albuquerque: Univ. New Mexico Press

Moseley, M. E. and K. C. Day 1982 (eds.). *Chan Chan: Andean Desert City*. Albuquerque: Univ. New Mexico Press

Moseley, M. E. and R. A. Feldman 1977. Beginnings of civilization along the Peruvian coast. *Geoscience and Man* 18: 271–6

Moseley, M. E. and C. J. Mackey 1973. Chan Chan, Peru's ancient city of kings. *National Geographic Magazine* (March), pp. 318–45

1974. *Twenty-Four Architectural Plans of Chan Chan, Peru*. Cambridge, MA: Peabody Museum Press

Moseley, M. E. and L. Watanabe 1974. The adobe sculpture of Huaca de los Reyes. *Archaeology* 27: 154–61

Moseley, M. E. and G. R. Willey 1973. Aspero, Peru: a reexamination of the site and its implications. *American Antiquity* 38: 452–68

Moseley, M. E., R. A. Feldman, and C. R. Ortloff 1981. Living with crises: human perception of process and time. In *Biotic Crises in Ecological and Evolutionary Time*, ed. M. Nitecki, pp. 231–67. New York: Academic Press

Mujica Barreda, E. 1978. Nueva hipótesis sobre el desarrollo temprano del altiplano, del Titicaca y de sus áreas de interacción. *Arte y Arqueología* 5–6: 285–308

[1981]. Desarrollo de las culturas prehistoricas en el area centro-sur Andina. Paper submitted for translation and publication in *Precolumbian Time of Troubles in the Andes*, ed. R. P. Schaedel, I. Shimada, and J. M. Vreeland

Murra, J. V. 1956. The economic organization of the Inca State. Unpublished PhD dissertation, Univ. Chicago

1962. An archaeological "restudy" of an Andean ethnohistorical account. *American Antiquity* 28: 1–4

1966. El Instituto de Investigaciones Andinas y sus Estudios en Huánuco, 1963–66. *Cuadernos de Investigación: Antropología 1*, pp. 7–21. Huánuco: Universidad Nacional Hermilio Valdizán

1968. An Aymara kingdom in 1567. *Ethnohistory* 15: 115–51

1970. Current research and prospects in Andean ethnohistory. *Latin American Research Review* 5 (1)

1972. El "control vertical" de un máximo de pisos ecológicos en la economía de las sociedades andinas. In *Visita de la Provincia de León de Huánuco* [1562], *Iñigo Ortiz de Zúñiga, Visitador*, ed. J. V. Murra, II, pp. 429–76. Huánuco, Peru: Universidad Nacional Hermilio Valdizán

1975. *Formaciones Económicas y Políticas del Mundo Andino*. Lima: Instituto de Estudios Peruanos

1979. El valle de Sama, Isal periferica del reino Lupaqa su uso dentro de la económia mineral colonial. *Collectanae Instituti Anthropos* 21: 87–91

1980. *The Economic Organization of the Inca State.* Supplement 1 to *Research in Economic Anthropology.* Greenwich, CT: JAT Press

Murra, J. V. and C. Morris 1976. Dynastic oral tradition, administrative records and archaeology in the Andes. *World Archaeology* 7 (3)

Nelken-Terner, A. 1980. Ground and pecked stone tools. In *Prehistory of the Ayacucho Basin, Peru,* III, *Nonceramic Artifacts,* by R. MacNeish, R. K. Vierra, A. Nelken-Terner, and C. J. Phagan, pp. 282–308. Ann Arbor: Univ. Michigan Press

Netherly, P. J. 1970. Conquerors and ethnographers: a new look at the cultural background of European ethnohistorical sources. Unpublished paper, read at the 10th Annual Meeting of the Northwestern Anthropological Association (Ottawa)

1976. Chimor conquered: the Inca occupation of the North Coast of Peru. Unpublished paper, read at the 41st Meeting of the Society for American Archaeology (St Louis)

1977a. On defining the North Coast of Peru. Unpublished paper, read at the 42nd Meeting of the Society for American Archaeology (New Orleans)

1977b. Local level lords on the North Coast of Peru. Unpublished PhD dissertation, Cornell Univ.

1978. Archaeological implications of North Coast social organization. Unpublished paper, read at the 43rd Annual Meeting of the Society for American Archaeology (Tucson)

1984. The management of late Andean irrigation systems on the North Coast of Peru. *American Antiquity* 49: 227–54

Nials, F. L., E. E. Deeds, M. E. Moseley, S. Pozorski, T. Pozorski, and K. Feldman 1979a. El Niño: the catastrophic flooding of coastal Peru, pt 1. *Field Museum of Natural History Bulletin* 50 (7): 4–14

1979b. El Niño: the catastrophic flooding of coastal Peru, pt 2. *Field Museum of Natural History Bulletin* 50 (8): 4–10

Nicholas, R. 1973. Social and political movements. *Annual Review of Anthropology* 2: 63–84

Niemeyer, F. Hans 1969–70. El yacimiento arqueológico de Huana. *Boletín de Prehistoria* 2 (2–3): 3–63 (Departamento de Historia, Facultad de Filosofía y Educación, Universidad de Chile, Santiago)

Nogami, M. 1976. Altitude of the modern snowline and Pleistocene snowline in the Andes. *Geographical Reports of Tokyo Metropolitan University* 11: 71–86

Nomland, G. 1939. New archaeological site at San Blas, Junín, Peru. *Revista del Museo Nacional* 8 (1): 61–6

Nordenskiöld, E. von 1917. Die Östliche Ausbreitung der Tiahuanacokultur in Bolivien und ihr Verhältnis zur Aruakkultur in Mojos. *Zeitschrift für Ethnologie* 49: 10–20

1924a. *Forschungen und Abenteuer in Südamerica.* Stuttgart: Strecker und Schröder

1924b. The ethnography of South America seen from Mojos in Bolivia. *Comparative Ethnographical Studies* no. 3

Nuñez, L. 1968. Subarea loa-costa Chilena desde Copiapo a Pisagua. *Actas y Memorias del XXXVII Congreso Internacional de Americanistas* (Buenos Aires) 2: 145–82

O'Laughlin, B. 1975. Marxist approaches in anthropology. *Annual Review of Anthropology* 4: 341–70

Oldale, R. N. and C. J. O'Hara 1980. New radiocarbon data from the inner shelf of southeastern Massachusetts and a local sea rise curve for the past 12,000 years. *Geology* 8: 102–6

Onuki, Y. and T. Fujii 1974. Excavations at La Pampa, Peru. *The Proceedings of the Department of Humanities, College of General Education, University of Tokyo* 59: 45–104

Orellana, S. 1973. Huacjlasmarca, un pequeño poblado Huanca. *Anales Científicas de la Universidad del Centro del Peru* 2: 69–132.

Ortiz de Zúñiga, I. 1920–5; 1955–61. Visita por Mandado de Su Majestad . . . [1562]. *Revista del Archivo Naciónal del Perú*

   1967. *Vista de la Provincia de León de Huánuco en 1562*, I, *Documentos para la Historía y Etnologia de Huánuco y la Selva Central*, ed. J. V. Murra. Huánuco: Universidad Naciónal Hermilio Valdizán

   1972. *Vista de la Provincia de León de Huánuco en 1562*, II, ed. J. V. Murra. Huánuco: Universidad Naciónal Hermilio Valdizán

Ortloff, C. R., M. E. Moseley, and R. A. Feldman 1982. Hydraulic engineering aspects of the Chimu Chicama–Moche Intervalley Canal. *American Antiquity* 48 (2): 375–89

Ossa, P. P. 1973. A survey of the lithic preceramic occupation of the Moche Valley, north coastal Peru. Unpublished PhD dissertation, Harvard Univ.

   1976. A fluted "fishtail" projectile point from La Cumbre, Moche Valley, Peru. *Ñawpa Pacha* 13: 97–8, pl. XXXVII

   1978. Paiján in early Andean prehistory: the Moche Valley evidence. In *Early Man in America from a Circum-Pacific Perspective*, ed. A. L. Bryan. Edmonton: Occasional Papers no. 1 of the Dept of Anthropology, Univ. Alberta

Ossa, P. P. and M. E. Moseley 1972. La Cumbre; a preliminary report on research into the early lithic occupation of the Moche Valley, Peru. *Ñawpa Pacha* 9 (1971): 1–16, pls. I–VIII

Parsons, J. R. 1971. Prehistoric settlement patterns in the Texcoco region, Mexico. *Memoirs of the Museum of Anthropology* no. 3. Univ. Michigan, Ann Arbor

Parsons, J. R. and C. M. Hastings 1977. Prehispanic settlement patterns in the upper Mantaro, Peru. Unpublished report, on file at Univ. Michigan Museum of Anthropology, Ann Arbor

Parsons, J. R. and R. Matos Mendieta 1978. Asentamientos prehispánicos en el Mantaro, Perú: informe preliminar. In *Actas y Trabajos del III Congreso del Hombre y la Cultura Andina*, ed. R. Matos Mendieta, II, pp. 540–56. Lima: Editora Lasontay

Parsons, J. R. and N. Psuty 1975. Sunken fields and prehispanic subsistence on the Peruvian coast. *American Antiquity* 40: 259–82

Patterson, T. C. [ms., n.d.]. The power of Pachacamac. Unpublished ms.

   1963. Contemporaneity and cross-dating in archaeological interpretation. *American Antiquity* 28 (3): 289–392

1966. Early cultural remains on the central coast of Peru. *Ñawpa Pacha* 4: 145–53, pls. XIX–XX

1971a. Chavín: an interpretation of its spread and influence. In *Dumbarton Oaks Conference on Chavín, 1968*, ed. E. P. Benson, pp. 29–48. Washington, DC: Dumbarton Oaks Research Library

1971b. The emergence of food production in Central Peru. In *Prehistoric Agriculture*, ed. S. Struever. Garden City, NY: Natural History Press

1971c. Central Peru: its population and economy. *Archaeology* 24: 316–21

1973. *America's Past: A New Archaeology*. New York: Scott, Foresman and Co.

1983. The historical development of a coastal Andean social formation in Central Peru, 6000 to 500 BC. In *Investigations of the Andean Past*, ed. S. Sandweiss, pp. 21–37. Ithaca: Cornell Univ. Latin American Studies Program

Patterson, T. C. and E. P. Lanning 1964. Changing settlement patterns on the central Peruvian coast. *Ñawpa Pacha* 2: 113–23

Patterson, T. C. and M. E. Moseley 1968. Late preceramic and early ceramic cultures of the central coast of Peru. *Ñawpa Pacha* 6: 115–33

Paulsen, A. C. [1980]. Huaca del Loro: the transition to the Middle Horizon on the South Coast of Peru. Paper submitted for publication in *The Precolumbian Time of Troubles in the Andes*, ed. R. P. Schaedel, I. Shimada, and J. M. Vreeland

Pearsall, D. M. 1978. Paleoethnobotany in western South America: progress and problems. In *Nature and Status of Ethnobotany*, ed. R. I. Ford, pp. 389–416. Ann Arbor: Anthropological Papers of the Museum of Anthropology. Univ. of Michigan, vol. 67

1979. The application of ethnobotanical techniques to the problem of subsistence in the Ecuadorian formative. Unpublished PhD dissertation, Univ. Illinois, Urbana

1980. Pachamachay ethnobotanical report: plant utilization at a hunting base camp. In *Prehistoric Hunters of the High Andes*, ed. J. W. Rick. New York: Academic Press

Pease, G. Y., Franklin 1977a. *Collaguas 1*. Lima: Pontífica Universidad Católica del Perú

1977b. Ethnohistoria andina: problemas de fuentes y metodología. *Estudios Andinos* 7 (13)

1978. *Del Tawantinsuyu a la Historia del Perú*. Lima: Instituto de Estudios Peruanos

Petersen, G. 1970. Minería y metalurgía en el antiguo Perú. *Arqueológicas* 12

Pickersgill, B. 1969. The archaeological record of chili peppers (*Capsicum* spp.) and the sequence of plant domestication in Peru. *American Antiquity* 34: 54–61

Pickersgill, B. and C. B. Heiser Jr 1977. Origins and distribution of plants domesticated in the New World tropics. In *Origins of Agriculture*, ed. C. A. Reed, pp. 803–35. The Hague–Paris: Mouton

Pires-Ferreira, J. Wheeler 1975. La fauna de Cuchimachay, Acomachay A, Acomachay B, Telarmachay, y Utco 1. *Revista del Museo Nacional* 41: 120–7

Pires-Ferreira, J. Wheeler, E. Pires-Ferreira, and P. Kaulicke 1976. Prehistoric animal utilization in the central Peruvian Andes. *Science* 194: 483

Pizarro, H. 1968. *Carta de Hernando Pizarro "A los magníficos señores oidores de la*

audiencia real de su magestad que residen en la ciudad de Santo Domingo."
Biblioteca Puerana, Primera Serie, vol. I. Lima: Editores Técnicos Asociados SA

Plaza Schuller, F. 1976. *La incursión Inca en el septentrion andino ecuatoriano.*
Otavalo: Instituto Otavaleño de Antropología, Serie: Arqueología no. 2

Plowman, T. 1979. Botanical perspectives on coca. *Journal of Psychedelic Drugs* 11
(1–2)

— 1984. The origin, evolution, and diffusion of coca, *Erythroxylum* spp., in South
and Central America. In *Pre-Columbian Plant Migration*, ed. D. Stone. *Papers of
the Peabody Museum of Archaeology and Ethnology* 76: 125–63

Pollard, G. C. and I. M. Dres 1975. Llama herding and settlement in prehispanic
northern Chile: application of an analysis for determining domestication
American Antiquity 40: 296–304

Polo, J. T. 1899. La piedra de Chavín. *Boletín de la Sociedad Geográfica de Lima* 4:
192–231, 262–90

Ponce Sanginés, C. 1969. La ciudad Tiwanaku. *Arte y Arqueología* 1: 5–32
(Universidad Mayor de San Andres, La Paz)

— 1970. *Las Culturas Wankarani y Chiripa y su Relacion con Tiwanaku.* La Paz:
Academia Nacional de Ciencias de Bolivia, Publication no. 25

— 1971. Tiwanaku: espacio, tiempo y cultura. *Pumapunku* 3: 29–44

— 1972. Tiwanaku: espacio, tiempo y cultura. *Pumapunku* 4: 7–24

— 1979. *Nuevo Perspectiva Para el Estudio de la Expansion de la Cultura Tiwanaku.*
La Paz: Instituto Nacional de Arqueología, Publication no. 29

— 1980. *Panorama de la Arqueología Boliviana.* La Paz: Libreria y Editorial
"Juventud"

Porras, P. 1975. Fase Pastazca, el formativo en el oriente ecuatoriano. *Revista de la
Universidad Católica, Quito* 10: 75–135

Posnansky, A. 1945. *Tihuanacu, The Cradle of American Man*, I–II. New York: J.
Augustin; La Paz: Ministerio de Educacion de Bolivia

Pozorski, S. G. 1976. Prehistoric subsistence patterns and site economics in the Moche
Valley, Peru. PhD dissertation, Dept Anthropology, Univ. Texas

— 1979. Prehistoric diet and subsistence of the Moche Valley, Peru. *World Archaeology* 11 (2): 163–84

Pozorski, S. G. and T. G. Pozorski 1979a. Alto Salaverry: sitio precerámico de la costa
peruana. *Revista del Museo Nacional* 43 (1977): 27–60

— 1979b. Alto Salaverry: a Peruvian coastal preceramic site. *Annals of Carnegie
Museum* 48: 337–75

— 1979c. An early subsistence exchange system in the Moche Valley, Peru. *Journal of
Field Archaeology* 6 (4): 413–32

Pozorski, T. G. 1976a. Caballo Muerto: a complex of early ceramic sites in the Moche
Valley, Peru. PhD dissertation, Dept Anthropology, Univ. Texas

— 1976b. El complejo Caballo Muerto: los frisos de barro de la Huaca de Los Reyes.
Revista del Museo Nacional 41 (1975): 211–51

— 1982. Early social stratification and subsistence systems: the Caballo Muerto complex. In *Chan Chan: Andean Desert City*, ed. M. E. Moseley and K. C. Day, pp.
225–54. Albuquerque: Univ. New Mexico Press

Proulx, D. A. 1973a. The development of urbanism in the Nepeña Valley, Peru. Paper presented at American Anthropological Association Annual Meeting (San Francisco)

1973b. *Archaeological investigations in the Nepeña valley, Peru.* Andover, MA: Research Report no. 13, Dept Anthropology, Univ. Massachusetts

Pulgar Vidal, J. 1972. *Las Ocho Regiones Naturales del Perú.* Lima: Editorial Universo

Raffíno, R. 1978. La ocupación Inka en el N.O. Argentino: actualización y perspectivas. *Relaciones de la Sociedad Argentina de Antropología* NS 7: 95–121

Rappaport, R. 1967. *Pigs for the Ancestors: Ritual in the Ecology of a New Guinea People.* New Haven: Yale Univ. Press

Ravines, R. 1965. Ambo: a new preceramic site in Peru. *American Antiquity* 31: 104–5

1967. El abrigo de Caru y sus relaciones culturales con otros sitios tempranos del sur del Perú. *Ñawpa Pacha* 5: 39–57

1970a. El sitio arqueológico de Chucuimarca, Huancaválica. *Revista del Museo Nacional* 36: 234–55

1970b. Introducción. In *100 Años de Arqueología en el Perú*, ed. R. Ravines, pp. 11–28. Lima: Instituto de Estudios Peruanos

1972. Secuencia y cambios en los artefactos líticos del sur del Perú. *Revista del Museo Nacional* 38: 133–84

1982. *Panorama de la Arqueología Andina.* Lima: Instituto de Estudios Peruanos

Ravines, R. and J. Alvarez 1975. Fechas radiocarbónicas para el Perú. *Arqueológicas* 11

Ravines, R. and W. H. Isbell 1976. Garagay: sitio ceremonial temprano en el valle de Lima. *Revista del Museo Nacional* 41: 253–75

Raymond, J. S. 1972. The cultural remains from the Granja de Sivia, Peru: an archaeological study of tropical forest culture in the montana. PhD dissertation, Dept Anthropology, Univ. Illinois, Urbana

1976. Late prehistoric and historic settlements in the upper montana of Peru. In *Papers of a Symposium on Canadian Archaeology Abroad*, ed. P. L. Shinnie and J. Robertson. Calgary, Alberta: Univ. Calgary Archaeology Association

1979. A Huari ceramic tapir foot? *Ñawpa Pacha* 17: 81–6

Raymond, J. S., W. R. DeBoer and P. G. Roe 1975. Cumancaya: A Peruvian Ceramic Tradition. *Occasional Papers* no. 2, Dept Archaeology, Univ. Calgary, Alberta

Raymond, J. S., J. G. Marcos and D. W. Lathrap 1980. Evidence of early formative settlement in the Guayas Basin, Ecuador. *Current Anthropology* 21 (5): 700–1

Reichel-Dolmatoff, G. 1965. *Excavaciones Arqueológicas en Puerto Hormiga (Departamento de Bolívar).* Ediciones de la Universidad de los Andes, Antropología 2, Bogota

Renfrew, C. 1982. Polity and power: interaction, intensification, and exploitation. In *An Island Polity*, ed. C. Renfrew and M. Wagstaff, pp. 264–90. Cambridge: Cambridge Univ. Press

Richardson, J. B. III 1973. The preceramic sequence and the pleistocene and post-pleistocene climate of northwest Peru. In *Variation in Anthropology*, ed. D. W. Lathrap and J. Douglas, pp. 199–201. Urbana: Illinois Archaeological Survey

1978. Current research: Peru. *American Antiquity* 43 (3): 524–5 [T. F. Lynch, asst ed.]

Rick, J. W. 1980. *Prehistoric Hunters of the High Andes*. New York: Academic Press
    1983. *Cronología, Clima, y Subsistencia en el Precerámico Peruano*. Lima:
    Instituto Andino de Estudios Arqueológicos
Rivera Dorado, M. 1971. Diseños decorativos en la ceramica Killke. *Revista del
    Museo Nacional* 37: 106–15
    1978. Procesos de aculturación en Tawantinsuyu. *Revista del Instituto de
    Antropología* 6: 105–10 (Facultad de Filosofía y Humanidades, Universidad
    Nacional de Córdoba, Argentina)
Roe, P. G. 1974. A further exploration of the Rowe Chavin seriation and its impli-
    cations for north central coast chronology. *Dumbarton Oaks, Studies in Pre-
    Columbian Art and Archaeology* no. 13
    1978. Recent discoveries in Chavín art: some speculations on methodology and sig-
    nificance in the analysis of a figural style. *El Dorado* 3 (1): 1–41
Rosas La Noire, H. 1976. Investigaciones arqueológicas en la cuenca del Chotano,
    Cajamarca. *Actas del XLI Congreso Internacional de Americanistas* (México,
    1974) 3: 564–78
Rosas La Noire, H. and R. Shady 1970. *Pacopampa: Un Centro Formativo en la
    Sierra Nor-peruana*. Lima: Seminario de Historia Rural Andina, Universidad
    Nacional Mayor de San Marcos
    1974. Sobre el período formativo en la sierra del extremo norte del Perú.
    Arqueológicas 15: 6–35
Rostworowski de Diez Canseco, M. 1967–8. Ethnohistoria de un valle costeño
    durante el Tawantinsuyu. *Revista del Museo Nacional* 35
    1970. Los Ayarmacas. *Revista del Museo Nacional* 36: 58–101
    1972. Breve ensayo sobre El Señorío de Ychma o Ychima. *Arqueología PUC,
    Boletín del Seminario de Arqueología* 13: 37–51
    1975. La "visita" a Chinchaycocha de 1549. *Anales Científicos de la Universidad
    del Centro del Peru* 4: 71–88
    1977a. Coastal fishermen, merchants, and artisans in pre-Hispanic Peru. In *The Sea
    in the Pre-Columbian World*, ed. E. Benson, pp. 167–86. Washington, DC:
    Dumbarton Oaks Research Library and Collection
    1977b. *Etnía Sociedad: Costa Peruana Prehispánica*. Lima: Instituto de Estudios
    Peruanos
    1978a. Una hipótesis sobre el surgimiento del estado Inca. In *El Hombre y la
    Cultura Andina*, ed. R. Matos Mendieta, I, pp. 91–100. Lima: Universidad
    Nacional Mayor de San Marcos, III Congreso Peruano
    1978b. *Señoríos Indígenas de Lima y Canta*. Lima: Instituto de Estudios Peruanos
    1981. Guarco y Lunaguaná. Dos señoríos prehispánicos de la costa sur central del
    Perú. *Revista del Museo Nacional* 44 (1978–80): 153–214
Rowe, J. H. 1944. An introduction to the archaeology of Cuzco. *Papers of the
    Peabody Museum of American Archaeology and Ethnology* 27: 2
    1945. Absolute chronology in the Andean area. *American Antiquity* 10: 265–84
    1946. Inca culture at the time of the Spanish Conquest. In *Handbook of South
    American Indians*, ed. J. H. Steward, II, pp. 183–330. Washington, DC: Bureau
    of American Ethnology, Bulletin 143
    1948a. The kingdom of Chimor. *Acta Americana* 6: 26–59

1948b. On basic highland culture. In *A Reappraisal of Peruvian Archaeology*, ed. W. C. Bennett. Memoirs of the Society for American Archaeology no. 4, p. 20

1956. Archaeological explorations in southern Peru, 1954–1955. *American Antiquity* 22 (2): 135–51

1960. Cultural unity and diversification in Peruvian archaeology. In *Men and Culture, Selected Papers, 5th International Congress of Anthropological and Ethnological Sciences*, ed. A. F. C. Wallace, pp. 627–31. Philadelphia: Univ. Pennsylvania Press

1962a. Stages and periods in archaeological interpretation. *Southwestern Journal of Anthropology* 18 (1): 40–54

1962b. *Chavín Art: an Inquiry into its Form and Meaning*. New York: Museum of Primitive Art

1963. Urban settlements in ancient Peru. *Ñawpa Pacha* 1: 1–28

1967a. Form and meaning in Chavin art. In *Peruvian Archaeology: Selected Readings*, ed. J. H. Rowe and D. Menzel, pp. 72–103. Palo Alto: Peek Publications

1967b. An interpretation of radiocarbon measurements on archaeological samples from Peru. In *ibid.* pp. 16–30

1967c. Stages and periods in archaeological interpretation. In *ibid.* pp. 1–15

1967d. Urban settlements in ancient Peru. In *ibid.* pp. 293–320

1976. El arte religioso del Cuzco en el Horizonte Temprano. *Ñawpa Pacha* 14: 1–20

1977. Religión e imperio en el Peru antiguo. *Antropología Andina* 1–2: 5–12

Rowe, J. H. and C. T. Brandel 1970. Pucara style pottery designs. *Ñawpa Pacha* 7–8: 1–16

Rowe, J. H., D. Collier, and G. R. Willey 1950. Reconnaissance notes on the site of Huari, near Ayacucho, Peru. *American Antiquity* 16 (2): 120–37

Ryden, S. 1947. *Archaeological Researches in the Highlands of Bolivia*. Goteborg: Elanders Boktryckeri Aktiebolag

1957. *Andean Excavations I: The Tiahuanaco Era East of Lake Titicaca*. Stockholm: The Ethnographic Museum of Sweden, Monograph Series, Pub. no. 4

Salazar-Burger, L. and R. L. Burger 1983. *La Araña en la Iconografía del Horizonte Temprano en la Costa Norte del Peru. Beiträge zur Allgemeinen und Vergleichenden Archäologie* 4: 213–53. Kommission für Allgemeine und Vergleichende Archäologie des Deutschen Archäologischen Instituts, Bonn

Samaniego, L., E. Vergara, and H. Bischof 1985. New evidence on Cerro Sechin, Casma Valley, Peru. In *Early Ceremonial Architecture in the Andes*, ed. C. Donnan, pp. 165–90. Washington, DC: Dumbarton Oaks Research Library and Collection

Sanders, W. T. 1965. *The Cultural Ecology of the Teotihuacan Valley*. University Park, PA: Pennsylvania State Univ.

1973. The significance of Pikillakta in Andean culture history. *Occasional Papers in Anthropology* 8: 379–428. Dept Anthropology, Pennsylvania State Univ.

1978. Ethnographic analogy and the Teotihuacan horizon style. In *Middle Classic Mesoamerica: AD 400–700*, ed. E. Pasztory, pp. 33–44. New York: Columbia Univ. Press

Santos Ramirez, R. 1977. Presencia de Wari en el valle de Siguas. In *Jornadas*

Peruano-Bolivianas de Estudio Científico del Altiplano Boliviano y del Sur del Peru, II, pp. 393–409. La Paz: Instituto del Investigaciones Arqueológicas

Sauer, C. O. 1952. *Agricultural Origins and Dispersals*. New York: American Geographical Society

Savoy, G. 1970. *Antisuyo: The Search for the Lost Cities of the Amazon*. New York: Simon and Schuster

Sawyer, A. R. 1963. *Tiahuanaco Tapestry Design*. New York: Museum of Primitive Art, Studies no. 3

1972. The feline in Paracas art. In *The Cult of the Feline Conference*, ed. E. P. Benson, pp. 91–112. Washington, DC: Dumbarton Oaks Research Library and Collections

Schaedel, R. P. 1948. Monolithic sculpture of the southern Andes. *Archaeology* 1 (2): 66–73

1951. Major ceremonial and population centers in northern Peru. In *Civilizations of Ancient America: Selected Papers of the 29th International Congress of Americanists*, pp. 232–43. Chicago: Univ. Chicago Press

1957 (ed.). *Arqueología Chilena*. Santiago: Talleres Gráficos "La Nación"

1966. Incipient urbanization and secularization in Tiahuanacoid Peru. *American Antiquity* 31 (2): 338–44

1978. The Huaca Pintada of Illimo. *Archaeology* 31 (1): 27–37

Scheele, H. G. 1970. The Chavín occupation of the Central Coast of Peru. Unpublished PhD dissertation, Dept Anthropology, Harvard Univ.

Schoffeleers, J. M. 1977. Cult idioms and the dialectics of a region. In *Regional Cults*, ed. R. P. Werbner, pp. 219–39. New York: Academic Press

Schreiber, K. J. 1978. Planned architecture of Middle Horizon Peru: implications for social and political organization. PhD dissertation, Dept Anthropology, State Univ. of New York, Binghamton

Sébrier, M. and J. Macharé 1980. Observaciones acerca del Quaternario de la costa del Perú Central. *Boletín del Instituto Frances de Estudios Andinos* 9 (1–2): 5–22

Shady, R. and H. Rosas 1977. El Horizonte Medio en Chota. *Arqueológicas* 16

1980. El complejo Bagua y el sistema de establecimientos durante el formativo en la sierra norte del Perú. *Ñawpa Pacha* 17: 109–42

Shady, R. and A. Ruiz 1979. Evidence for interregional relationships during the Middle Horizon on the north-central coast of Peru. *American Antiquity* 44 (4): 676–84

Sharon, D. G. and C. B. Donnan 1977. The magic cactus: ethnoarchaeological continuity in Peru. *Archaeology* 30: 374–81

Sherbondy, J. 1980. Water in the ritual calendar of Cuzco. Paper prepared for the symposium: Myth and Ritual in Andean Societies, 79th Annual Meeting of the American Anthropological Association (Washington, DC)

Shimada, I. 1978. Economy of a prehistoric urban context: commodity and labor flow at Moche V Pampa Grande, Peru. *American Antiquity* 43 (4): 569–92

Silva, J. Elías 1975. Excavaciones en Bermejo: 1972. Unpublished Bachelor of Social Science thesis, Archaeology Program, Universidad Nacional Mayor de San Marcos, Lima

1978. Acercamiento al Estudio Histórico de Bermejo. *Actas y Trabajos del III Congreso Peruano El Hombre y la Cultura Andina* (Lima, 1977), I, pp. 310–24

Silva Galdames, O. 1977–8. Consideraciones acerca del período Inca en la cuenca de
    Santiago (Chile Central). *Boletín del Museo Arqueológico de la Serena, Chile*
Smith, C. E., Jr 1980a. Plant remains from Guitarrero Cave. In *Guitarrero Cave: Early
    Man in the Andes*, ed. T. F. Lynch, pp. 87–119. New York: Academic Press
    1980b. Vegetation and land use near Guitarrero Cave. In *ibid.* pp. 65–83
Spickard, L. E. 1982. The evolution of Huari administrative architecture. Paper
    presented at the 10th Annual Midwest Conference on Andean and Amazonian
    Archaeology and Ethnohistory (Ann Arbor)
Squier, G. E. 1877. *Peru: Incidents of Travel and Exploration in the Land of the Incas.*
    New York: Macmillan
Stehberg, R. L. 1976. *La Fortaleza de Chena y su relación con la Ocupación de Chile
    Central.* Publicación Ocasional del Museo Nacional de Historia Natural,
    Santiago, no. 23
Steward, J. H. 1948. South American cultures: an interpretative summary. In *Hand-
    book of South American Indians*, ed. J. H. Steward. Washington, DC: Bureau of
    American Ethnology, Bull. 143, 5: 669–772
    1949. Cultural causality and law: a trial formulation of the development of early
    civilizations. *American Anthropologist* 51: 1–27
Steward, J. H. and L. C. Faron 1959. *Native Peoples of South America*. New York,
    Toronto and London: McGraw-Hill
Steward, J. H. and A. Metraux 1948. Tribes of the Peruvian and Ecuadorean
    montana. In *Handbook of South American Indians*, ed. J. H. Steward.
    Washington, DC: Bureau of American Ethnology, Bull. 143, 3: 535–656
Stone, J. 1978. Lithics and trade at Huari, Peru. Unpublished paper, presented at 77th
    Annual Meeting of the American Anthropological Association (Los Angeles)
    1979. The socio-economic implications of lithics from Huari, Peru. Unpublished
    paper, presented at 44th Annual Meeting of the Society for American Archae-
    ology (Vancouver, BC)
    1981. The socio-economic implications of lithic remains from Huari, Peru.
    Unpublished PhD dissertation, Dept Anthropology, State Univ. of New York,
    Binghamton
Stothert, K. E. 1980. Review of *Guitarrero Cave: Early Man in the Andes* (ed. T. F.
    Lynch). *Lithic Technology* 9: 61–3
Stothert-Stockman, K. 1967. *Pre-Colonial Highways of Bolivia. Part I: The La Paz–
    Yungas Route Vía Palca.* Academia Nacional de Ciencias de Bolivia, La Paz, pub.
    no. 17
Strong, W. D. 1948. Cultural epochs and refuse stratigraphy in Peruvian archaeology.
    In *A Reappraisal of Peruvian Archaeology*, assembled by W. C. Bennett.
    Memoirs of the Society for American Archaeology (Menasha), no. 4, pp. 93–102
    1957. Paracas, Nazca, and Tiahuanacoid cultural relationships in south coastal
    Peru. *Memoirs of the Society for American Archaeology, no. 13*, 22 (4) pt 2
Strong, W. D. and C. Evans Jr 1952. Cultural stratigraphy in the Viru Valley, northern
    Peru: the Formative and Florescent epochs. *Columbia Univ. Studies in Archae-
    ology and Ethnology* 4
Strong, W. D., G. R. Willey, and J. Corbett 1943. Archaeological studies in Peru,
    1941–42. *Columbia Univ. Studies in Archaeology and Ethnology* 1

Stumer, L. M. 1954a. Population centers of the Rimac Valley, Peru. *American Antiquity* 20 (2): 130–48

1954b. The Chillon Valley of Peru: excavation and reconnaissance, 1952–53. *Archaeology* 7: 171–8

1954c. Report on the south Peruvian coast: Chala to Arica. *American Antiquity* 19 (4): 384–6

Sturtevant, W. C. 1968. Anthropology, history and ethnohistory. In *Introduction to Cultural Anthropology*, ed. J. Clifton. Boston: Houghton-Mifflin

Tabío, E. 1972. Asociación de Fragmentos de Cerámica de los Estilos Cavernas y Chavinoide-Ancón en un Basural de las Colinas de Ancón. *Arqueología y Sociedad* 7–8: 27–9

Tello, J. C. 1930. Andean civilization: some problems of Peruvian archaeology. *Proceedings of the 23rd International Congress of Americanists* (New York, 1928), pp. 31–43. New York: Science Printing Company

1939. Sobre el descubrimiento de la cultura Chavín del Perú. *Actas de la Primera Sesión del XXVII Congreso Internacional de Americanistas* (Mexico, 1939), I: 231–52. Mexico: Instituto Nacional de Antropología e Historia

1943. Discovery of the Chavin culture in Peru. *American Antiquity* 9 (1): 135–60

1956. *Arqueología del Valle de Casma: Culturas Chavín, Santa o Huaylas Yunga, y Sub-Chimú*. Publicación Antropológica del Archivo "Julio C. Tello" de la Universidad Nacional Mayor de San Marcos, I. Lima: Universidad Nacional Mayor de San Marcos

1959. *Paracas. Primera Parte*. Lima: Empresa Gráfica T. Scheuch SA

1960. *Chavín Cultura Matriz de la Civilización Andina*. Publicación Antropológica del Archivo "Julio C. Tello" de la Universidad Nacional Mayor de San Marcos, II. Lima: UNMSM

1970. Las ruinas de Huari. In *100 Años de Arqueología en el Perú*, ed. R. Ravines, pp. 519–25. Fuentes e Investigaciones para la Historia del Perú, III. Lima: Instituto de Estudios Peruanos

Terada, K. 1979. *Excavations at La Pampa in the North Highlands of Peru, 1975*. Report 1 of the Japanese Scientific Expedition to Nuclear America. Tokyo: Univ. Tokyo Press

Thoden van Velzen, B. 1977. Bush negro regional cults: a materialist explanation. In *Regional Cults*, ed. R. P. Werbner, pp. 93–118. London and New York: Academic Press

Thompson, D. E. 1962. The problem of dating certain stone-faced, stepped pyramids on the North Coast of Peru. *Southwestern Journal of Anthropology* 8: 291–301

1964a. Formative period architecture in the Casma Valley, Peru. *Actas y Memorias del XXV Congreso Internacional de Americanistas* (México, 1962) 1: 205–12. Editorial Libros de México

1964b. Postclassic innovations in architecture and settlement patterns in the Casma Valley, Peru. *Southwestern Journal of Anthropology* 20 (1): 91–105

1967. Investigaciones arqueológicas en las Aldeas Chupacho de Ichu y Auquimarca. In Ortiz de Zúñiga, Iñigo, *Visita de la Provincia de León de Huánuco en 1562*, I, pp. 357–62. Huánuco: Universidad Nacional Hermilio Valdizán

1968. An archaeological evaluation of ethnohistoric evidence on Inca culture. In *Anthropological Archaeology in the Americas*, ed. B. J. Meggers. Washington, DC: The Anthropological Society

1970. Habitantes del período intermedio tardío en la sierra central del Perú (I). *El Serrano* 19 (250): 16–20

1973a. Archaeological investigations in the eastern Andes of northern Peru. *Atti del 40 Cong. Int. degli Americanisti* (Genoa) 1: 363–9

1973b. Investigaciones arqueológicas en los Andes orientales del norte del Perú. *Revista del Museo Nacional de Antropología y Arqueología* 39: 117–25

1974. Arquitectura patrones de establecimiento en el valle de Casma. *Revista del Museo Nacional* 40: 9–29

1976. Prehistory of the Uchucmarca Valley in the North Highlands of Peru. *Actas del 41 Cong. Int. de Amer.* (Mexico) 2: 99–106

Thompson, D. E. and J. V. Murra 1966. The Inca bridges in the Huanuco region. *American Antiquity* 31: 632–9

Topic, J. 1982. Lower-class social and economic organization at Chan Chan. In *Chan Chan: Andean Desert City*, ed. M. E. Moseley and K. C. Day, pp. 145–75

Topic, J. and T. Topic 1978. Prehistoric fortification systems of northern Peru. *Current Anthropology* 19 (3): 618–19

Topic, T. L. and J. R. Topic 1982. *Prehistoric fortification systems of northern Peru: preliminary report on the final season, January–December 1980*. Unpublished paper, Dept Anthropology, Trent Univ., Peterborough, Ontario

Tosi, J. A. Jr 1960. *Zonas de Vida Natural en el Peru: Memoria Explicativa Sobre el Mapa Ecológico del Perú*. With an Appendix by L. R. Holdridge. Instituto Inter-americano de Ciencias Agrícolas, Boletín Tecnico 5. OAS, Zona Andina, Proyecto 39

Towle, M. 1961. *The Ethnobotany of Pre-Columbian Peru*. Chicago: Aldine

Trigger, B. 1978. *Time and Traditions: Essays in Archaeological Interpretation*. New York: Columbia Univ. Press

Trimborn, H. 1973. Nuevas fechas radiocarbónicas para algunos monumentos y sitios prehispánicos de la costa Peruana. *Atti del 40 Cong. Int. degli Americanisti* (Genoa) 1: 313–15

1979. *El Reino de Lambayeque en el Antiguo Perú*. St Augustine, Germany: Hans Volker und Kulturan-Anthropos Institut, Collectanea Instituti Anthropos, vol. 19

Trimborn, H., O. Kleeman, K. Narr, and W. Wurster 1975. *Investigaciones Arqueológicas en los Valles del Caplina y Sama, Depto. Tacna, Perú*. St Augustine, Germany: Studia Instituti Anthropos, no. 25

Troll, C. 1958. Las culturas superiores andinas y el medio geográfico. *Revista del Instituto de Geografía* 5: 3–55

1970. The cordilleras of the tropical Americas. In *Geo-Ecology of the Mountainous Regions of the Tropical Americas*, ed. C. Troll, Proceedings of UNESCO Mexico Symposium (1968), 9: 15–56. Bonn: Ferd. Dümmlers

Tschopik, M. 1946. Some notes on the archaeology of the Dept of Puno, Peru. Cambridge, MA: *Papers of the Peabody Museum of American Archaeology and Ethnology* 27 (3)

Tsunoyama, Y. 1977. *Textiles of the Pre-Incaic Period: Catalogue of the Amano Collection*. Shimogyo-Ku Kyoto: The Dohosha

Turner, V. W. 1974. *Dramas, Fields and Metaphors, Symbolic Action in Human Society*. Ithaca: Cornell Univ. Press

Ubbelohde-Doering, H. 1959. Bericht über archäologische Feldarbeiten in Peru, II. *Ethnos* 24 (1/2): 1–32

    1967. *On the Royal Highways of the Inca: Civilizations of Ancient Peru*. New York: Praeger

Uhle, M. 1903. *Pachacamac. Report of the William Pepper, M.D., LL.D. Peruvian Expedition of 1896*. Philadelphia: Dept Archaeology, Univ. Pennsylvania

    1910. Uber die frühkulturen in der Umgebung von Lima. *Verhandlungen des XVI Internationalen Amerikanisten-Kongresses* (Vienna and Leipzig, 1908), pp. 347–70

    1923. Las ruinas de Tumbebamba. Quito: Imprenta Julio Saenz Rebollendo

    1924. Explorations at Chincha. *Univ. of California Publications in Archaeology and Ethnology* 21 (2): 55–94

Valastro, S., E. M. Davis, and A. G. Varela 1978. University of Texas at Austin, radiocarbon dates. *Radiocarbon* 20 (2): 245–73

Valcárcel, L. E. 1934–5. Sajsawaman Redescubierto (3 pts). *Revista del Museo Nacional* 2 (1–2): 3–36, 211–40; 4 (1): 5–24

Van Binsbergen, W. M. J. 1977. Regional and non-regional cults of affliction in western Zambia. In *Regional Cults*, ed. R. P. Werbner, pp. 141–75. New York: Academic Press

Van Der Hammen, T. 1973. The quaternary of Colombia: introduction to a research project and a series of publications. *Palaeogeography, Palaeoclimatology, Palaeoecology* 14: 1–7

Vázquez de Espinoza, A. 1948 [1630]. *Compendio y descripción de las indias occidentales*. Washington, DC: Smithsonian Miscellaneous Collections, vol. 108

Vierra, R. K. 1975. Structure versus function in the archaeological record. Unpublished PhD dissertation, Univ. New Mexico

von Reiss Altschul, S. 1967. Vilca and its use. In *Ethnopharmacologic Search for Psychoactive Drugs*, ed. D. Efron, pp. 307–14. Washington, DC: US Govt Printing Office

Wachtel, N. 1977. *The Vision of the Vanquished: The Spanish Conquest of Peru through Indian Eyes 1530–1570*. Hassocks, England: Harvester Press

Wallace, A. 1956. Revitalization movements. *American Anthropologist* 58: 264–81

Wallace, D. T. 1957. The Tiahuanaco Horizon styles in the Peruvian and Bolivian highlands. PhD dissertation, Dept Anthropology, Univ. of California, Berkeley

    1962. Cerrillos: an early Paracas site in Ica, Peru. *American Antiquity* 27: 303–14

Wassén, S. H. 1967. Anthropological survey of the use of South American snuffs. In *Ethnopharmacologic Search for Psychoactive Drugs*, ed. D. Efron, pp. 233–89. Washington, DC: US Govt Printing Office

    1972. A medicine-man's implements and plants in a Tiahuanacoid tomb in highland Bolivia. *Etnologiska Studier* (Göteborg) 32

Watanabe, L. 1976. Sitios tempranos en el Valle de Moche (Costa Norte del Peru).

Unpublished PhD dissertation, Programa de Ciencias Histórico-Sociales, Especialidad Arqueología. Universidad Nacional Mayor de San Marcos, Lima

1979. Arquitectura de la Huaca Los Reyes. In *Arqueología Peruana*, ed. R. Matos Mendieta, pp. 17–36. Seminario "Investigaciones Arqueológicas en el Perú, 1976." Lima: Universidad Nacional Mayor de San Marcos and Comisión para Intercambio Educativo entre los Estados Unidos y el Perú

Weberbauer, A. 1945. *El Mundo Vegetal de los Andes Peruanos*. Lima: Estación Experimental Agrícola de la Molina

Wendt, W. E. 1964. Die präkeramische Siedlung am Rio Seco, Perú. *Baessler-Archiv* NS 11 (2): 225–75

Werbner, R. P. 1977a. Introduction. In *Regional Cults*, ed. R. P. Werbner, pp. ix–xxxvii. London and New York: Academic Press

1977b. Continuity and policy in South Africa's high god cult. In *Regional Cults*, ed. R. P. Werbner, ch. 7. London and New York: Academic Press

West, M. 1970. Community settlement patterns at Chan Chan, Peru. *American Antiquity* 35 (1): 74–86

Wheeler, J. C. 1984. On the origin and early development of camelid pastoralism in the Andes. In *Animals and Archaeology*, III, *Early Herders and their Flocks*, ed. J. Clutton-Brock and C. Grigson. BAR International Series 202

Wheeler, J. C., R. Cardoza, and D. Pozzi-Escot 1977. Estudio provisional de la fauna de las Capas II y III de Telarmachay. *Revista del Museo Nacional* 43: 97–109

1980. Faunal remains. In *Guitarrero Cave: Early Man in the Andes*, ed. T. F. Lynch, pp. 149–71. New York: Academic Press

Willey, G. 1945. Horizon styles and pottery traditions in Peruvian archaeology. *American Antiquity* 11: 49–56

1948. Functional analysis of "horizon styles" in Peruvian archaeology. In *A Reappraisal of Peruvian Archaeology*, ed. W. C. Bennett, pp. 8–15. Memoirs of the Society for American Archaeology, no. 4. Menasha, WI: Society for American Archaeology and the Institute of Andean Research

1951. The Chavin problem: a review and critique. *Southwestern Journal of Anthropology* 7 (2): 103–44

1953. *Prehistoric Settlement Patterns in the Viru Valley, Peru*. Washington, DC: Bureau of American Ethnology, *Bulletin* no. 155

1962. The early great styles and the rise of the pre-Columbian civilizations. *American Anthropologist* 64: 1–14

1971. *Introduction to American Archaeology*, II, *South America*. Englewood Cliffs, NJ: Prentice-Hall

Willey, G. and J. Corbett 1954. Early Ancon and early Supe culture: Chavin horizon sites of the central Peruvian coast. *Columbia Univ. Studies in Archaeology and Ethnology* 3

Willey, G. and P. Phillips 1958. *Method and Theory in American Archaeology*. Chicago: Univ. Chicago Press

Williams León, C. 1971. Centros ceremoniales tempranos en el Valle de Chillón, Rimac y Lurín. *Apuntes Arqueológicos* 1: 1–4

1972. La difusión de los pozos ceremoniales en la costa peruana. *Apuntes Arqueológicos* 2: 1–9

1980a. Arquitectura y urbanismo en el antiguo Perú. In *Historia del Perú*, VIII, *Perú Republicano y Procesos e Instituciones*, pp. 369–585. Lima: Editorial Juan Mejía Baca

1980b. Complejos de pirámides con planta en U, patrón arquitectónico de la costa central. *Revista del Museo Nacional* 44: 95–110

Williams León, C. and F. Merino 1979. *Inventario, catastro y delimitación de sitios arqueológicos en el valle de Supe*. Lima: Manuscript Files Centro de Investigación y Restauración de Bienes Monumentales del Instituto National de Cultura

Wilson, D. 1981. Of maize and men: a critique of the maritime hypothesis of state origins on the coast of Peru. *American Anthropologist* 83: 93–120

Wing, E. 1972. Utilization of Animal Resources in the Peruvian Andes. In *Andes 4: Excavations at Kotosh, Peru, 1963 and 1966*, ed. S. Izumi and K. Terada, pp. 327–54. Tokyo: Univ. Tokyo Press

1977. Animal domestication in the Andes. In *The Origins of Agriculture*, ed. C. A. Reed, pp. 837–59. The Hague: Mouton

1980. Faunal remains. In *Guitarrero Cave: Early Man in the Andes*, ed. T. R. Lynch, pp. 149–71. New York: Academic Press

Winterhalder, B. P. and R. B. Thomas 1978. *Geoecology of Southern Highland Peru: A Human Adaptation Perspective*. University of Colorado, Institute of Arctic and Alpine Research, Occasional Paper 27

Wright, H. E. Jr 1980. Environmental history of the Junín plain and the nearby mountains. In *Prehistoric Hunters of the High Andes*, by J. W. Rick, pp. 253–6. New York: Academic Press

1984. Late glacial and late Holocene moraines in the Cerros Cuchpanga, central Peru. *Quaternary Research* 21: 275–85

Yabar, J. 1972. Epoca pre-Inca de Chanapata. *Revista Saqsaywaman* (Cuzco) 2: 211–33

Yellen, J. E. 1977. *Archaeological Approaches to the Present*. New York: Academic Press

Zevallos, C., W. Galinat, D. W. Lathrap, E. Leng, J. Marcos and K. Klump 1977. The San Pablo corn kernel and its friends. *Science* 196: 385–9

Zuidema, R. T. 1964. The Ceque system of Cuzco, the social organization of the capital of the Inca. *International Archives of Ethnography*, Supplement to vol. L. Leiden: E. J. Brill

1979. El puente del río Apurimac y el origen mítico de la Villca. *Collectanea Instituti Anthropos* 21: 322–34

1982. Catachillay – the role of the Pleiades and of the Southern Cross Alpha and Beta Centauri in the calendar of the Incas. In *Ethnoarchaeology and Archaeoastronomy in the American Tropics*, ed. G. Urton and A. Aveni. *Annals of the New York Academy of Science* 358: 203–29

INDEX

Italic figures refer to pages on which illustrations appear.